S0-EST-046

CHILDCRAFT
YOU AND YOUR FAMILY

Childcraft

IN FIFTEEN VOLUMES

•

VOLUME TWELVE

YOU AND YOUR FAMILY

FIELD ENTERPRISES, INC.

CHICAGO

CHILDCRAFT
Reg. U. S. Pat. Off.)

Copyright © 1954, U. S. A.
by Field Enterprises, Inc.

Copyright © 1949 by Field Enterprises, Inc.
Copyright © 1947, 1945, 1942, 1939 by The Quarrie Corporation
Copyright © 1937, 1935, 1934 by W. F. Quarrie & Company

THE CHILD'S TREASURY

Copyright © 1931, 1923 by W. F. Quarrie & Company

International Copyright © 1954, 1949
by Field Enterprises, Inc.
International Copyright © 1947
by The Quarrie Corporation

All rights reserved. This volume may not be reproduced in whole or in part in any form without written permission from the publishers.

Printed in the U. S. A.

EGA

On Being a Parent

NOTHING in all the world is more fascinating and challenging than being a parent. Parenthood is as old as the human race, and as young as the most recent parent. It can bring you the greatest joys and the most satisfying rewards. But being a parent also brings you face to face with situations and problems which tax your greatest wisdom, ingenuity, and patience.

From day to day you watch your child grow. He gains control of his body. His mind develops. He responds to and communicates with the people around him. He acquires the values and the faith his forefathers cherished. Your affectionate encouragement and the setting you provide can make it possible for him to do his best growing. Yours is a full-time job which is one of life's great adventures. It calls for love and for some understanding of what is known about children's development.

In this machine age, we can hardly practice a trade or follow a profession without special training. Yet most of us parents face the delicate and demanding task of rearing our children with little or no preparation. We have to learn about parenthood on the job. This is where CHILDCRAFT can help. It brings us basic principles which have been tested in actual situations and found to be helpful. We want the best available information in bringing up our children, just as we would in any other difficult undertaking.

CHILDCRAFT brings you this help through the practical knowledge and experience of 155 leading child-guidance specialists who have written for these volumes. Among them are parents, teachers, doctors, and other specialists who have intimate, first-hand knowledge of children. They are sharing with you what they themselves have learned. They are passing on to you, too, the wisdom they have gained from contacts with thousands of other parents, and from the research centers where many of them work.

What the authors have written has been woven into a carefully unified program. The blueprint for this program was worked out in detail in collaboration with the distinguished members of CHILDCRAFT's Editorial Advisory Board. You will find this blueprint on the next two pages.

CHILDCRAFT will add to your understanding and enjoyment of day-to-day family living. But it offers no sure-cure prescriptions for solving family problems or for securing children's co-operation. What succeeds in the case of one child may fall flat when you try it out with another, even in the same family. What worked almost like a charm with a boy or girl last year or last week may produce only black looks and tears in that same boy or girl today. Children are ever changing, and family relationships take many different shapes through the years.

Volume 12
You and Your Family

I. UNDERSTANDING YOURSELF
1. Joys and Disappointments of Being a Parent — Katherine Clifford
2. Parents Are Important — L. K. and M. H. Frank
3. You Had a Family, Too — Ernest G. Osborne
4. You as a Person — William C. Menninger
5. Parents Are also Husbands and Wives — David R. Mace

II. YOUR FAMILY IN TODAY'S SETTING
6. Things Aren't the Same — Freda S. Kehm
7. Grandparents and Other Relatives — Jean Schick Grossman
8. If Three Generations Live Together — Robert G. Foster

III. WAYS OF GROWING
9. What Children Need from Life — James L. Hymes, Jr.
10. How Do Children Grow? — Mary Fisher Langmuir
11. Children Play Many Parts — Helen Ross
12. Each Child Is Different — Marion L. Faegre

IV. LIVING TOGETHER IN THE FAMILY
13. Families Shape Personality — Lois Meek Stolz
14. Discipline for Self-Reliance — Ruth W. Washburn
15. The Family Council — William E. Blatz
16. The Father in the Family — Russell C. Smart

V. RELATIONSHIPS AMONG CHILDREN IN THE FAMILY
17. Sometimes Rivals, Sometimes Friends — Edith G. Neisser
18. Building Friendlier Feelings — Joan Kalhorn Lasko
19. Some Combinations Are a Special Challenge — Edward Liss

VI. SHARING PLEASURES AND RESPONSIBILITIES
20. Sharing the Work — Dorothy Lee
21. Family Celebrations — Anna Rose Wright
22. Family Vacations — Helen W. Puner
23. The Family Keeps Records — Marjorie K. Reynolds
24. Reading Together — Jean Betzner
25. Building a Home Library — Annis Duff

VII. FAMILY CRISES
26. Losses Through Death — Adele Franklin
27. Divorce and Separation — Dorothy W. Baruch
28. Family Ups and Downs — James Lee Ellenwood

VIII. SPECIAL FAMILY SITUATIONS
29. The Adopted Child — May Reynolds Sherwin
30. Stepparents and Stepchildren — Mary H. Frank
31. Gifted Children — Harvey Zorbaugh
32. The Handicapped Child and Your Child — Eleanor P. Eells
33. The Handicapped Child in the Family — E. M. Stern and E. Castendyck
34. Special Needs of Various Handicaps
   - Children Who Cannot See — Berthold Lowenfeld
   - Helping Children Who Have Defective Hearing — Richard G. Brill
   - Children Who Are Crippled — Jayne Shover
   - Children Who Have Cerebral Palsy — Mildred Shriner
   - Children Who Are Epileptic — John W. Tenny
   - Children Who Are Mentally Retarded — Elise H. Martens
   - Children with Rheumatic Fever — Irene M. Josselyn

IX. HAPPY FAMILY LIVING
35. Building the Strong Family — E. C. Lindeman and M. A. Glasser

Volume 13
Your Young Child

I. THE BABY IS BORN
1. Before the Baby Arrives — Charlotte del Solar
2. Mother and Child Are Doing Nicely — Anna W. M. Wolf
3. Rooming-in — Edith B. Jackson
4. For Fathers Only — Richard W. Olmsted

II. THE INFANT
5. Early Growth Is Swift and Dramatic — Frances C. Perce
6. Keeping a Baby Comfortable — J. C. Montgomery and M. J. Suydam
7. Feeding Has Many Meanings — Richard E. Wolf
8. Helping Your Child Learn to Use the Toilet — A. G. Trainham
9. He Discovers His Own Body — Donovan J. McCune
10. He Finds Out Who Is Important — Katherine M. Wolf
11. He Learns Through Activities and Toys — Lili E. Peller

III. THE TODDLER
12. The Age of "Me-Can-Do" — Frances L. Ilg
13. Caution—Toddler at Work Here — Mary E. Keister
14. What Does His "No, No" Really Mean? — Gertrude E. Chittenden
15. Guiding Him Tactfully — Arnold Gesell
16. What Does He Like to Do Best? — Terry Spitalny

IV. THE NURSERY YEARS
17. He Likes to Be Busy — Mollie S. Smart
18. His Language Is Rich and Fluent — Evelyn M. Beyer
19. He's a Great Pretender — Roberta Collard
20. He Learns About Differences Between Boys and Girls — M. I. Levine and J. H. Seligmann
21. Other Children Become More Important — Cornelia Goldsmith
22. When Are Children Spoiled? — Marjorie Momyer

V. THE KINDERGARTNER
23. He Is Ready for New Experiences — Lynette M. Messer
24. He Asks Endless Questions — Nina Ridenour
25. He Still Learns Through His Play — L. Joseph Stone
26. He Has a Conscience — Maria W. Piers
27. He Gets Along Better with His Playmates — Christine M. Heinig

VI. NORMAL DIFFICULTIES IN EARLY CHILDHOOD
28. "My Child Doesn't Like to Eat" — Mary M. Aldrich
29. Some Children Have Trouble Sleeping — Milton J. E. Senn
30. Some Children Resist the Toilet — Gustave F. Weinfeld
31. Difficulties in Living with Others — Eveline B. Omwake
32. When Children Are Anxious — Mary Fisher Langmuir

VII. FIRST EXPERIENCES AWAY FROM HOME
33. What Leaving Home Means to a Small Child — Virginia M. Stapley
34. Traveling with Young Children — Carmen Stone Allen
35. What Nursery Groups Offer — Frances R. Horwich
36. If You Want a Play Group — Elizabeth L. Woods

VIII. THE HEALTH OF THE YOUNG CHILD
37. Keeping Your Young Child Healthy — Sally A. Provence
38. The Doctor and the Dentist—Your Child's Friends — Julius B. Richmond
39. Your Child's Teeth — J. H. Sillman
40. If Your Child Goes to the Hospital — Mary E. Mercer
41. Keeping a Convalescent Child Happy — Mary R. Osborne

IX. WHAT CAN I DO NOW, MOTHER?
42. Toys and Play Materials — Rowena M. Shoemaker
43. Stories for Young Children — Pauline Hilliard
44. Young Children and Music — Emma D. Sheehy
45. Excursions for Young Children — Ethel Wright Kunkle
46. Will My Child Be Ready for First Grade? — Celia B. Stendler

Volume 14
Your Child Goes to School

I. GROWING IN INDEPENDENCE
1. Your Child Moves Beyond the Family Circle — Alfred L. Baldwin
2. "Us Kids" — Lois Meek Stolz
3. Friends Are Important — George V. Sheviakov
4. Sex as a Part of Life — Adrian H. Vander Veer

II. PERSONALITY GOES ON DEVELOPING
5. Personalities Need Balancing — R. G. and L. S. Barker
6. When Things Go Wrong — Frederick H. Allen
7. Children in Trouble — A. Whittier Day

III. GROWTH AND HEALTH
8. Growth in Size, Strength, and Co-ordination — Herbert R. Stolz
9. What Your Child Needs for Health — Katherine Bain
10. "Anything to Eat in This House?" — Miriam E. Lowenberg
11. When Children Get Sick — Henry H. Work

IV. PLAY IN CHILD LIFE
12. What Play Means to Your Child — Barbara Biber
13. Children Need Time for Play and Hobbies — Joseph Prendergast
14. Children Need Space and Play Materials — Grace Langdon

V. SCHOOL IN THE LIFE OF THE CHILD
15. What Is the Modern School Trying to Do? — Wilbur A. Yauch
16. What School Means to the Child — Alice V. Keliher
17. Schools Influence Personality — Esther E. Prevey
18. The Handicapped Child in School — Leo F. Cain

VI. THE WAYS OF SCHOOLS
19. Discipline — Hillis L. Howie
20. Reports and Promotions — Harold G. Shane
21. Measuring Achievement and Ability — Morris Krugman

VII. THE WORLD OF KNOWLEDGE
22. What Reading Means to a Child — A. Sterl Artley
23. The Art of Spelling — Ernest Horn
24. Writing and Speaking the Language — Ruby M. Schuyler
25. Experiences with Numbers — Lowry W. Harding
26. Discovering the World of Science — Glenn O. Blough
27. How We Live Together — J. U. Michaelis and F. R. Shaftel

VIII. CHILDREN NEED TO CREATE
28. Music for Children — Emma D. Sheehy
29. Painting, Drawing, and Modeling — Jane Cooper Bland
30. Creating Through Language and Dramatics — Moyne Rice Smith

IX. WIDENING HORIZONS
31. Making the Most of Your Public Library — Ruth E. Hewitt
32. Adventuring Through Excursions — E. G. and P. W. Olsen
33. Organized Groups for Children — Hazel Osborn

X. EXPERIENCES AWAY FROM HOME
34. Traveling Alone and Visiting — Helen S. Burgess
35. Camps and Camping — Helen L. Haskell
36. Boarding Schools — A. E. Hamilton
37. Looking Toward the Teens — Florence Clothier

Volume 15
Your Child in Today's World

I. THE WORLD COMES TO OUR CHILDREN
1. Our Changing World — S. M. Gruenberg and H. S. Krech
2. Radio and Television — Robert L. Shayon
3. The Child and the Movies — Edgar Dale
4. Comics — Arensa Sondergaard
5. Interpreting the News — Agnes Snyder

II. KNOW-HOW FOR TODAY'S WORLD
6. Family Life Is Preparation for Adult Life — Ralph H. Ojemann
7. Accident Prevention Is Your Responsibility — Harry F. Dietrich
8. Becoming Resourceful — James L. Hymes, Jr.
9. Children Learn to Handle Money — Rhoda W. Bacmeister

III. THERE ARE NEW PROBLEMS THESE DAYS
10. Some Mothers Go Out to Work — Dorothy H. Beers
11. Some Fathers Must Be Away from Home — Edith M. Dowley
12. When the Family Moves — Gladys G. Jenkins
13. Sitters Have an Influence — Marion Lowndes

IV. LIVING WITH YOUR NEIGHBORS
14. Neighborhoods Influence Personality — Paulette K. Hartrich
15. Children Learn About Other People — Wanda Robertson
16. Your Neighbors—Dictators, Troublemakers, or Friends — Hilda Taba
17. Neighbors Can Work Together — Ernest G. Osborne
18. What Kind of Manners for Our Children? — Rose H. Alschuler

V. PARENTS IN ACTION
19. Your Role as a Parent — E. T. McSwain
20. Home and School Are a Team — Bess B. Lane
21. Family Guidance Services — Robert L. Sutherland
22. Your Greatest Gift to Your Child — M. F. Ashley Montagu
23. A Healthy Personality for Every Child — Leonard W. Mayo

THE INDEX

All volumes of CHILDCRAFT are fully indexed at the end of Volume 15. Through this index in Volume 15, you can find quickly what you are looking for if you know the author, title, or subject. You can also find a poem if you know the first line. Be sure to look in the index, if you want to use CHILDCRAFT quickly and easily.

There is no set pattern of behavior for you to follow in dealing with your children. In fact, no such pattern is possible, for the personal make-up of each parent and each child is different. Yet studies of children and of families in recent years have added greatly to what is known about human behavior.

CHILDCRAFT can give you helpful ways of thinking about some of the puzzling situations mothers and fathers must meet. These new approaches may go far toward clearing up doubts and worries. A fresh viewpoint may make it easier to accept and live with a problem that cannot be solved at the moment.

The sound knowledge in these volumes will not replace or hinder your spontaneity with your children. It will, in fact, add richness and warmth to family relationships.

Knowing what makes your child behave as he does and understanding how to live with him will help you take prompt action when that is necessary. Part of this understanding is knowing what to expect. Then you do not worry over behavior that is a normal part of growth, even though it may be inconvenient to you.

Volume 12 deals with the over-all problems of YOU AND YOUR FAMILY. The growth and development of the preschool child is taken up in Volume 13, YOUR YOUNG CHILD. Volume 14, YOUR CHILD GOES TO SCHOOL, discusses the characteristics and problems of the school-age child up to the age of ten. Such topics as Radio, Television, Comic Books, and Motion Pictures are discussed in Volume 15, YOUR CHILD IN TODAY'S WORLD.

When you act naturally as a parent, you are likely to be on the right track. How you *feel* about your youngster and about what you do, counts for more than what you may actually do at any particular moment.

Bringing up children with healthy personalities is of deep concern to the nation as well as to individual parents. Because this is so vital a question, leaders in education, religion, medicine, and child development were called together for the Mid-Century White House Conference on Children and Youth in Washington, D. C. The purpose of this Conference was "to consider how we can develop in children the mental, physical, emotional, and spiritual qualities essential to individual happiness and to responsible citizenship." These volumes of CHILDCRAFT are dedicated to the achievement of this purpose.

Parenthood is a high calling. It calls for an understanding of the interests and basic needs of children. With this interest and understanding as a foundation, you will be better able to enjoy the satisfactions that go with parenthood. You will be better able to meet your responsibilities toward your children. You will, too, be giving your children the warm appreciation, the confidence in themselves and in life, so necessary to their wholesome growth.

The Editors

CONTENTS

Understanding Yourself

JOYS AND DISAPPOINTMENTS OF BEING
A PARENT . . *Katherine Clifford*   3
- Why Do We Want Children   3
- There Are Deep Satisfactions   4
- Responsibilities Can Be Heavy   5
- Overcoming Disappointments   6
- When You Are Puzzled   9

PARENTS ARE
IMPORTANT . . *Lawrence K. and Mary H. Frank*   10
- Hidden Values in Parenthood   10
- Why "Disturbed" Children?   12
- Not the Event, but How You Handle It, Counts   13
- Preventing Damage   15
- Today's Parents Want Help   16
- You Need Not Be Perfect   16

YOU HAD A FAMILY,
TOO . . . *Ernest G. Osborne*   18
- You Carry Childhood with You   18
- Understand the Causes   19
- Childhoods Affect Marriage   19
- Children Bring Back the Past   21
- Childhoods Affect Parenthood   23
- Face the Past to Deal with It   23

YOU AS A
PERSON . *William C. Menninger*   24
- Personality Is Complicated   24
- This Is Mental Health   26
- Mental Health Rules   28
- Emotional Maturity   30

PARENTS ARE ALSO HUSBANDS AND
WIVES . . . *David R. Mace*   32
- Good Marriage—Good Parents   32
- Building a Good Marriage   32
- Children Change Things   35
- When Parents Disagree   37
- Marriage Is for Grownups   40

Your Family in Today's Setting

THINGS AREN'T THE
SAME . . . *Freda S. Kehm*   43
- Family Means Partnership   43
- New Demands on Fathers   46
- New Demands on Mothers   47
- What Do We Expect of Children?   48
- What Are the Permanent Values?   48

GRANDPARENTS AND OTHER
RELATIVES . *Jean Shick Grossman*   49
- Grandparents Are Here to Stay   49
- Grandparents Make a Contribution   51
- If Grandparents Interfere   53
- Grandparents Are Human Beings   54
- The Cousins and the Aunts   56
- Lest Auld Acquaintance Be Forgot   56

IF THREE GENERATIONS LIVE
TOGETHER . . *Robert G. Foster*   57
- Reasons for Sharing a Home   58
- Sharing Has Different Meanings   58
- Problems Connected with Money   62
- Worries of Older People   64

Ways of Growing

WHAT CHILDREN NEED FROM
LIFE . . . *James L. Hymes, Jr.*   67
- Surface Needs   67
- Children Are Seekers   67
- Parents Are Givers   68
- Needs That Go Deep   68
- Love and Affection   69
- A Feeling of Independence   70
- A Sense of Achievement   71
- Encouragement   72
- Parents Who Understand   73

		PAGE
How Do Children Grow?	Mary Fisher Langmuir	74
Growth Comes from Within		74
Growth Is Orderly		75
Growth Is Uneven		77
Growth Is Individual		78
Growth Can Be Helped		79
Growth Fulfills Itself		81
Parents Play Many Parts	Helen Ross	82
Mothers Are Givers		82
Father Is the Outside World		83
Parents Become Teachers		84
Family Circles Become Triangles		85
The Family Is a Proving Ground		86
Each Child Is Different	Marion L. Faegre	90
Some Differences Are Inborn		90
Environments Are Never Alike		91
Each Responds in His Own Way		93
When Temperaments Differ		95
Variety Is the Spice		96

Living Together in the Family

Families Shape Personality	Lois Meek Stolz	99
What Is Personality?		99
How Personality Grows		100
Parents' Personality a Force		100
Effect of Brothers and Sisters		102
Each Year Is Important		102
Accepting Change in Children		103
Training Affects Personality		104
Readiness Is the Key		105
What Home Stands for		106
Not Perfection but Progress		106
Discipline for Self-Reliance	Ruth Wendell Washburn	107
Discipline Is Teaching		107
Basic Principles of Discipline		109
Conflict Can Be Constructive		112
Discipline Is in the Situation		114

		PAGE
The Family Council	William E. Blatz	115
Everyone Expresses Himself		115
How the Council Works		117
Working Out Difficulties		119
The Values of a Family Council		120
The Father in the Family	Russell C. Smart	121
Father Is the Model		121
Father Brings a Wider World		122
Discipline—a Two-Parent Job		123
Fathers Are Only Human		125
How Can You Deal with Anger?		125
How Can You Share Interests?		127
Father's Hobbies Fascinate Youngsters		127
To Keep Them Close, Let Them Go		128

Relationships Among Children in the Family

Sometimes Rivals, Sometimes Friends	Edith G. Neisser	131
Rivalry Has Justifiable Causes		131
New Babies Are Puzzling		132
Older Girls Care for Small Fry		135
Jealousy of Older Brothers		136
Expect Ups and Downs		139
Building Friendlier Feelings	Joan Kalhorn Lasko	141
Create a Friendly Atmosphere		141
Teachers Can Provide a Balance		144
What Makes Them Good Friends?		145
How Much Companionship Can We Expect?		146
Keep Your Eye on the Goal		148
Some Combinations Are a Special Challenge	Edward Liss	149
Twins		149
When Twins Have Different Interests		150
One Girl with Several Brothers		150
One Boy with Several Sisters		151
How to Balance Petticoat Rule		152
Wide Differences in Age		153
The Only Child		155
The Child of Older Parents		156

Contents

xi

Sharing Pleasures and Responsibilities

	PAGE
SHARING THE WORK . Dorothy Lee	159
A Child Copies Your Feelings	162
What About Jobs and School?	163
Teaching Responsibility	163
Should You Pay for Work?	165
FAMILY CELEBRATIONS . . . Anna Rose Wright	167
Making Traditions	167
Spotlight on Birthdays	170
Surprises for Mother and Father	172
Some Occasions Have No Labels	172
The Values in Celebrations	174
FAMILY VACATIONS . Helen W. Puner	175
Vacation Give-and-Take	175
Planning Is Half the Fun	177
Enjoying the Journey	178
While You Are Away	180
Making Vacations Endure	180
THE FAMILY KEEPS RECORDS . Marjorie K. Reynolds	182
Some Vital Facts and Dates	182
It's Fun to Remember	186
A Log Reinforces Solidarity	188
READING TOGETHER . Jean Betzner	189
Enriching Family Life	189
Happy By-Products for Adults	190
Understanding Their Tastes	192
Suit Reading to the Listener	192
BUILDING A HOME LIBRARY . . . Annis Duff	195
Choosing the Books	195
Books About Children's Reading	196
Booklists and Reviews	197
Books for the Family Library	197
For Children Two to Four	197
For Children Four to Six	198
For Children Six to Eight	199
For Children Eight to Ten	201

Family Crises

	PAGE
LOSSES THROUGH DEATH . . . Adele Franklin	207
What Does Death Mean to a Child?	207
Are the Children "Bloodthirsty"?	207
Explaining Death	209
If Death Comes to the Family	212
Should Children Go to Funerals?	214
DIVORCE AND SEPARATION . . . Dorothy W. Baruch	215
What Divorce Means to a Child	215
Feelings Can Be Shared	217
Should a Child Have Two Homes?	218
When a Parent Remarries	219
What of the Part-Time Parent?	220
FAMILY UPS AND DOWNS . James Lee Ellenwood	222
Let Children Know	222
What Shall We Tell?	222
Responses Differ	222
Belonging Is Essential	223
Facing Financial Reverses	224
It Has Happened Before	225
Daily Life Goes On	226
When Fortune Improves	226
If a Parent Is Ill	227
Ready for Anything	228

Special Family Situations

THE ADOPTED CHILD . May Reynolds Sherwin	231
This Is Adoption	231
Two to Get Ready	233
Becoming Acquainted	233
Explaining Adoption	236
A Favorite Story	236
STEPPARENTS AND STEPCHILDREN . . . Mary H. Frank	239
Your Feelings About Yourself	239
Feelings About Your Marriage	240
What Are Stumbling Blocks?	240
What Causes the Antagonism?	240
Strengthening the Relationship	243
Stepparenthood No Secret	246

	PAGE
GIFTED CHILDREN . Harvey Zorbaugh	247
Gifted Is as Gifted Does	247
The Gifted Child and His Family	248
The Gifted Child's Friends	250
The Gifted Child and His School	251
THE HANDICAPPED CHILD AND YOUR CHILD . . . Eleanor P. Eells	253
The Handicapped Need Friends	253
Explaining a Handicap	254
Values in Handicapped Friends	256
THE HANDICAPPED CHILD IN THE FAMILY . Edith M. Stern and Elsa Castendyck	258
Facing a Handicap	258
See the Child, Not the Handicap	259
Finding Medical Care	262
The Parents Have Needs	262
Consider the Whole Family	264
SPECIAL NEEDS OF VARIOUS HANDICAPS	266
CHILDREN WHO CANNOT SEE . . . Berthold Lowenfeld	267
Where Special Help Is Needed	268
Educating the Blind Child	269
Booklets to Read	269
HELPING CHILDREN WHO HAVE DEFECTIVE HEARING . Richard G. Brill	270
Deafness and Hearing Loss	270
Learning the Meanings of Words	271
How About Speech Training?	271
Hearing Aids for Children	271
School for the Deaf Child	272
Books to Read	272
CHILDREN WHO ARE CRIPPLED . . . Jayne Shover	273
Use All the Resources	273
School for the Crippled Child	274

	PAGE
New Help for the Crippled	274
Helpful Reading Material	274
CHILDREN WHO HAVE CEREBRAL PALSY . . . Mildred Shriner	275
What Is Cerebral Palsy?	275
Meeting the Special Needs	275
Resources for Help	277
What to Read	277
CHILDREN WHO ARE EPILEPTIC . . . John W. Tenny	278
All Convulsions Not Epilepsy	278
Medical Care for Epilepsy	278
Contact with the Outside World	279
Books to Read	280
CHILDREN WHO ARE MENTALLY RETARDED . . Elise H. Martens	281
Needs of the Mentally Retarded	282
Where Can I Get Help?	283
Materials to Read	283
CHILDREN WITH RHEUMATIC FEVER . . . Irene M. Josselyn	284
Facts About Rheumatic Fever	284
Acute Illness	285
Convalescence	285
After Convalescence	286

Happy Family Living

BUILDING THE STRONG FAMILY . . Eduard C. Lindeman and Melvin A. Glasser	289
The Strong Family Is Flexible	289
Rules Are Necessary	291
A Strong Family Reaches Out	293
Facing Misfortune Bravely	294
Humor Goes with Confidence	294
The Anchor of Society	294

These Are the Authors

Dorothy W. Baruch

family counselor, psychologist, trainer of teachers, and author of *Parents Can Be People* and a score of other books and articles. In the chapter DIVORCE AND SEPARATION (page 215), she discusses specific ways of helping a child maintain security and confidence in his parents when his home is broken. She has won recognition for her study of children's illnesses in relation to troubled family situations.

Jean Betzner

author of *Exploring Literature with Children* and a member of CHILDCRAFT's Editorial Advisory Board, is visiting Professor of Education at Queen's College, New York City. In the chapter READING TOGETHER (page 189), she shows how parents, by reading good books with children, can inspire them with a deep love of good literature.

William E. Blatz

is Professor of Psychology and Director of the Institute of Child Study, University of Toronto, Ontario. He is also a member of CHILDCRAFT's Editorial Board. Doctor Blatz was appointed by the Government of Ontario (Canada) to act as advisor for the Dionne quintuplets when they were born in 1934. He is the author of *The Five Sisters* and many other books and articles on family life. In his chapter THE FAMILY COUNCIL (page 115), he stresses how the family is strengthened when parents and children discuss problems together.

Richard G. Brill

Superintendent of the California School for the Deaf at Riverside, is the author of many articles about the education of hard-of-hearing children. In his article CHILDREN WHO ARE HARD OF HEARING (page 270), he shows how parents can help children with defective hearing to lead useful and reasonably normal, happy lives.

Elsa Castendyck

a consultant in research, and author of several books on behavior problems. She is also co-author with Edith M. Stern of *The Handicapped Child: a Guide for Parents*. These two authors, in THE HANDICAPPED CHILD IN THE FAMILY (page 258), discuss what handicapped children need from their families if they are to grow up with courage and confidence.

Katherine Clifford

is the mother of six children, and author of JOYS AND DISAPPOINTMENTS OF BEING A PARENT (page 3). Drawing on her rich experience as a mother, she brings assurance that parenthood pays rich dividends in spite of occasional trials. Children may not be perfect, nor indeed are parents.

Annis Duff

in the chapter BUILDING A HOME LIBRARY (page 195) offers important practical helps as to what books to select for family use. As a mother, librarian, and editor of children's books, she knows at first-hand children's reactions to different stories and poems. *Bequest of Wings*, her own sensitive book about reading with children, is a favorite with parents, teachers, and librarians.

Eleanor P. Eells

is Co-Director of Herrick House, Bartlett, Ill., where children with handicaps live and play happily together. In the chapter, THE HANDICAPPED CHILD AND YOUR CHILD (page 253), she points out how you can help your child accept a handicapped playmate, and how such experiences can result in benefits to all concerned.

James Lee Ellenwood

well-known writer and lecturer on family life, and author of *It Runs in the Family*, *There's No Place Like Home*, and *Just and Durable Parents*. His down-to-earth advice in FAMILY UPS AND DOWNS (page 222) will be a source of inspiration and comfort to countless parents and children in helping them to weather family reverses.

Marion L. Faegre

co-author of *Child Care and Training* and of many other books and pamphlets, is Consultant in Parent Education for the Children's Bureau in the United States Department of Health, Education, and Welfare. In the chapter, EACH CHILD IS

DIFFERENT (page 90), she emphasizes the importance of recognizing each child as an individual in his own right.

Robert G. Foster

author of *Marriage and Family Relations*, is Director of Marriage Counseling Service at the Menninger Foundation at Topeka, Kan. In IF THREE GENERATIONS LIVE TOGETHER (page 57), he discusses practical ways of solving difficulties which sometimes arise when grandparents live with parents and children.

Lawrence K. Frank

educator, author, and authority on family relations, and Mary H. Frank have truly inspiring things to say about your job as father and mother in PARENTS ARE IMPORTANT (page 10). The author was formerly Director of the Caroline Zachry Institute for Human Relations in New York City. Among the honors he has received is the Lasker Award in Mental Health Education. He and his wife, Mary H. Frank, are the authors of *How to Help Your Child in School*.

Mary H. Frank

writes from first-hand experience, for she has five stepchildren in addition to her own child. In STEPPARENTS AND STEPCHILDREN (page 239), she discusses difficulties which sometimes arise between a stepfather or stepmother and stepchildren, and how these can be solved happily. She is also co-author of *Parents Are Important*.

Adele Franklin

co-author of *The Happy Home* and *Your Best Friends Are Your Children*, is Assistant Administrative Director of the All-Day Neighborhood Schools of New York City's Board of Education. In her chapter, LOSSES THROUGH DEATH (page 207), she tells how we can explain death to our children without making them unduly anxious.

Melvin A. Glasser

is co-author with Eduard Lindeman of BUILDING A STRONG FAMILY (page 289). This chapter discusses how families develop solidarity through faith, affection, flexibility, and fun. Melvin A. Glasser was Executive Director of the Mid-Century White House Conference on Children and Youth. He was responsible in a large measure for the success of that important conference. He is now Assistant to the President of the National Foundation for Infantile Paralysis.

Jean Schick Grossman

wrote *Life with Family* and *Do You Know Your Daughter?* With wide experience as editor, lecturer, mother, and grandmother, she has warm and deep understanding of family living. In GRANDPARENTS AND OTHER RELATIVES (page 49), she brings wise counsel as to how family life can be kept on a smooth and even keel.

James L. Hymes, Jr.

Professor of Education at George Peabody College for Teachers, Nashville, Tenn., is one of the most widely read writers on child guidance. He has a rare ability to express ideas clearly and simply. He is author of *Understanding Your Child*, and is a member of CHILDCRAFT's Editorial Advisory Board. In his chapter, WHAT CHILDREN NEED FROM LIFE (page 67), he emphasizes basic principles for raising happy children, and gives you renewed confidence in yourself as a parent.

Irene M. Josselyn

is a member of the staff of the Institute for Psychoanalysis in Chicago, and has written for parents and for professional people on the emotional problems of children who are ill. In CHILDREN WITH RHEUMATIC FEVER (page 284), she indicates how parents can aid a child's recovery by emphasizing the things he can safely do and the activities that are permitted him.

Freda S. Kehm

as Director of the Association for Family Living in Chicago, is in close touch with the everyday problems of thousands of parents. She brings to her chapter, THINGS AREN'T THE SAME (page 43), keen understanding of changing trends in family relationships.

Mary Fisher Langmuir

a member of CHILDCRAFT's Editorial Advisory Board, is Chairman of the Department of Child Study at Vassar College and Director of the Vassar Summer Institute on Family and Community Relations. She knows from close contact with parents, teachers, doctors, and other lay and spiritual leaders, the questions which are uppermost in their minds on child care and development. In How DO CHILDREN GROW? (page 74), she tells how parents can provide the setting children need for all-around wholesome development.

Joan Kalhorn Lasko

was formerly Clinical Psychologist at the Children's Mental Health Center, Columbus, Ohio. As one of the younger members of a large family, she is well qualified to write BUILDING FRIENDLIER FEELINGS (page 141). Through her special interest in the relationships of brothers and sisters, she brings you practical suggestions as to how to help children get along together.

Dorothy Lee

mother of four children, and Chairman, Division of Social Development at the Merrill-Palmer School, Detroit, Mich. In her chapter, SHARING THE WORK (page 159), she discusses how children can share in the responsibility for some of the household tasks that are a part of the life of every family.

Eduard C. Lindeman

as co-author with Melvin A. Glasser of BUILDING A STRONG FAMILY (page 289), helped show how family unity can be developed. As Professor of Social Philosophy at the New York School of Social Work, Columbia University, and as author and editor, he gained a wide experience in family relationships and their effect on the community.

Edward Liss

Lecturer in Psychiatry at State University College of Medicine, New York City, and specialist on relationships of children in the same family. In the chapter, SOME COMBINATIONS ARE A SPECIAL CHALLENGE (page 149), he points out how you can avoid some of the difficulties which arise when there are twins, wide age differences, or all girls or all boys in the family.

Berthold Lowenfeld

author of many articles and books on the child who is blind, is Superintendent of the California School for the Blind, Berkeley, Calif. In CHILDREN WHO CANNOT SEE (page 267), he brings helpful suggestions to those parents whose children have defective vision or no sight at all.

David R. Mace

author of *Marriage Crisis*, *Marriage Counseling*, and *Marriage: the Art of Lasting Love* is Professor of Human Relations at Drew University, Madison, N. J. In PARENTS ARE ALSO HUSBANDS AND WIVES (page 32), he shows how the relationships between wife and husband have an important bearing on the attitudes and lives of their children.

Elise H. Martens

teacher, writer, and author on the education of exceptional children. In her chapter, CHILDREN WHO ARE MENTALLY RETARDED (page 281), she brings a rare sympathy and a note of positive encouragement to parents in providing for the needs of the mentally retarded child.

William C. Menninger

is General Secretary of the internationally famous Menninger Foundation, Topeka, Kan., author of *Psychiatry in a Troubled World*, and co-author of *You and Psychiatry*. In YOU AS A PERSON (page 24), he brings you an understanding of the principles of mental hygiene as well as suggestions as to how emotional security can be achieved.

Edith G. Neisser

is author of *Brothers and Sisters*, numerous pamphlets and articles on family relations, and is CHILDCRAFT's Child Guidance Editor. As mother and grandmother, she brings practical experience to her chapter, SOMETIMES RIVALS, SOMETIMES FRIENDS (page 131). Here she shows how parents can minimize jealousy and quarreling when children have trouble in getting along together.

Ernest G. Osborne

is Professor of Education, Teachers College, Columbia University, N. Y., and Chairman of CHILDCRAFT's Editorial Advisory Board. In the chapter, YOU HAD A FAMILY, TOO (page 18), he brings out the fact that feelings which have persisted from your own childhood can influence the way you act toward your children or marriage partner. Ernest Osborne's leadership in education for family living and his sensitivity to family relationships give this chapter sound practical meaning.

Helen W. Puner

is author of *Daddies: What They Do All Day*, and of many other books and articles. In her chapter, FAMILY VACATIONS (page 175), she outlines practical ways to plan and manage family vacations so that they will satisfy every member of the family.

Marjorie K. Reynolds

is one of those gifted mothers who manages to give her family affectionate care and companionship, and still finds time to write articles on various phases of family life. In her chapter, THE FAMILY

KEEPS RECORDS (page 182), she demonstrates how family records can be kept so that they will bring lasting satisfactions.

Helen Ross

Administrative Director of the Institute for Psychoanalysis, Chicago, Ill., is the author of *Fears of Children*. In her chapter, PARENTS PLAY MANY PARTS (page 82), she explains how the roles of the father and mother change as children change and grow. Teachers, parents, and professional people who work with children draw renewed confidence from the gentle wisdom, constructive counsel, and reassurance of her teaching and writing.

May Reynolds Sherwin

author of *Children from Seed to Sapling* and of numerous magazine articles, brings a rich combination of study and experience to THE ADOPTED CHILD (page 231), for she and her husband adopted and brought up four children. She is familiar with the problems, the rewards, and the amusing and touching moments that fall to the lot of adopting parents.

Jayne Shover

is Associate Director of the National Society for Crippled Children and Adults, and is intimately familiar with the newest developments in treating, rehabilitating, and educating crippled children. In CHILDREN WHO ARE CRIPPLED (page 273), she brings you her special awareness of the hopes and fears of crippled children and their parents.

Mildred Shriner

with years of experience as classroom teacher of cerebral-palsied children, has worked closely with doctors, teachers, and therapists. She was formerly consultant for the National Society for Crippled Children and Adults. In CHILDREN WHO HAVE CEREBRAL PALSY (page 275), she passes on her thorough knowledge of how children suffering from this handicap can lead a better life.

Russell C. Smart

is Head of the Department of Child Development and Family Relations at the University of Rhode Island. With his wife, Mollie, he has written *It's a Wise Parent* and *Living and Learning with Children*. In the chapter, THE FATHER IN THE FAMILY (page 121), he, himself a father, brings you practical suggestions as to how fathers can help their children.

Edith M. Stern

co-author of *The Handicapped Child: A Guide for Parents* and other books on mental hygiene, has collaborated with Elsa Castendyck in writing THE HANDICAPPED CHILD IN THE FAMILY (page 258). These two authors tell what handicapped children need from their parents to grow up with courage and confidence.

Lois Meek Stolz

is Professor of Psychology, Stanford University, Calif., author of *Your Child's Development and Guidance*, and a member of CHILDCRAFT's Editorial Advisory Board. In her chapter, FAMILIES SHAPE PERSONALITY (page 99), she brings you things she has learned as the result of a lifetime of research in the field of child development and family relationships.

John W. Tenny

is General Adviser in Special Education at Wayne University, Detroit, Mich. In CHILDREN WHO ARE EPILEPTIC (page 278), his understanding of and experience with children who have this handicap bring hope and strength to their parents.

Ruth Wendell Washburn

consultant in child development, is author of *Children Have Their Reasons* and *Children Know Their Friends*. In her chapter DISCIPLINE FOR SELF-RELIANCE (page 107), her sympathetic understanding is helpful in showing how parents can arrange daily routines so that children learn acceptable ways of behaving and of achieving independence.

Anna Rose Wright

housewife and author of the popular book, *Room for One More*, is an advocate of generosity and good common sense. In her chapter, FAMILY CELEBRATIONS (page 167), she stresses how family ties can be strengthened by making the most of holidays, birthdays, and those unlabeled traditions treasured in closely-knit families.

Harvey Zorbaugh

is Director of the Counseling Center for Gifted Children, New York University. In his chapter, GIFTED CHILDREN (page 247), he brings you suggestions for letting the talented child use his gifts fully and satisfactorily at home and at school, without becoming set apart from other children.

UNDERSTANDING YOURSELF

1. JOYS AND DISAPPOINTMENTS OF BEING A PARENT
2. PARENTS ARE IMPORTANT
3. YOU HAD A FAMILY, TOO
4. YOU AS A PERSON
5. PARENTS ARE ALSO HUSBANDS AND WIVES

Many of our feelings about our children, our joys as well as our doubts and worries, have their roots in our feelings about ourselves, about our own parents, about our husbands, and about our wives.

In order to give our children the affection, the understanding, and the guidance they need from us as parents, we need to understand ourselves, and our relationship to those closest to us.

On such understandings are good, strong, satisfying families built. Such understandings can prevent many difficulties in family life and they can make it easier to work through those difficulties that are unavoidable.

JOYS AND DISAPPOINTMENTS OF BEING A PARENT

KATHERINE CLIFFORD, M.A.
Mother and Author, Upper Montclair, N. J.

Some days, they act like angels . . .

. . . other days, like little demons.

ARE YOUR children perfect? Ours are not. They are nice, normal children. Sometimes we think they are wonderful. Then there are days when everything goes wrong and we think we must be the world's worst failures as parents. That is when we stop and remember that satisfactions and heartaches are both a part of parenthood.

The pride you feel the day your six-year-old marches off to first grade has in it more than a twinge of regret. You know the bloom of his baby charm will soon be rubbed off, and, besides, you will miss having him around the house.

Confusing, contradictory feelings, existing almost at the same instant, are really the core of our emotional life.

If we understand ourselves, and the causes of our joys and disappointments, we will do better in the great task of understanding our children and guiding them toward happy, effective adulthood.

Why Do We Want Children?

Most people know with a certainty, born more of feeling than of logic, that marriage would not be complete without the kind of satisfaction children bring. Children are the fulfillment of love between a husband and wife. One of the characteristics of a person who is grown up in feeling is the willingness, in fact the desire, to assume the responsibility of caring for and giving to children. Perhaps one of the deepest reasons for having children is that our world values good, sound, everyday families. Could it also be that we want children because we are sure families are fun?

When you see your child take his place with his friends, you know you are doing well as a parent.

Families are fun. Families are the most lasting and rewarding kind of fun.

There Are Deep Satisfactions

From the day that your baby is born, you have the thrill of pride in creation. You look at this new life and think, "If it weren't for us, this child wouldn't be here." Even if yours is an adopted child, you make it over into something that is uniquely your own.

You find your heart swelling with pride, and a wave of affection sweeping over you, when you single out one small figure in a milling group of youngsters and think, "That's my own little boy." Being human, you probably also think, "How superior he is to all the other children there." You watch him in a school play, and you get a lump in your throat. He is so awkward, so inept, so intent, and so sincere—and he is yours! When he comes home, a mixture of braggadocio and sheepishness, you tell him over and over again how wonderful he was, and you mean every word of it.

It is fun to watch family traits cropping out, even though the traits themselves are not inherited. It is love that makes you so proud of having your children imitate you, even when the imitation is not flattering.

When Each Has a Place

It is satisfying to see a youngster take his place in the family, especially if there are other children. You wonder how the same parents could have offspring so different in every way. Each is unique in appearance, temperament, personality, and outlook. You prize each one of them just because he is yours. You take each one as he is, enjoying him for his own self.

In the whole of childhood, each day seems so long in the living, and so short when you try to recall it. You do not want to feel, too late, that you have not savored to the full each phase of your child's development. Your feeling is not "I hate to see this child grow up," but "I know that each step on the way up is too precious to lose."

You cannot afford to miss some of the pleasures that come at the most unexpected moments. A little boy snuggles down under the covers, after saying goodnight, then jumps up again to give you one last hug. "I'm the best hugger in the business," he says, "and all my hugs have Mommy and Daddy written on them."

When You Share Experience

While your children are small, your best moments are apt to arise out of experiences shared with them. You cannot depend on time left over from your work or your own amusement to be with them. You do better to *plan* times to do things with them. Sometimes you may do big, expensive things, such as going to the circus, or on a sightseeing trip. More often you can do little things, such as a walk in the park or a picnic in the country. Whether you take them to big-league ball games or play catch in the back yard, take them to concerts or sing nonsense songs with them, it is the "togetherness" that counts.

New pleasures crop up when your children go to school. You have the thrill of seeing their minds grow and develop. Now you can talk to them about things that interest you. You exult when they report progress, and, from your own past experiences, sympathize when they find it hard going. You are happy to see them make new friends and develop new interests. Perhaps you are a bit sad, too, because here is a new step toward independence. Of course you want them to be independent, but you miss the old dependence. The time when Mommy and Daddy were their whole world, when all they needed or wanted was you, had a joy all its own.

DOING THINGS TOGETHER IS FUN

It may be a trip to the circus . . .

. . . a walk in the park . . .

. . . or reading a story at bedtime.

Responsibilities Can Be Heavy

Years later, you look back on these early days fondly. But when you live around the clock with small children, you sometimes get bogged down in the day's routine.

One of the biggest changes a child brings to a young couple is that they can no longer come and go as they please. From the minute the baby comes home from the hospital until the day the youngest child starts school, Mother is on call twenty-four hours a day. She cannot even run around the corner for a loaf of bread unless she arranges for someone to stay with the baby.

The knowledge that this period is comparatively short-lived helps tide you over it. There will be many years when you can come and go without a thought. Then you may wish you could hear a small voice calling you again. You cannot escape the restrictions that come with children, but you can make up your

There will be days of worry when the work is heavy, or your child is sick or gets into mischief.

mind to value the rewarding moments.

Living with small children is physically exhausting. The lack of sleep, the noise, the dirt, the bickering, the ever-present laundry, the toys strewn over the house and the sidewalk are at times discouraging. The constant efforts to get children to do things they do not want to do, the continual questions and incessant demands on time and energy take a strong back and all kinds of patience.

Patience is the quality parents need most. There are times when it is the quality hardest to muster. The mother or father who can still say cheerfully, "Yes, honey, what is it?" the sixteenth time a two-year-old comes in crying, deserves a citation for "valor above and beyond the call of duty."

You Do Better than You Think

As children grow older, tests of your physical endurance decrease, but there may be some mental anguish. The children have more chances to get in trouble. More personality problems may bewilder you. Because they are older you expect more of them, yet their ideas do not coincide with yours any more than they did earlier. There is still the same old clash of wills. On many days, life with Junior and his sister is a struggle. But even when you are the most tired, irritated, and annoyed, you still would not trade your life for anyone's, or your children for any others.

You may get too conscious of your responsibilities. You have heard that a child's first years determine the whole course of his life. As a result you may be "scared to death" that you will do something that will ruin him forever.

Relax. All parents go through this. It is one of the occupational hazards of parenthood. Don't magnify your responsibilities. If you are honest, loving parents, trying to do a good job with your children and enjoying them most of the time, the chances are they will grow up just about the way you hope they will.

Overcoming Disappointments

It would not be fair, either to you or to the children, for you to make them your whole life. You might turn into one of those overdevoted, possessive parents. Fathers usually escape this fate, because their business interests occupy part of their attention and energies. It is mothers who are likely to sacrifice their own interests for the children's to an unwholesome extent.

You need fun on your own level, with friends your own age. It is good for you, occasionally, to be one in a group. A steady diet of being the central, directing, parent figure may make a mother a shade too queenly. You need to have interests outside the family circle. These interests help to prepare you for the day when the children no longer need you. Even when you cannot leave home physically, there is nothing to prevent your mind from roaming through the farthest reaches of books, music, and the world around you. You will be a better person, and a better parent, if you take a little time to refresh yourself physically, mentally, emotionally, and spiritually. Mothers and fathers need, and are entitled to, time for each other.

Don't Expect Children to Fulfill Your Dreams

Not all parents have the same kind of dream for the children's futures, but all the visions are rosy. In our house, for instance, we debate quite seriously whether it would be proper for our oldest boy, who plans to be President some day, to appoint as Chief of Staff his brother, who has his heart set on being a General.

That is the kind of dream that is fun to share with your children, because you do not have to believe in it, and there is not much danger that you will use undue and constant pressure to make it come true.

We exert more pressure—sometimes too much—to bring about the fulfillment of some of our dreams. It is natural for a father who is doing work he enjoys to hope that his son will follow in his footsteps.

It is natural for parents who have fallen short of realizing their own ambitions to be eager for their children to reach their goal for them. There is no harm in hoping or wanting, but the danger comes when pressure is put on children who do not want to, or cannot, fulfill their parents' hopes.

A boy may be so caught up with the love of his father's profession that he cannot imagine following any other trade or calling. That is fine. But his interests might lie along completely different lines, even though he admires his father greatly. It is not fair to mold him into a dissatisfied copy of his father just because he has not the courage to disappoint his parents.

If parents' hopes for the future are firmly set in one direction, the parents may be heartbroken when a youngster strikes off on pursuits of his own. But it is far better for the children to go their own way. Eventually parents become reconciled. The best way to avoid this kind of heartache is not to set your heart on your children becoming anything but nice, normal, happy adults. Then you will be able to accept the choices they make and the way they run their lives.

How Can You Take Their Troubles?

Parents may want to save their children from all heartaches, however slight. It cannot be done. We do not expect our children to be perfectly healthy, with never so much as a sniffle. Why should we expect them to be perfectly happy, with never a cloud in the sky? They will have to learn to take disappointments in their stride, if they are to become truly grown up.

You know how you tend to suffer more for your child than he does for himself. If Doris comes home completely downcast because three other fourth-graders have formed a club and excluded her, you feel a surge of anger against those spoiled little snobs who do not appreciate Doris. You would like to tell their mothers a few things! The next day, while you are still composing a fine speech to make to the first one of these mothers you chance to meet, Doris dances into the house beaming, because now she is in the club. You saw the situation with adult eyes and read more into it than your nine-year-old did.

You will have the same reaction to things that happen in school. You have to be on guard lest you magnify every fancied slight into evidence that friends are false or teachers unfair.

Your child needs to have you believe in him. He needs your confidence in his ability to solve his own problems, but you cannot continually do his thinking for him. If he needs help and asks for it, you are there to give it. If he is learning to stand on his own feet, he may not want help.

You Need Faith

There are few things in life that approach the tension of parents hanging over a sick child's bed, fearful that each minute may bring a turn for the worst. That is when you need faith and hope. Fortunately such moments do not happen often, for they are among the hardest that any parent has to face.

You may go through agonies of doubt when your children get into trouble. They can run into small troubles, such as the clashes with the teacher at school. Then there are the bigger troubles, when they do something like destroying a neighbor's property. You worry about what you may have done to make them behave that way. This is the time you need faith. You need faith in the basic soundness of your way of raising children. You need faith in your ability to discover, perhaps with professional help, what the cause of the trouble may be.

Are Your Standards Too High?

Most children go through stages when it is hard even to live with their disagreeable behavior. They will answer you in a nasty tone. They will be sulky, stubborn, aggrieved, or remote and unapproachable. They will just slide by in school when you know they could do much better if they would only try. They will be lazy and unco-operative, demanding and ungrateful.

The knowledge that other people's

Gendreau

Sulkiness is a part of growing up.

children do the same things will help you over many rough spots. Books about child development will tell you what to expect of children at different ages. Taking part in study groups and Parent-Teacher Association discussions will convince you that all children go through some difficult and unhappy stages. Reading and discussion can give you an idea of what may be expected in the course of normal development, and of what may be a danger signal.

Many of us set our standards too high. We feel guilty every time we fall short of our picture of the Ideal Parent. But even the experts do not expect us to live up to all their suggestions all the time. They assume we will do our best and will not worry if our best is far from perfection.

One of the finest things you can do for your children is to enjoy them. Don't let other things crowd out your fun with your children. Don't let them suffer because you are too busy keeping house, or keeping up with the Joneses. Save your energy for the things that really matter.

A Sense of Humor Saves the Day

One of your most valuable assets is a sense of humor. We knew a little girl who once shrilled at her mother "You're mean. You're just like Cinderella's mean old stepmother." Her mother could have been angry because her daughter was behaving badly. Instead, she laughed.

"Oh, I don't know," she said, "I always thought I was more like her fairy godmother." The little girl laughed, too, and the whole thing blew over in an exchange of hugs and kisses. That is the kind of mother who will enjoy her children. She does not take the things they say too seriously.

When You Are Puzzled

We all occasionally run up against problems too big to be dismissed lightly. Then is the time to look around for advice from someone qualified to give it. Many parents are afraid to consult people trained to give them just the kind of help they need, because they feel it is an admission of failure. Going to a child-guidance clinic or to a psychologist or psychiatrist does not mean you have a serious problem, but rather that you want to keep a problem from becoming serious. Seeking help does not mean you are less effective as a parent than your grandmother was. After all, she never took penicillin when she was sick. They did not have that in her day, either. The chapter FAMILY GUIDANCE SERVICES, in Volume 15, will suggest where to look for help if you need it.

Nobody can feel love for anyone all the time, and nobody needs to try to do so. You enjoy your children most if you learn to prize every satisfaction and minimize the disappointments. When things go wrong, you can take an "into each life some rain must fall" attitude. Do what you can to improve matters, by all means, but don't expect the impossible of yourself, of your husband, of your wife, or of your children. Part of being grown up is taking things as they are.

Of course you want your children to be a credit to you and an asset to their community. But remember that the measure of your happiness and effectiveness as a parent is not how high your children climb, but how much fun you had with them along the way.

PARENTS ARE IMPORTANT

LAWRENCE K. FRANK, B.A.
Formerly Director, Caroline Zachry Institute,
New York, N. Y.

and

MARY H. FRANK, B.S.
Co-author "How to Help Your Child in School"

Lapham

Everything that is good in human beings, all the art and poetry, the song and music, the generosity, the gladness, the kindness, the love of people for one another, is nurtured by fathers and mothers living together and creating human family life.

The family is a group of people who live together more closely and for a longer span of time than any other group. In any such intimate group you may find in miniature most of the problems of humanity. But you will also find the strength of humanity.

World War II, with its direct effect on the lives of parents and children, jostled us into a realization of how precious parents are to their children. It brought us to the full awareness that although what parents do for children may seem like simple tasks, yet no other persons can be immediate substitutes for parents. The war also brought home the necessity of preserving for families the good things in parenthood. The wisdom of parents, their confidence in themselves, in their lives, and in the future deserve careful cultivation.

Hidden Values in Parenthood

We might call these good things the "hidden values" in family life. Doctors and those who study human behavior have made the discovery that babies need a mother's close love to be healthy and happy. Clear proof is now at hand that babies in institutions, with the best of scientific care, feeding, and cleaning, are still not as happy and as energetic as babies who are cared for at home.

But, surprisingly, many persons do not know how greatly every baby needs its mother and her love. Her cuddling as well as her feeding, clothing, bathing, and other physical care help him thrive.

How Can Love Give Protection?

As babies grow into young childhood, the "hidden values" of a parent's love—

Mother's arms provide the comfort, love, and warmth every child needs.

that is, such values as warmth and encouragement—help the little child grow. He needs these if he is to be happy and healthy, to enjoy playing with other children, and to be friendly. Those hidden values help children to meet the "bumps" in life. The frightening times, the unhappy times, the difficult lessons of growing up become less disturbing when parental love and encouragement act as shock-absorbers for a child. They help him meet life's upsets without permanent damage. His courage, his friendliness, his happiness in living are far less likely to be dampened if a youngster knows Mother and Father will stand by him, come what may.

To prove that this is so, once again we have to find out what happens to children who do not have their parents, or their parents' love, in frightening times. During World War II, Dr. Anna Freud and Dorothy Burlingham worked in England with little children who had lived through bombing experiences. The children who stayed with their parents during the bombing were much less upset and anxious than children who had been kept in a safe place, but separated from their parents.

Also, over and over again, in studying disturbed children, psychiatrists find that, just at the time of some hurtful or frightening event, the child has not had the "shock-absorber" he needed. The love and reassurance of a parent, the hidden values, might have told him that things were all right and helped to tide him over his difficulties.

In modern times we have thus discovered an old truth in a roundabout way. Parents and parents' love are important. Without them children are unhappy or disturbed as they grow into adulthood.

Your Importance Increases

As your children grow out of early childhood and begin to "talk back" to you, or to fuss about family rules, you might assume that this means "My child is beginning to dislike me." There are times when you wonder, "Have my children outgrown the need for my love?— All they seem to need is a little discipline now." But no matter what happens, no matter who you are or what you do, you, the parents, are the most important persons in the world to your children.

You Teach Through What You Are

As your child grows he depends more and more on his parents, and on his home and his family for everything that he will take to his own future as a man or a woman. Ways of talking to others close to him, ways of working in the family, ways of having fun and sharing things are all learned from what Mother and Father say and do. Most especially a way of *giving* to other human beings, giving without getting a receipt for what is given, or without asking for something in return, is absorbed from the behavior of Mother and Father and the atmosphere of home.

This learning, again, is what we like to call a "hidden value" in parenthood and family life. *Parents are so important that they are the cornerstones of democracy, or of any society. By what they do to each other and to their children, they build the nation.* Parents do much of this silently, without "preaching at" their children or knowing what they are giving. Many a mother or father admires his sons and daughters and their good qualities without realizing what he or she has done to help produce those qualities!

Hidden Values Are the Roots

These are the "good" things. These hidden values of parenthood live with children, like the roots of a plant, as long as the children live. Parents in each family give their children something special, to make them different persons, interesting persons. Without knowing it, your children, and their children, and their children's children will continue to do many things in the same ways their parents did, because it has become part of them.

Both parents are important. Not just a mother, not just a father, but a mother and a father working and living together, solving problems together, laughing, quarreling, ironing out difficulties, show a child how to live.

When a baby smiles and reaches out his hands to his father or to his mother, you have a deep something in him that grows as he grows. You have that peculiar, indescribable quality of wanting to be alive, wanting to learn, wanting to explore. You see the desire to be close to Mother or Father, who gives the important love.

Why "Disturbed" Children?

Now, as you begin to see what a parent can give a child and, incidentally,

Shune Snow

The courage to learn and to explore grows from trust and confidence.

what parents can give the world, it is difficult to understand the other side of the picture. Why are there so many unhappy children and adults? Some children cannot learn or work with others because of deep hurts that are still bothering them.

If only a parent's love can start the growth of those priceless, rich human qualities, then, in the many problem cases you read about, there must have been something missing in the family. What was wrong with the parents and their love?

There are never any clear-cut answers to questions such as these. We must hesitate to explain any one instance without a great deal of study and research. But we can make some general observations about those disturbed children.

Not the Event, but How You Handle It, Counts

In most cases something happened to hurt a child deeply. If a new baby has taken all Mother's and Father's attention, there may be upset and unhappiness. A child may have had a frightening experience. A father or mother may have gone away for awhile, and not left a loving person to care for the child. Perhaps a parent died or was divorced and left the home. Also, scores of events that we do not consider out of the ordinary may be hurtful to children.

Experiences that *might* be hurtful, whether big or little, take place in every family and happen to almost every child. They are a part of life. A toy breaks, a doll smashes, a dog dies. There is an automobile accident, or the child is ill for a long time, or he has an operation. Most children are able to take the majority of these experiences in their stride. Why then do they leave scars on some?

It is the people around a child who count when these incidents occur. What the persons who are important to him do or say in such cases is more crucial than the event itself. Parents are often unaware that they can help, with reassurance and love for their child.

How Can Reassurance Give Strength?

A little child does not realize fully why things happen as they do. He is confused when he is hurt, when people leave, get sick, or die. To him, many ordinary events seem like the end of the world—or at least the end of his world and his happiness. He needs to be reassured again and again by his mother or father, or others close to him. This steady reassurance, or trust and protection of his parents, gives him strength. The hidden values parents offer children help them meet the hurts of everyday life in our world.

Hurtful experiences may be harmful when a child has the feeling that his parents or their love and reassurance have been taken away.

Take a jealous child who feels that his parents' love has been given to someone else—to a new, tiny baby, for example. The jealous child is not happy, and so for awhile he may be what his parents call "nasty." He may hurt the baby, his mother, his grandmother, or himself. He may cry, refuse to sleep, to play, or to pick up his toys. He wants his mother's love, for without it, he feels that life will be bleak and miserable.

Fears Can Cause Misbehavior

Continued jealousy is one of the experiences that may hurt a child deeply if no one helps him feel better. If he has a deep fright and no one comforts him, he may get a feeling of panic, a feeling that no one will protect him.

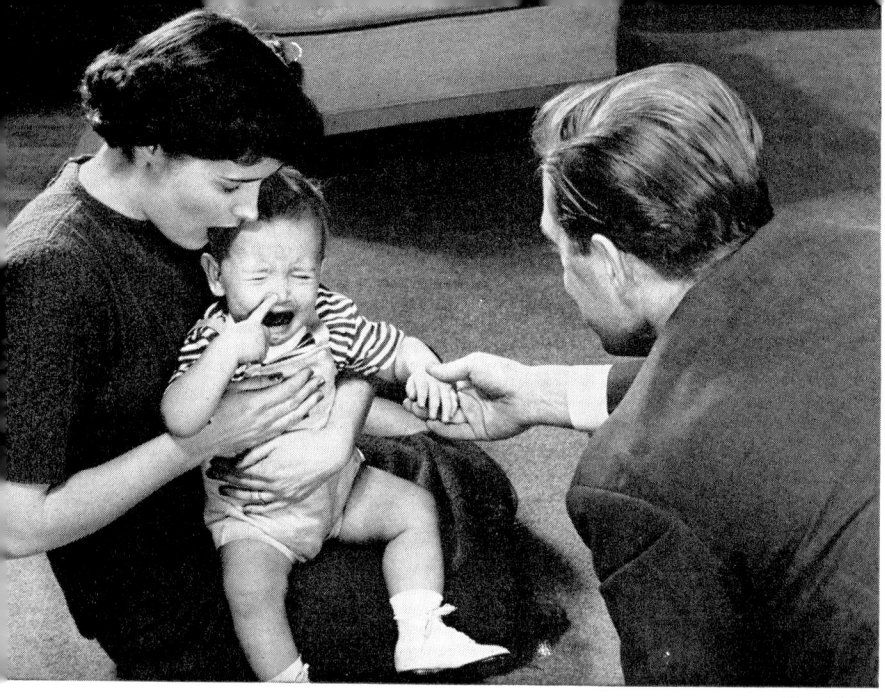

When things go wrong is the time your youngster needs to be reassured again and again.

Tana Hoban

For most children in frightening situations there is usually someone at hand to help smooth feelings; or a child may have had enough previous reassurance to draw on in a bad moment. It is the persistent pattern, the accumulation of these disturbing experiences, that often warps the growing child or damages his confidence.

In a well-meant but misguided effort to "toughen" a child, sometimes adults think it is better to ignore his fears. A parent may neglect to reassure a child to help him feel better before an operation. Or a parent may not realize that a divorce, or death, hurts the child. The mother or father may go away for a long time without leaving the child in a happy state with a person who loves him.

What Makes a Child "Unlovable"?

A parent may misunderstand a child's behavior and punish him for showing fright or unhappiness, instead of reassuring him. Frequent harsh punishments leave a child tense and mixed up.

A baby boy nine months old was extremely ill. He cried at night, he was irritable, and he was frightened by the doctor who came often to give him the medicine he needed.

The baby cried at night for a long time, even when there was no more pain or fever. He continued to be irritable, too. He shied away from strangers, and ate only a little.

The baby's mother was told by her mother-in-law that the child was "spoiled," but actually the baby was cross and fearful because of what he had gone through. A severe illness, with a hurtful cough, pains, doctors, and medicines, would make even a puppy mixed-up and "nasty."

But the baby's mother liked to do what was right. She was tired. Maybe the baby was spoiled, she felt! She started a program of letting him cry himself to sleep, and of spanking him, so he would "get over" his fussiness. To most babies, under ordinary circumstances, a crying spell or a spanking might do no harm. But this baby had been frightened badly before. He became tense and un-

When Mother's patience has worn thin, Father can take over.

happy, and everybody called him "unlovable."

Even older children can be hurt unintentionally by such a train of events, Gradually they really seem like "mean" children, when perhaps the trouble is that an old problem or a past experience is still bothering them. Certainly parents do not mean to hurt their children, but sometimes, even with good intentions, parents fail to understand the reasons for behavior, and, because of this, they get off on the wrong track.

Preventing Damage

In most families, fortunately, the "bad" experiences do *not* turn into deep problems. What happens to keep the children in good mental health? Probably *both* parents take a hand in giving the child love and attention. If Mother is tired or cranky, Father slips in a little extra kindness and love.

At the time of frightening events, parents may not always be near by. If they help reassure the child afterward, many troubles may be avoided. When they see he is frightened, they do not shame him, or force him to be brave. They give him reassurance and quiet consolation when he needs it. Gradually, he loses the deep fright.

Probably most parents are equipped with good solid common sense. Each day just by being there they help a child see that he can go on living, playing, and working. Life then is not just full of fears or hurts, but is also exciting and rewarding.

Two Heads Are Better than One

Two parents, with two personalities and two points of view, often save the day for the family, and prevent a problem for the child. A little girl may seem fussy to her mother, but her father's "attention" sweetens her up in no time! It is so often the second parent who can do the trick. The one who comes to the situation "fresh," who is not all upset at the time, or all tired out from a day's care of the children, has, often, a wonderful, healing quality. Here we see why fathers are so important for children.

In most families, humor, happy experiences, interests, and talking things out together also help dissolve a child's glumness or misery. Of course, if there is an especially severe problem for the child to deal with, such as death or divorce, it is more difficult to keep a youngster on an even keel. The section on FAMILY CRISES in this volume discusses these situations in detail.

Today's Parents Want Help

Problems are not new in families; nor are they new for children. Why is it, then, that today's parents seek so much advice about child care from books, lectures, pamphlets? Are there more problems for families today? Are there more reasons for children to have problems? The changes that have come about in families in the last two or three generations have tended to make our communities less unified. A family today is smaller, and more isolated from both its neighbors and its relatives, than it would have been fifty or seventy-five years ago. You can read more about these changes and how they affect families in the chapters THINGS AREN'T THE SAME, in this volume, and OUR CHANGING WORLD and YOUR NEIGHBORS—DICTATORS, TROUBLEMAKERS, OR FRIENDS, in Volume 15.

Exchanging Ideas Can Be Useful

Parents are not less intelligent nowadays, though they may be more lonely, more isolated, and more in need of sympathetic advice. Many parents seek help through getting in touch with one another. They find reassurance in hearing each others' problems. They want to find ways of solving problems in common with other parents. They want to feel that there is a way of talking to children, helping children, disciplining children, and talking *about* children that they can share with other mothers and fathers. Most parents want to feel: "When I do this, I am helping myself and my child to live more happily and more humanly with other people."

The chapter HOME AND SCHOOL ARE A TEAM, in Volume 15, has valuable suggestions for ways parents and schools can work together. Unfortunately, today parents (and teachers) get scolded more often than the youngsters in their charge! Also, they are blamed (more often than other groups) for *all* the evils in the world. Most often, parents need help in their own living, security with other people, understanding from schools and community leaders. In order to help their children, and in order to do it well, they need to know they are doing a great and difficult job. Often parents find the help they need in a child-guidance center or family-counseling service, but emotional tangles are more readily unraveled in their early stages. The chapter FAMILY GUIDANCE SERVICES, in Volume 15, tells how qualified counselors can help you.

You Need Not Be Perfect

Parents are important, not because they are perfect, but because they are human. In talking together, making mistakes, making plans, quarreling and making up, in all the daily experiences, parents give children a pattern of living that is hopeful and ongoing.

Children learn to live and to be happy from watching the adults closest to them. But, for generations, parents have felt that they should know all the answers, and *not* make mistakes.

Of course there is no human being who could live up to these specifications. Yet parents have tried, with their children, to appear absolutely sure of themselves. In most cases children can feel it when parents are "pretending." But, in many cases, children are frightened and bewildered by such extreme sternness, especially if it never turns to softness, laughter, or kindness.

How Are the Human Values Handed On?

Children learn to be human from watching human beings live. They learn not only how to be "mad," but also how to be "glad." They learn from their own experiences how to live with people in a family year after year, giving others, too, a chance to speak, to act, and to have their own interests.

Children learn to enjoy living from the adults closest to them. They learn to be curious, to be alive, to have new ideas. They learn to enjoy both work and rest, and to work happily—if the adults enjoy their work as parents. It is not strange that curious, lively, intelligent minds are often found in happy children.

Children learn to meet their own problems from watching adults meet theirs. It does not matter that the problems of each are different. When the adults around continually try to do the wisest thing by talking things out, asking the opinions of others in the family, children learn to do the same. Then the children are better able to try going ahead without too much fear or distrust of themselves.

How Do Families Teach Democracy?

Children learn to live in a democratic society by living in their families with their parents. They learn that no one person is perfect, but that everyone learns by working and living each day. They learn to respect and to like authority, when they have found that their closest authorities—that is, their parents —usually try to help them, listen to them, and offer fair rules.

Children also learn the necessity for some wise authority who does not control with an iron hand but who helps them look at all sides of a problem. Probably most important, in such families children learn more and more to use their own judgment and to use it wisely and with conviction.

Parents are important to their children because in everything they do, no matter how simple, they are showing youngsters what it is to love, to grow, and to give to others.

A Good Parent Can Give Faith in Life

Children need to meet problems, to make mistakes as they grow. They need to know that problems can be "licked." They need to see how adults tackle problems. They need to find that the best fun in life comes if one believes in other people. The best kind of strength arises from the feeling that one can "put his thinking-cap on." Children can get the feeling, too, that, if one is admired and loved, life really *is* good—and *can* be good for their own children and their children's children.

We need faith in living today. In difficult, troublesome times we try to find what it is we believe in most deeply, most certainly. We believe in the close love bonds of parents who are generous and warm, and who know the satisfaction of rearing children who are able to be happy and to give.

YOU HAD A FAMILY, TOO

ERNEST G. OSBORNE, Ph.D.
Professor of Education, Teachers College,
Columbia University, New York, N. Y.

Have you ever come into a theater when the first act was nearly over? Or have you ever had the experience of coming into the motion-picture house in the middle of the picture? If so, you know what a wrong impression you may get of some of the characters. How different your feeling about them is when you have seen the entire performance!

So it is with everyday, flesh-and-blood people. When we see them as husbands and wives, as fathers and mothers, some of the things they do are hard to understand. But if we can get a picture of their place as children in their own families, things may come clearer.

You Carry Childhood with You

Here is Charles Moody. He is father of four children, and a hard-working, responsible business man. But he expects to be waited on hand and foot when he is at home. He is nice enough about it, but he gets the idea across. Yet Mr. Moody does not realize that he expects more than do most other men. He grew up in the kind of home where mother and sisters always waited on the menfolks, and seemed to like it. To him, this is the natural order of things. He would be shocked if told he is selfish.

The Roots Are Deep

Mary Manson is a "perfect housekeeper." She cannot bear to have any ashes in ashtrays, or the slightest hint of dust in the corners of the room. In some ways, life is made rather unpleasant for her husband and the children. They get the feeling that a clean house is much more important to Mom than anything else. Mrs. Manson, herself, fails to realize that the roots of her cleaning "bug" go back to the days of her childhood. Her mother made her feel, as a little girl, that the only way you could really be sure you were approved of or loved was to keep yourself and everything around you in apple-pie order.

Dr. Louis Maynard is a big man in town. He is the outstanding physician.

He is also a civic leader, president of his service club, an active member of the chamber of commerce, and prominent in the church. Yet, at home, there are unmistakable signs that he is jealous of the attention his wife gives to their ten-year-old son.

Doc's family background tells the story. His mother died when he was only five. For the next ten or twelve years he was shunted about among relatives who had children of their own. Over and over again, he was made to feel that he came second. Even though his aunts and uncles were kind, the boy Louis could not get over the feeling that he was a sort of stepchild. When he married, he felt that at last he would come first in someone's affections. In spite of himself, he felt pushed into second place again when his son was born, and Mrs. Maynard had to give the baby a great deal of attention.

Understand the Causes

In one way or another, everyone brings to his own family as husband or wife, father or mother, attitudes and expectations that have been laid down in the family in which he grew up. The first step in being able to come to terms with these influences, to use them constructively, to control them, is to understand them. There are innumerable ways in which your early family life may have affected you. By looking at some of the more commonly occurring ones, you may find cues to understanding yourselves and your husbands or wives.

Childhoods Affect Marriage

The degree to which you work out a good marriage relationship has much to do with your effectiveness and your happiness as parents. Of course, this is a matter of degree. Some may not have entirely satisfactory husband-wife relationships. Yet they are fine parents. Others may get along well as husband and wife but are inadequate as parents. But these are definitely exceptions. For most of us, there is a close relationship between satisfaction in marriage and effectiveness as parents.

In Search of a Parent

Some individuals have never been fathered or mothered enough. Like Dr. Maynard, they may quite unknowingly be looking for a father or a mother in their marriage partner. In childhood, perhaps, the boy received little warmth or attention from his mother or the girl from her father. One way of reacting to such a situation is to go on hunting for the lost parent in other relationships. Older, or at least more mature, members of the opposite sex are the ones to whom such a dependent individual is attracted.

This need not be an undesirable relationship if the marriage partner gets satisfaction out of being fatherly or motherly. But most husbands find the perpetual "child-wife" something of a strain. Most women want men, rather than everlasting little boys, as husbands. The husband or wife who first and always needs a parent rather than a partner may become something of a burden. But, of course, even the bravest *sometimes* needs to be dependent!

You Cannot Relive the Past

Sometimes the dependent relationship to a wife or husband is due to the fact that such deep satisfaction was found in a close tie to the parent of the opposite sex that the same sort of thing is sought in marriage.

This variation on the theme might be called, "The Case of the Prince Charming" or, with the sex reversed, "The Princess and Her Court." When an individual is the one child of his or her sex in the family, it can happen that father and mother, even sisters or brothers, focus a great amount of attention on the

The girl who is the center of attention will get a false idea of her own importance.

beloved one. He or she may never be really satisfied with anything less than the center of the stage in later life. For such a person the give and take that marriage usually requires is hard to learn. Such a person always needs an excessive amount of attention and affection. Even the children are expected to play the role of courtiers to mothers or fathers with that kind of background.

Men or women raised in a family where little affection is shown between parents often find it "unnatural" to show affection openly. Sometimes a reserved individual marries a person in whose family love and affection were constantly and openly demonstrated. That couple will have some adjustments to make. What is embarrassing to one may be an essential proof of love to the other.

How to Get Rid of Ghosts

Remember that affection is not the only childhood experience that is carried over into adult marriage relationships. David Wright's mother had tried to control his every thought and action. As a matter of self-protection, he had learned to resist. Sometimes he could handle the situation calmly. Sometimes he "blew up."

Though his wife was a different sort of person from what his mother had been, his defensive reactions showed themselves often in the early years of their marriage. He saw, in every suggestion she made, the old dominating approach of the senior Mrs. Wright. His wife was puzzled and distressed by his behavior until she realized that her husband had been treated to an overdose of petticoat rule in his early years. Once she recognized this, she saw that his anger was not really directed at her. Before long she was able to help her husband see the difference between her approach and that of his mother.

Beulah Jones' family life had been an unhappy one. Her folks were constantly bickering. She swore to herself that when she married there would be none of this. But her fear of quarrelling and unpleasant words was so strong that she could not cope with healthy difference of opinion. She was afraid that any question she might raise about her husband's ideas would lead to the same sort of thing she had so disliked in her childhood home.

She made a tremendous effort to keep quiet, even though she was boiling inside. Often her unnatural restraint led to an icy politeness, much less healthy than a warm argument. Fortunately, as her husband began to recognize her difficulty, he was able to help her to express her point of view. Eventually she saw that she could even quarrel with his ideas without having things go to pieces.

In almost any kind of husband-wife relationship the effect of childhood experiences may be felt. Differences may arise over the control and use of the family income, the kind of responsibility each should have for the care of the home, entertaining and friendships, or a hundred other things. If you recognize that all these may have their roots in the past, if you are willing to try to understand each other's backgrounds, such differences usually can be handled. They can become a challenge to overcome rather than a barrier to happiness.

The man who grew up under too much petticoat rule is likely to resent constant suggestions from his wife.

If things were different when you were a child, you may feel life is too easy for your own children.

Children Bring Back the Past

As children are born into the family, and as you live with them day by day, memories and feelings of your own childhood are aroused.

Perhaps this past that children bring back is made up largely of warm memories, of happy times with parents, brothers, and sisters. The spontaneous picnics, the fun on summer holidays, when Dad was with the family all day long, come back to you as you bring up your own children. Memories of the nor-

Some parents want to give their youngsters all the things that they did not have as children.

mal, everyday "fights" now have pleasant overtones and come flooding back to you in your job as parent. What fun it is to see your child discover the exciting world about him! What satisfaction to tie that up with your own memories of similar discoveries!

There are other things in the past, too, that may not be so pleasant. Perhaps you feel resentful that your children "have it so easy," and you had such struggles! One father thought his eight-year-old boy would become soft if he did not have to walk three miles to school, as he had. Sometimes you look at your own past, decide that you have come through pretty well, and feel that the only way your children can turn out as well is to go through the same experiences.

Can They Avoid Your Heartaches?

Sometimes you do just the opposite. You make every effort to make up to the children for what you may have missed. You shower your youngsters with gifts, for you remember how little you had as a child.

Arthur Thompson, though nearly forty, still remembered how unhappy he was because he could not play games as well as the rest of the boys. When Arthur, Jr., came along, big Arthur dreamed of the time when he could go to the high-school football games and see his boy star. Almost as soon as Junior could walk, his father began coaching him to hold a ball, to throw it, to kick it, and to run. But this was not the kind of thing the boy liked to do. Before long, a tense relationship was built up, which caused great unhappiness.

Sylvia Stern had been something of a wallflower when she was a girl. Her dreams, her expectations for her daughter centered in a series of social triumphs. Like Arthur Thompson, Sr., she was going to make up through her child for what she had missed.

Sometimes these plans work. But, usually, your desire to make up for the past through your children brings only unhappiness, stress, and strain for all concerned.

History Repeats Itself

In other interesting ways, too, the past is resurrected by your children. When James Adams overheard his nine-year-old daughter rather sharply order her younger brother to do something, he, himself, was surprised at the violence of his own reaction. Sternly he ordered her to go into the house, and never let him hear her speak that way again. The little girl was upset, for much of the ordering around was in play. Later, Mr. Adams spoke of the incident to his mother, who was visiting.

"I wonder, James," she said, "whether you weren't so upset because Sandra's ordering Danny around reminded you of the way your sister used to talk to you?" As a grown man, James Adams had forgotten about these early experiences with a bossy sister. When he recalled those incidents, the reasons for his anger became clearer. He had been so upset because he saw himself, without realizing it, in the same position as his son.

It is harder than you think to separate early relationships with your own brothers and sisters from present relationships with your children. If one of your own youngsters reminds you strongly of a favorite sister, that child is likely to get a little more attention, a bit more approval, than the other children. The boy whose mannerisms remind you of the brother with whom you competed bitterly may well get the short end of the deal from you on occasion. Nobody does such things purposely, but your emotions may play tricks on you.

Your own early family experiences intrude upon your relationships with, and your feeling about, your children. Recognize the possibility of the tie between your childhood experiences and your behavior as parents. Then you can usually guard against undesirable feelings and build on the good points.

Childhoods Affect Parenthood

Parents often disagree about discipline of children. The root of these disagreements is rarely a matter of principle, but much more a matter of personal feeling. That was the case with the Williams family.

Albert Williams had been brought up in a family where the father's word was law. Children were literally to be seen and not heard. Father was always right, no matter what the facts of a situation happened to be. Punishment was dispensed freely. For some youngsters, this might not have been too bad, but Albert was desperately unhappy. As a father, he went to the opposite extreme. It was almost impossible for him to use any sort of discipline with the children. He always would take their part and protect them.

Mrs. Williams had grown up in a different sort of home. Her parents had seemed almost indifferent when it came to controlling the children. Often, as she grew older, she wished that one or the other parent had set some limits, had given her some direction. It was painful to be so entirely on one's own in making decisions. When she thought about bringing up her own children, she decided that they were not going to be deprived of discipline in the way she had been.

Of course, the Williamses worked at cross purposes, with unhappy results, until they were able to face the reasons for their own attitudes. When they realized that they were reacting to their extreme personal backgrounds, they were able to work out agreements on most questions.

Face the Past to Deal with It

Sometimes you find that the things that happened to you as you were growing up cling like burrs to a soft sweater. In spite of yourself, you feel things you know are not right. Fortunately, your children are usually tolerant and understanding. They can accept certain weaknesses in you, if you give them the chance, when they realize how these have developed. Facing the facts with husbands or wives, and even at times with children, will counteract the unfortunate effects of old attitudes.

The business of fact-facing will help in all the situations that have been discussed, and in others like them. Husbands and wives can help each other discover the ways their early experiences are being carried over. Sympathetically, they can give each other aid and comfort in their mutual attempts to do away with the disadvantages, and to build on the advantages, of their early backgrounds. If they can continue to discuss things honestly and frankly, they can go a long way in coming to terms with deeply buried attitudes and reactions.

You can face squarely the fact that you each had a family. You can acknowledge that that family had much to do with what you are at present. Then your own family life can be more deeply satisfying.

YOU AS A PERSON

WILLIAM C. MENNINGER, M.D.
General Secretary, The Menninger Foundation, Topeka, Kan.

Taking a good look at yourself may help all members of the family.

"KNOW THYSELF!" words made famous by Socrates more than 2,000 years ago, is good advice. The more clearly we understand our feelings, the better we can build relationships with other persons. The better we understand our relationships with our children, the better we can do our jobs as parents.

If we look at ourselves carefully, we can now and then recognize some of the disguises that our angry feelings take—stubbornness, willfulness, neglect, or forgetfulness. We can see how we take out our annoyance and disappointment, not on the real source of irritation, but on some innocent bystander, even on our children. A headache or stomachache may be caused by an emotional rather than by a physical problem.

Personality Is Complicated

You cannot understand how any machine works unless you know something about its structure and the interrelations of its parts. The same principle applies to understanding that delicate and complicated machine, your own personality.

Certain of our qualities are the result of the biological union of the two cells from our parents. It is generally agreed that our capacity to learn and to use what we learn is inherited. In all probability, too, we inherit the capacity to develop certain skills. Even more important than inheritance in forming personality is our environment. It is really impossible to separate the two forces, for one actually inherits part of his environment.

Parents, brothers and sisters, other members of the household, immediate friends, and schoolteachers participate in molding the young personality. Customs and events in the wider community where you live help to shape your personality as you grow up. Every individual is unique, for each is shaped by a unique combination of forces.

What Is Personality?

Even though people differ widely as individuals, each has a heart, a stomach, a brain, and a personality. Scientific study has led to the conclusion that personality is made up of the unconscious, the conscious, and the conscience. In order to understand oneself, one must have some information about the way these three parts work.

The Unconscious Supplies Energy

The unconscious is a portion of the personality with which we are born. We are rarely aware of our unconscious, and we have little control over it. For all practical purposes the unconscious, like the heart or the liver, is vital to life but not subject to conscious control. All through our lives, the unconscious part of our personality is the powerhouse from which our energy comes.

The unconscious is primitive and animallike in its nature. Its impulses have to be modified and controlled through training. When one does not succeed fully in modifying the energy that comes from these primitive impulses, it may show up in childish acts, in behavior that seeks to hurt others or to avoid them. Unreasonable fears, anxiety, physical symptoms are almost always due to emotional causes. They may be the expression of unconscious impulses which have not been controlled or modified.

The Conscious—the Familiar "You"

The conscious part of our personality begins to develop at birth. Its growth is directed at first by our parents, and later by all the forces which contribute to our education. The conscious part of the personality is the part we know as ourselves. It is the remembered accumulation of ideas and attitudes, memories, and beliefs. The conscious part of our personality directs our behavior and sets the pattern for the way we act.

If there are difficulties in establishing healthy early relationships, behavior that might be acceptable in a baby or a small child continues long past the time that it would be useful. The man who feels he must fight for everything he receives is using the only technique he found successful in babyhood and childhood. The little boy who is unable to establish a happy relationship with his father may go through life resenting authority in any form. The individual who, as a child, was forced to stay dependent long after he should have been looking after himself in many ways, is apt, as an adult, to continue to be dependent on others instead of relying on himself.

The Conscience Is a Policeman

The conscience begins to develop as we take over from our parents some responsibility for our own behavior. The child is likely to make the ideals and standards of his parents his own. Parental standards are modified and further developed by religious training and by the early contacts a child has with people. The conscience is, all through life, our own internal policeman. We feel its effects most often as dissatisfaction with ourselves, or as guilt. Sometimes these feelings seem unjustified by any conscious yardstick. Conscience is discussed in detail in the chapter HE HAS A CONSCIENCE, in Volume 13.

Why Should We Understand Ourselves?

Reasonable or unreasonable acts can

The boy or girl who is bossed too much may grow up to resent a boss of any kind.

be explained by the performance of one or another of these three related parts of the personality. Knowledge about the make-up of our personalities helps us see how we use our early ways of behaving to meet situations in adult life. Such knowledge helps us understand that our mistakes are due to being human, not to being stupid or lazy.

This Is Mental Health

Mental health concerns various kinds of "psychological pains" such as anxiety, fear, depression, excitement, and hate. These usually occur in our relationships with people in everyday living.

It is apparent that we all fall short of having a healthy mind at times. We each have our inadequacies and our weaknesses in our relationships with other people. When our child is failing in school, when our neighbor is unfriendly, when our boss is irritable, or when we are worried about the state of the world, we are subject to emotional stress. We may show evidences of varying degrees of mental ill-health as pressures affect our lives, but, fortunately for most of us, our less-healthy moments are brief and not too disturbing to the people around us.

Unhappy childhood experiences, emotional blows or constant pressures, do, unfortunately, disable some of us. It is reassuring to know that nowadays the great majority of individuals who become mentally ill can be restored to health.

Freedom from Internal Conflict

To be mentally healthy, one must have relative peace of mind. The word "relative" is important since it is also true that one must be willing to go all out in working for socially approved hopes, desires, and ambitions.

Consider the young mother who at one time expected to use her real musical gifts as a pleasant hobby, if not actually in a career. Her three small children, her home, and her husband give her great satisfaction, but they take every minute of her time and every ounce of her energy. On the rare occasions when she sits down at the piano, she realizes what lack of practice is doing to her touch.

She regrets giving up her interest in music, for it was often a source of comfort as well as pleasure to her. It occurs to her that here and there she can cut some corners on her housekeeping, and save a little time to play the piano. She still has some twinges of conscience as she plays, because she thinks she should be ironing the sheets instead, or perhaps mending clothes for the children.

She has the relative peace of mind of the mentally healthy person, for she is making an effort to realize her desires and ambitions. She is keeping the demands life makes on her in a reasonable balance.

If she never went near the piano and gave up all thought of playing, she would probably experience the dissatisfaction a person with emotional well-being usually feels when she cannot use a talent constructively. In this case, because she is finding deep satisfaction in making a home and caring for her children and husband, the disappointment would probably not be overwhelming, even if she could not use her abilities to the fullest and include her music in her daily life. But she is happier if she can do so.

Mental health does not mean resignation, nor does it mean an absence of any conflicting desires. Everyone has conflicts. Those who have good mental health are able to handle those conflicting desires without becoming unduly restless, jumpy, or worried.

Ability to Adjust to People

The greatest satisfactions in life come from our relations to people. A person in good mental health is able to find happiness in his relationships to at least some of the persons around him most of the time. Life from birth to death is a series of varying relationships. The rewards we covet most are not bought with money, nor are they represented by material things. They come from our everyday relationships.

The mentally healthy person is able to derive personal pleasure from life. At the same time he can make life worthwhile for others.

Making life worth-while for others might be making a home and caring for a family. It might be opening new doors to children as a teacher in a classroom. It might be creating in one of the arts, or assisting in the production of things people need. It might be earning a livelihood for a family or engaging in one of the professions that serve people's material, emotional, or spiritual needs. Making life worth-while for others may sound like a nobler calling than most of us follow. Yet in many of the situations in which we gain the greatest satisfaction, mothers, fathers, teachers, and even the children are making life more worth-while for those around them.

Childhood experiences add to or take away from our ability to get along with other people. If a child's efforts to be friendly are welcomed, he is likely to grow up to be a warm outgoing person. But if these efforts are rebuffed, he may develop into a reserved, cold, and distant person.

You will be a better mother if you take time out from your chores to do those things you like to do.

Press Syndicate

The mentally healthy person accepts the principle that his own welfare depends on the welfare of the group. He assumes responsibility for his share of a friendship, of his family, of his community, of his nation, and of the world in which he lives.

There are those individuals whom one would have to judge mentally unhealthy because they must live entirely by themselves. Angry feelings express themselves in any contacts such people manage to make. We can only understand these people when we recognize that, in their earliest days, they did not learn how to be interested in, or to get along with, other people in ways appropriate to their age and to the situation. Learning to get along with people is a slow process. Small children cannot be expected to be good at it, but adults are expected to do better.

Ability to Adjust to the World

Good mental health implies an ability to get along in the world by meeting and conquering obstacles without fighting or fleeing from the real situation. Suppose you planned to catch a train early Sunday morning to meet some friends in the country. Through a chain of mishaps, you arrive at the station a minute or two after the train has left. You may be angry, but you will not be so angry that you cannot act, if you are a well-balanced person. You start inquiring about other ways of getting to your destination. Perhaps you find there is a bus that will take you almost to the spot where you had planned to meet your friends and you hurry to the bus stop.

Now, suppose you were a person not in good mental health. You might fly into a rage and scream at the station attendants. You might even decide that missing the train was the result of a plot by someone to keep you from enjoying this excursion. Or you might decide nothing ever turns out right, and go home to spend the day sulking. You would be fighting or fleeing from the real situation instead of doing something about it.

In meeting the demands of life, the mentally healthy person relies more upon his intelligence than his feelings. In making plans or tackling problems, he accepts the world as it is rather than as he wishes it were, or fears it might be. He accepts responsibilities and does his best to carry them out.

The ability to fight for principles and convictions helps you to be a constructive person. Mentally healthy people get angry. They sometimes get "fighting mad," but they get fighting mad when there is just and real cause, rather than expending unnecessary energy on trifles.

Mental Health Rules

What mental health rules will help Johnny when father forbids him to play baseball with the gang? Or what rules will help father when Johnny gets into serious difficulties in school?

There are no simple rules for mental health, but there are some principles that may be applied to one's own experiences. They all revolve around the central theme of one's ability to accept the cards that are dealt him in the game of life and to play them "with a maximum of effectiveness and happiness." None of us can do this under all circumstances, but with special efforts, special knowledge, and sometimes special help, we can do a better job of it.

Finding security and satisfaction within the framework of things as they are, is an indication of mental health.

Security and satisfaction are difficult to obtain at times, and continued lack of them may result in mental ill-health.

You Need Security

Each of us wants and needs to believe that he is acceptable to himself, to those he loves, and to those with whom he associates. Much of our psychological energy is spent in devising ways of protecting ourselves from disapproval by explaining any assumed or real misbehavior. Any major threat of being pushed aside results at least temporarily in uneasiness, or perhaps in fear.

The little girl who is excluded from the secrets of the other third-graders will feel like asking, "What is wrong with me?" So will the college freshman who is not elected to the sorority of her choice. The wife whose husband refuses to go out in the evening with her; or the child whose parents are too busy to play with him or listen to him will feel hurt.

Conflicting feelings and desires produce some degree of insecurity for us all at times. Nobody is constantly secure emotionally, or perhaps completely secure at any given moment. The degree of security we achieve depends on our ability to solve our problems, to accept our disappointments, and to live in the world as it is.

If we ourselves are reasonably secure, we are able to make others feel comfortable with us. We may not choose everyone whom we meet as a close friend. But it is the mentally unhealthy who are condescending, or feel they must discriminate against their neighbors, relatives, or associates, for one reason or another.

Physical health, economic security, and many other conditions can threaten the well-being of each of us. The degree of success with which we face these realities of life determines our mental health, too.

You Need Satisfaction

From the point of view of the mental hygienist, satisfaction is almost the same as happiness. Sometimes one cannot have satisfaction, and, in its absence, the individual is to some extent likely to be mentally unhealthy. If you believe that the lack of satisfaction is only temporary, often you are able to adjust to it. You may figure out a compromise, or a plan for achieving satisfaction eventually. You may deny wanting it or you may fight the situation by complaining or by being destructive in one way or another.

Sometimes the lack of satisfaction is due to the fact that an individual has no ideas about anything interesting to do. Sometimes anxiety prevents satisfaction.

When a child is critically ill, a father finds little satisfaction in his job. When his business is going badly, he may get less than full satisfaction in a happy home life. A wife may find little satisfaction in community activities during the day if her husband is *never* willing to talk to her in the evening.

How Can I Improve My Mental Health?

No set of instructions can solve the problem for the insecure and dissatisfied individual, but there are some suggestions worth trying.

Weigh, insofar as possible, your own contribution to the cause of the problem confronting you. If the situation is sufficiently serious, talking it over with an understanding friend may help.

Try to discover some constructive opportunity in the situation. Talk it over with the other persons who are also involved in it. What do they think are the causes of the difficulty? Can you use their suggestions?

Have the courage to change your pattern of life. Perhaps a new system of keeping the family accounts, or a change in your usual habits of getting up, going to bed, or doing the marketing, will help you out of a possible bad spot. Maybe you need some new friends. Perhaps you should take up a new hobby or revive an old one.

You can try to find activities that make up for the things you do not like or cannot change. If your job is monotonous, it is especially important for you to find spare-time activity that is rewarding.

If necessary, get professional help. The chapter on FAMILY GUIDANCE SERVICES, in Volume 15, will give you more definite suggestions about where to find qualified, reliable help with personal problems.

Emotional Maturity

Our main goal should be to develop adult feelings and to become emotionally mature. In assuming our responsibilities as parents, no goal is more important. If children are to be healthy, happy, and effective, parents must become mature themselves. One extremely young mother said to her husband, "Do you think I'll really make a good mother?"

"That depends on whether you or the baby matures first," he answered jokingly. Actually, there was a great deal of truth in his teasing remark. The most successful parents have grown on the job.

To develop feelings that are truly adult, we need to have some idea of what emotional maturity means.

Finding Satisfaction in Giving

It is essential to the very life of an infant that he be on the receiving end of any situation. But the emotionally-mature person finds giving more satisfying than receiving. He can be both the giver and the receiver.

Parents give their babies and children love. The capacity to give is somewhat dependent on what has been given. Being loved is preliminary to loving in return. In order to love, one must give of one's self. This really means being willing to go to some trouble for another person, or showing some concern for him. It is difficult to separate the giving and the receiving of warmth and friendliness. The friendly person attracts friends and receives approval because he gives friendliness.

As we set up a family, we give to our children. This in turn gives us satisfaction and helps us mature. As we continue to mature, we are able to include a wider group in our interest and concern. The mature person derives satisfaction in being considerate in a variety of situations.

The friendships of the psychologically mature person are strong and lasting, regardless of the stresses that may intervene. Maturity enables us to take slights in our stride.

Using Leisure Creatively

Maturity is easier to maintain if one has a constructive, creative hobby. Unfortunately there is a tendency on the part of many persons to use their leisure only in seeking entertainment. But mental health depends in no small degree on how we utilize leisure.

Our most valuable leaders are those who contribute their time, energy, money, and themselves to the causes to

This young mother finds teaching Sunday school a refreshing change. Time and energy spent in volunteer work in the community can be satisfying and rewarding. Many of our finest services depend on such leadership for their success.

which they are dedicated. One of our responsibilities as parents is to work for the improvement of the environment in which our children develop. Our community and our nation need "pillars" who find their greatest satisfaction in contributing, building, and leading. The mature individual has a mission in life, a mission much bigger than his own personal interests.

Profiting from Mistakes

Many individuals go through life making the same mistakes over and over. An essential characteristic of a mature person is the ability to learn from experience. This implies ability to recognize unprofitable and unhealthy behavior.

Under sufficient stress, we all develop anxieties. The mature person learns to work through his tensions and fears by developing constructive compromises.

The Capacity to Love

Probably one is born with the ability to love, if the opportunity is provided. Love is the only constructive force that can neutralize hate. But the capacity to love can be smothered in childhood.

We learn early to love ourselves. "Love thy neighbor as thyself" is a commandment that recognizes our capacity to love ourselves, but we cannot fully love our neighbors if we do not like ourselves. If and when we as individuals are able to love our neighbors as we do ourselves, we will be emotionally mature and we will have a happier world in which to live and bring up our children.

PARENTS ARE ALSO HUSBANDS AND WIVES

DAVID R. MACE, Ph.D.
Professor of Human Relations,
Drew University, Madison, N. J.

To be a good wife or a good husband is a real accomplishment. It is reassuring to discover that usually the more satisfaction, the more sustaining strength, and the more enjoyment you are drawing from your marriage, the better able you are to be a good parent.

Good Marriage—Good Parents

A child definitely needs two parents for steady and happy normal development. That is his birthright. It is not enough to say that the child should have each parent playing a part in his unfolding life. The harmony of your marriage is vitally important in the lives of your children. There are those who believe that nothing contributes more to success in rearing children than mutual happiness in the relationship between the father and mother.

There is probably no greater service you can render your children than to bring them up in a home where the overflowing love of parents for each other gives a warm feeling of security. In an atmosphere of abundant love, the child knows he can find healing for all kinds of hurts. He knows, too, that parents like his will not forsake him or forsake each other. This assurance brings a deep sense of confidence as he embarks upon the great adventure of growing up, and helps him to free himself later.

Building a Good Marriage

If you wish to be successful parents, therefore, you must aim to be successful marriage partners. In the months or years before the children come, you can put down foundations for a good adjustment to each other. Two young persons who care for one another usually find this the most pleasant of assignments. Still, it is a matter requiring some consideration. Life is not all dates and parties, as it may have been before marriage. Every step you take toward the understanding and acceptance of each other as husband and wife will mean progress toward later understanding and acceptance as father and mother.

Many parents, for one reason or another, do not work out their relationship as well as they might wish, before the children come. You can still grow closer, but you will have to be willing to give thought and attention to the matter. Good marriages seldom "just happen."

Companionship Goes the Extra Mile

Good partnership in marriage is essential if there is to be real teamwork in managing all the complexities of a family. Inevitably, complexities do accompany satisfactions. Children are fun, but at the same time they can disorganize a household and create a great deal of work. There will be times when mother will be desperately tired. There will, too, be times when father will be burdened with a heavy sense of responsibility. Such situations demand effective co-operation in the everyday tasks, as well as understanding.

Young husbands and wives need to learn the art of sharing the work and responsibility of the home. It is a new kind of partnership, different from any either parent has known. One young husband expressed it well when he said, "At home, in the army, or at school the idea always was to see how little you could do and how much you could make the other fellow do for you. Now I don't keep looking to see whether I'm doing more than my share. Maybe I am sometimes, but who cares? After all, our home is what I'm hustling for."

Doing more rather than less than his or her share is a stage not immediately or easily reached by every young married person. It takes time to learn to give one another encouragement and comfort, as well as help in running the family. If you have made a start on sharing and giving in the comparatively simple twosome of the first year or years of marriage, you will be better able to take the next step and give to your children. Giving is an art, and takes practice.

A small person in a bassinet imposes

Luoma, Monkmeyer

For a good marriage, husband and wife should be both partners and lovers. The happier you are in your marriage, the happier you are likely to be as parents.

a decidedly more-complicated relationship than the twosome of husband and wife. Several small persons who have emerged from the bassinet stage and begun to move around on their own create still more complications. Family ties must have strength and elasticity to stand these strains.

Affection Is the Keystone

Husband and wife need to give one another affection as well as sexual satisfaction. Continuously satisfying another adult's need for affection is an art. This art, too, comes only with practice. Such practice gives you a feeling for each other's needs and a sensitivity to each other's moods.

Two young wives were discussing their husbands. Said the first, "I've found out that when Joe comes home at night he's tired and he wants me to make a fuss over him. If I have any troubles—and pretty often I do have—I keep them until the next morning. Then he's cheerful as a bird and nothing bothers him."

The other young woman smiled at her, "I guess it takes all kinds to make a world. Now Tim—well, he's not worth anything before he's had two cups of coffee. If I need his help, or if I want sympathy, I know I have to wait for a better moment."

Even in the best of marriages, there are times when husbands and wives may fail to give one another the affection each needs. We all dream of someone who is completely and everlastingly understanding. But no human being can completely satisfy the emotional needs of another, day in and day out through the years. You are more than fortunate if *most of the time* you can give each other the affection each needs.

If a husband and wife can be satisfyingly affectionate to each other, they will be inwardly free to give their children the patient, undemanding care of true parental love.

Satisfactory Sexual Relations

A satisfactory sexual relationship is another cornerstone of a good marriage. This relationship, too, needs cultivation, if it is to grow richer and deeper with the passing of time.

When the physical adjustment of a husband and wife is steadily unsatisfactory, tensions arise. They may mount to such a point that the flow of mutual tenderness is dammed up in one or both partners. If the persons involved are to be satisfied and happy in each other, they need tenderness. They also need the kind of communication a satisfying sexual relationship gives. No matter how fine your marriage may be, there will probably be some variation in the quality of your sexual relationship from time to time.

There are many sources of help for husbands and wives whose intimate relations for any reason are constantly falling short of their expectations.

The kind of family-counseling services discussed in the chapter FAMILY GUIDANCE SERVICES, in Volume 15, can be helpful. In many churches and synagogues, ministers, priests, or rabbis are themselves good marriage counselors. In any case, they would probably be able to refer you to sources that would be helpful. Some prefer to start by consulting their doctor. He also can be a valuable source of help, for doctors are concerned with emotional health.

Neither man nor woman stands alone either biologically or emotionally. Each needs the other to fulfill his or her life

Pick the best time to talk over problems.

Spending leisuretime with each other and sharing experiences will help you grow closer together.

Ewing Galloway

completely. Each needs the companionship, affection, and sexual satisfaction that the other has to give. Those who find some satisfaction in a combination of companionship, affection, and sexual relations are among those who are doing well with their marriage.

Children Change Things

The arrival of the first child in the home provides a new focus of shared interest for husband and wife. It can stir powerful new emotions, create pride of achievement, and heighten the sense of unity. It should be a wonderful experience, and usually is. At the same time it makes exacting new demands. These the young couple may not find themselves entirely ready to meet.

When you graduate to parenthood, you have to face radical changes in the pattern of your life together. You must break the tight, cozy little circle to take in a newcomer who seems to make nothing but demands. You must be ready for disorganized days and disturbed nights. You are no longer as free to go out together. Your social life falls to a low ebb. Family finances may be heavily strained.

"My Wife Is So Busy With the Baby She Has No Time for Me"

All this can amount to a real crisis in the marriage. Mrs. Green, absorbed in her baby, almost forgot her husband. He became hurt and annoyed by the accumulating irritations of a disorderly household. There was a stack of new bills, a bathroom cluttered with unfamiliar equipment. His shirts had buttons missing. His suit was not pressed. All this contributed to his feeling of being neglected. A sexually disinterested wife added to that feeling. His exaspera-

The new baby brings new demands on husband and wife, but he also is the tie that makes their marriage stronger.

Tana Hoban

tion piled up till he resented the baby as an intruder and disturber of the peace. His wife failed to understand his attitude, and accused him of not loving her or the baby. The first serious crack in a marriage might have started right there.

The Greens were intelligent and managed to surmount their difficulties. They realized that they must work out a new pattern. There would need to be some changes in their life. Yet they saw that their own needs as a married couple could not and need not be sacrificed to the baby. The bills would have to be paid. The bathroom might remain cluttered, and a few buttons might be missing, but they must manage to find time for each other.

Mrs. Green discovered it was worth making an effort to talk about something besides the baby, and to remember what her husband liked for dinner. Like all wives, and husbands, too, she found it took the skill of a juggler to balance the demands of marriage with the demands of parenthood. But she found, as most parents do, that she *could* handle both demands.

Parents, particularly the most responsible parents, may get the idea that only the child matters. Anything they want or need is to be set aside, if it clashes in the least degree with their great undertaking.

Extreme self-sacrifice does good to nobody. It can result in the children expecting everyone else to treat them with the same doting devotion their parents have shown. Without neglecting the children, mothers can be companionable wives most of the time. Fathers can still be affectionate husbands.

"My Husband Only Thinks of Me As the Mother of His Children"

You need to recognize that you have legitimate rights. Even your children must not deprive you of these rights. You also have duties to each other. You had better clarify these rights and duties at the outset. Otherwise the unsuspecting mother may wake up one day to find she has been too preoccupied with her children and may have failed to be a wife to her husband.

So, too, the harrassed father may strive devotedly to achieve a high standard of living. He may discover that in

Pop sometimes grumbles when Baby takes over the bathroom.

years of ceaseless hard work he has so neglected his wife that she has ceased to love him. The material things he has striven to give his wife and children are worth little compared with their love and comradeship.

Husbands and wives who live amid a houseful of boisterous and demanding children will do all the more justice to their offspring if they are determined to do justice to each other. They need time alone together. They need time away from the pressure of their parental duties; time to talk, time to relax, time to keep in love.

Family outings and activities are fine and have their place. Children can also learn that there is a relationship between their parents which they cannot expect to share and upon which they must not intrude. Their own understanding of marriage, and their intelligent approach to it in later years, will be better if the quiet insistence of their parents makes this point clear.

Junior may prefer to have his mother stay home with him to being left with a baby-sitter. He will learn a valuable lesson as he finds out that his mother has obligations to other persons as well as to him. The "baby-bound" mother, who will never leave her child, is not necessarily the best mother. She is failing as a wife if she *always* compels her husband to take his outings alone.

Naturally, when parents are away from home even for a few hours, someone who is thoroughly reliable must be left with the children. That is another story. You will want to read the chapter SITTERS HAVE AN INFLUENCE, in Volume 15, in this connection.

When Parents Disagree

Competition is so strong a force in our world that it even enters the relations of husband and wife. There is probably a degree of competition in every marriage, whether it is openly expressed or not.

There is an important distinction to be made when we talk about disagreements between husband and wife. There are the everyday differences of opinion and the normal squabbles common to every marriage. If there is a basic understanding, these are like summer showers. There may be some lightning and thunder, but everybody knows it will be sunny soon. Altogether different is the deep conflict coloring every phase of living in a marriage that is not working out.

How Does Conflict Affect a Child?

There are unhappy homes where parents are constantly in conflict with each other. The tensions between them are passed over to the child, even though nothing is said, or the child seems too young to understand. Here is a difficult situation for the youngster to handle.

He naturally has a loyalty to both his mother and his father. When they are at loggerheads with each other he may feel a kind of civil war going on in his own heart. Many of the kinds of behavior in children which we refer to as problems result from the vague sense of uneasiness they feel when their parents have difficulties. Children can sense tension in the atmosphere.

How Can You Work Out Problems?

Fortunately, the usual disagreements in a family are of a less serious nature. It is often possible to prevent situations from getting to the point where they are loaded with emotional dynamite. One of the ways that has proved most effective is to keep the channels of communication open between husband and wife. Once you get your feelings out in the open and your wife or your husband listens to you, you have started on the road to working things out. Brooding over slights or wrongs, whether they are real or fancied, saps energy you might more profitably put into finding a way out of your difficulty.

"So I won the argument and had the last word this time," a young husband told a friend in relating an incident that occurred in his family.

"Maybe you've paid a pretty high price for that victory," his friend replied. "After you've been married as long as I have, you'll find out that there's sometimes no sense in winning the argument. What winning does to the feelings between you is what counts. If your wife feels beaten down and mad, well . . . you aren't much ahead. Maybe you think I'm a milksop, but at our house we talk things over and try to reach a compromise."

Many couples whose marriages are happy have developed the habit of talking over their difficulties without being aware that it was a technique of solving problems. It just seemed the natural thing to do.

Everyone does not express himself with equal ease. Everyone is not born a sympathetic listener. You may be skeptical at first about the value of opening your hearts to one another, but it is a way of communication worth cultivating. It has been of real help to husbands and wives who found that many of their misunderstandings could be prevented, many others talked out.

Differences Over Discipline

At no point will the teamwork of husband and wife be more severely tested than when they disagree on some important issue in rearing their children. Sometimes these disagreements are honest differences of opinion. It can also happen that husband and wife are blocking each other's desire for affection. Then they may use some difference of opinion about their child as an opportunity to let out the resentment they feel against each other.

"You aren't insisting Mary go to bed at eight o'clock just because you believe it's good for her. You want to prove you are right and I am wrong, and that you can get your own way," one exasperated husband told his wife.

Unfortunately, exactly that situation had developed. If Mary's parents had been able to give one another the affection each needed and wanted, they would not have found their difference of opinion over Mary's bedtime a cause for bitter argument.

If you recognize *why* you disagree, you will not let the children's upbringing become a battleground. Settle all ar-

His Majesty takes a good look at his adoring parents.

guments out of the children's presence, too.

"Should Parents Try to Make Children Believe They Never Differ?"

There is nothing wrong with letting the child know that you disagree, or in taking his view into consideration. He must learn sooner or later that grown-ups are not perfect, and that the clash of wills is a common enough event in human society. It will be valuable for him to see how his parents have composed their differences.

There are stages in the working-out of the solution, however, which belong to the privacy of the relationship between husband and wife. Wise parents will have a clear understanding about this. At the appropriate point they will adjourn the family council with the announcement, "We'll talk this out by ourselves and let you know what we decide."

Marriage Is for Grown-Ups

Settling disagreements calls for mature emotions. We are not yet as stable or mature in our feelings as we would like to be. You AS A PERSON, the preceding chapter, discusses what you can do about your mental health and emotional well-being.

If one of the marriage partners clings to childish types of relationship, it puts a great burden on the other. Some women seem to expect all the tender, protecting care from a husband that their fathers gave them. They want to go on being little girls. One young woman who had worked through a difficult time in her marriage with the help of a skilled counselor put it well when she said, "I've learned one thing. I can't have Daddy." Husbands are not and cannot be expected to be fathers to their wives, nor can a wife expect her husband to act like her own father.

Some men who are not entirely grown up in their feelings may likewise expect their wives to take the place of their mothers. There are times when everyone wants to be childlike. Anyone has the right to an extra measure of dependence and care *occasionally*. Every wife may need to do some mothering. Every husband occasionally plays a fatherly role to his wife. When the "little-girl wife" or the "little-boy husband" is the *consistent* pattern, it is hard to build a good marriage. If one of you is failing to make a grown-up contribution to your marriage, it may be well to look for help through one of the sources mentioned early in the chapter.

Sustaining Strength for Marriage

In marriage and parenthood we are all learners, right to the end. What matters is that we should try sincerely to be teachable.

When husband and wife are happy and united in a strong mutual love, they have the resources to meet each crisis which arises, to find a way out of most difficulties. By keeping their marriage in good repair, they provide for themselves a source of constant renewed satisfaction. Neither has an unbearable internal conflict. They look out on the family they are raising from the inner sanctuary of their own security and delight in each other. Once that private kingdom of their own was all they had. In time, as the children one by one achieve independence and pass on their way, it will again be all they have. This experience they will meet not with rebellion, not even with resignation, but with acceptance. It is the law of life.

YOUR FAMILY IN TODAY'S SETTING

Ewing Galloway

6. THINGS AREN'T THE SAME

7. GRANDPARENTS AND OTHER RELATIVES

8. IF THREE GENERATIONS LIVE TOGETHER

      A family is influenced by the customs, by the values and the pressures of the community, by the country, and by that combination of forces we call "the times." The make-up of your family, the responsibilities it carries, the sources of help available to it, and the position of various members are different today from what they were fifty years ago.

      As you build a strong family and guide your children, you need to see your family in today's setting. You need to understand the relationship among people of different generations, and among people who do different kinds of work.

      It helps to understand how changes in relationship in the last fifty or seventy-five years have come about. Then you can make the most of the good in life for your children today and minimize the unfortunate aspects.

THINGS AREN'T THE SAME

FREDA S. KEHM, Ph.D.
Director, Association for Family Living, Chicago, Ill.

"IF I had talked that way to my father, I would have caught it, but good." "Imagine our parents letting a two-year-old (or a six-year-old, or a ten-year-old) do this!" "I must say nobody expected me to know that at five-and-a-half." Have you found yourself using expressions like these many times in the course of a week? Parents, uncles and aunts, even grandparents borrow standards from the past.

Things aren't the same. We need to take into consideration the new pressures, the new demands that television, airplanes, and thousands of other inventions, constructive and destructive, bring to bear on our children and on us. In the light of these demands and pressures what kind of guidance is most helpful for our children? Certainly, more than ever children need warm, loving, understanding parents who can give them order and independence. How does a family provide a flexible kind of order and opportunities for independence in today's world? How does a family preserve the child's individuality and at the same time teach him to conform to the present-day world?

Family Means Partnership

One of the changes in family relationships that has come about in the last fifty years is the shift from the heavy-handed father who often dominated the family through fear, to the "partnership" family. Today respect and consideration for each member of the family is the goal.

While Mother was often as much in awe of Father as were the children, she had an authority of her own. "Mother knows best." Parents never—well—hardly ever—were wrong. You may feel that the parents of an earlier time were far more fortunate than you are today when your home echoes to "Why must I wear rubbers? Nobody else does!"

Being a parent today presents more of a challenge. You are not perfect, and certainly you and your children know it. A parent who admits to making occasional mistakes, has a sounder basis for a good, durable relationship with his (or her) children than one who could never afford to be wrong.

In the good family today, rules are not made to show who is boss, but because everyone understands that regulations are necessary if people are to live together happily. Mother and father work out those rules together. In many instances they take the children into their confidence as they plan for the family's welfare. How such planning works out in actual practice is discussed in the chapter in this volume on THE FAMILY COUNCIL.

Are Our Children Obedient?

What has happened to the time-honored idea of obedience? Everyone would agree that there are moments when prompt obedience is necessary. If you tell a small child to "get out of the street," or if you tell an older one to "stay off that thin ice," you want obedience, and you want it immediately. Many people wonder whether you can get a child to follow your directions when that is necessary if you have not enforced the rule of "Do as I say because I say so—and do it quickly," on all occasions.

Right here a fundamental change in thinking about parent-child relationship comes in. Knowledge gained from careful studies of hundreds and hundreds of children over a long period of time points to the fact that children learn to conform because they want to please the parents they love and admire. They want to do what their parents do, and be like them. Children do not profit from being drilled in obedience like puppy dogs. Drill of that sort may even defeat its own purpose and create rebellious and unco-operative youngsters.

Children who love and trust their parents, who have been treated reasonably, sense the tone of special urgency in mother or father's voice when an emergency arises. The emergency may not be a matter of life and death. It may be only "Dad just phoned. We've got company coming for supper. This house is in a mess. The icebox is empty. We've all got to pitch in so things'll be in apple pie order when Dad gets home and supper will be something special. We can't let him down."

We can't let him down! Loyalty, self-respect, family solidarity, secure the co-operation of the youngsters in this family. They rise manfully to the occasion, and help mother straighten the house, get the supplies, prepare the meal, and welcome the guests.

Today's thinking is that, in most of the day-to-day events, parents can set the stage and plan the routines so that discipline lies in the situation itself rather than in too many spoken commands and directions. You can read more

The children learn through imitating grown-ups. Here is a first step toward pride in good housekeeping.

H. Armstrong Roberts

When angry feelings come out openly, they can be drained off. When they are bottled up they tend to spread.

about that question in the chapter DISCIPLINE FOR SELF-RELIANCE in this volume.

Conflict Is Not Feared

There is another way in which things are not the same as they were a few generations ago. Formerly, the family ideal was a calm, serene home. "Nobody ever said a cross word" was the perfect tribute to family life. Now we know that this ideal was unhealthy. It would not be good for anyone to live in such a rarefied atmosphere, even if it were possible. Everyone gets angry at times. Just because we love our children, our wives, our husbands, even our brothers and sisters, they can make us angrier than casual acquaintances can. But we get over it.

We have learned that bottling up resentments inside ourselves tends to make them fester and spread. If children, and adults too, feel it is wrong to express or even feel resentment, the guilty feelings that result can be damaging.

Today we are not afraid of the occasional differences, the arguments, the spats that are a part of family living. Devotion and basic unity do not need to mean complete continual agreement. The fact that family members get cross with one another at times is not serious, but the way those feelings of annoyance are handled is important. Children need opportunities to let off steam in vigorous play. In their play, too, they can do to toys and dolls what they cannot do to people, and that can be an excellent safety valve. Parents are beginning to understand the value, indeed, the necessity of letting children talk about their angry feelings at appropriate times and places and in appropriate doses. Of course, if either a child or an adult does nothing but express anger that may be a danger sign.

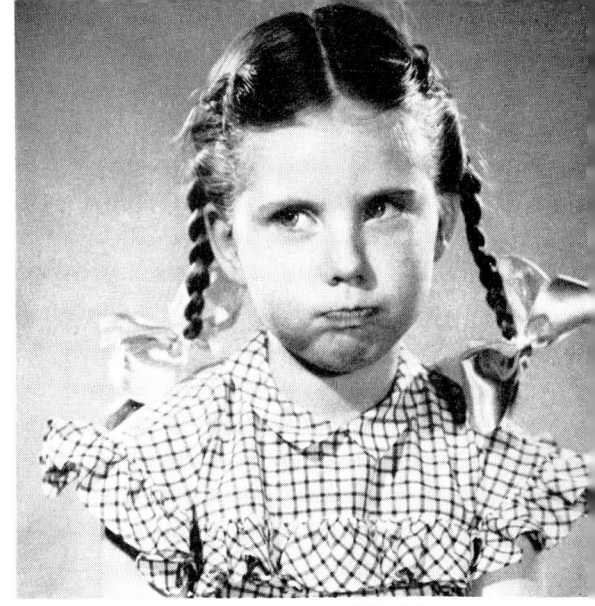

We are finding out that we may in the past have gone too far in demanding that feelings of all kinds be pushed aside. Now we know that if the children are allowed to talk about their feelings, if we admit these feelings exist, and accept them, it is easier to guide the children toward reasonable and appropriate control.

Are Children Less Respectful?

We often hear it said that children today are not respectful to their parents. Definitely there is little of the self-effacing, unquestioning, "Yes, papa," and "As you wish, mamma" that our parents tell us they were taught to give their parents. It is a curious fact that nobody ever talks about the countless boys who ran away from home or became misfits of one kind or another because they could not endure the continual "Yes, papa" that was demanded of them. Nobody mentions the numberless girls who grew up afraid of their own shadows (and their own husbands) because their behavior and even their thoughts were so strictly limited. Perhaps that brand of respect was not so valuable after all.

There is a different and a deeper kind of respect that we strive for today. That kind sees the worth and dignity of every human being, and admits the right of each to be himself. Children who are themselves treated with that kind of respect are capable of showing the same regard for others. If the basic feeling is there, it is not hard to build agreeable manners on such a foundation.

That kind of respect is made of sturdy stuff. It will not be destroyed by a few words of doubt or even of anger. It can withstand the attack of a six-year-old who calls his mother a "dope" because she doesn't know one type of airplane from another. True respect will not even be withered by a ten-year-old who dismisses her father's opinions as hopelessly out-of-date. We can still suggest, teach, and set an example of more acceptable ways of disagreement. But we need not be horrified or upset by the children's words.

New Demands on Fathers

There have been changes in what we expect of each member of the family, too. Perhaps fathers have had the greatest variety of roles demanded of them. For thousands of years the father in the family knew what was expected of him and what he had to do. He was the provider; his was the last word. Everything went along smoothly—or at least at this distance in time it looks as if things went along smoothly—while a man's work was centered around his home.

The children could follow him around, watch his work, and even take part in it. He was a part of their daily life. He was, in fact as well as in name, the head of the household.

About a generation ago we woke up to the fact that fathers spent most of their time away from home and had lost touch with their own children. Jokes and catchwords often reveal our real feelings. The father who was referred to by his small son or daughter as "that man who spanks me" or "that man who hangs around here on Sundays" was a standing joke—though not a humorous one.

In an effort to correct this sad state of affairs, fathers were urged to be "pals" to their boys and girls. It did not take long to find out that neither father nor children found that relationship particularly satisfactory. Boys need the example of the adult father to pattern after as they grow up. A father should be stronger and wiser than his children. If he were not more competent, how could he offer them the protection and guidance they want and need from him?

What Is Father's Job Today?

At present our feeling is that fathers can have fun with their children. But even when they play with the youngsters, they are still fathers.

In the meantime, another demand has been made on papa. The helping hands of extra female relatives have become less available, and paid help almost as extinct as the buffalo. Fathers often are pressed into service to help in the day-to-day care of the small babies and children. Father's importance to Mother during pregnancy and at the time the baby is born is now recognized, too. The whole question of father's

For up-to-date fathers, baby care is all in the day's work. It is a good basis for later understanding.

Mother leads a triple life today as her children, her husband, and her community make demands on her.

contribution to the family is discussed in detail in THE FATHER IN THE FAMILY, in this volume, and FOR FATHERS ONLY, in Volume 13.

New Demands on Mothers

The last two or three generations have brought dramatic changes in what we expect of mothers, too. Time was when a woman was expected to be proficient in a long list of household arts. If she was good at these, she could take pride in them. As for bringing up her children, that was something she knew well how to do, without advice from experts.

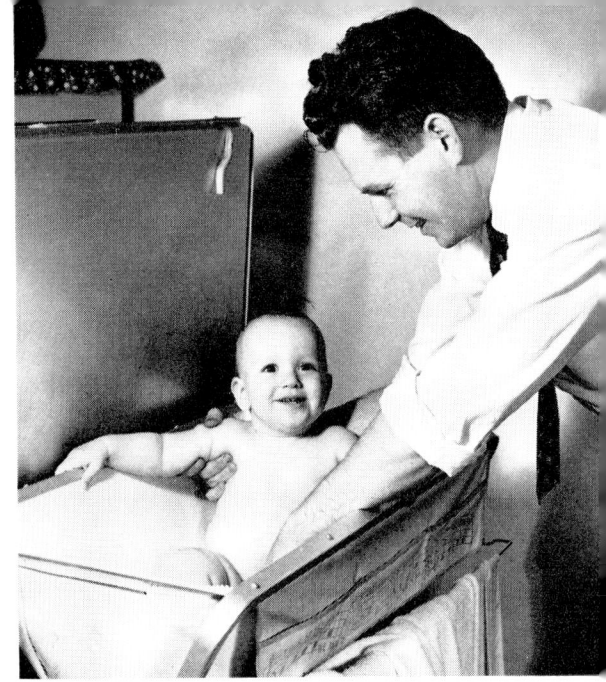

Now the experts know more than she does, and a bright array of gadgets deprives a woman of the satisfactions that can come from being highly competent at a difficult job. Nobody wants to turn the clock back, and, on balance, the changes are undoubtedly an improvement. Mothers today should be less hurried since they have less actually time-consuming, back-breaking work to do. It would seem as if they would have more time for leisurely companionship with their children. Actually, a young mother is often under greater pressure. In place of the evenly-paced cooking, cleaning, and sewing often shared by several women in a household, a young woman is expected to take part in activities in the community. Since she cannot leave her children, she tends to feel resentful at times. She must steadily say "no" both to the actual requests that are made of her by friends and neighbors and to her own desire to keep in touch

47

with or be part of the wider world. Even the most deeply maternal woman grows tired of the exclusive company of two-, four-, and six-year-olds after a spell of bad weather or a bout of children's illnesses. Being a mother is not easy when you are bombarded with advice and warnings on all sides, either.

Are Your Children Proud of You?

At the same time every advertisement insists the mother must be well-groomed, smart, and youthful to keep her husband's love and have her children be proud of her. She is supposed to be a companion to her husband, and probably also a kind and devoted daughter to her own parents. In order to resolve her dilemma, she must continually make a variety of choices, a number of compromises. She needs to be flexible enough to be able to make different choices each year as the demands on her time and strength vary with the change in the number of children and their ages.

How Can Parents Keep on Learning?

If your parents wanted to find out more about how their children grew and what made them tick, they probably had to turn to a textbook on psychology. Twenty-five or thirty years ago, there was little material for parents about normal children. Discussion groups where parents could think through problems together were few and far between, except in one or two of the largest cities.

Today, parents are bombarded with sound, readable material written expressly for them. Study groups and discussion groups are fast becoming a part of the program in every parents' organization in school, church, or community center. Indeed, the hundreds of thousands of parents who take part in these programs are in themselves a sign of the times. Parents are eager to learn more about the job of parenthood. They have a growing sense of responsibility about taking part in the institutions that affect their children.

What Do We Expect of Children?

Our standards for a satisfactory child have changed. The "good," quiet, docile boy or girl is no longer the ideal. Even allowing for the great individual variations in interest and in temperament, we recognize that continual quietness and docility are not part of the nature of a healthy, growing child. The children have undoubtedly profited by our greater understanding of their need to be active and sometimes noisy.

Our demand that they be "successful" is often hard on them. We may talk about accepting each child as he is, but almost from the day a child is born we ask "Is he as big as the baby next door?" "Does the little girl down the block talk better?" "Will his cousin who is the same age do better in school?" This increasing pressure to be at the top is one of the less fortunate attitudes toward our children that is characteristic of our generation. If we recognize our tendency in that direction, we can watch ourselves.

What Are the Permanent Values?

Changes of all kinds in our world have been rapid. We cannot tell what lies ahead. The understanding warmth that fosters the feeling in our children—"you are able to do it"—is the best way of preparing them to meet life unafraid. If we can give our children happy, satisfactory relationships in the family in their earliest years, we are giving them the only security that endures.

GRANDPARENTS AND OTHER RELATIVES

JEAN SCHICK GROSSMAN
Author, "Life with Family," New York, N.Y.

GRANDPARENTS were under discussion at a community center mother's meeting. "But you can't talk about grandparents in mass form! They're all so different!" one member protested.

Some grandmothers and grandfathers are vigorous women and men in early middle life who have more resources of all kinds than their grown children. Equally many are lonely souls failing in health and dependent on those around them for support of every kind. Usually grandparents are somewhere in between these two extremes. No matter how hale and hearty your parents and your older relatives may seem today, the time will come when they will need care and consideration. Then the relationship with them may not be so easy and may require more giving on your part.

Grandparents Are Here to Stay

Science has lengthened the span of human life. As a result, more alert, interested older people will increasingly be part of the scene. These older people are not likely to retire to a corner and become mere onlookers. The advantage in this state of affairs is that the contribution they make to their grandchildren's lives is greater. The disadvantage is that their presence may at times create problems. Their interference in their children's lives is almost sure to cause difficulties.

Mixed Feelings About Relatives

We might as well face the fact that, much as we love our relatives, we also resent them at times. Granted that they have many praiseworthy qualities, grandparents may offer unasked-for advice. They may find fault and interfere. They may be scornful of current theories of child-rearing. Even when grandma tries to be most tactful, she reminds young parents that they were once small children. Mothers and fathers find themselves recalling the times when, as children, they were angry at these same parents, even though they loved them dearly.

Contradictory feelings, such as affection and annoyance, exist side by side in every relationship. It is not easy to trace these feelings to their sources, nor do we need to try to do so. We can accept the tendency in ourselves and in others to like and to dislike the same person at almost the same moment. It is neither good nor bad. It is only human.

It may be helpful to air these mixed feelings by putting them into words occasionally at an appropriate time and place. If we can get some of the weight off our chests, we will be less inclined to blame our parents for our own faults. We will be less irritated with our in-laws over the shortcomings of our wives or husbands. We may still be annoyed, but we will perhaps not feel so guilty over our annoyance.

Resentment is not confined to the parent caught between his or her own children, and his or her parents. Grandfathers have been known to protest that in their sons' homes "All we are supposed to do is *come, bring, look,* and *listen!*"

What About Disrespect?

The children, too, may become impatient with the ways of grandparents or aunts and uncles. Being human, they, also, have mixed feelings toward those they love. Usually, we describe any expression of these feelings as disrespect and try to put a stop to it promptly. Nobody would question the fact that children should learn consideration for other persons, especially for older folk. But we can teach consideration without insisting that all adults are perfect just because they are adults.

Children need a time and a place for getting their feelings out in words. If Sally at five or at eight declares her great aunt Cora is an old crosspatch, she can hardly be allowed to say so in Aunt Cora's presence without reprimand. But Sally will be less likely to be disagreeable if her feelings have been relieved. Sally's mother can say, "Everyone gets angry sometimes. You can say anything you like about Aunt Cora to *me,* but when she comes here you are still going to be nice to her. Even if we don't always like people, we don't want to hurt them, and I won't let you hurt Aunt Cora by being rude to her."

Children can learn through what their parents say and the way their parents act that affection does not mean complete and continuous agreement. Parents can explain the peculiarities of the older relatives. In fact, sometimes children will be more co-operative and considerate if oddities are interpreted, and if they know that their parents, too, must make an effort to be agreeable.

True respect is not likely to vanish with a few casual criticisms. True respect means admitting the right of other people to be themselves. The child who feels loved and is friendly will be better able to find satisfaction in his relationship with his grandparents, even if he knows they have their little ways. The child who is sternly prohibited from expressing his feelings at any time, gets the idea that those feelings are bad. He will, in the long run, tend to have more stored-up anger and to be less capable of genuine warmth and friendliness.

Grandparents Make a Contribution

Grandparents and other members of the older generation contribute in many ways to children's development. The child who has no contacts with older relatives is definitely the loser. Parents can do a great deal to build up the happier side of the relationship, so that both grandparents and youngsters can reap benefits.

Grandma to the Rescue

If there is illness, if mother and father are to have a well-earned vacation, at holiday times or under special stress, the older relative, usually grandma, is invaluable. The children look to her as a sort of extension of mother. Or perhaps grandma can fill in on something mother does not do too well or has no time to do. Maybe grandma comes to put up the currant jelly and can the peaches. Perhaps she brings her portable sewing machine and attacks the mountain of mending. She may be the one who knows the best rhymes and stories.

Grandmother or grandfather may be a refuge when things are rough at home. There are some situations in which a grandparent may listen to troubles with more sympathetic tolerance, and offer wiser counsel than a parent could. Grandparents are more experienced. They are more detached than a parent would be. Both these facts combine to make them helpful allies of the young persons who confide in them.

Grandma Widens the Child's Horizon

During a child's earliest months and years, his most important relationships are with his parents. Soon grandparents enter the scene. They add one further dimension to the encircling arm of parental devotion.

One young woman recalls how, as a child, she loved to visit both her grandmothers. "Grandma Landers would always ask if I had washed my hands before we sat down to lunch. She complimented me if I took pains to comb my hair neatly. Luncheon was a solemn occasion and I felt like a guest. Grandma Foster was much more informal. Two drawers in her living-room chest, reserved for visiting grandchildren, were filled with games and toys. She loved to watch us play and hugged, kissed, and fussed over us. She'd feed us cookies any time at all—with no thought of 'spoiling our appetites' for lunch. She never seemed to notice whether we looked neat and clean! I loved both grandmothers dearly."

This incident is an answer to the claim that, because the ways of a grandmother or grandfather differ from the ways of a parent, a child will be confused. On the contrary, grandmother's house (or her apartment) is an excellent place to discover that there are many good ways to carry on the business of daily living. Small babies may not profit by different kinds of handling, but that is another matter.

Grandma's house is a second home . . .

but everything has new flavor there.

relatives and see how it feels to be away from home for a night, or even for a few days.

Betty was almost four the first time she stayed overnight at grandma's house. Toward her bedtime, she had not felt comfortable about separation from her own parents; but she managed fairly well. Next morning at breakfast she remarked to her grandparents, "I want to go home and I *don't* want to go home!" Betty was expressing her dawning recognition that one can accept more than one kind of love, and that one can want and not want at the same time.

Finding a Meeting Ground

Providing ways for young and old to get together may take some imagination on the part of the middle generation. Reading together often draws young and old closer. Stories about grandparents' early days make for a cozier relationship. Those early days may go back to nothing

Grandparents, and other relatives as well, contribute to the development of a child's personality precisely because they show him that it is safe to be somewhat flexible. There is room in a child's life for many kinds of people.

When a child visits his grandparents' home he may be taking a first real step into the "outside world." He has been learning to conform to the routine of his own household. He has become familiar with the attitudes and behavior of immediate family members. In grandma's house he hears new words, observes different facial expressions, handles other objects, hears other kinds of laughter. He senses that here, too, there may be periods of sadness and disappointment, as well as happiness and fulfillment. He is enjoyed or found fault with in new ways. Perhaps he tastes another kind of cooking, or meets a new set of friends and neighbors.

New Experiences—New Feelings

It is a fortunate child who can visit

more adventurous than the Model T Ford or having seen Babe Ruth hit a home run, but they are a far-off and fascinating time to the youngsters. A grandfather who will share a hobby with a young person brings added joys to the child.

Grandparents are often the ones who have time to take the children on short trips. Suggestions for such excursions for younger children can be found in the chapter EXCURSIONS FOR YOUNG CHILDREN in Volume 13. The chapter on ADVENTURING THROUGH EXCURSIONS, in Volume 14, will suggest neighborhood trips for the boys and girls over six years of age.

Small jobs that the oldest and youngest generations can do together around the house give them a chance to become better friends.

As a foundation for good relationships, parents can play up the qualities and abilities boys and girls admire in grandparents or other relatives. "Get grandma to show you how," or "Ask Gramps to tell you about the time. . . ." may prepare the ground for an hour in which the grandparents' contribution can be realized more fully.

Grandma can be the extra help that keeps things moving smoothly.

Do Grandparents Spoil a Child?

Grandparents are often accused of being overindulgent. They bestow too many gifts and offer too many between-meal sweets. It is safe to say that children have rarely been known to suffer because they were precious and "special" to a number of people. There can hardly be too much of the right kind of love. That kind of love protects, cherishes, and also helps to set free.

If Grandparents Interfere

It is not always easy for an older generation to accept new or different ways. A grandfather confided to a contempo-

Age is no barrier to comradeship when the fish are biting.

rary that he "just couldn't take it" when his son permitted his little boy to refuse to eat "all that good food." "Crackpot theories," he muttered.

Older people are not always wrong. Frequently, they have valuable ideas and experiences to share.

If you find yourself *always* rejecting older people's suggestions you might ask yourself why you feel the need to do so. It takes a degree of maturity to be able to accept help graciously and gracefully. It is good to recognize older folks' needs as individuals. Such recognition helps us see why they may be interfering.

When Do You Stand Your Ground?

You cannot and should not put up with real interference or opposition. Your own marriage and your children's well-being should not be sacrificed because of dissension and strife with the older generation. You will need also to find ways of letting the older persons know through what you do and what you say that you appreciate them. There are likely to be times when you will be obliged to take a firm stand. You may find it profitable to use existing counseling services when things seem to have become especially tangled. The chapter Family Guidance Services, in Volume 15, may be helpful to you.

Tact Is Oil on Troubled Waters

Neither parents nor grandparents should expect to be perfect. You are entitled to your low moments and your periods of less than noble behavior. But there are some steps you can take to smooth matters. *How* you say something may count for more than *what* you say.

"How would you like to do this?"
"Maybe you can help me out here."
"What do you think or feel about that?" "What were your experiences in this sort of thing?" "Thanks for helping us." "It means so much to us to know you are with us." "I never would have thought of that myself." These simple phrases and others like them are useful in preventing the slights and the hurt feelings that all too often characterize the relationships between relatives.

Parents will find that it is more effective and less irritating to reserve their ammunition for the vital issues in standing firm on a question. Sometimes it will be possible to clear the air by sitting down to talk things over. On other occasions avoiding a hear-all and see-all attitude will be effective. Techniques of management will matter less than the spirit. Winning a point or getting one's own way is not so important as achieving success in the preservation of fundamentally good living relationships. *All* the members of a family profit when, over the years, they learn what it takes to live, work, and play with older persons with a degree of relative satisfaction for all concerned.

Grandparents Are Human Beings

It is not always the fault of the older people if they try to find their satisfactions through the lives of their children or their grandchildren. Perhaps they lack purposeful interests and activities of their own.

"I know I meddle too much in the young people's lives," admitted one widow in her late fifties. "I only wish I knew *what else* to do with myself!" Here is a sad comment on how much needs to be done to open new avenues for recreation, education, and new business or professional opportunities to people in and beyond middle life.

When old and young enjoy playing together, true respect is likely to grow and flourish.

There are many steps that the wider community needs to take. What can be done here and now for the older person in one's home who is restless and unhappy because he or she no longer feels needed? There are, in many communities, organizations set up to provide for the needs of the older person who wants to find new interests in life. Your local welfare council or council of social agencies, if you live in a large city, or your church or community center may be helpful in suggesting where to look for such organizations.

Older persons need friends of their own. The middle generation can encourage them in making or keeping friendships. Young parents are sometimes thoughtless in expecting grandma to take care of the children at times when she might have some plans of her own. It is a good idea to inquire "What are you doing Sunday?" before you announce "You can have Jimmy all to yourself all day." If grandma and grandpa devote themselves to their grandchildren to the exclusion of their own friends and interests, they may lose out on many experiences that would contribute to their happiness and their mental health. If the lives of our older relatives are more interesting, they will have less time and less reason to criticize or interfere.

Grandparents Want to Be Useful

Everyone feels better if he feels he is pulling his weight in the boat. A grandmother visiting in her married daughter's home was peeling potatoes in the kitchen. The delivery boy arrived with the groceries.

"Are you the help?" he asked.

When she replied that she was the grandmother, he grinned and said, "Then you *are* the help—and how!"

Being either "a help" or "the help," or both, is good for men or women whose children are grown. Grandparents may resent being turned to *only* when their help is needed. Being of service brings satisfaction, but they want to be accepted first for themselves. They are hardly expecting too much if they ask that their children pay some slight attention to them when no favors are wanted.

It is gratifying to older persons, too,

if occasionally you ask their advice about something, or at least listen when they want to express an opinion.

The Cousins and the Aunts

We are not required to like all our relatives all the time, even though we strive to be understanding and accepting. When relatives live near by, some of the young members of the family may resent too frequent visits. They may rebel against remembering such occasions as birthdays and anniversaries. When older children are absorbed in activities with their own friends, they are likely to object to "being dragged along" when their parents go calling on relatives. Some relatives seem to be highly prized. This is especially true in the cookie, present, and fun-producing stages of earlier childhood, and, again, much later on. If the eight-, nine-, and ten-year-olds are not enthusiastic, don't worry!

Lest Auld Acquaintance Be Forgot

Many relatives live far away and may rarely, if ever, be seen or heard of. One need not glorify absent kith and kin, but there are values in keeping their existence (and in some cases their memories) alive. Some families put real effort into corresponding with relatives with whom they want to keep in touch. Some families have produced home-made phonograph records, movies, and photographs to bridge the miles and the years. Occasionally, they indulge in long-distance telephone calls.

In talking about the relatives to the children, they describe little peculiarities and elaborate on interests, capacities, handicaps, achievements, problems faced, and difficulties surmounted. Mrs. Brown shows seven-year-old Marie a colored picture of her Aunt Clara. "Now do you see why so many people say you have eyes like hers?" she asks. For Marie it is fun to think that an aunt, whom she has never seen, has in her eyes an expression and a blueness like her own!

We do not wish to become excessively sentimental about either ancestors or living relatives. We do not take foolish pride in people *just because* they have grown older or are related to us. But we do recognize a real need for cultivating a sense of continuity in the lives of all family members. In life's high moments and in moments of great loss or sorrow we sense the need of being related to a special group in a unique way. A group in which the individuals differ one from the other and yet have a unity, a sense of belonging, gives strength to all its members.

Distance need not tarnish family affection, when letters keep it fresh.

IF THREE GENERATIONS LIVE TOGETHER

Fritz Henle

ROBERT G. FOSTER, Ph.D.
Director, Marriage Counseling Service
The Menninger Foundation, Topeka, Kan.

IT IS not unusual these days for three generations to share a home. It was not unusual in earlier days, either, but seventy-five or a hundred years ago houses and back yards were more spacious. People were more likely to have elbow room. Then, too, in an earlier day, many activities carried on in households put the skills of the older people to good use. They felt wanted, while now they often feel useless and out of place.

Perhaps the fundamental difference between sharing a home today and those earlier sharings lies in people's attitudes. Formerly, if young couples moved in with the old folks, if middle-aged or aged parents lived with married sons or daughters, it was accepted as a good way of life. Today our ideal is "a home of one's own."

"It's not what we would choose," says an elderly couple living with their children. "It's not what we would choose" expresses the prevailing attitude today when three generations live together. It is often the best arrangement, under the circumstances. It can be a good arrangement, but it takes patience, good will, a sense of humor, and compromise.

Reasons for Sharing a Home

One of the most frequent reasons for the doubling-up of families is that either the younger or the older generation, or both, cannot afford to maintain a home independently. Sometimes the older person is not in good enough health to live alone. Or again, it might be the young wife or husband who is ill. Then the older generation moves in to care for the house and the invalid, while the breadwinner goes out to work. If the young wife needs, or, in some cases, wants to work outside her home, the older person may be called upon to come and take care of the children. Housing shortages also are a frequent cause of doubling-up.

If Mother goes out to work, Grandma is the one who gives the youngsters the loving care they need.

Is This Move Necessary?

These are all good, sound, practical reasons why three generations may need to share a home. Sometimes the reasons are not so valid. An older woman confided to a friend, "I wouldn't care how tiny or how bare a place I had, if I could only live by myself. But my son and his wife would be offended if I suggested such a thing."

In another family the daughter felt, "We couldn't leave Dad in this big house. He's so lonely since Mother died he needs us here." As a matter of fact, it is just possible that her father would have preferred selling the house and living quietly by himself.

Before you decide to share a home, be clear in your own minds as to why you do it. If you started sharing a home with parents as a temporary, emergency measure, have the courage to review the situation in frank discussions between yourselves and then with the parents.

Sharing Has Different Meanings

When three generations share a home, the situation has different meanings, depending on the reasons for the sharing. One middle-aged couple whose daughter and her husband came to live with them, willingly went out of their way to make the young family feel welcome. They realized their son-in-law was having uphill work as he prepared for a profession. A few years before, they had not been so gracious to another daughter and her husband, for they felt that son-in-law was an idler.

Sharing a home has a special meaning to each individual, depending on his relationship to the other persons involved. For one young woman, living under her parents' roof meant that she had welcome help from her mother and sister in caring for the children. To her husband it was a bitter pill, for he knew his parents-in-law had opposed the marriage.

If you consider what the sharing means, you have a possible clue to the feelings and behavior of each member of the group. On the basis of such understanding, it is easier to work together.

What Is a Husband's Attitude?

The man who is neither afraid of nor dependent on his parents, who can look upon them as good friends, can be a stabilizing influence if he and his wife must share a home with the older generation. Many men are still tied to their parents to some extent. Perhaps they feel that their marriage amounts to a desertion of Mom and Dad. Others may resent Mom's and Dad's overprotection. Still others are so emotionally dependent on their parents that they lack the courage and ability to break away.

If an immature young man must live in the same house with his wife and his mother, difficulties are likely to crop up. He feels his mother's suggestions on how to hang the living-room curtains, how to carve the Sunday roast, how to bring up the children, are good and should be followed. His wife feels he is turning back to his mother, and she is rightfully resentful.

"That woman!" the wife says to herself and to anyone else who will listen, "You'd think she wrote the book on everything. Since when does she know all the answers?"

His wife's attitude is probably a shock to the husband, who sincerely believes that his mother's greater experience and age merit respect. For a man who cannot see that his wife comes first, the situation is confusing. If his wife really takes first place with him, then he and his wife, standing shoulder to shoulder, can usually work things out. The older woman may have a better head on her shoulders, but the important thing is for the wife to feel that her husband is backing her. If she is sure of his loyalty and his support, she can often shrug her shoulders at criticism and suggestions. Maybe she can even take the suggestions if nobody is forcing her to do so. The suggestions may turn out to be reliable, for older heads often are wiser.

If a man resented his own parents, he may transfer that feeling to his in-laws. If he is not tied up with his own mother, he can frequently establish a good relationship with his wife's mother. In spite of all the threadbare mother-in-law jokes, for there is not much competition between a man and his mother-in-law and they can be good friends.

If the father has been extremely attached to his daughter, competition, and consequently disagreement with the husband, is more likely to come from him. Again, if a man and his wife feel that each comes first with the other, they can usually make it clear, without being unpleasant, that no one can come between them. They have one another's full confidence.

How Does a Wife Feel?

A woman spends so much of her time at home that she necessarily runs up against whatever difficulties may exist at every hour of the day. By the same token, there can be greater benefits in the situation for a woman if a home is shared. A woman's home is her business. It is the show window she presents to the world. Because her stake in running her home just as she pleases is so great, she resents any interference from a mother-in-law, and often from her own mother. Wouldn't a man resent an outsider interfering with his job?

Two women may find themselves

competing for the approval of one man. This happened when Mrs. Chandler came to live with her son and his wife. Each day things seemed to go along

Two homemakers may sometimes tread on one another's toes, in spite of their efforts to be considerate.

nicely at breakfast and lunch, but at dinner the older Mrs. Chandler was almost sulky. One Sunday she suggested that she get up and prepare breakfast. During the meal, Molly Chandler found herself resenting her mother-in-law.

Between mouthfuls of biscuits, Bob Chandler exclaimed, "These are the most wonderful muffins, Mother. Best eggs I've tasted for a long time, too."

Suddenly, the wife realized why her mother-in-law had been downcast each night at dinner. Bob invariably would say, "Molly, this is a super supper," or "Mother, don't you think Molly feeds us pretty fancy? Smart girl, my wife."

Not every young woman would have been capable of seeing, as Molly did, that she and her mother-in-law were competing for Bob's approval. Such competition can come about in many ways, but if you are aware of what is going on you can often take steps to avoid the sensitive spots. Molly told her husband, laughingly, "Maybe you'd better not tell me how good my mashed potatoes are unless we're alone. As long as I know you appreciate me, it won't do me any harm to have you give Mother credit in public. Of course, if I didn't know you thought I was pretty good, I probably couldn't take it."

Here is the heart of the matter. The wife who knows she takes first place with her husband can more readily accept her mother-in-law, even if the older woman is a bit difficult at times. It probably never is necessary for the husband to say to his mother in so many words, "My wife and I make our decisions about the running of the house and the bringing up of the children." A man can,

... But there are times when two heads are better than one in solving family problems or in raising children.

by his actions, make it clear in a good-humored way that interference is unwelcome.

In the many-sided problems that may arise when three generations live together, one fact stands out clearly. If the husband and wife can agree on a policy, tensions will be greatly eased. You need to talk matters through honestly and thoroughly.

What Is the Older Woman's Position?

A woman cannot expect to be the final authority in her son's home, or with his family, as she may have been in her own home.

When two women keep house together, each needs to understand the other's strengths and weaknesses. Each must be aware that the other has real needs. Each should respect the things the other does well, and be willing to come to the rescue in the spots where the other may be less competent. If they can talk over their situation frankly and acknowledge that they will probably occasionally annoy one another, they will have taken a big step toward a good relationship. Either the older or the younger may be the kind of housekeeper who wants no one in her kitchen. Nevertheless, she *has* someone in her kitchen, and unless she works out a way of living with that person things are going to be extremely difficult.

The two generations will tread on one another's toes far less often if responsibilities are carefully divided and duties worked out in advance. It helps, too, if both the younger and the older woman can see that the details of housekeeping are not nearly as important as a good relationship in the family. There are bound to be some sacrifices on everyone's part, but neither side should make all the sacrifices.

How About the Older Man's Predicament?

The man who has been head of a household for many years, who has made decisions at home and perhaps in his business, may be disappointed and easily offended when he lives in a home where his word carries no weight. If he can no longer make any kind of contribution to the home in which he finds himself, his is, indeed, a sorry lot.

It takes courage but it is sometimes necessary for a son to make a decision contrary to his father's wishes. It takes more courage sometimes for a grown man to admit his father is right. Both these courageous acts are necessary at times if your father lives with you.

The younger woman in the family takes the brunt of the responsibility, whether it be her father or her father-in-law. It is she who must plan the day's routines to include the older man's needs. A widower, accustomed to a great deal of attention from a devoted wife, may make demands that a busy housewife cannot meet. If the younger woman has to make that fact clear to a father or a father-in-law, she can still be good-humored and tactful.

If a man is to live contentedly in a son's or daughter's home, interesting activities that he can pursue need to be discovered. If they live on a farm, or have a house and yard, there may be ways an older man can make himself useful. If he has a mechanical bent, or even a faint artistic interest, he may develop a satisfying hobby.

Many communities, aware of the need for recreation for older persons, are sponsoring clubs and hobby groups for those past middle life. The preceding chapter, GRANDPARENTS AND OTHER RELATIVES, suggests where you might find such groups.

Sons and daughters need to take considerable trouble to find activities the older man can enjoy. If they let him feel he is contributing to the family, if they help him find friends his own age, if they look for ways grandfather and the smaller children can have fun together, their efforts will be well rewarded. Grandfather will tend to be less demanding, less critical, and more willing to make compromises if he has a reasonable degree of satisfaction out of life.

How About the Children's Rights?

The relationship of children and their grandparents is discussed in the preceding chapter, GRANDPARENTS AND OTHER RELATIVES.

It is hard on children when they and their parents are living in the home of a grandparent. Children have a right to bring their friends home. They need space and a chance to play noisily at times. Finger marks on the walls or spots on the rug are not really major calamities. Yet older people may object to the noise and dirt that result from the play of even well-behaved children.

If you make your home with the older generation, it may take considerable ingenuity and effort on your part to give your children the chance to be hospitable and still not upset grandma or grandpa. Some mothers have found that taking the child and one or two of his friends to the park or a playground often is a good solution. Excursions to near-by places, such as are described in EXCURSIONS FOR YOUNG CHILDREN, in Volume 13, and ADVENTURING THROUGH EXCURSIONS, in Volume 14, can be part of the week-end program. If your child invites a friend to come along, you are carrying your share of the neighborhood hospitality and making up for the times your youngsters play at someone else's house.

Picnics, or cookies and ice cream for classmates, served at recess in school, may be the substitute for the usual birthday party, which is out of the question at grandpa's house.

If you are willing to go half way in keeping the older people's house quiet, it is likely that they will be more willing to let the grandchildren have a friend over for an occasional afternoon of relatively quiet play.

Problems Connected with Money

The middle generation must make choices of many kinds. Will grandfather be provided with a hearing aid or will young Jimmy have his tonsils out? If there is money for meeting only one of these needs, the answer takes careful thought. You cannot make a cut-and-dried policy that "youth must be served" or that "deference is due to age."

Many older persons have no money of their own and are completely dependent on their sons and daughters. It is downright humiliating to be forced to ask for money for a pair of stockings or a few postage stamps. Older persons who are without any resources of their own should be considered when the family draws up its budget. An allowance, which the older man or woman can use without accounting to anyone, may go a long way toward helping him or her maintain self-respect.

Can the Older Generation Earn?

More than one family has found it practical and helpful to pay grandma a modest "wage" for her baby sitting, dishwashing, and mending. This wage

⟶
Grandpa is more contented when he feels he is pulling his weight in the family. His daughter considers him a help; his grandchildren think him a hero.

O. V. Gordon

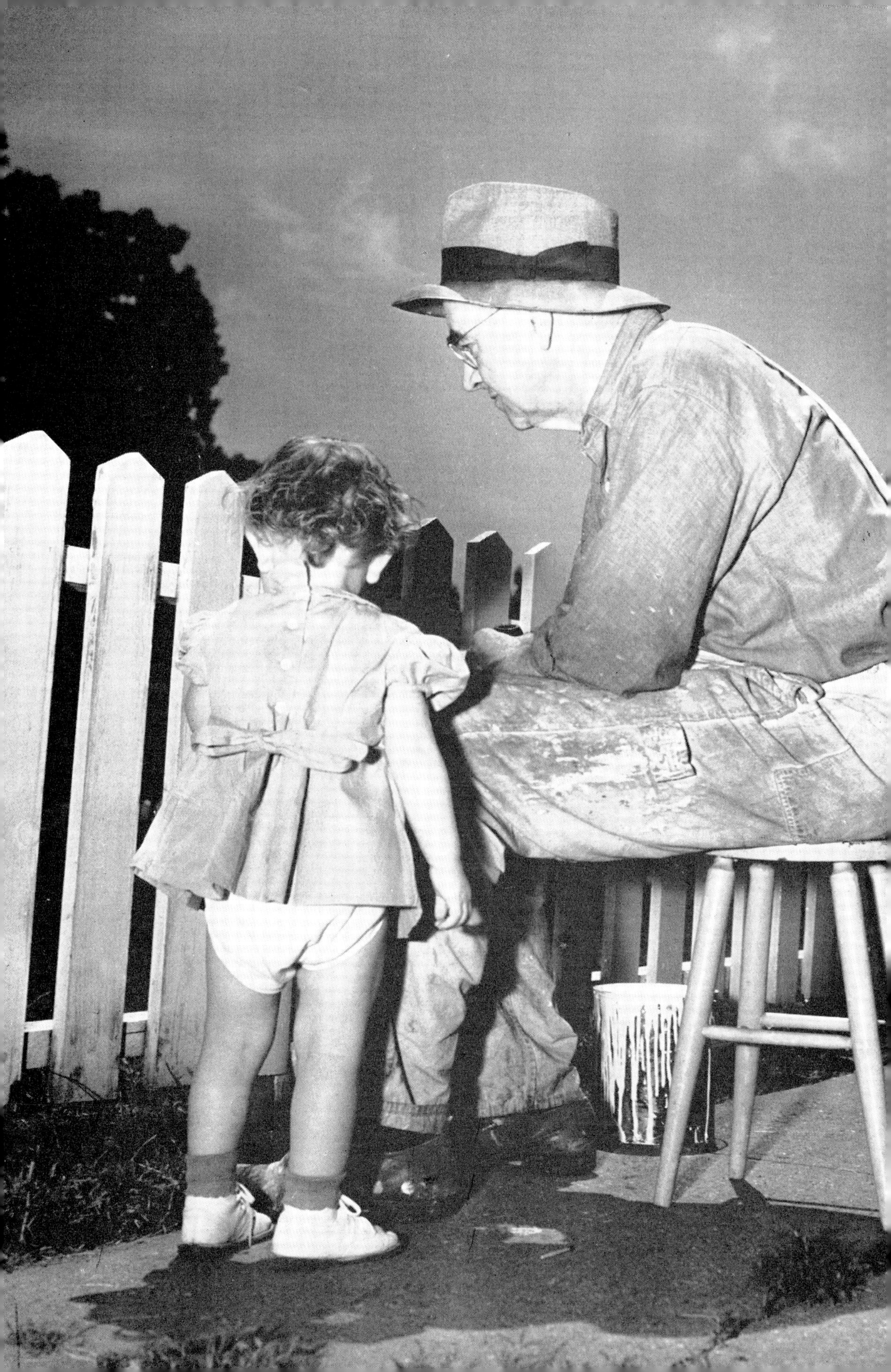

makes for better feelings all the way around. Grandma feels she is pulling her weight in the boat. Her son or son-in-law is less likely to regard her as a financial burden. Her daughter or daughter-in-law does not feel guilty about asking for her help. Grandma may turn around and use her "wages" to give the family an extra treat rather than spend the money on herself, but the choice is hers. Similar arrangements might be worked out for an older man.

Many communities are offering opportunities for older persons to earn money at home by using a special skill to make a simple product. Older women can pick up a fair amount of pocket money by baby-sitting outside the family. Let no false pride about "letting people think I'd make my poor old mother earn her living" stand in the way of an interesting, even mildly profitable, job for your parent.

Worries of Older People

When people pass the age of sixty or sixty-five, they may be troubled by all kinds of questions. Younger persons often fail to realize how hard it is for a widow or widower to get along without the companion of a lifetime. Loneliness increases as relatives and friends in their own age group die or become incapacitated. Some of the problems older people face are related to different kinds of physical illnesses, sometimes real, sometimes only feared. The loss of physical vigor and energy is often a source of concern. The prospect of becoming increasingly dependent in every way is frightening.

Older persons often feel unloved, unneeded, and in the way. You can make the older person feel he is still part of the family by taking him or her into your confidence. Ask for an opinion, even if you do not always follow it. Listen to him. Encourage him to have his own friends and interests. Make him feel he is useful, and you help the older person retain self-confidence and self-respect. You may be surprised at how much more agreeable older people are, how much more ready to compromise, when their lives are more satisfying. When three generations share a home, each one needs to have the satisfaction of knowing he or she is a contributing, valued member of the group. Then each one can do his share toward realizing the benefits inherent in the situation and avoiding some of the difficulties.

WAYS OF GROWING

Ewing Galloway

9. WHAT CHILDREN NEED FROM LIFE

10. HOW DO CHILDREN GROW?

11. PARENTS PLAY MANY PARTS

12. EACH CHILD IS DIFFERENT

All children go through similar stages in growing, but each grows on his own timetable. It is exciting to watch children grow in size, strength, and co-ordination from year to year, sometimes almost from week to week.

Their growth in ability to express ideas, to understand, and to reason is thrilling, too. Not always so clear-cut, but equally important for the development of healthy personality, is their growth in feelings, in relationships, in ability to get along with others, and in needs.

You will be better able to enjoy and foster your children's wholesome development if you remember that every step in growth does not necessarily bring with it improvement in behavior. If you understand ways of growing, you will realize that some phases of growth may be hard to live with, but that, in the long run, these phases too may be useful.

WHAT CHILDREN NEED FROM LIFE

JAMES L. HYMES, Jr.
Professor of Education
George Peabody College for Teachers, Nashville, Tenn.

CHILDREN, like all human beings, are always in need of something. Their needs come in two layers. One is a surface layer, while the other is deep and basic.

You, as a parent, have had much experience with the top layer, the surface needs for food, clothing, and toys. But there is another layer of needs deep down inside your child. If you succeed in satisfying these hidden needs, you make an important contribution to your child's well-being, health, and happiness.

Surface Needs

Youngsters can tell you about their top-layer needs. When he cries, your baby is telling you about his needs to be comfortable. Your three-year-old tells you, "I need some candy," or "I need some gum." You can see these top-layer needs right out on the surface. You sometimes say, "Billy needs new shoes. Look at those scuffs and the hole in the sole."

These top-layer needs include the buyables, the loseables, the holdables, and the breakables. The more fundamental, intangible needs are buried within your child. They are deep in the fiber of his being. They are the very fuel on which he runs.

Children Are Seekers

It is good to talk first about the child's material needs that we all know so well. They teach us something about all needs. They teach us, for one thing, that children are always seeking something. We get annoyed at this at times. It frightens us when we have to pay the bills. But it is good to understand from the very outset that this is the way all children are. This is the way they are made, and this is the way they have to be. The normal person is a seeking, wanting, needing kind of animal.

This top-layer group of needs teaches us, too, that children have different needs at different ages. You feel sad when you realize this.

Look at the wooden trains bought for his first birthday. Your child no longer plays with them. Look at the puzzles he loved when he was four; now that he is seven he does not care a whoop for them. But here is a fact that you have to accept—children must have certain satisfactions, both top-layer and fundamental, at certain ages. As they get them, new needs arise which are more fitting to the age of your child. You must meet these as they come up. This is hard to take at times, but it will help if you remember that this is the child—this is what a youngster is like.

Parents Are Givers

As you look back on all you have bought and made and given, you learn one more important idea from these top-layer needs. You learn something about yourself. You are generous with children. You want them, if possible, to have what they need. Maybe some people say you are soft. The truth is that you don't like to hold out on youngsters.

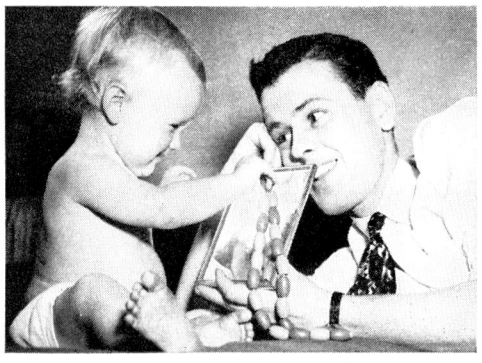

Pinney. Monkmeyer

Play with him . . .

It is true that we all say "No" to children at times. Each of us sets certain limits and we stick by them. But we don't say "No" just for the sake of saying it, or because we think that children do not count. We want them to have what is important to them during the period of growing up. But there are always situations where we cannot give in.

Those "No's," when you feel you have to say them, are not too important in the top-layer realm. Your youngster

H. Armstrong Roberts

Comfort him . . .

wants an ice-cream cone. Maybe you say "yes," or maybe you don't. He is pleased one way, sometimes a little mad the other. But it does not make much lasting difference, one way or the other. His tears soon stop if he is upset, and life picks right up again.

Needs That Go Deep

But you cannot say "no" to supper . . . and to breakfast and lunch and supper again. Your child has to have his basic food. If he were always hungry, he would always be demanding something to eat. Eventually he would become undernourished. The same thing holds true for his other fundamental needs. If a youngster does not get what he really must have, he cannot give up. These needs go so deep that he keeps trying to meet them, one way or the other.

If you hold out, put off, or deny these basic needs, your child must continue to want and need and search for them. He stays stuck, hungry, wanting what he must have more and more. Help him

Feed him . . .

get what he is after and the satisfaction makes your child go—and grow—and glow!

Love and Affection

What does your child need fundamentally, at the start of his life? It is your love. He has to have complete trust in you. You are his whole world. He has to be sure that you will comfort him and protect him, hold him and cuddle him, be head-over-heels in your feeling about him.

You give your very young child this assuring security through the words you use. Babies make us all say silly but so-good-to-hear talk. Your youngster interprets it as "I love you. . . . We all love you." But you build this good feeling even more through your actions. Feed your child when he is hungry. Relax so

Enjoy him . . .

that he really gets full and does not feel rushed. Be gentle with him, laugh with him, enjoy him, and play with him. You don't ignore him; you are *with* him. You don't let him cry endlessly; you comfort him. You are not afraid he will break; you hold him and cuddle him.

Every little deed in every minute gets your meaning over: "You are welcome here." And that is what a baby has to know. This is a safe world. People are for me. I am all right.

A child never outgrows needing to know this. Even adults must have this surety inside. But the start of life is the time above all times when a youngster must have his fill of this warm feeling. This is really what infancy is for, so that you can give him your love and warmth and joy. When a child knows he has it, he is free to move on along to a search for other satisfactions.

What Is the Right Kind of Love?

Your full and complete love frees him to grow. That means you must feel a special kind of love. Not the binding, worrying, keep-him-close type, but a

. . . and he will have courage to stand on his own more and more as he develops.

H. Armstrong Roberts

freeing love that makes you feel glad when your youngster starts branching out.

"Gosh, do I *have* to go on that old picnic with you and Dad Saturday? I wanted to work on our club house with Tim," may be your eight-year-old's response to the announcement of an event planned for his special enjoyment.

Right here is where you may find it hard to hit a balancing note. When your baby is small you show your love by your closeness to him. As he grows you show it by your willingness to hold the reins loose. Your love is always there but, more and more, your child comes back to you for it, instead of your advancing it constantly, as you must when he is a baby.

A Feeling of Independence

No bell rings, no birthday party is held when a youngster has had enough of your affection to feel safe in stepping out. But the loved and trusting baby does move into new fields. Sure of the support of the people around him, he sets out to be BIG. He wants now to find himself, to be a real person in his own right.

Although the change-over from one peak need, security, to this new peak, independence, comes at no set time, you begin to see a difference in your child's behavior. He has his own ideas. He runs away sometimes. He wants to do everything for himself—dressing, feeding, and deciding. He goes overboard on the language he uses, with "No's" abounding. This is followed later by some bad words and much tough talk. He wants so much to set himself off, to say "Look at me, I am here."

You did it! He never would dare if you had not loved him so well. Your good start gave him the courage to be a person and to stand on his own. If you find all the strong will that goes with this search for independence hard to take, two or three facts may comfort you.

Is Self-Assertion Necessary?

Remember, these are the years when children are supposed to assert themselves. This is their special use, just as infancy has to give itself over to the search for security. A two-year-old or three- or four- or five-year-old can be a little over-bossy or over-insistent. But if a youngster does not find himself during these years, think how hard it will be to live with the thirty-two-year-old who always wants his way (and how unhappy he will be).

Do you worry over your youngster's tough talk or his strong words when he tries to be so big? Don't be alarmed. He is not the only one. All children act the same way. They have to. This sense of strong independence is a building stone in human growth.

It is a comfort, too, to remember that each peak need subsides after a while. Of course, another new need arises to take its place. But you can keep your good, friendly spirit going if you know that no single need flares up and stays high forever—if each need is met satisfactorily.

Everything Will Not Become a Habit

That is the hardest fact of all to believe. So many people worry about habits. If you comfort your child when he needs you as an infant, won't he start a habit of always wanting his way? If you take his strong preferences into account when he is two years old, and try to adjust to them, won't he get a habit of being stubborn? If you don't make a major issue out of his wilfulness, and break it the first time it shows up, won't he form a habit of acting that way?

Worries like these are so logical that many people feel them. But you will see the answer if you keep your eye on your child. You won't have to break his "habits"; he will break them himself. His growth will break them. As he acquires the sense of security first, and then the sense of being a real person, he is free to mature. Old concerns that once were everything subside, but new needs arise.

A Sense of Achievement

Once your youngster has proved to the world, to you, and to himself that he is big, you will see him settle down. He is still seeking satisfactions. During the elementary school years his great need is for achievement. He feels safe, for his satisfactory infancy gave him an excellent start. He knows he is real, for you gave him enough freedom and a chance to do things in his early childhood to start him on the right track. Now he wants to put himself to work, to use himself, to accomplish.

Friends begin to matter even more than they did before, especially people his own age with whom he plays and works. Skills—in games, reading, riding a bike, hammering—begin to matter even more than they once did. You begin to see your child industriously engaged in his work, in his play, and in his school life. He is a bubble of collections, of hobbies, and of enthusiasms. These all have more point to them than in the years just gone by.

How Do You Supply a Sense of Achievement?

You give children this sense of achievement when you encourage them. "Seems to me you sound much better on that clarinet than you did last month. I still don't think you're ready for a name band, but you're coming along," is the kind of remark from father that tells Junior he is accomplishing something.

If Jane tries her hand at knitting, you can pick out the good features of the sock to comment on, even as you suggest something not so ambitious for her to try. It helps if you plan with the children so that they will have their share of successes, rather than a procession of outstanding failures.

You give them a sense of achievement as you give them more opportunities to choose, more leeway to decide and to carry out plans on their own. They want to make things; they plan plays and entertainments. Some project is always afoot. Your approval gives an undertaking status. Your support and constructive suggestions let them know you think it's worth-while.

Of course, you can get impatient with all this, too. No one time in the child's process of growing up is a bed of roses for you. Your youngster's messes may

Kaufmann & Fabry

Encourage your children to carry out their own plans. This will give them a most satisfying sense of achievement.

get you down. The way he is all wrapped up in one thing, and then later in another, may make you impatient. The wholeheartedness with which enthusiasms grab hold of him may occasionally wear you to a frazzle. The strong way he wants to pursue his own interests, and his nonchalance about some of the ideas you think are important, may be sources of irritation. You can manage to live with this with a smile, however, if you see that it all feeds into the growing person. Your child utilizes each one of these satisfactions. He puts them to work inside himself. They give him what he needs for growing.

Encouragement

Not that you never say "No," during this span of years, or at any other time. When your child is a baby your "No's" have to be rare. At that one time he is so dependent on your approval that it is good to give in. You feed, hold, comfort, about as much as he wants you to.

Even in these very early years, though, you must want to give in and feel good about it. If you say "Yes" because you think you should, your youngster catches your reluctant feeling. He does not get from you the real thing he is after: your joy, your gladness, your comfortable willingness. The once-in-a-while when you are too pressed or tired or harried, it is better to have him wait than for you to come gritting your teeth.

When Do You Say "No" and Mean It?

Gradually, the more sure he feels, the more he will be able in the later years to take a "No." Not that you must be harsh about it, or careless—dropping *no's* and *don'ts* and *mustn'ts* whenever you talk. But when it seems necessary—if the puppy's tail is being pulled; or the youngster next door is being pummeled; if your five-year-old selects the railroad embankment as a place to play or experiments with a scissors on the living room curtains—he must be stopped. Never hesitate to call a halt and mean it when your boy or girl is hurting somebody; when he is in danger himself; when he is needlessly destroying something; or even when he is presenting you with more than you can

When they hurt others

When they are in danger

There are times when you should say "No"!

take at the moment. Never hesitate to say (and to mean it), "This must stop."

Far from hurting your child, such reasonable limits help him. One of his fundamental needs, running through all the years, is to have some sensible limits set. If *anything* goes, you worry your child. The complete absence of "No's" makes him wonder if you really care. It shakes his sense of trust and he feels too much on his own.

A child has quite a job to do, to move from being a self-centered infant to being a socially sensitive, mature person. He wants to do this job and he is working at it all the time. Your gentle but firm limits, your reasonable limits, your occasional limits all buck him up. They help him do what he wants to do, for he does not have to do the job of maturing all by himself.

Parents Who Understand

We speak here of trust and security as the great needs of infancy. Your youngster does not want you to memorize this. He wants you to keep your eye on him, to try to figure out from his behavior: What is he after now?

Infancy is the peak time for this concern, but there will be many other times all through the growing years when this need will surge up and become, for the moment, the most important.

We speak of independence and the discovery of self as the great concerns of the age period from two to six years. Your child does not want you to copy this down and then learn it from your notes. He wants you, most of all, to glue your eyes on him and to learn from what he is doing.

There will be times earlier in his life than the book says and later in his life than the book says when independence will matter most to him, and be the be-all and end-all of what he does, for the while.

Being Aware of Needs Is All-Important

We speak of the need for achievement, of the need for your setting some limits. One final need is maybe more important than any of these: *Children need to grow up with people who know they have needs!* Feel this way about your child and you will keep asking yourself: What is he after now? Why does he do that? What does it bring him?

His behavior will talk to you. It will let you know what matters most to him and you will be able to satisfy what he is really after. You will keep him moving toward a healthy maturity if you keep your eye on him, and if you remember that he always needs something, that he is supposed to have needs because he is human, and that these needs are not waste or luxury but the stuff of growth.

HOW DO CHILDREN GROW?

MARY FISHER LANGMUIR, Ph.D.
Chairman, Department of Child Study, Vassar College, Poughkeepsie, N. Y.

To LEARN to let live is the most helpful thing parents and teachers can do for children. Since we are the adults who care for and teach children day after day, year after year, what we do or fail to do makes the greatest difference in their lives. We are the ones who must understand the changes that come slowly or swiftly as the years of childhood pass. The plan for growth is all there. It is we who must learn about it. Problems are a necessary and valuable part of changing and growing and living. We are the ones who must help children meet them.

It will help us if we see how children grow, and if we map out the ways and by-ways of their growing. Looking ahead, as well as backward, can help us see the over-all plan. Knowing what may happen, and why, can make it easier to keep our sense of direction when the going is difficult. We can be certain there will be rough places as well as smooth ones. Unless we know what to expect, we may create or prolong difficult times by expecting too much too soon of our children—or too little too late.

Growth Comes from Within

No one knows the whole plan of growth. Perhaps it can never be completely understood, for the mystery of life itself lies behind and beyond the miracle of growing. The fact that growth comes from within makes it difficult to study and observe. We can see the changes in size and shape and ability that growth brings about, but we cannot see the process itself. We can study the parts, but the whole eludes us.

The plan for growth begins to reveal itself from the moment of conception. Once begun, development goes on with incredible sureness and swiftness. Growth continues as long as the conditions for development are possible. Never again in so short a time will the child grow so much, or so fast, or in so many different ways, as before his birth.

In nine months the almost invisible fertilized egg, weighing nothing, develops into a six- to nine-pound infant. If prenatal growth and birth have gone well, the newborn can survive separation from his mother. He is completely equipped for all further physical development—and for learning the ways and the customs of his particular family and his world.

At birth, the infant has already come far in his development. He can do his own breathing, his own sucking, his own eliminating. But he cannot even begin to do his own questioning, his own knowing, his own loving, his own giving. These are the most precious of all human capacities, but they develop slowly and mature late. Like walking upright, knowing and loving are developments possible only in the plan for human growth. If children are given barely enough food and a minimum of shelter, they may be able to survive and to grow up physically. But they cannot grow up emotionally, mentally, and spiritually under such conditions. They cannot become mature and truly adult without love, protection, and wise and patient guidance. This is why parents and teachers make so much difference in children's lives.

Growth Is Orderly

After birth, as before, growth continues to be orderly, continuous, and predictable. At the right time and in the right order, new skills and new capacities develop. Each infant in his own good time repeats the pattern of the human race as he lifts his head before he can crawl, crawls before he can walk, walks before he can run. Before he can master or "learn" any new skill, his nervous system must mature, he must become "ready." Then if we give him a chance, he practices and practices until finally he achieves whatever is next on the calendar of growth.

How Can You Tell They Are Ready?

Each child, as he learns to grasp, to throw, to stand, to walk, to talk, to read, to write, and even to co-operate or to share, follows a definite pattern. That pattern is readiness—practice—achievement. There are no short cuts, no passing quickly from immaturity to maturity. There is no skipping of stages of growth, like skipping a grade in school. We can ignore, we can hinder, we can help—but we cannot hurry growth. The part of wisdom, then, is to co-operate with growth, to learn to know the signs which tell us "what next."

Restlessness is usually the first sign that a new stage is about to begin. A baby of six to nine months "ready" to crawl is no longer content in his chair or carriage. He fusses and struggles. It is not enough for him to watch and to

This baby has a good start. Love and protection are the foundation for wholesome growth of all kinds.

Korling

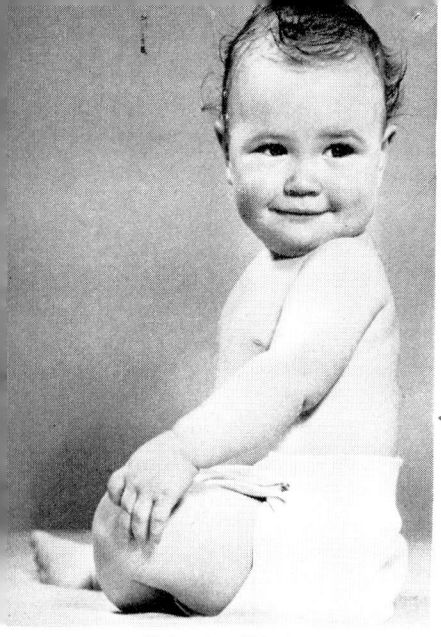

Everything comes in its due season. Sitting up is a big advance. Crawling is a mark of progress. The final triumph is getting on two feet.

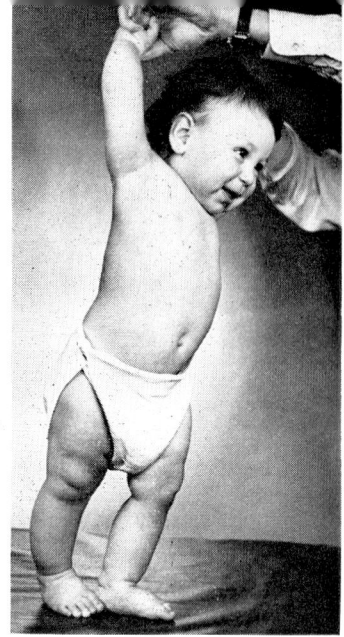

practice using his hands. He must be up on all fours. He must get his back into it and begin to conquer space. Later, when he is ready to walk, even more room will be needed. "Don't fence me in" is the theme song of every child as he learns to crawl, to walk, to run, and to explore.

The same child four or five years later will be getting "ready" to read. He will no longer be content to be read to, or to repeat the story from memory as he turns the familiar pages. He begins to notice that the black marks on the page are both different and alike. He wants to find out. He *must* find out. He is impatient that it takes so long! If we are impatient too—or if we ask him to begin before he is "ready"—we will hinder, not help, his learning to read. Learning to read, like all other important learning, is complicated and takes time.

Interest Makes Practice Worthwhile

Interest is another definite sign that a child is getting ready to practice and learn something new. He watches and tries to imitate. We see this when younger boys watch older boys play baseball, or when younger girls watch older girls closely and begin to practice the art of using lipstick. Usually we are more willing to let boys practice baseball than we are to let girls practice being attractive. In either case, unless we understand the signs and co-operate in letting the child *begin* to learn, we are asking for trouble. Holding growth back, or limiting growth, always creates problems. Children become defiant and rebellious, or they lose interest and become bored and restless.

In most families, fortunately, children take matters into their own hands when they are "ready," and we are not. Their going-ahead-on-their-own causes many crises, and also creates real problems for them and us. On the whole independence and initiative are healthy and should be welcomed. To know that "misbehavior" is frequently a sign of growth is comforting. When children rebel at rules and regulations, it is time to re-examine the family "do's" and "don'ts." It may well be that we are trying to treat our children as though they were still much younger. It helps to remember that schedules, as well as shoes,

Investigating a new toy is one way of learning.

Even getting a hat on one's head takes careful practice.

Away he goes when success has given him confidence.

can be outgrown. The shoes—or the rules—that fitted six months ago may have become too tight for comfort or further growth.

Growth Is Uneven

Every child grows in spurts. He starts and stops, and starts again. He forgets about words, for example, when the urge to walk is strongest. We often say, "But my child seems to go backward in one direction whenever he goes forward in another." This is good observation. Growth is uneven. The child does go backward many times, and then retraces his steps. He cannot concentrate on too much at once. It takes energy, as well as time and confidence, to learn to walk, to talk, to dress oneself, to make friends, to do arithmetic, or even to play baseball. There will be many slow starts before the gains begin to show.

How Shall We Handle Backsliding?

There is another important reason for the unevenness of growth. All through their growing years we can expect children to forget, or lose interest, in much that they have already learned. This happens when they become absorbed in new interests, new skills, or in "just growing." Their forgetfulness about manners, or grammar, or how to wash thoroughly is annoying but not serious. Teachers also must expect that much will be forgotten and lost over every summer vacation. They, too, must start over, review, and help children by beginning slowly.

Every child can be expected to go backwards not once but many times. We can expect him to lose ground when something new and difficult is happening in the family like a new baby, a move to a new house, or when he begins school. Then he may wet again, want help in dressing, or begin to stutter or talk baby talk. If we understand this is part of growth—not naughtiness—we help him out, encourage him, and try to build up his confidence. Sooner or later we can be sure he will be back on his growth schedule.

We need not be worried, then, when our children seem to lose ground and make many detours. If we keep track of the major landmarks, and concern ourselves with each child's *total* progress, we can tell whether or not his growth is going well. If we are in doubt, or if there seem to be no gains to cancel the losses over several months, we should seek advice. Doctors, teachers, and psychologists can help. They have studied and observed many children and understand the ways and needs of growth. The chapter FAMILY GUIDANCE SERVICES, in Volume 15, will be helpful here.

What Landmarks Can We Watch?

In general, we can tell how growth-as-a-whole is going if we watch for certain major events in the early years. We can reasonably expect each child to walk by the time he is two, to talk by the time he is three, to keep dry by the time he is four. When he is six he can probably dress and bathe himself, and when he is eight, he can read. Yet even after these important landmarks in growth and independence have been reached and passed, we must not count on steady performance.

This brief timetable tells us, of course, only what *most* children have achieved and are able to do at certain ages. Happily there is no "ideal," no "average" child. There are only individual children, growing at their own rates and in their own ways—but all according to the basic plan.

Growth Is Individual

In spite of the basic plan for growth which all children must follow, no two children can or do develop in the same way—nor even in the same family. The fact that each member of the human race is "born to be different" is almost more than we can get our minds around. Each person is unlike every other person who has ever lived—or who ever will live—because his own special inheritance can never be matched or duplicated in all human history. He is also different because the exact conditions under which he grows and lives can never be repeated.

Being the only child, the oldest, the youngest, or in the middle makes another important difference. No one position in the family is necessarily better or worse. All positions have their advantages and disadvantages. The chapter EACH CHILD IS DIFFERENT in this volume discusses the reasons for and ways of handling individual differences in detail.

Even though we really *know* that all children are individual and different, we worry when their differences show up. We are concerned if Johnny does not walk as soon as the cousin who is only six days older. Later we are concerned because he does not learn to read as early or as easily. Unless we can really accept the fact that each child *must* grow at his own rate, in his own way, we may hinder or slow up his development.

Different Styles in Growing

It helps our acceptance of children to know that there are many normal patterns and rates of growth. The specialists who have studied and observed many children over many years tell us about *the fast grower, the slow grower, the split grower, and the harmonious grower*. These terms describe the general rate of growth and its evenness or unevenness. The *fast grower* does everything earlier than most children of his age. The *slow grower* gets there, but it takes him longer. The *split grower* grows more unevenly than most. His body may be slower in developing than his mind. He may be sexually immature when most boys of his age and intelligence

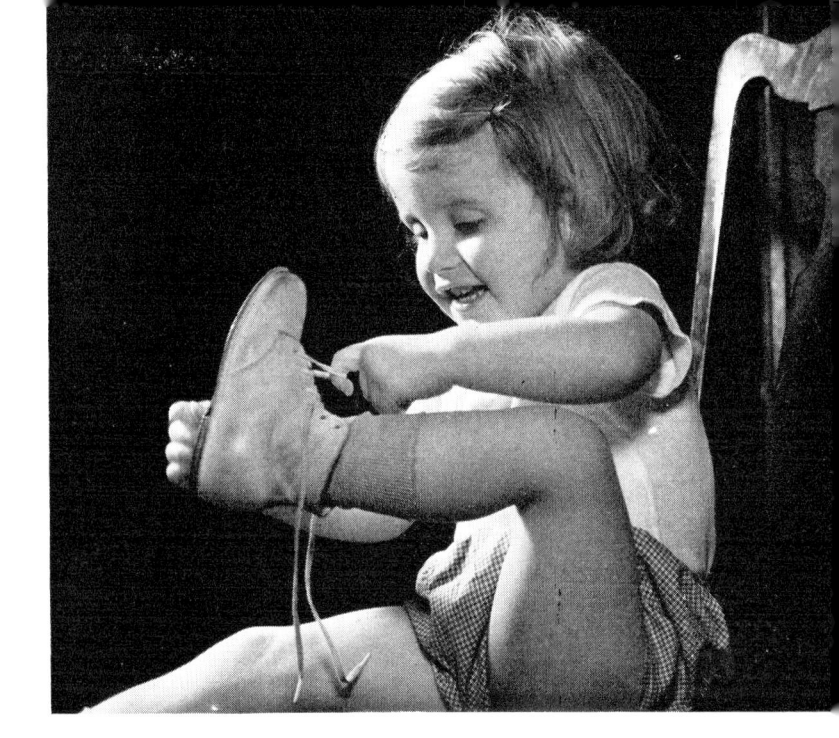

Each age has its own satisfactions. Six-year-olds can dress themselves.

New doors open to the eight-year-old as he discovers he can read and that reading is fun.

Korling

have reached puberty. This is only one of many possible and familiar combinations of split growth. The *harmonious grower* always grows more evenly, and more of a piece.

Each of these patterns of growth is *normal*, although obviously different. Many of the problems and troubles we have at home and at school are the result of our trying to make children more alike. It takes patience and wisdom, for example, to keep a slower-growing brother from being discouraged or defeated by his faster-growing older brother. We easily get impatient with a slower child, and feel he is not trying. It often seems to him that he can never catch up, never do as well, never be as loved or appreciated. He may even become slower because his discouragement sets the brakes on his growing.

No matter how "different" our children are, we may be sure that each can be trusted to pass through the stages that lead to maturity in his own way. But he can do this only if we value and accept him for himself, and can free him to do his own growing.

Growth Can Be Helped

It is important for all parents and teachers to know that growth comes from within—that growth is orderly and continuous—that growth is uneven and highly individual. It is even more important for us to know that growth can and must be helped. Without the right conditions, without guidance and protection, the plan for growth cannot be fulfilled. For growth is indivisible. Body, mind, and spirit all grow together, all influence each other, as the child's "self," his unique personality, develops.

What Does Personality Need for Growth?

The more we study how the "self" or the personality is developed, the more clear it becomes that each period of growth has its critical stage and its special requirements. Each stage must build on what has gone before. This is as true of the personality as of the body.

The infant must have loving and patient care if he is to learn that living is comfortable, and that people are to be trusted. Without such basic trust, all future growth will lack a firm foundation.

The two- and three-year-old must be disciplined with friendliness, firmness, and tolerance if later he is to be friendly, firm, and tolerant with himself. "Conscience" begins at this sensitive period. It must become neither too strict nor too lax, if growth is to proceed according to plan.

The child of four and five must have freedom *and* sensible limits if his zest for living and learning is to remain strong and vital. The school-age child must have, *each year of school*, the continuing satisfaction of learning to do things well. Otherwise he cannot become a creative and productive person with confidence in *his* ability to learn and to achieve.

If we take this long view of the growth of personality, it becomes clear that *with whom the child lives and learns, and how he is taught and guided, are of crucial importance*. By the time he is ten—or six, or four, or even two—every child has seen, heard, felt, and ex-

When the things the children make are appreciated, personality blooms.

perienced far more than we can ever know or appreciate.

How Do Feelings Influence Personality?

In terms of his personality, the most important parts of his environment for growing have been *people* and *relationships* and *feelings*. Even the most loved and protected child experiences failure, doubt, anger, and fear. This is part of human growth. Every child knows what it is to be weak, dependent, and helpless. This is part of human childhood. At best it is not easy to help a child keep his initiative and confidence intact. Yet this is, perhaps, our greatest responsibility. Without initiative and confidence, growth cannot be fulfilled.

One of the most difficult things about helping the plan for growth is that a child so easily learns the wrong feelings. Often without our knowing it, or being able to prevent it, he may learn to feel that it is not "safe," "possible," or "comfortable" to try new things, to take on greater responsibilities that come with growing up. He may get caught by his own fears and doubts and begin to stand in his own way. Then his wonderful urge to do, to find out, to try, to create, becomes damaged and weakened.

When and if this happens—and it happens to all children to some extent—it is a sign that the going is difficult, that the child needs special help. At such times we must go gently and carefully, not rush in to push and put the pressure on. Growth so quickly resists force and attack. Children so easily retreat and defend themselves when life, or parents and teachers, demand too much. Then they may develop, or return to, what we are pleased to call "bad habits." Yet, this, too, is part of growing.

Growth Fulfills Itself

Growth can be trusted to fulfill itself, but it cannot be trusted to suit our convenience, or to fit easily into the rush and pressure of modern life. Every time we get discouraged or impatient and say, "But I have done all the right things and my child *still* has problems," we have lost sight of the meaning and purpose of the plan for growth. Growth leads to maturity; but not easily, not automatically. The way is long, difficult, and demanding, as well as wonderful, rewarding, and deeply satisfying. Our children must take the same journey, face the same tasks, and learn from their own experiences and mistakes just as we have, and just as their children will in their turn. We can stand by, we can respect, we can help, we can value, we can love—but we cannot take the journey for them or shorten it. There are no short cuts to maturity, no substitute for striving and learning, and living.

And how can we tell how they seem to be faring? There can be no single yardstick to measure growth. But if our children—*most of the time*—are friendly and interested, if they like to learn and find out, if they are usually helpful and co-operative, then their growth is going well. If they are not afraid to show their feelings, if they can stand up for their rights—then we are learning to "let live."

If they are happy, friendly, and interested most of the time, their growth is going well.

PARENTS PLAY MANY PARTS

HELEN ROSS, B.S.
Administrative Director,
Institute for Psychoanalysis, Chicago, Ill.

Hibbs

THE family is the foundation of happy living in our modern society. The stronger the family, the more solid, substantial, and progressive our society will be. The family is usually made up of a wide variety of interesting and complicated relationships between the parents, among the children, and involving parents and children.

These day-to-day relationships, or feelings, make for good family life or tend to break it apart. Such feelings include love, sympathy, envy, fear, distrust, jealousy, and a host of others.

The forces within the family shift and vary. Indeed, the strength of the family, and the welfare of each person in it, depend upon changes. These come with the growth and experience of each individual. Every day the child is older and the parents more experienced, in a world that constantly changes. The family is dynamic. It never stands still.

Mothers Are Givers

The birth of the first child makes new people out of the parents, and the child's life of relationships begins. The first, the mother-child relationship, is the groundwork of the child's later attitudes toward the world. The mother is the child's first contact with people, and so she becomes the pattern of what the child can expect from others. The way she feeds him, fondles him, cares for him, determines his anticipation of the ways other grown-up people will feel about him now and later.

The usual mother is ready to give her child the warmth and comfort that he needs. If she cannot feed him at the breast, she gives him the bottle in her arms. The child's first learning is through his body. To the baby, food equals love and love equals food.

If the mother enjoys feeding him, he usually responds with satisfaction. He eats well, he settles down to sleep. If there is uneasiness in the mother, as often happens with the young mother and her first child, her movements may not be so easy and gentle. She cannot make him as comfortable as when she is relaxed. Her tenseness goes from her

When Father, as well as Mother, gives loving care, a baby's trust expands. Then his confidence in the world around blossoms, and he reaches out.

body into his. If she does not love the child, as sometimes happens, the child responds uneasily even though she be careful about everything she does for him.

Comfort to the baby spells security; discomfort comes to mean anxiety. An anxious child becomes restless and "hard to handle." Even the baby with a good relationship to his mother will sometimes get sick or fretful. Then he needs more closeness to the mother than when he is well. It is true, too, that happy, well-satisfied babies are usually healthier than unhappy, dissatisfied babies.

How Do Babies Become Friendly?

Confidence in his mother makes the baby interested in the people about him. Happy infants begin to notice things earlier, to reach out earlier, and to recognize people earlier than those children to whom only routine care is given. The foundation for good relationship seems to start with one person.

The mother is the key person in the infant's life. But the father is also ready to help with the baby. If he follows as nearly as possible the mother's way of handling the baby, he can make him feel more secure. The child soon learns there are two people who love him and he knows what to expect from each. If there is a baby sitter, she should handle the infant as the mother does.

The mother-child unit is extremely important. The mother's happiness and contentment are reflected in the baby's smile and in his general well-being. The mother is the bridge from the prenatal growth to the adventure of the whole life. She is the first provider of food and comfort. She is the pattern for the child's feeling about the world, and she is the buffer against pain and uneasiness. She is at first the center of the child's world. The security he feels with her leads him to include others in his ever-widening orbit.

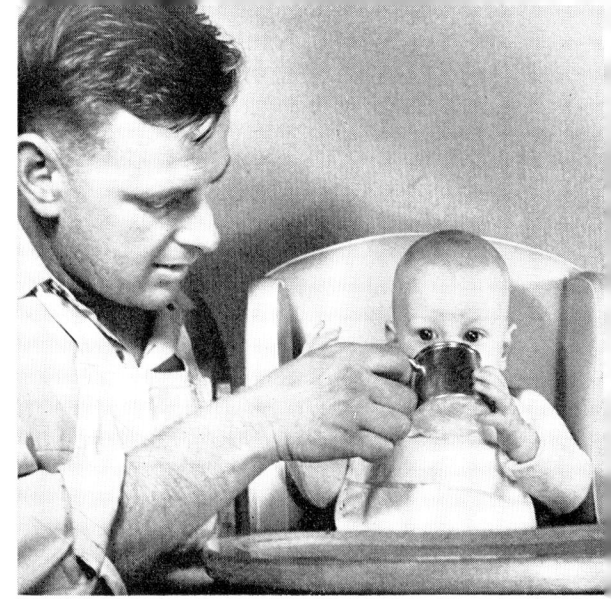

Father Is the Outside World

The father's importance grows as the child begins to toddle. He becomes to the little child the big, important person who leaves home every day and returns with a warm smile, with new games to play, high on his shoulders, or ride-a-cock-horse. The little child learns quickly to anticipate this fun. He knows when to go to the window to watch for Daddy's homecoming. Sometimes the mother who has worked hard all day feels a little hurt that father gets such a big hand. But the child rewards the mother with his need for her when he is tired or hungry or not well, as well as at other times. And fathers and mothers learn to share each other's joy in the child's growth and accomplishment.

Learning is worth the effort when Mother is pleased. Her approval is both reward and encouragement.

Parents Become Teachers

Toward the end of the first year, the parents start to train the child to habits of cleanliness. "Too early" or "too late" can cause trouble. But what *is* the best time and what *is* the best way? The young mother asks for an answer. The older mother has learned from experience, and it is interesting to note that the youngest children in the family are usually the easiest to train. There is no one "right way," but there are a few good leads to follow.

The child should be ready. In other words, the muscles involved in eliminating should be under control. He should have some understanding of what his mother is asking him to do. His development should be average, and his health must be good. The observant, sensitive mother usually knows instinctively when the right time has come.

The mother should be "ready," too. She should have the necessary patience, for she is asking the child to respond to new expectations on her part. At first, perhaps, there will be relapses. Heretofore she has been satisfied when the child's elimination was healthy and regular. Now she shows her special pleasure only when he eliminates in the right place. It is often difficult for the child to learn, though many children "learn before they know it," especially if there are older children to imitate. HELPING YOUR CHILD LEARN TO USE THE TOILET, in Volume 13, is concerned with the details of toilet training. Here we are concerned only with what it means to the child.

How Do Children Learn?

In this period, the mother has a new role. She is the teacher. The child enjoys learning because he pleases his mother. Learning for its own sake comes much later in his life. At first he conforms because he wins his mother's smile. This smile is his fun, his reward. To be sure, the child will respond, also, to threats and punishment. In that kind of training he has no part. He just acts on the demand of another. Such learning does not "get into his backbone" and become automatic. It remains always mixed up with feelings of uneasiness and distress.

The healthy child enjoys learning to do new things, but in his own good time. Since toilet training is one of the first important lessons in his life, how it is accomplished may easily influence the way he tackles new demands from then on. Some children undertake any new activity with pleasurable anticipation. Some hold back and have to be reassured over and over.

Another point to emphasize to the mother is the importance of being casual about the training. Her confidence in the child's response, her recognition that she cannot impose her timing on the child, will make her less concerned about immediate results of the training.

Too much pressure at this time slows up the whole process. It may make an anxious child or it may create physical symptoms and influence character. Stubbornness often results when the child is high-pressured into doing what the parents wish. The bowel and bladder functions should fall into their normal place in the child's life. They should not hang over him as a threat of losing the good will of his parents.

Every parent takes pride in his child's accomplishment, but comparisons with other children too often make children over-ambitious or discouraged and unwilling to make ventures. Every child's development and growth follow a certain order, but the tempo varies with the individual.

Mother Interprets the Rules

As the child's first teacher, the mother becomes the interpreter also of what society demands. To be lax or neglectful of training may let the little boy or girl grow up without a sense of responsibility for his behavior. This responsibility is at first the parents'. The child learns gradually to take it over as a part of himself. This is easier to do when the parents are consistent, when they present a "united front." Through the father this notion of responsibility is widened. He represents law and order outside the home. From him the child learns of government and protection on a larger scale. To make good citizens, parents have to be responsible people themselves.

Family Circles Become Triangles

Quite early, little children learn that there are two kinds of people in the world, like Daddy or like Mommie. They discover that they belong to a certain sex. The little girl finds in her mother not just the good protector but also someone to imitate. The little boy tries to be like the father. The twosome of mother and child now becomes a triangle of mother-father-child, and the child has to work out new relationships. Mother belongs to him, but not exclusively. Father and Mother belong to each other.

The child normally tries to be like the grown-up of his own sex. At the same time, he turns to the other parent with new interest. The little girl says, "Some day I'll marry Daddy." The little boy expresses himself to the mother: "Let's have a big house together some day." These common expressions of children show they are trying to take the first steps toward later, important relationships in life, when they will get married and start families of their own. This is a rehearsal for adulthood. Little girls practice how to please their fathers. Little boys practice being protective with their mothers. Fathers and mothers are models for the future.

This is not always an easy period for the child to work through. The three- to four-year-old likes to be with the grown-ups and often feels shut out by the parents when he is not allowed to come into their room any time he wishes. The boy competes with his father. The girl becomes impatient with her mother. It is especially hard for the little girl, who needs her mother and tries to be like her, to discover that Mother comes first with Daddy.

With the discovery of sex differences, children become curious about their own bodies and about those of other people, sometimes to an embarrassing degree. But this normal curiosity should

"I'll always love my Daddy best," insists this enchantress, size three. Daddy knows this is one phase of growing up, and knows it will not last.

not be forbidden. Curiosity is the mainspring of learning. If it is frowned upon or punished, the child drives his curiosity underground, and he will have to ponder alone or get wrong information outside the home. Questions should be answered as they come, but not expanded beyond the child's understanding. If he has confidence in his parents, he will come back for more information when he needs it. Again the parents are teachers in the best sense. They await the readiness of the child for the learning, and they are patient with his efforts to understand. HE LEARNS ABOUT DIFFERENCES BETWEEN BOYS AND GIRLS, in Volume 13, discusses in detail children's feelings about sex in the early years.

In all these early stages, the mother is the axis about which the child's feelings revolve—his willingness and his resistance; his "goodness" and his "badness;" his love and his hate. (Hate to a little child is just the other side of love.) The parents give to the child, but they also ask him to do what they say. Society makes demands, too. One might say the child makes his experiments with the parents as far as society is concerned.

The Family Is a Proving Ground

Parents must be prepared for the child's badness as well as his goodness, and the home is the place for experimenting with behavior. The naughtiest child at home is often the best at school. This happens not because he loves the teacher more than the mother but because he has experimented at home and knows what is acceptable behavior. He controls himself at school, but he is in the process of learning control at home. Knowing his parents' loving tolerance, he can try things out. The parents, therefore, hold the reins of aggression in their hands. If they are wise and patient, they will know when to slacken and tighten the reins, not just for their own comfort but for the child's future good.

Brothers and sisters belong in the family picture, too. How the young child feels about them and how these feelings develop, have much to do with his growth. It is easier at three or older to share the mother with a new baby than it is at an earlier age. At eighteen months, for example, the child still needs the concentrated attention of his mother. He often finds this so hard to give up that he will act like the baby, thinking this will reinstate him in her favor. He may return to wetting or soiling himself. He may begin sucking his thumb, or he may even have temper tantrums.

The younger child may remain an object of the older one's envy even after he

Korling

"What'll Mommy say to this?" That is the question small children are trying to answer as they test their own strength and test their parents. If limits are set with gentle firmness, they gradually learn how far it is safe to go.

himself has grown up. Jealousy is normal, for each child wants to be loved the most. Gradually, under the guidance of the parents, children learn to share with each other, not only things, but also the attention and love of the parents. You will want to read the section in this volume on RELATIONSHIPS AMONG CHILDREN IN THE FAMILY, for a fuller presentation of how brothers and sisters feel toward one another.

Sometimes parents get impatient with the child's failure to behave in a more grown-up way. Parents are likely to remember themselves as more mature at four or five than they actually were! But pressure to achieve beyond the child's capacity usually discourages and slows him up. Children normally try to please their parents, although they sometimes *seem* not to care.

Widening Circles of Interest

Around the age of six comes the time for school, a time about which the mother may have mixed feelings. She wants him to go but she hates to give him up. The father usually is more ready for this step. New experiences and new companions await the child at school. New authorities come into his life. Soon parents have to reckon with, "Well, my teacher says we must do so and so." It may be, "Bobby's father lets him do this or that," or "My dresses are not as short as Mary's." Some new words the parents do not like may even be brought home. This is normal. Parents learn how to help the child put all these differences together and to understand that there are family standards to which they wish the child to be loyal. Parents must help children be selective of new modes of expression, new standards, new friends. These are steps toward independence.

To make a child feel naughty and guilty is to hold back his progress.

As the children go to school, fathers and mothers are released a little from the closeness so necessary in infancy. They now have more time and can take more interest in the neighborhood the child plays in, in his school, and in their own friends. This turning outward of interest for both parents and children makes a healthier, more colorful home life. The family dinner table with its sharing of what each member did during the day is a picture which is a part of our way of life.

Do They Care Less for Home?

This enrichment of the child's life outside the home only *seems* to make the child less interested in his home. Sometimes parents are fearful that the child now loves home less. But the family remains his bulwark, his city of refuge. Though he may not expect to stay in the house with his mother after school, he wants her to be there. This is his protection.

As he comes into pre-adolescence, he grows more independent, even to the point of criticizing his parents. He now looks for new authorities outside the family. These may include an older boy or older girl, a teacher, a coach or camp counselor, or someone else to imitate. Hero worship is a normal stage in development. Sometimes the choice seems odd to the parents— "What do you see in Miss Jackson?" or "How can you like Mr. Stone?" Often these models change, not because children are emotionally fickle, but because they are learning about people and are sampling new relationships. Parents should stand by, sympathetically, giving the child guidance when he needs it. Too severe criticism may turn the child away from parental opinion altogether and drive him into undesirable companionships.

From the time of the mother's first smile, the little child knows that he can please the parents with what he does. This smile foreshadows the conscience. This is not born but grows slowly as the child takes into himself the "yes" and "no" of the parents, and as he gradually absorbs their standards in general. These parental attitudes are first accepted as the only "right and wrong." Later the boy and girl learn that attitudes and customs vary.

The ability to live on friendly terms with one's conscience is one of the important ingredients of a healthy personality. Many children think they are bad, and need to be reassured. It is a good practice to talk things over with the child as soon as he is able to understand.

Enjoying Each New Step

Growing pains have to do with feelings as well as with physical make-up. Pre-adolescents are often querulous, demanding, and unreasonable. They are so unsure of themselves that they swing from babyishness to bravado. Then they may get frightened and return to childish behavior. They may become morose and want to stay out of school to avoid situations they are not ready to meet. It is not always easy to be patient with such seemingly irrational behavior. But all boys and girls go through an unreasonable, confused period as they try to figure themselves out.

The family tries to help a child become independent. Sometimes this is overdone. Children have to learn to dress themselves, to be watchful at street corners, and to let the gas burners alone. But they do need help and watchfulness and patience in acquiring this self care. As they grow older, wise parents consult them in making such decisions as those that concern their fun or their clothing.

Some parents, in their ambition to make the child independent, turn over too much responsibility and expect decisions far beyond the capacity of the individual. This is more discouraging than helpful. Children need to feel the wisdom and responsibility of their parents as a guide and support, something to fall back on. They realize their own inability to work things through alone, even though they want the experience of trying. At the same time, they like the assurance that the parents will stand by in case of failure. There is a good middle ground in helping adolescents to maturity. It is a compromise between restriction and indulgence.

Those parents, especially mothers, who have enjoyed their children and cared for them intimately while they were small, usually find it easier to relinquish the reins as the children grow up. This is one of the reasons for encouraging a mother to take the chief care of her baby. It is good for the baby, but it is good for her, too. It enriches her own womanhood. If the parents have not satisfied their needs for the children's affection and tenderness in the early years, they are inclined to hang on, trying to make up for the past. The time of child care is brief at best, but fathers and mothers can have an abiding pleasure as they see their efforts bearing fruit in the child's healthy personality and success. Then there is the later reward of being grandparents, the gilt-edged certificate of a long-term investment in both the pain and pleasure that rearing children entails.

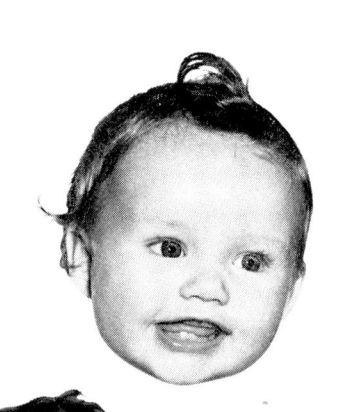

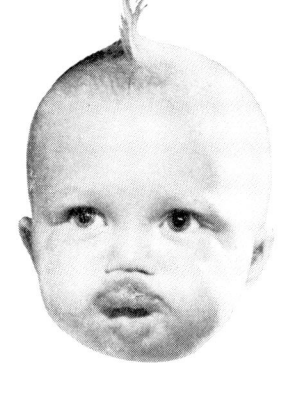

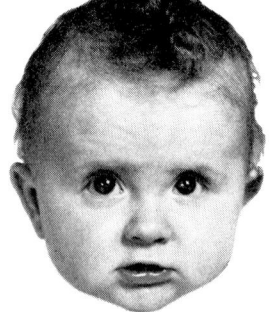

EACH CHILD IS DIFFERENT

MARION L. FAEGRE, B.A.
Consultant in Parent Education, Children's Bureau, Washington, D. C.

ANY impression you may have had that babies are much alike vanishes once you have one of your own. When a second one comes along, differences are proved even more dramatically. The miracle is, that no matter how many children are born, no two are alike. From earliest infancy, there are differences in the way babies react. One nurses fast and hungrily. Another goes at it more slowly. One baby likes to be cuddled and held, another seems more independent. One baby sleeps as readily at grandma's as at home, another is slower to accept change.

Some Differences Are Inborn

Every child is different from every other child. That is the important thing to remember. It is important because it helps us to take proper care of children, to do a better job as fathers and mothers and teachers. Johnny and Bobby and Mary may seem to be much alike. They may play with toys in the same way or be upset by the same things. They may even look alike, but they aren't. Each is different from the other in the same way that grown-up persons are different.

Some of these differences seem to be inborn, because they appear early, before environment has had a chance to have much effect. All through a child's growing years these traits may continue to identify him as a person, unique and special in his behavior.

How Much Is Inherited?

The differences between children that you can see, like the color of their eyes and hair, the shape of their faces and their body build, are clearly inborn. You cannot be sure about what differences of temperament and personality are present at birth. Some may seem so deeply ingrained that you are tempted to think they may have at least a basis in heredity. One of two brothers is quite cagey about making up his mind. He takes a long time. When he goes into a dime store, he looks over everything and may, after pondering long and hard, come out with his money still unspent. His brother knows exactly what he wants when he makes such a trip. He has made a definite decision days before. He makes a beeline for the counter, picks out the thing he wants, and does not stop to look at anything else. Maybe the traits that cause these differences are inborn, maybe not. We don't know.

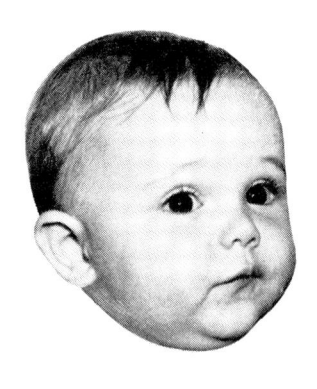

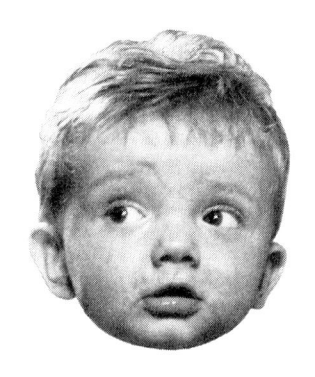

When a child seems shy, you can easily see that it may be a learned, rather than an inborn, trait. Is it because Laura played alone so much that it takes months in kindergarten before she mingles freely with other children? Or did she inherit this characteristic from her shy, reserved father? Isn't Paul's bashfulness with strangers partly explained by the fact that his family has rarely had guests? Each child's life-experience piles up, overlaying his original nature with its results. Sometimes experience and nature reinforce each other. Sometimes, perhaps, one even counteracts the other to a certain extent. By creating the kind of home atmosphere in which children have a chance to grow, parents can have a big part in making these layers of experience good ones. Teachers can help the child's growth in this way, too.

Environments Are Never Alike

Familiar as you are with the fact, you need to remind yourselves now and then that no two children, even in the same family, have the same environment. You take it for granted that you are a unit as a family, that you love all your children equally, that you treat them all alike. Yet there are inescapable differences in their life experiences. You yourselves—your living conditions, your finances, your neighbors, your attitudes, even some of your beliefs—keep changing. Each child as a result is riding a different horse in the family merry-go-round. Each is getting a different view of family living.

What Effect Has Position in the Family?

In a way, you experiment on the first baby. The wonder is that oldest children turn out as well as they do! Your great expectations, your tremendous pride, your overconscientiousness, and your equally great lack of experience tend to make life hard for them in some ways. No second child ever has to undergo the painful experience of learning to share his parents in quite the same way the oldest does. Later children may be envious of older ones who have, or seem to have, great privileges. Don't they go to school first? Don't they have a bicycle first? Keeping up with an older brother or sister is sometimes hard for the younger child in the family, but his environment is easier to cope with in an-

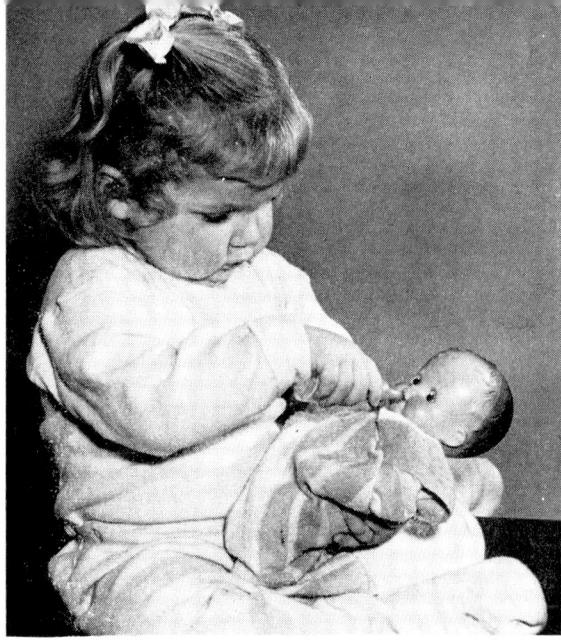

Boys are expected to be boys, tough enough for football, but girls are expected to be gentler. Everyone approves when they are good mothers to their dolls.

other way. He never has quite the same feeling about being supplanted by a new baby as the oldest one had. Each child after the first is somewhat accustomed to the idea that mother and father are to be shared.

How About the Middle Child?

Middle children are in a tough spot. They are neither young enough to be as free of responsibility as the smallest ones, nor old enough to have as many privileges as the oldest. Almost everything they wear, play with, or read is a hand-me-down. Even their triumphs are likely to be somewhat "cut down to size." "Nancy made me a basket like that when she was in kindergarten," Mother says when Nancy's little sister proudly presents her handiwork. Remember, the experiences and achievements of the middle child are new to him. You are giving him the support he needs only when you take a fresh and vital interest in his affairs. Don't take the edge off his experiences by giving the impression that "this is old stuff to me." Once in a while brand new clothes and playthings for the middle one may save many heartaches and arguments. Consider the extra expense as a good investment in peace and emotional well-being!

The Ever-Changing Environment

A child born when his parents are better off financially than they were when the first baby came, grows up in a different environment from that in which the oldest grew up. A child born during a depression or a war will live in and be affected by an environment different from that of a child born in more fortunate times.

You are not the same persons in your thirties or forties that you were in your twenties. You are more anxious or more carefree, noisier or quieter, more of a spendthrift or more of a hoarder. The youngest and oldest children often might almost be said to have different parents! Many of the traits we see in our children reflect the influences of varying family situations.

Each Sex Has a Different Environment

Almost from the beginning you emphasize the different roles you expect boys and girls to play. Teddy is "grandpa's little man" from the time he can toddle, and grandpa may frown on your giving him a doll. The play interests of babies and young children are similar, but you give the girls one kind of toy and the boys another. You add to the differences laid down by their sex. You protect little girls more, then wonder why they are timid! You expect little boys to be brave, and then wonder why they have nightmares sometimes!

Might the feeling that boys are "harder to handle" come from the inability of a mother to understand her son's nature as well as she understands her daughter's? Are you more interested, sometimes, in keeping boys clean and neat than in seeing that they have the excitement of building dams, climbing trees, or making scooters? A knife to a woman means cut fingers, but to a little boy it is indispensable to experimenting.

In the same way, fathers may encourage little girls to be fussy and conscious of their pretty clothes. A father may, by his gentle and indulgent treatment, teach his daughters to expect all the breaks, and none of the responsibilities, in their relationships with men. Again, a father who has no sons may encourage a daughter to be a tomboy.

Sometimes you make unfavorable comparisons between boys and girls. Girls care more about their teachers' approval, and about school marks. It is hard on Jamie if you ask him, "Why is your spelling so poor? Marcia never gets such low marks!" You may have to wait a good many years to see Jamie equal or forge ahead of Marcia in studiousness. You may never see him realize his possibilities if you discourage him with comments that favor his sister. His talents may show up in so many other ways than school marks! Why not be on the lookout for things in him that you can cheer about? Do you appreciate sufficiently his good sportsmanship in games, or his pluckiness in sticking at learning to dive well?

Boys and girls show enough differences without emphasizing them by your expectations. Quarrels and struggles over what is the proper work for boys and girls may be less frequent now that more little boys see their fathers run vacuum cleaners, shop for the family food, and even cook it on occasion.

Each Responds in His Own Way

You are prepared for your children not to look alike, but you are surprised that they do not act alike. When it comes to discipline, the lightest word is enough to stop Mary when she does something displeasing to her mother or her teacher. In fact, they have to be careful, for her sensitive nature is crushed by reproof. She does not bounce back the way Dickie does when he has to be reminded not to repeat a misdeed. Dickie, the irrepressible, has quite honestly forgotten, the next minute, what he is supposed "not to do." But he never holds a grudge, never sulks or whines, if his parents or his teachers have to be firm with him about something. His merry good nature goes a long way to make up for the innumerable door-bangings, lost mittens, and mischievous pranks that are another way of saying "Dickie."

Some children wear you out with their eagerness to talk.

Others worry you because they keep their troubles to themselves. In a happy family, there is room for both.

Should You Hurry the Slowpoke?

A difference that is often interesting in a family is the difference in the children's tempo. One child may be speedy, another slow. Both, even at their widely varying rates of activity, may accomplish about the same amount. Suppose Jackie is always being hurried. His deliberation is quite the opposite of his mother's briskness. His dawdling irritates her and she rushes him. This may slow him up even more. He is confused and frustrated when his natural way of doing things is interfered with. He's *not* "poky," he *doesn't* "dawdle," and he's bothered by being told that so often.

As parents, and teachers, too, you will find it pays to observe children closely, so that you do not make the mistake of misreading their behavior. Once you have looked thoughtfully at your ways and your children's ways, you can take in your stride some of the things that might otherwise be annoying. You should be careful to see that Jackie's slow, cool approach, his mind that weighs, measures, and comes out with something sound, can well be an asset instead of a liability. Of course you need to give him more time! To manage that is far easier than to deal with a child made stubborn and resentful by being pushed too hard.

When Temperaments Differ

As each child gets older, his personality becomes more complex, for experience deepens and enriches it. Many of the events in his life are experiences about which parents or teachers know nothing. You cannot follow your older children through the day. If ten-year-old Ellen seems subdued when she comes home from school, you may never know what bruised her this time. When Bobby comes to school in a grouchy mood, his teacher may not be able to find out why the day started off wrong. You can always leave the way open for a child to tell you his troubles, but sometimes it is wiser to respect his silence for the moment. Ellen may be the kind who will talk about her troubles later on when she is relaxed and alone with you. Perhaps you would only close the door more tightly for Bobby if you were too eager to console him or to offer help. Keeping the channels of communication open for each child is necessary, but even that is done in a different way for each child.

Children who have not been as easy to see through as a pane of glass may, through the years, become more comprehensible. Sometimes a new interest brings about a bond between parent and child. The friendship between Tom and his father ripened when the boy developed a keen ambition to play football. Tom suddenly awakened to the fact that those old photographs of his father in football togs, with a letter proudly displayed, had meaning for him, too.

Differences May Make for Squabbles

Perhaps one of the hardest things for parents to deal with is the kind of difference between two children that leads to bickering and quarreling. Alan's boister-

Patience, not punishment, helps the slowpoke and cuts down resistance.

Nina Leen-Pix

ous behavior, his tendency to make light of his brother Ned's opinions, caused clashes. Because the parents were sensitive to what might be back of these outbursts, and were able to help, the boys became more companionable. The parents understood that Alan's attempts to dominate were his effort to make up for his less distinguished work at school. They realized they must find things to praise in Alan, so that he would not need to demonstrate in disagreeable ways that he was "as good as" Ned. Ned, once the pressure of Alan's sneers was lifted, was less often reduced to tears.

How Can You Balance Their Needs?

Some of the qualities that make your children most puzzling are those you need to cherish in them. Take Chucky, who is always asking questions. A busy mother is sometimes inclined to try to turn off this flow, to wish she were "blessed" with a quiet child who didn't pester her for information. To be followed around while you're getting dinner with questions about what kind of trees potatoes grow on, or why they have "eyes," can be distracting. But actually, isn't it the double job, not Chucky himself, that irritates you? When he is so alert, so eager, is the time that you ought to be able to do a fine teaching job. But you have to divide your thoughts between the bubbling on the stove and the bubbling Chucky—and you can't do justice to either. That's what really gets you down.

This outgoing, demanding son, whose curiosity leads him into trying out all manner of things, from matches to mucilage, may claim so much of your attention that you are less aware of the unspoken, less obvious demands of a quieter, more reserved child. Sometimes you may even feel that a child is harder to understand and to get close to because his quiet strengths are overshadowed by the bouncing, lusty, ready response of another. You need to look twice to be sure you are really giving him what he needs, that you are not brushing him away and causing him to withdraw because he is so sensitive.

Variety Is the Spice

You can learn much that is valuable about children if you watch for the differences and take your clues from them. The infinite variety in a family or classroom gives you color and spice. Of course, the differences can irritate you if you let them.

What a dull affair family life would be if all its members were reduced to the grayness of similarity. You need this child's startling imagination even though at one point you may worry over the child's ability to be truthful. You can cherish the bubbling humor of that one even though it is disconcerting when it bursts out in church over a spider about to drop on a bald head. The quieter child who is not a leader nor the life of the party may grow up to make a contribution of his own. When you recognize, respect, and accept differences, life is pleasanter. Accepting each child for what he is, and as he is, at home and at school, is the best safeguard against insecurity, jealousy, or undue rivalry. Each child needs to have you be on the alert to discover his own special gifts and capacities, his own pace, and his own way of meeting his problems. You need to keep in mind that you will help a child most if you see him as an individual who cannot and should not be like any other individual who has ever lived.

LIVING TOGETHER IN THE FAMILY

Chicago Daily News

13. FAMILIES SHAPE PERSONALITY

14. DISCIPLINE FOR SELF-RELIANCE

15. THE FAMILY COUNCIL

16. THE FATHER IN THE FAMILY

The unique personality of each member of the family is influenced by, and, in turn, influences day-to-day living in the family circle.

What you are, what you say and do and feel, the kind of discipline you set up can teach your children to give and take, to make sensible choices and decisions, to be self-respecting, self-confident, and self-reliant, and to respect the individuality of others.

The way your children will meet their problems and get along with others, the beliefs they will hold to, and the values they will cherish all through life are largely determined by the experiences they have in the family in their early years.

FAMILIES SHAPE PERSONALITY

LOIS MEEK STOLZ, Ph.D.
Professor of Psychology, Stanford University, Stanford, Calif.

No matter how much alike they look, each is unique, and differences will become more marked through the years.

Mothers and fathers are interested in the personalities their sons and daughters are developing. A mother says, "Billy is independent, just like his Dad." A father remarks, "The twins look alike, but Babs is so much more forceful than Bee." No two personalities in a family are identical. Even though Billy is like his Dad in independence, in other ways he is unlike him. In his early outbursts of anger, he is entirely different from his father. His parents often wonder how Billy got that way.

What Is Personality?

This word *personality* is used in different ways. Sometimes a person says, "My, she has a lot of personality," meaning, of course, that she is attractive.

Personality in this sense is something a person has or has not. But we mean something quite different. We mean the uniqueness of each particular person. Each human being *is* a personality, different from all others. He feels he is different and unique. He is conscious of his selfhood. A man's personality is what he does and how he feels—what he is.

Heredity Gives the Basic Constitution

All newborn babies are somewhat alike, but each differs from the others in many ways, due to the great variety in hereditary patterns. Newborns differ in muscular equipment and in energy. Some will develop early, others more slowly. They differ in how big they can be, how beautiful, and how smart.

Such inherited differences will influence the personality each child develops as he moves along the path to maturity. For example, an "early developer" will probably gain self-confidence more easily than other children. His parents will be proud of his early accomplishments and he will feel secure and important. But, in adolescence, he may feel awkward and ill at ease, when new emotions and desires arise in him while his friends are less mature. These experiences affect his personality through the way people respond to him. Also, his own attitude

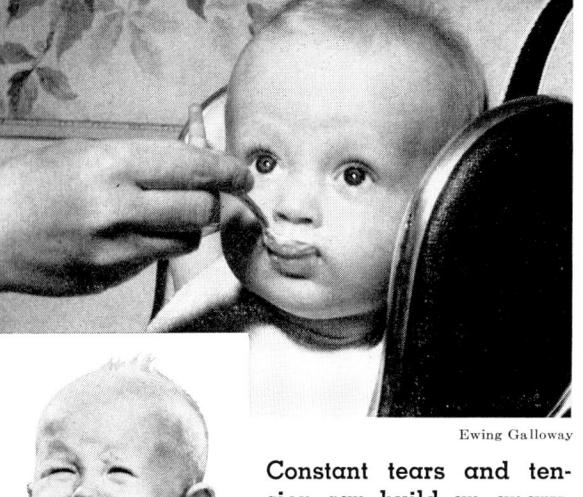

Constant tears and tension can build an angry, anxious personality. But if needs are met promptly, contentment and trust will take root, as a rule.

Ewing Galloway

toward himself is influenced as he continuously compares himself with others.

This is only one example of the way an inherited difference can influence personality. In any child, many such forces are interacting constantly. They determine to some extent how a child will respond to life and how others will respond to him. You can read more about the influence of heredity in the chapters EACH CHILD IS DIFFERENT and HOW DO CHILDREN GROW?, in this volume.

How Personality Grows

No two children in the same family, not even twins, ever have the same experiences in growing up.

When we talk about personality, we speak of life's experiences as pressures. An experience presses a child to do something, to behave in some way, to adapt to it. His personality is really formed through the adaptations he makes to these pressures.

Pressures from Inside and Outside

Pressures come from various sources. Some of them come from within the child. Hunger is a pressure. The infant responds by a lot of activity, a whimper, and then a loud howl. If food comes soon, the baby relaxes, his tensions go. If food is slow in coming day after day, the infant may gradually build up tensions that do not leave easily. Sometimes these early tensions from hunger are the beginnings of what we later call a tense personality. These tensions contribute to making the high-strung, "nervous" child who has difficulty in relaxing.

Pressures from outside also demand adaptations. Some of these come from the physical environment. Conditions such as bright, piercing sunshine or sticky, humid weather, low or high altitude, dry winds of the desert or fogs of the seacoast, demand adaptations. It is difficult for some children to make the necessary adjustments. For example, a child whose skin is extremely sensitive may develop irritable traits if he lives in a windy, dry place.

But the most important outside pressures for a child come from people. Early in life it is mainly the members of the family who *press* the child in certain directions. Later other children and teachers play a part. But babies and young children also depend on their parents to help relieve the tensions that come from hunger, cold, pain, or from being lonesome or unhappy. Thus what parents do and say, and *the way* they do it, affect a child's behavior and his feelings most deeply. The family's influence on the developing personalities of children is our concern here.

Parents' Personality a Force

Children's personalities are strongly influenced by what parents are; far more, in fact, than by what parents say.

How a woman feels about herself and

her life will affect the quality of the relations she builds with her child through the years. This is just as true for a man. These feeling tones will determine to a large extent what the child means to each parent and how each acts as father or mother.

If a father is a basically satisfied person, he will probably have positive, friendly relations with his child that will increase the child's confidence. His child will be influenced toward developing affectionate, sympathetic, generous qualities. But where life has made the father irritable, distrustful, or bitter, his child may be influenced toward developing undesirable qualities too, though these may differ from his father's.

Mothers who have enthusiasm for what they are doing influence their children toward zestful living. Those who are worried or unhappy are likely to magnify their children's problems. The woman who has never grown up, who is still emotionally immature, does not usually give her children the feeling of trust they need to grow toward independence.

But the effect on a child of any quality in a parent's personality depends on the whole picture. A child of a "bossy," dominating mother *might* turn out to be a quiet, mouselike person. He *might* become rebellious and defiant. Circumstances *might* combine to make a child develop a tenacious, indirect persistence quite effective in getting his own way. Other influences in a child's life will determine just how he will adapt to any quality in his mother or father.

Relations Between Parents Affect Their Children

The love of parents for a child is one phase of their love for each other. Where the relations between husband and wife give to each a feeling of emotional security, there is likelihood that children will be wanted and that they too will find emotional security as part of the family unit.

A child who is part of a warm, loving home can develop warm, loving,

When Father is too disturbed to answer, the world looks bleak. The worrying habit may be contagious, too.

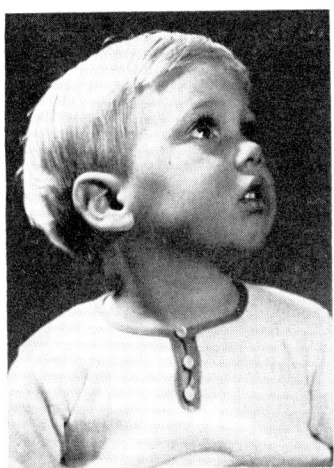

F.P.G.; Ewing Galloway

friendly characteristics. A child who grows up where there is mutual respect and consideration can learn to be respectful and considerate. Unhappiness between husband and wife usually brings stress to a child, and that may affect his developing personality in a variety of ways. A child may take on the ways of his parents if he feels close to them, or he may develop different characteristics as a reaction against his parents. More information about the effect on children of the relations between par-

When each is loved and accepted, they are fonder of one another, too.

ents will be found in PARENTS ARE ALSO HUSBANDS AND WIVES, in this volume.

Effect of Brothers and Sisters

When there is more than one child in a family the situation changes. The forces that influence the development of the children's personalities become different.

There are normal stress situations that develop for any child when he is one of several in a family. Feeling tones about how much he is loved, whether he will get his share, whether he can be his age, whether he can compete fairly, influence a child's personality development. A child must make some adjustment to such stresses. His spontaneity, his generosity, his sympathy, his affections, his hatreds will all be influenced.

To help in the development of the positive qualities, parents have to try to give each boy and girl a feeling that there is plenty of love for each child. Mother and father can make it clear that a child may have to give up sometimes but not always. They can let each child feel that he will get plenty of chances to grow and do big things. They can give assurance to each that he will get his share of comfort and sympathy when things go wrong.

Some of the specific ways brothers and sisters influence each other's development are set forth in the chapters in the section RELATIONSHIPS AMONG CHILDREN IN THE FAMILY, in this volume.

Each Year Is Important

The personality of a child begins to develop early in infancy and continues to develop throughout life. Day after day, new threads are woven into the pattern of the individual's behavior and feelings. Each particular stage brings with it special needs for adequate development. How these needs are met will influence what a child is like, how he behaves, and how he feels about himself and other persons.

What happens during infancy seems especially important in helping to develop within a child a feeling of security. This comes about through the care he receives from his parents in his everyday needs. The right kind of food when he is hungry, clothing that keeps him comfortable, and cuddling and loving affection when he is lonesome, assure him he can depend on his parents. Attention and smiles when he wants to play, and freedom to move about and to handle things as he grows are satisfactions that help him to build confidence in the people around him. In these simple ways, parents help their baby lay the foundation for one of the essential ingredients of a healthy personality. This ingredient is sometimes called a sense of trust.

Gradually a child will ask more of his parents than security. Each child needs to use his increasing abilities to walk, to taste, to feel, to pound. He will struggle to be independent, to assert himself. The "me do," the running away, the grabbing, are all signs of growing consciousness of self and the independence that comes with power to do. It is thus he begins to learn that he is a person in his own right. All through childhood and into adulthood he will continue the process of understanding his "me-ness," of realizing what he is. In some ways this growth of one's own sense of being unique and different, separate from others, is really the core of personality development.

Through using his increasing abilities in early and later childhood he can gradually develop such qualities as initiative, creativeness, and satisfaction in doing. Parents can influence this aspect of personality development through their attitude toward their child's natural desires for activity. As a child grows, what he needs from his parents to insure wholesome personality development will change. Volumes 13 and 14 will help you to determine what your children need for best development in infancy, early childhood, and later childhood.

Accepting Change in Children

How well a parent can accept the normal behavior of his child as he grows will greatly affect the personality of his child. Children are continually changing.

It is sometimes difficult for parents to adjust to these changes. A mother who loves a soft, cuddly, dependent infant may not be pleased when he wiggles out of her lap to crawl on the floor, or yells for freedom from the play pen. A father who has gained a great deal of satisfaction from the admiration of his young son may not be so pleased when that same boy gets old enough to question his father's knowledge of airplanes.

As children change from complete de-

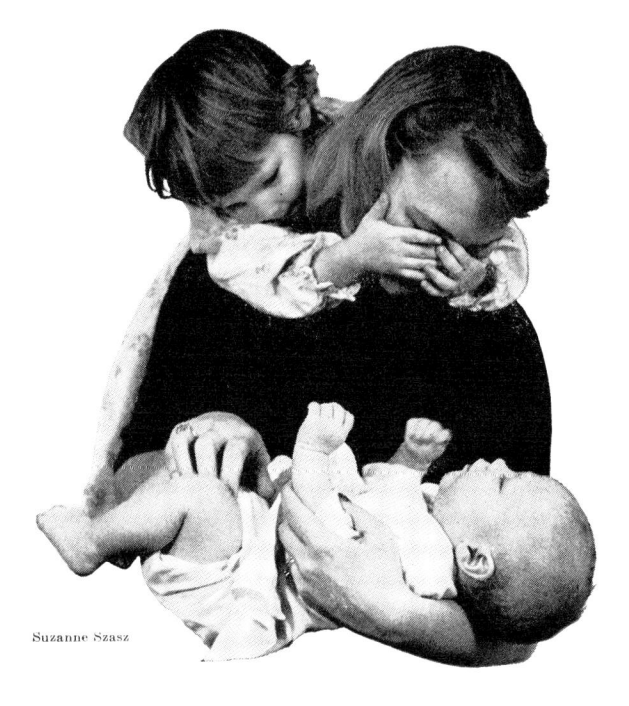

Small as he is, the new baby has an influence on his brothers and sisters. Their personalities will affect him as he lives and grows with them, too.

Suzanne Szasz

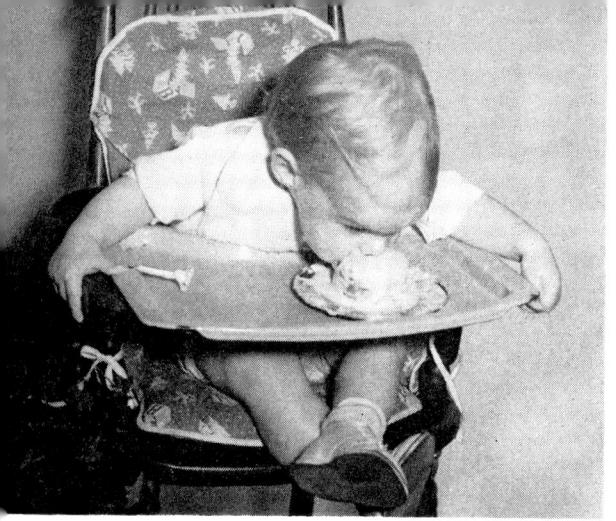

This is a good sign of growing independence, even though it may not look like an advance in manners.

"That's me!" is a great discovery, for the feeling of being a separate person is the core of personality.

pendence to increasing independence in activity and thought, parents are continually faced with accepting and loving a changing child. This isn't easy, but it is important. A child's feeling of self-worth depends on being loved and accepted by his family. A child who, deep down, feels that his normal impulses are bad because his parents have not accepted them, lacks the core for developing strength in character.

A child should feel that each new sign of progress is as important to his parents as his first step was. If a child has this basic feeling of acceptance through the changing years, he can learn the many things his parents ask of him without losing his zest for living. He will build that self-respect essential for good adjustment and happiness.

Training Affects Personality

One of the strongest urges of parents is to make their child develop according to their ideals. They try hard to get their child to think, to act, and to feel as they would like him to. Each parent has his ideas of what is good and right. He has just as strong ideas of what is bad and wrong. These he tries to pass on to his child.

But parents often do not realize that while they are teaching their child to behave, they are also influencing his feelings. If a boy's mother continually tries to make him quiet and gentle, he may eventually learn. But at a price. He will certainly learn to doubt himself, to feel that his own normal urges for activity and noise and roughness are somehow bad. When he forgets and acts like a real boy, he is apt to feel guilty and ashamed.

A child needs freedom to grow, and freedom to use his developing skills and abilities. This is the only way he can build self-confidence. A child has to mess in his food not only because messing is fun at one year of age, or because it is the only way he can begin to learn

Families Shape Personality

to feed himself. There is a deeper reason. This touching and messing with his food helps him to gain confidence in himself. It is only through practice that he can develop the skills that give him feelings of adequacy and of courage to tackle the next step in learning.

What About Rewards and Punishments?

A child's freedom can only be freedom within limits. A child gains a sense of security if those limits are clearly set. Then he knows where he stands. If the restrictions are inconsistent, a child lacks the help he needs for gaining stability. If they are not clear, he has only his own urges to guide him, and they sometimes cause him to trespass on other people's rights.

The rewards parents give and the punishments they inflict affect personality development, too. If parents offer ice cream for good behavior, children soon learn to offer good behavior only for ice cream. Punishment that is too severe, or that is given inconsistently, builds resentment or fear and sometimes hate within a child. When a child feels that punishment is fair and the natural consequence of his acts, he can take it and still keep his confidence in his parents.

The chapters on WHAT CHILDREN NEED FROM LIFE and DISCIPLINE FOR SELF-RELIANCE, in this volume, will be helpful to read.

Readiness Is the Key

What you teach your child must be geared to what he is ready to learn. *Readiness* is a key word for any parent. If you push your daughter too soon, she may become unsure of herself and doubtful of you. If you hold her back when she is ready, she becomes frustrated, angry, irritable, and perhaps unstable. Or if she is a more passive type, she may

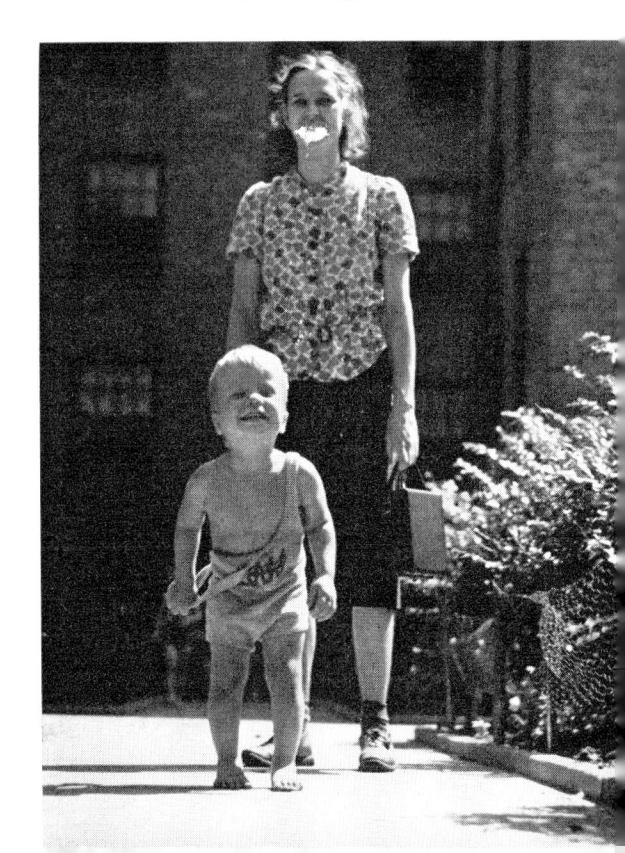

Have fences outlived their usefulness in her life? Now is the time for the next step in independence.

He is ready for more freedom while Mother keeps a watchful eye on him.

give up the struggle, become dull, placid, "good" on the outside, unhappy on the inside. Young ones are often like colts champing at the bit, all ready to go, with parents holding the reins tight and saying, "Wait now; you are too young, you don't know enough."

If we would keep a child outgoing and eager for learning, we must not expect too much, not more than the next step. The father or mother who must have perfection usually gets a child who feels inadequate and inferior. He can't live up to his parents' standards, and what is more he really never has had a chance to learn. Such a child too often resents his parents' superiority and takes out his feelings in petty, irritating ways. Volumes 13 and 14 will help you adjust your teaching to your child's readiness.

What Home Stands For

The family has a subtle influence on a child's personality, through the way certain things are given emphasis in the home. These are the everyday aspects of life that are considered important by mother or father. For example, in some homes, time schedules and routines are given unusual emphasis. One can sometimes see the effect on a child in his dependence on routine, his lack of self-direction, his feeling of being lost when there is freedom to choose. Such a child feels most secure in situations that are planned and where directions for behavior are clear. He likes to be told exactly what to do and when.

There are other homes where cleanliness and order are given high values. We may see this reflected in the cautious, almost timid way a child plays. It may show in his worried look when finger paints are presented. Sometimes it is revealed by his dismay over dirty hands or a messed blouse.

Not Perfection but Progress

We must remember that we want our children to make progress through the years, not to be perfect. Each child lives through a series of events in life that are unique for him. He is constantly learning from these experiences. Each new event changes him to some extent.

You can feel reassured about your child's personality if you can see him making progress along these general lines: Is he gaining a clearer sense of self, of his own identity as a person in his own right? Is he learning to respond to other people as individuals, to treat each as a person in his own right? Is he developing interests that engage him in a wholehearted fashion? Are his guiding principles of good and bad, right and wrong, fair and unfair, becoming increasingly his own and based upon his own experiences?

You can rejoice at progress. Never mind if perfection is still far off.

Mary Eleanor Browning

DISCIPLINE FOR SELF-RELIANCE

RUTH WENDELL WASHBURN, Ph.D.
Author of "Children Have Their Reasons" and
"Children Know Their Friends," Boston, Mass.

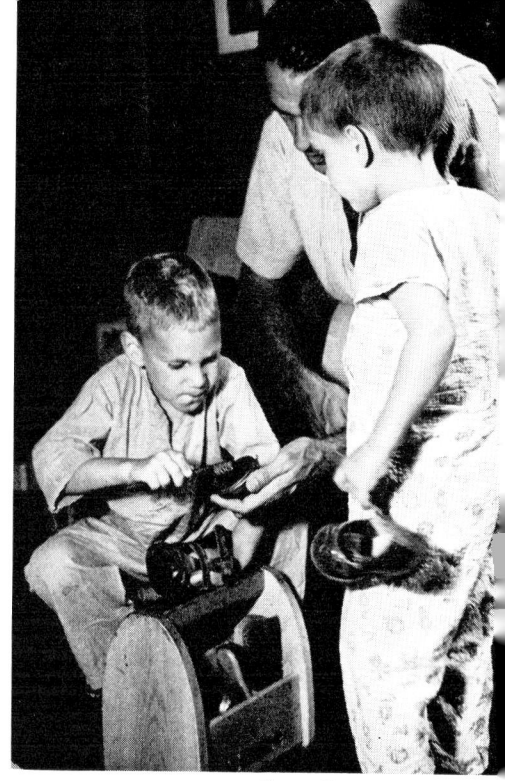

Suzanne Szasz

MANY people talk about discipline as if it were something to be applied from time to time in some special, usually painful, way. Bothered parents say, "We must discipline Frank," or critical outsiders think, "That child needs discipline." Often they would like to spank if they were free to do so. But in its broadest sense discipline means teaching or training, or helping to learn. This important subject cannot be discussed with understanding unless it is agreed that discipline begins at the moment of birth and continues throughout life.

Discipline Is Teaching

Everyone must learn some lessons about living in a world with other people. These lessons are made vivid by special action, or by any one of a large variety of rewards or punishments. These are the disciplinary acts which people remember and plan to repeat (or avoid) when it is their turn to bring up children. The pleasant surprise earned by brave behavior at the dentist's office takes its place in memory beside the spanking which followed a raid on the icebox. Every child who is making his way toward self-reliant maturity is much more constantly, though less clearly, disciplined. He is taught by the physical laws of the universe, as well as by the little undramatic daily acts, attitudes, and feelings of the people with whom he comes into contact at home and abroad.

If we think of discipline in this way it is clear that it is not only children who are its subjects, but everyone who is capable of growth and self-management. There is even a great deal of give and take about it, for sometimes children discipline their parents in important ways.

Good Discipline Looks Ahead

We certainly want children to become friendly, independent, continuously-developing citizens. Thought about their discipline is more profitably given to the conditions and relationships of their daily lives. Those needs and motives underlying their behavior, which they will gradually learn to understand and control, can be taken into consideration. Those questions so often uppermost in the minds of discipliners, such as "What shall I do if John or Mary does this or that?" are not as important as they seem at the moment.

Fruit trees can be forced by various techniques to grow against sunny walls. In their stunted, dependent, molded way they may make a creditable showing. How different they are from the trees in the orchard which have been given good conditions for the fullest possible growth! Even the orchard trees, however, are subject to the laws of wind and weather and must be restrained if they overstep a neighbor's territory.

Children need the security which comes from the knowledge that their parents or teachers, who are themselves living under the terms of just laws, are strong enough to help them curb immature interests. Laws in any household or school need frequent reconsideration. Outgrown, unjust, or drastic rules stir up rebellion or else their enforcement requires constant policing. It may be, for instance, that more quiet is required in a classroom than young children are capable of maintaining. Work periods can often be shortened, or occasions made when accumulated energy may be run off.

How Do You Get Co-operation?

Parents and teachers must be enforcers until children are strong enough to accept laws and rely on their inner control. On this account it is important to find ways and means to discipline children without arousing resentment. Children are the people in a household or school to whom directions are given. They often "take it personally," and feel that they are the only ones who are restricted. "I wish that I had as much money in my purse as you have in yours," said Charlie to his mother. "You could have just as much if you spent it for the family, as I have to," she replied. Then she told him how some of it went for the family dinner, some for his shoes, and so on.

The most successful disciplinarians make it clear that law is universal. Parents and teachers are there to introduce children to the responsibilities and restrictions that are so inevitable a part of life. The clock which keeps good time, refusing to hurry up or slow down because it would suit somebody better if it did, can be one of the best disciplinary aids. If someone says to a child in the yard, "I want you to come in to dinner," his free spirit may rebel. He will say, as Josie did, "That great big boss told me

When banked-up energy is run off in play, it will not cause mischief.

Snyder, Monkmeyer

to come in." But if the direction is, "It's time for dinner," or "It's time to come back to work," personal antagonism is less apt to be aroused. The child knows that his elders are just as much dominated by the clock as he is.

Basic Principles of Discipline

There are a few basic principles to keep in mind when setting forth with a child on the long trail of growing up.

First of all, children need what might be called developing patterns in the conditions of their life as day succeeds day. They are unlike the grown-up who knows quite well what his capacities are and has settled down, not only into routines that make the mechanics of life easy for him, but also into occupations that make it interesting.

Rules That Fit

For children, last year's plans may not fit any better than last year's blue jeans. A mother who likes to organize her household may find that she can tie the bows on a few shoes between putting the cereal on the stove and washing her own face. She may continue to do so long after the wearers of the shoes could quite easily have tied the bows themselves.

Since daily ways need constantly to be looked at, and sometimes revised, it is reassuring that the children help to set the time for these revisions. When the pattern they have outgrown is uncomfortable, they are quick to register their discomfort. The playpen offered just the right opportunity to the baby from ten to eighteen months old. But it will prove cramped quarters for the two-year-old, and he finds ways to make this clear.

The four-year-old feels uncertain

Suzanne Szasz

Each new experience is welcomed by the self-reliant who can leave home cheerfully and without regrets.

about the adventures he might have between the school gate and the door of his schoolroom. He needs to have his mother go with him to the place where he can transfer his trust to his teacher. For a time Tad's mother took him to the school gate, then sat in the car while he went in alone. He turned to wave to her every few feet. At the same time he called loudly to his teacher, "Mitz Chennins! I's comin'." By the time he was five, Tad, too, had learned that the trip from car to schoolroom was a safe one.

The freedom given a child to roam, first in the house and then in the neighborhood, is another example of the patterns of daily life in which developing self reliance plays an important part. Many questions have to be kept constantly open for consideration. What traffic conditions exist between eight-year-old Mary's home and that of the best friend with whom she wants to

It is hard to find the right combination!

spend the afternoon? When and where can the children be allowed to stay out after dark?

It is just as important not to run ahead of a child's developing patterns as it is not to lag behind them. Ways can be found to keep him stretching without subjecting him to the strain of too much responsibility. Self-reliance may be threatened rather than strengthened if we expect too much.

Providing the Props

A second fact to keep in mind is that children can learn many of the most important lessons about taking care of themselves if their stage is properly set. These lessons are among the most important because they can be learned almost entirely without adult help, interference, or insistence.

The playpen is an excellent illustration of a well-planned arrangement to help a child become self-reliant. He can learn independently as his development reaches the point where he is ready to go on. Without argument, it imposes boundaries assuring his safety. When he is nine or ten months old, the pen provides the opportunity most longed for by every child of this age—something to pull on. Each one finds out for himself how best to take advantage of opportunity.

As confidence is gained, the playpen gives the hint as to what comes next. When the art of pulling up to a standing position and getting safely down again has been mastered, the continuous railing is always within reach. It suggests to the baby that he can go on a short tour, and he begins to cruise about. With practice in taking steps, safe because the support is at hand, he is soon brave enough to give up the use of the railing. Presently the miracle has happened. He is walking about alone and unaided.

Routines Are the Teachers

Flexible routines can be considered a kind of stage setting. They keep the number of necessary suggestions down to a minimum. Certainly the ten-year-old does not go to bed at the same time as the two-year-old. The changes in routine times have come with the years, not because a fresh decision is made every night as to when to go to bed.

It is probably fair to say that the more insecure the parent or teacher, the more he or she falls back on the spoken word. Such a one multiplies commands and reminders. Routines, or the child's developing self-reliance, can be depended on more than we realize to help with the teaching. Parents or teachers do well to listen to themselves every once in a while. If they hear too much of their own voices, it is one indication that their disciplinary plans need overhauling.

But "if at first you don't succeed, try, try, again," is a lesson best learned early and through experience.

Let Them Help Themselves

With self-reliance as a goal, a third good rule is: do for children only those things they are incapable of doing for themselves. This is often a hard rule to remember. A mother's affectionate tendency is to help a child who seems to be having a hard time. Then, too, there are so many things the older person can do more easily and more quickly. Young children have a good deal of time to spend. How could it be more profitably employed than in solving some of their own problems? They enjoy working to get back a toy that has fallen out of reach. Putting shoe laces in and out of holes or finding ways to make blocks stand up are satisfying accomplishments to a young child. Cooking the supper without anyone hovering about in the kitchen is a great achievement for a nine- or ten-year-old.

This does not mean that a tired or sick child should not be helped. If a child temporarily needs added assurance that he is loved, he should have the kind of help that gives him such reassurance. If a child has undertaken some impossible task, such as trying to get a big toy through the railings of a pen, he must be spared the frustration of defeat. But make sure that defeat is inevitable before rushing in to help.

It was a great temptation to help Jessica, aged two, as she tried to seat herself on a somewhat high chair in order to read a book to her doll. Each time that she succeeded in sitting on the chair she dropped either the book or her baby and had to clamber down again. But there was nothing else that Jessica especially needed to do at that time. She was interested in solving her problem and kept working at it. Since she was successful before her patience gave out, she might be expected to work over her next task even more hopefully. Nothing succeeds like success!

Early Teaching Is Important

Children's need to grow up and to do for themselves is basic and contributes greatly to self-reliance. It often means you must take more time today to let them accomplish something. Still, you know that they are learning to do it for themselves, and the same thing will require much less parental time another year.

When a baby begins to want to feed himself, either with his hands or his spoon, it is hard to sit by watching him mess up his bib, the table, and the floor. Who does not long to seize the spoon and scrape all that spinach off the baby's chin? But the time spent in cleaning up around the high chair this year will be entirely freed next year when the toddler has had time to perfect his techniques. If the mess cannot be tolerated and the child's eager hands are brushed away from the spoon, he may learn to rely on the service. Time to feed him will have to be included in the day's schedule far longer than necessary.

The same thing is true of help in the kitchen in later years. Heidi's mother really dreaded it when the child said, "Heidi holp" and moved a stool close to the dishpan. As the years went on, she was glad she had put up with this early "holp" because she found that, by the time Heidi was nine or ten years old, she could go to the kitchen and proudly get supper with almost no help.

Tailor-Made Discipline

A fourth important truth to keep in mind is this: each child in a family is so different from every other child in the same family that plans which have successfully disciplined one child will often be found to be unsuitable for disciplining his brother or sister.

Jimmy was merry and happy-go-lucky most of the time. But he seemed to need a few moments of violent protest before he could get to sleep, no matter what was done to help him with this period. His twin sister found her crib her stronghold and settled down immediately and contentedly.

To Spank or Not to Spank?

The same experience affects different people in different ways. This must be especially considered in the use of a disciplinary tool such as spanking. While children are little, it may be wise occasionally to build in painful associations like slaps on the hand or spanks to discourage such activities as reaching for forbidden things. It is wise only if the slap or spank can follow the bit of behavior so closely that the child can easily make the connection between the two. It is certainly a waste of time and effort to spank at bedtime for something a young child did in the morning.

Before using any sort of spanking, the child and the nature of his relationships with the spanker must be well known. For some children, a spanking clears the air just as a thunderstorm does. But the same effect might be more safely produced by washing their faces with cold water. If things get to the spanking point too often, the reasons underlying the need for this discipline should be carefully explored.

Some children will retreat after a spanking and store up angry feelings against the spanker. They tend to brood and learn nothing from the treatment. Planned spankings, administered in "cold blood," are practically never justified. Spankings given at heated moments are justified only as they can release primitive feelings and quickly restore friendly relations between the spanker and the spanked.

Best Discipline Can Be Self-Discipline

It is because of these personality differences in children and their parents that it is hard to give or to get specific suggestions as to what should be done about disciplining a child. If he is to gain control of himself and learn that the best discipline is self-discipline, plans for teaching him will of necessity take his traits with their glories and difficulties into consideration. Discipliners must also feel comfortable and confident about the plan or the measure. Mrs. Smith's disciplinary techniques won't fit Mrs. Bent's household any better than Mrs. Smith's size five shoe would serve Mrs. Bent's size nine foot.

Conflict Can Be Constructive

Everyone would like to think that his

"I can do it by myself" is the theme song of the four-year-old, who takes great pride in her accomplishments.

family or his schoolroom went along without conflict among its members, but this is an impossible standard. If children were like putty in our hands we would indeed have cause to be worried. A healthy child, with the vitality to make his way in the world, is certain to find that other people's interests and needs run counter to his. He is hardly worth his salt if he does not at least try to fight through to the satisfaction of his own vividly-felt wants, no matter what happens to those of other persons. "There's just one person I can't imagine the world without," said eight-year-old Ken. "Myself!" Certainly such a one will encounter and stimulate conflict as he presses forward. It is only as conflict is constantly present in marked degree in family or classroom that it need be considered a problem. There is bound to be some normal friction as wants and needs of different personalities are fitted together.

Feelings Can Come Out

Children experience strong feelings and understand them in others. It is far better for the disciplining adult to lose her temper occasionally than to try so hard for control that she seems cold and distant to the child. If his parents are too self-controlled in the expression of such feelings as affection or anger, the child may use uncomfortable ways to find out whether they are capable of feeling.

The child who is to become a reasonably happy, self-reliant man or woman must be taught not to be afraid of or feel guilty about his feelings. Without emotion, life would indeed lose its savor. It is to be hoped that any child will continue to suffer from or enjoy feelings and emotions as long as he lives. He can and must, however, learn to take responsibility for, and to control, his behavior when his emotions have been aroused. Eventually he is not driven by feeling. He is able to make a decision as to whether to take when he wants, strike when he is angry, try to possess when he loves, or even laugh when he is amused. Most people learn to behave in a civilized manner even when they are in the throes of strong feeling.

Mrs. Harris felt that she understood the nature of Katy's feelings about her baby brother better after she had watched the child playing with her doll's house one day. The baby in the miniature family proved to be a remarkable

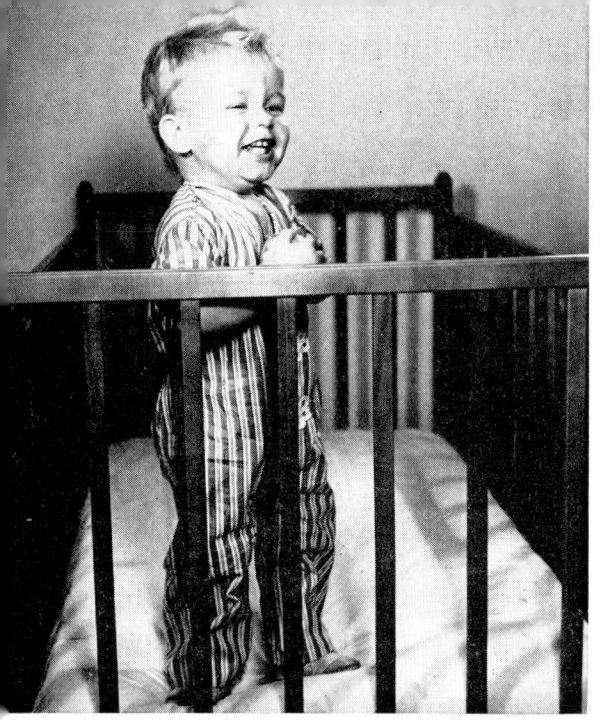

Discipline is in the situation itself when the crib sets the limits.

one. Not only could he feed himself and carry himself upstairs, but he could take himself out for walks in his baby carriage. It is to be hoped that Mrs. Harris said to Katy at some later time, "I don't blame you for feeling that the baby gets a great deal of care. When you were a baby I used to do all those things for you, but now you can do them for yourself so you and I have time to do together things that are more fun. If you could not feed yourself I would not have time to sit with you while you play." Katy might say nothing, but she would be relieved to know that her mother understood without blaming her for wishing the baby were different.

Discipline Is in the Situation

Much of what has been discussed can be summed up in Cedric's experience. Cedric's parents were anxious about him because he did not learn to rely on himself. At his age his brothers and sisters had been much more responsible people. He cried too easily in tight places. He was too apt to feel that he was more punished than the others, and that he was the only one to whom laws were applied. His mother knew that Cedric would not learn in a day or in one experience, but she thought she had tried every way known to her. How could she help Cedric to realize that no one else could live his life for him and that other people were just as restricted as he?

One summer when Cedric was about eleven, the family vacation was spent at the seaside and the children had the use of a little sailboat, so small that it could be manned by a crew of one. Cedric knew a good deal about the management of boats. The harbor in which the boat was to be used was a safe one and visible from the house. Because older members of the family sailed the boat alone, Cedric was eager to do so. Knowing that currents, winds, and tides had ways of their own and could not be argued with, Cedric's parents thought that sailing the boat alone would make it crystal clear to him that he could rely on himself to bring the boat safely home only if he understood and obeyed the laws which govern all sailors.

They knew that they could reach him in any real emergency, so they summoned their courage and gave him permission to go out alone. Often with her heart in her mouth, especially if the wind came up, Cedric's mother watched the little white sail far out across the harbor. She knew that Cedric was happy, that the boat, in its wordless but lively way, would teach him as people could not.

The situation itself, as so often happens, gave the best kind of discipline for self-reliance.

THE FAMILY COUNCIL

WILLIAM E. BLATZ, Ph.D.
Director, Institute of Child Study,
University of Toronto, Toronto, Canada

"Family council!" scornfully cried a friend of mine. He was the father of four boys, whose ages ranged from six to twelve. "I'll have none of it. Let me tell you what went on in our house last week! In school the older children were told to urge their parents to have a family council—everyone should have a vote, and so on. My oldest boy got the other three together and arranged for them all to vote whatever way he told them to. Then he asked us to have a council.

"My wife and I, willing to take on anything and try it out at least once, consented. The first item on the agenda was —we should have ice cream every night for dessert. The vote was 4 to 2 in favor. The next item proposed that all allowances be raised. This resolution passed 4 to 2. The next resolution was 'no more family council.' It passed, I'm telling you—but not by voting. Family council, forsooth—buncombe!"

Everyone Expresses Himself

If my friend had understood the uses of a family council, he might have turned either the ice-cream situation or the allowance motion to good account. A family council is something far deeper, more subtle, and more educational than mere majority rule. A family council, in most households that use it, means bringing all the members of a family together to work out situations that concern everybody. There are always questions to be settled. Through discussion, these can usually be worked out with less tension.

Now let us write the story as it might have happened in a family where the council idea was used to good advantage.

Reasons Are Carefully Examined

The oldest boy had made the suggestion that ice cream be the dessert every night. Father ventured the opinion that even ice cream might grow tiresome if it appeared on the table every night. Mother declared that there is such a thing as a balanced diet and you could hardly achieve a good balance if you limited yourself to the same dessert seven days a week.

"But come to think of it, there isn't

any law that people can have ice cream only for Sunday dinner, is there?" Father asked, with a twinkle in his eye.

"Why, I suppose there's no law, but—well, ice cream for Sunday dinner was the way we did at home when I was a little girl and I guess I just always have planned it that way," Mother answered.

One of the children said that even if there was not to be ice cream seven days a week, at least they ought not to have to eat that old apple betty Mother was always making. This statement found support from everyone. Even Father inquired why there had been such a run on apple betty lately.

Mother reminded the boys that Grandfather had sent them a barrel of apples. With the apples in the basement and bits of stale bread in the breadbox, an apple-bread-crumb dessert had seemed to be hearty and economical.

"One of you big boys might dig around in the cookbooks or watch the cooking page in the newspapers for some new apple desserts. I run out of ideas for things to satisfy your he-man appetites," Mother suggested.

The ten-year-old volunteered that "anything would be worth it to get rid of that dead old goo we usually have."

The eight-year-old, like many eight-year-olds, was beginning to be a master of the art of trading and compromising. He had the inspiration that ice cream could make its appearance on the family table at least as often as "that apple stuff."

This plan was hailed as nothing less than the wisdom of Solomon.

"So," Father said, "it's ice cream and apple betty, or something appleish, on a matching basis. All those in favor say 'Aye.'"

Of course the "ayes" had it, but the six-year-old insisted somebody explain what a "matching basis" was.

Many Kinds of Learning Take Place

As the curtain falls on this scene, we cannot assume that this particular family ate happily ever after. There may still have been grumbling and some teasing—more or less good-humored. Nobody claims that a family council settles any question definitely and forever.

Consider the values that did come out of this session. The children learned that you can put forth your opinion and air your grievances in a reasonably friendly way. They had the highly educational experience of using their wits to look at a problem from several angles as they sought to solve it. They discovered to their satisfaction that a working solution in which everyone gives up something is possible. They also found out, in case they had any false ideas on the question, that a family council does not mean ganging up on Mother and Father in mob-rule fashion.

Mother and Father took time to make explanations. The children learned on what basis Mother planned the meals, and that planning meals takes some thought. New ways of getting along with people, new ideas, even new words and phrases were among the by-products of this session. And all this took half an hour between supper and the bedtime of the smallest boy!

It is noteworthy that neither the Mother nor Father in this family gave the children the feeling that ice cream for dinner every night was out of the question just because it is traditionally children's favorite dessert.

How Can I Interest My Family in a Council?

Many families are doubtful about the

Everyone likes to air his views. The family council table is the place to express ideas, give suggestions, and complain if you have been wronged.

way a council would work. If you are trying it out, start with something easy. As a matter of fact, ice cream for dinner every night or "What shall we do next Saturday afternoon when Daddy has the day off?" are typical of the questions that are good for beginners to help solve. Allowances, jobs around the house, measures to end carelessness in leaving lights burning, can come when the family group has had a bit more practice.

As you tackle the knottier problems, you will find some that cannot be worked out to everyone's satisfaction. You may go through a few weeks or months when your family council seems to be losing its grip. You need not be afraid of these small failures. Listen to yourselves as you talk together. Compare the times when the council went well with the times it seemed to fall flat. Perhaps you can learn from your mistakes.

How the Council Works

How can a family council be made to work so that the rights of each member of the family may be retained, along with the fun and spontaneity of family life?

Without some regular time, meetings may be put off indefinitely. Hidebound rules are not a part of the plan, but once a month is certainly the minimum for council meetings. Most families prefer to hold them weekly. Special occasions or emergencies may call for an additional get-together.

Who Attends the Family Council?

Everyone who is directly concerned with the matter being discussed and who has to accept some responsibility about it can attend the council meeting.

Some parents may be afraid that the affairs of the household will be spread throughout the neighborhood. If you take children into your confidence, they tend to be more careful than if they listen at keyholes.

What Does the Council Discuss?

Anything that affects the family and needs to be worked out may come up for discussion. Money matters are a fre-

Family councils consider...

Shall Sister's allowance include money for lunch?

When do big brothers look after smaller ones?

What kind of vacation shall we take this year?

quent topic. The way the family spends, saves, and shares its money should be an open agreement openly arrived at. Many misunderstandings arise within a family because of mismanagement of the family income. Responsibility for spending and saving is a joint affair.

Allowances for the children, expenditures within the home, food budgets are discussed at the council. Unpleasant? It need never be! Time-saving? Yes. Temper-saving? Astonishingly so.

Finances are only one of the many topics family councils can thrash out. In one household there were eight- and ten-year-old girls and two-year-old twin boys. The questions most frequently discussed centered about play space, free time, and guest privileges for the older children. Arrangements needed to be made carefully in order not to conflict with the care, needs, and activities of two toddlers. As the older girls realized what it meant to plan routines and arrangements for a family with such diversified interests, they became more willing to help their mother look after the little boys. They became resourceful, too, in figuring out ways and means of having their own friends come to play without putting too much strain on the resources of a small house.

In other families, responsibilities in caring for the house and the children's possessions, or plans for leisuretime activities, may be the chief concern. In some families, arrangements for the use of the telephone, radio, or television need to be made. A place to do homework, who uses the shower in the morning, and who gets it in the evening are often questions that need frequent discussing and reviewing. Nothing is ever settled once and for all!

When Do Parents Decide?

In many discussions the children do not have a voice in the decisions. It is better if nobody leads them to believe they will have, either. The responsibility would be unwelcome and overwhelming, as it was in the case of Lois. When Lois was eight or nine or ten her parents, after discussing some important matter, would turn to her and say, "Now you decide what we should do." Their reasoning was that if she thought the decision was hers, she would be more willing to accept any resulting inconveniences more cheerfully. In later life, she often said that she usually felt confused and cross with her mother and father when these incidents occurred. Deep inside herself she knew that it was their responsibility, not hers, to settle these matters. She resented her parents instead of feeling closer to them.

When there is a serious question to be considered, such as the mortgage on the house, the older children may sit in on the discussion. They can learn that problems are met without panic. At the same time Jack may find out why he is not getting a new bicycle. Martha may know why this is not the moment to ask for a new dress.

Jack and Martha understand that they are not qualified to decide the real issues, but they do absorb the reasoning process. They get the idea that questions can be approached with a problem-solving attitude. The feelings back of such phrases as "You can usually find a way," "Will this really help us in the long run?," "Let's be clear about the next step," or "There are likely to be stumbling blocks. How will we get around them?" influence the way a child will work at his own problems, now and as he grows up.

Mother and father may differ on the principles of child rearing, but a united front toward the children is essential. Parents can work out their differences by discussing points of disagreement when the children are not present. Then many questions of discipline can be dealt with in council meetings with the children. Such discussions give children the feeling that rules are made because certain regulations are necessary if people are to live together. They get the feeling, so necessary for their security, that their parents are strong enough to guide them and protect them. A family council can actually reinforce parental control.

Working Out Difficulties

Authority in any body governed by

Indoors or out, no matter what the job, boys and girls work more willingly when they have had a part in choosing what task they will do.

Ewing Galloway
H. Armstrong Roberts
Gendreau

democratic procedures rests on competence. Parents are the ones who are competent to make the decisions on questions that affect orderly living together in the family. Discipline is really the teaching of an orderly way of living. As children have a chance to see why rules are necessary, they tend to be less resentful of control. They are more willing to comply with necessary regulations.

Assigning Family Jobs

Everyone has jobs to do in a family. It is enlightening to see the results of a general discussion where everyone can voice his complaints, put forth his views, and finally accept his just share of the many tasks a household demands of its inmates. There may be more co-operation and less dodging of tasks, if the children have a share in the assigning of jobs. The assignments can be made with an eye to the special requirements of each child's schedule. Everyone feels more like carrying out plans he or she has helped to make. The chance to make some decisions makes the children more, rather than less, willing to accept their parents' word when that is necessary. If, as jobs are discussed, the children volunteer for table-setting, snow-shoveling, or bedmaking, they will tend to perform the jobs less reluctantly.

The Values of a Family Council

As questions are tossed about in these informal meetings, everybody learns not only to speak up, but to listen. Because his own judgment is respected, each gains respect for the judgment of his fellow council members. Brothers and sisters who were feuding yesterday may find themselves on the same side of a question today, and realize they are friendlier than they thought. The line-up is by no means continuously children versus parents.

The Loyal Opposition

The children discover some important facts about minority rights. They find out, too, that it is safe to disagree, and that disagreeing does not lessen family solidarity. The training of the family council often carries over to the playground, to school, and even to later life. The ability to work out conflicting needs and interests through friendly discussion is no small asset in the wider community.

As a family thinks its problems through together, that invaluable sense of belonging is strengthened. In the course of time, everyone is sure to contribute some good ideas. The contributor grows in his own and his family's esteem as those ideas are accepted. Everyone also comes out with a few impossible suggestions. If the impossible suggestions are treated with good humor, much is learned about graceful give and take. The younger children may not be particularly graceful about taking criticism, but a friendly mother or father can usually find some good point in even the most outlandish idea. A small person can save face with brothers and sisters, and criticism becomes bearable.

Everybody Benefits When Everybody Shares

When one reads and hears of the many disrupting influences bearing on the family today—the automobile, the movies, the crowded homes, the working mother—it is refreshing to contemplate a device like the family council. It inevitably brings the family closer together. It does not cost a cent. It works. It can be fun.

THE FATHER IN THE FAMILY

RUSSELL C. SMART, Ph.D.

Chairman, Department of Child Development and Family Relations, University of Rhode Island, Kingston, R. I.

"Dear, would you mind taking the children to the office with you today so I can get some work done around here?"

Boys learn to be men by living with men. The first man a boy knows, and the one he has the most chance to copy, is his father. Long before a baby can talk, he recognizes differences between his mother and his father. If he could talk, he might say: "This is that person with the deep voice and the strong arms who lifts me up high." Or, another time, "This is the one who has soft arms, who cuddles me and talks in a gentle voice." As time goes on, he discovers other things that make differences between his parents.

Father Is the Model

Since the boy is the son of a father who loves him, what his father does becomes his model for measuring all men. Particularly does a boy measure himself, as a man-in-the-making, by his father's standards. His grandfathers, his uncles, his men teachers, the heroes of the stories he reads will all have their influence on the picture of himself as a man that he is trying to copy in his behavior. But the pattern of the longest standing, the pattern that is before him most often, is his father.

Boys Want to Be Men

Nine-year-old Jimmy shows promise of having hair and eyes of the same color as his father when he grows up. People comment on the similarity between Jimmy and Jim Senior, but nobody is really surprised. You expect parents and children to be somewhat alike in physical appearance.

If you were to look at the two Jims more closely, you would discover similarities not due to heredity. Jim Senior grew up in South Carolina and has never completely lost the softness and slowness of his talking. His wife grew up in Minnesota. Jim Junior has spent most of his life in New York state, but it does not take a trained ear to recognize that he talks more like his Dad than like his Mother. When he walks, he moves his shoulders and arms the way his Dad does. He has the same patience and gentle fingers when he takes burrs out of the ears of the family dog.

Young Jim may or may not be an engineer like his Dad when he grows up.

As Father comes and goes, he links the familiar scenes of home with the great world beyond the front door. He stands for the ways of that unknown region.

He shows some signs of turning in that direction, but Big Jim is determined not to force him. He realizes that there are lots of other ways of earning a living. Nobody can predict now what occupation young Jim will follow when he grows up. But we can predict with a great deal of certainty that he will be much the same kind of man that his father is. Big Jim would probably be embarrassed and a little flustered if we told him that, but it is true.

Girls Want a Man Like Daddy

Our daughters learn a similar lesson from us, appropriate to their needs. Part of the picture in each girl's mind when she chooses a husband is made up of what she has learned about men from her father. Anna and Margaret were sisters, five years apart in age. Both adored their father and each was loved deeply by him. When they were married, each one commented on how much her own husband resembled her father. To a third person to whom they made the comments it looked as though the two husbands were not at all like each other, but that each was like his father-in-law in some ways.

Just as boys learn to be men by living with men, so girls learn what men are like and what to expect of them. A girl whose father loves her learns ways of receiving and giving affection. The foundation for the love between herself and her husband is laid in her early years. The husband she chooses will represent for her the ideal of what is best in a man. Her experiences with other men as she grows up only add details to the basic picture of men she forms from her experiences with her father.

Father Brings a Wider World

Bringing up children is a job that takes two persons, not just because child-rearing takes time and energy, but also because children need to learn about both the masculine and the feminine ways of looking at life. In families in which father is the breadwinner, he is the person who brings in something of the outside world. The world of business and other people comes into the intimate circle of the family through father. He spends so many of his waking hours away from home, that he is in a position to see life at home in perspective. He knows his way around outside the home. Therefore, he may be in a better position to interpret the way things are done in the outside world. Because he has traveled, he can explain how to figure out a timetable when the children are going on a trip to grandfather's. He knows how much the tip should be in a dining car or at a hotel. He can explain the difference between the money he carries around in his pocket and the bank checks he sometimes writes. He can tell how the mailman gets the letters he brings to the house.

Discipline—A Two-Parent Job

Children learn from both their parents, not only in these minor ways of living, but also in the bigger moral issues of right and wrong. Discipline is the method used to teach children the accepted ways of behaving both at home and away from home. Discipline is far more than correction and punishment for wrongdoing. It is the teaching of an orderly way of living. Above everything else, children want their parents' approval. As we bring up our children, we sometimes give approval freely and sometimes withhold it.

Sometimes fathers want only to play with their children, and to leave the job of keeping the children in line to the mothers. There is another school of thought that operates on the principle that the unpleasant parts of child-rearing should be left to father. Then the time when Dad gets home from work becomes to Sam and Mary not a time to look forward to joyfully, but something to fear because their mother has said, "Just you wait until your father comes home. . . ."

Discipline is best for children when Mother and Dad agree on how they expect Sam and Mary to behave and when both parents share in giving approval and disapproval. Mother and Dad need not use exactly the same types of discipline. Generally fathers are stricter with their children and mothers more willing to give them the benefit of the doubt. It is part of our idea of masculine behavior to have father stick close to the letter of the law. It is part of our idea of feminine behavior to have mother be more indulgent. Boys and girls need to learn that men and women sometimes have different viewpoints, if they are to understand what it means to be masculine and what it means to be feminine.

In the job of being a father we need not overdo this business of being masculine. The tough he-man who sits in judgment on his children, who lives aloof from them because he is preoccupied with "man's work," is not our ideal. We need not put Papa on a pedestal labeled "Father, Who Is Beyond

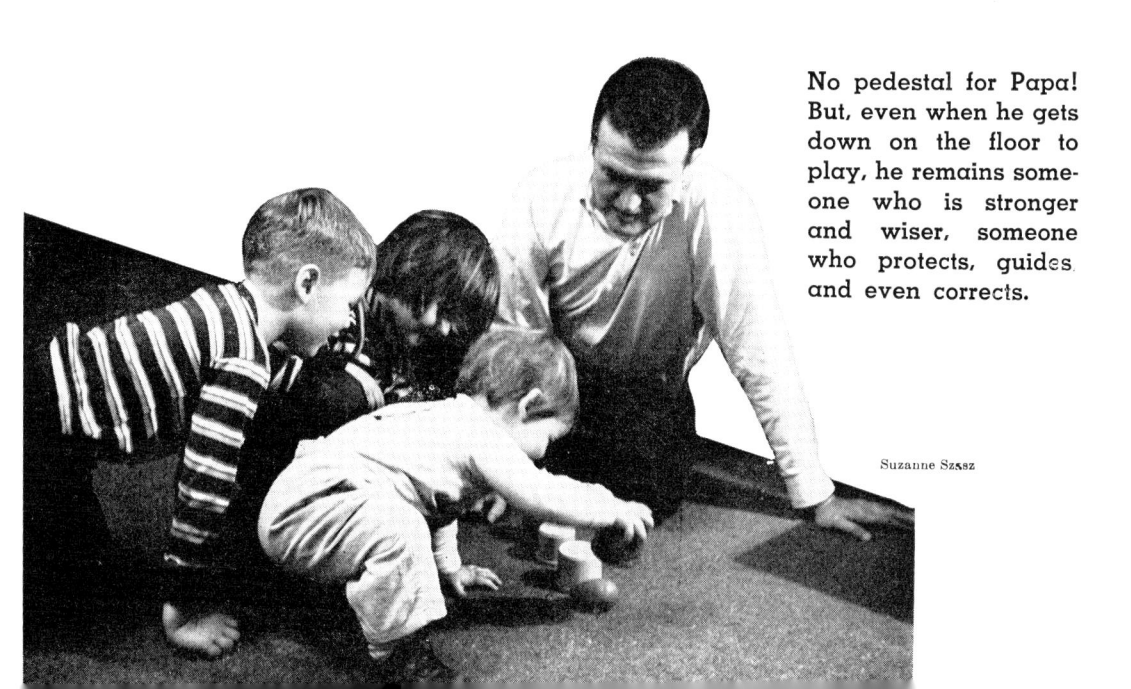

No pedestal for Papa! But, even when he gets down on the floor to play, he remains someone who is stronger and wiser, someone who protects, guides and even corrects.

Suzanne Szasz

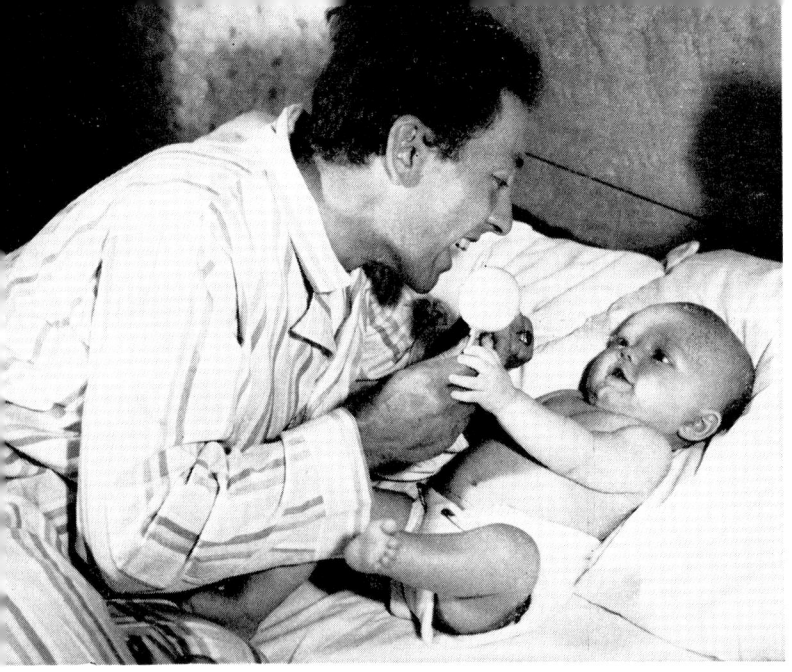

Babies want Father's attention, too. It is good for them to have both parents share in taking care of their needs.

Approach and also Above Reproach."

Why Is the Pal Idea False?

The other extreme, the father who is "one of the boys" with his son and his son's friends, lacks something in his relationship, too. There is a difference in years between Jack McDonald and his children. Being older and bigger, he must be stronger and wiser than they are. They need his strength and wisdom when they want protection.

Young Bill McDonald may do a pretty good job of hiding his hurts and fighting for his rights like a young devil when he is with the gang. When he gets home he needs a sympathetic shoulder to cry on, and a sympathetic ear to listen to his side of the story. If his side of the story is the wrong one, Bill needs an understanding person who has lived through the same kind of scrape and can now see what would have been the better thing to do.

Only Someone Stronger Offers Protection

Children need to be protected from things outside themselves that are too big for them to cope with. Equally great is the need for protection against the unpleasant feelings that sometimes rise up inside even well-adjusted youngsters and threaten to overwhelm them. Fears of doing poorly in school, fears of failing on the playground come to all children. Fears and hates of the big boys and girls at school, and huge, destructive feelings about things and people are part of childhood. These call for a father who can say, "Yes, you're in a tough spot. Let's figure this out together and see what needs to be done. It's mighty unpleasant to feel the way you do, but lots of people have had that happen to them. Now, how about . . ."

You don't pooh-pooh their feelings. You don't come out with a pat answer that fits too easily. You accept the way they feel and recognize that something needs to be done. Then you can help them figure out what course of action will be best for everybody. You are a friend; you are a stronger, wiser, more experienced guide who can help your children meet their problems.

Luckily for everybody, life is not all grim. It need not be serious day in and day out. Fathers can be fun. Private jokes and family jokes, hilarious nonsense that leaves everybody weak and gasping, are all part of life, too. But fun that fathers have with their children is fun between adults and children. A father is not another child. He doesn't need to act like another child. But he can still spend time with his children. This affection will be especially precious to them.

Fathers Are Only Human

Young Sylvia asks, "Why does the toaster get hot?" In reply to your answer she asks, "What is electricity? Where does it come from? How do they make it?" Maybe the knowledge she is seeking comes back to you in a flood. One day Sylvia will think up a question that stumps you completely. Do not try to bluff the answer or to change the subject. Tell her, "I don't know. We'll look it up together in the encyclopedia," or, "I'll stop in at the library and get a book that tells about that." You may even say, "Mr. Montgomery knows all about that kind of thing. We'll find out from him next time we see him."

You want Sylvia to keep her curiosity about all kinds of things. She will not think any less of you because of an honest "I don't know." If, coupled with that "I don't know," there is desire to find the answer, she will be learning that ignorance is no sin.

What If Father Makes a Mistake?

Sometime Sylvia is going to discover that you have made a mistake. After all, you are human! Unless you have been too harsh about the mistakes she has made, you can say, "Yes, I did. I'm sorry that I didn't see it was a mistake before it was too late. But that happens to us all. The only thing to do is to try to do better next time." If you have scolded her severely for her mistakes, or belittled her for errors of judgment, or held up an ideal of perfection for her, you will have some difficulty making that particular speech sound convincing. You can always turn over a new leaf. You can try to see her mistakes, and yours, as evidence that you are both human.

You can take the attitude that most of us try to do the right thing. Much of the time we are successful. This attitude shows that you have confidence in yourself. Your children will be better able to develop self-confidence if you have a degree of optimistic buoyancy.

How Can You Deal with Anger?

One of the most human things in the world, and one that nobody can avoid, is getting angry. This happens most

Luoma, Monkmeyer

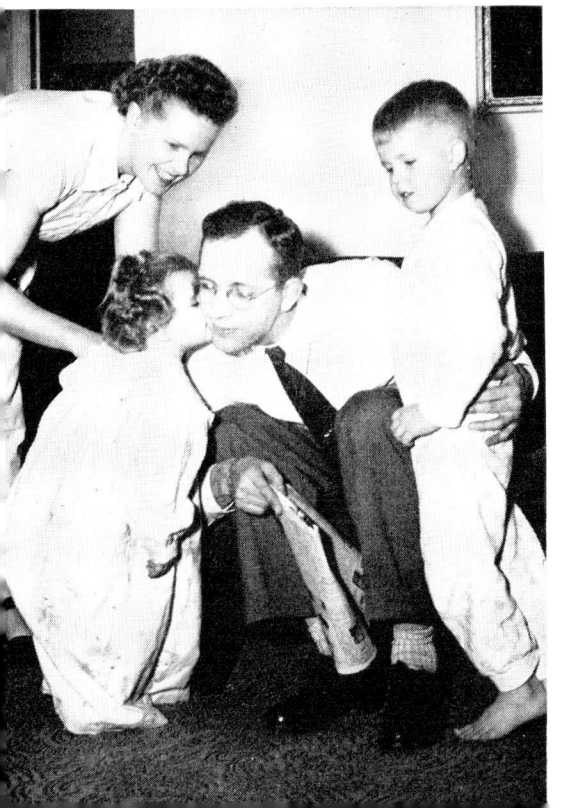

Father's goodnight kiss makes even going to bed in the dark seem bearable.

often if you feel hemmed in and are prevented from doing the thing you want to do. One of the spots where Father can be especially helpful is in showing his children how to deal with their overwhelming feelings. But he needs to understand what may be going on beneath the surface.

In the process of growing up we adults have learned, sometimes painfully, and not always completely, that there are some ways of behaving that are unacceptable. Young children hit out against whatever is preventing them from doing what they want to do. Pretty soon they get the notion that hitting is not permitted, and may even get them into worse trouble. Then they substitute "hitting-out" words, sassy words, rude words, for actual hitting. Even these words are usually discouraged. Sometimes, with children their own age, they can get away with the name-calling and the sarcastic wise crack.

Hitting out against whatever is holding you back is the inevitable response to frustration. Children inevitably meet frustration again and again as they are growing up, and after they are grown up. We need to accept anger as natural, but we do not need to accept or permit constant hitting-out in children. Our job is to teach children that it is possible to hit out in ways that do no harm and may even do good. We need to teach a double lesson, for children must accept their anger and channel it.

A Reasonable Father Turns Away Anger

An angry child needs help. He needs to be shown by word and deed that he is not an outcast because he is angry. He needs to be shown how he can get rid of his feelings. Adults can look for the cause of the anger. They can see if there is some way the situation may be avoided another time. A few minutes' warning that bedtime is coming up, or that it will soon be time to wash for supper, may prevent outbursts of anger at having to stop playing. If the broken toy is mended so it will work, if the too-complicated toy is put away until the youngster can handle it, frustration and anger in those situations can perhaps be avoided.

No amount of good management will do away with all disappointments for children, but it certainly helps everybody to keep the frustrations at a minimum. When Peter or Betty are blocked in what they want to do, you can say, "Lots of people get mad when that happens to them. But you mustn't hurt other people just because you're angry. You'll feel better if you run hard, or sock the ball as hard as you can, or something like that."

Saying rude things, being sassy, talking back are forms of hitting back that use words instead of fists. It helps children if fathers can look at the anger instead of talking back themselves. If Dad can control his own anger at the sassiness, Carol will be helped to control hers. Carol will be helped even more if Dad says, "I'm sorry it makes you mad at me when I say you can't go to the movie. Being rude doesn't make you feel much better, really, does it? I think you shouldn't go to the movie because . . ." After giving the real reasons, Dad can go on to say that everybody gets angry sometimes at restrictions, but as people grow up they find better ways of dealing with anger. Then he can explain some good ways people have found for getting rid of anger.

Children meet frustration at school and at play as well as at home. Over and over again, they will have that feeling of wanting to hit out against the people who are restricting them. It helps tremendously to have someone with whom they can talk things over. They need someone who can listen sympathetically to the injustice they suffered, and agree that they were in a tough spot. Dad can ask them what might have been a better way of meeting the situation. If they cannot think of anything else they might have done, perhaps Dad will be able to make a suggestion out of his own experience. They get the idea that Dad does not disapprove of their being angry, but is trying to help them.

Fathers are just as helpful when it is a question of such feelings as jealousy. The chapters in the section RELATIONSHIPS AMONG CHILDREN IN THE FAMILY, in this volume, suggest ways father can deal with the jealous child.

How Can You Share Interests?

Sometimes fathers say that when Belle and George get to such and such an age, they will begin to do things with them. But if you do not make friends with your children before they are five or eight or ten years old, you may find it difficult to get close to them. Taking care of young children is man's work as well as woman's work. Even diapers and bottles are not below the dignity of a man. They may be rewarding to a father, for they give him opportunity to watch his child's personality unfold.

Later on you can play blocks and balls and "tea parties" with them. There are stories to be read and told. You take the lead from what your children think is fun. You do not always need to show them a better way to catch the ball or pile the blocks. You take them with you when you go shopping for hinges for the new cupboards, or seeds for the garden.

Devaney

"Easy does it! That's the girl!" When Father is beside you it is easy to be brave. Father is a source of courage.

A trip to the zoo or the park with Dad somehow makes the animals or the boats seem different from what they are when Mother leads the way.

Some fathers can arrange to take their older children along with them on short vacations. Sometimes Mother goes away for a week-end visit, and Dad takes over running the house. Meals are probably different, and maybe the beds do not get made. Linda's braids may not be as neat and tight as when Mother does the hair fixing, but everybody is still well and happy when Mother gets back. She is refreshed by a change from cooking meals, making beds, braiding hair, and all the rest.

Father's Hobbies Fascinate Youngsters

Being close to your children is basically a day-to-day affair. Always remember that a child cannot keep up his interests, even in an absorbing activity, as long as an adult can. While you are planting the peas, or getting the fishing tackle ready, Phil works right alongside you for a few minutes. Then he is off on an adventure of his own. Later he comes back for another spell of "helping." His flitting probably makes him of less help, but it does not mean that his ability to concentrate is abnormally low for a lad his age. Later on he will be able to stick at helping for a longer time, because he will be able to wait longer to see the finished product.

Even when Phil can work along with you at your hobby for an appreciable length of time, you have to remember that you cannot expect a perfect performance or a prize-winning product to result from his efforts. This does not mean that you let him do the rough work, after which you take over and put a satiny finish on the piece of wood. Sometimes you let his performance stand. He needs to have the satisfaction of seeing the results of his labors rather than the craftsman's touch that you can achieve.

Father's Work Is Exciting

Children who know something about how Dad earns the family living have that much more understanding of what Dad is like. They have more understanding of men in general, too. Whatever Dad does every day at the office, the factory, or shop is glamorous because it is what "my Dad" does. To see the place where Dad spends his time between breakfast and supper, to see the tools and instruments he uses, perhaps even to use them, makes what he does more real. It is good to know he is doing something that helps other people in some way, or makes it possible for them to do their jobs, too. Even though Dad is away from home all during the day, what he is doing seems nearer to his children if they understand it.

To Keep Them Close, Let Them Go

When children get into school they become interested in clubs and gangs. Sometimes it seems as though they were never at home. They are always busy with youngsters their own age, doing things they do not want to share with their parents. This is part of growing up. In their adult lives, your children will be living and working more with people their own age than with people your age. Learning what their own age-mates are like, and how to get along with them, begins when children are seven, eight, or nine years old. If you insist on keeping them close at home then, they will be handicapped later on.

You need not fear that as you loosen the apron strings you are losing your children. They need your steadying hand, your wise counsel, your companionship even, as they are venturing out into their own world. They will turn to you if you are available. If you do not always preach at them, or complain to them, or hold up an impossible ideal for them, they will feel closer to you, too.

You do not have to be a perfect father to be a good one. You make mistakes. You feel a little foolish now and then. You are only human, after all. But, being human, you are also warm and friendly, loving and lovable. You are wise at some times and inconsistent at others. You are by turns cross and patient, and joking and stern and tender. And you find many moments that are richly rewarding.

RELATIONSHIPS AMONG CHILDREN IN THE FAMILY

Fishback

17. SOMETIMES RIVALS, SOMETIMES FRIENDS

18. BUILDING FRIENDLIER FEELINGS

19. SOME COMBINATIONS ARE A SPECIAL CHALLENGE

Children growing up together in a family can develop a basic loyalty and fondness toward one another. Friendly feelings toward brothers and sisters can enrich life for your children now and when they are grown.

Feelings about brothers and sisters carry over to feelings about other associations throughout life. It is worth devoting considerable thought and effort to the cultivation of friendliness and fondness among the children in the family. This cultivation is necessary, as the forces that make for resentment are strong and deep.

You cannot forbid or root out rivalry or jealousy, but through your attitudes and the arrangements of family life you can keep them within bounds.

SOMETIMES RIVALS, SOMETIMES FRIENDS

EDITH G. NEISSER, B.A.
Author, "Brothers and Sisters," Highland Park, Ill.

FEELINGS of brothers and sisters, or of sisters and sisters, or of brothers and brothers, toward one another, are as variable as the weather on an April day. But, as with the weather, there are signs that point to coming storms or mildness. There are, too, certain periods when emotional hurricanes may be expected.

The relationship of children in the family is totally unlike the weather in one important respect, for something can be done about it. If you understand the causes and the meanings of the variations from almost frenzied anger to protective tenderness, you are in a position to act. You can take steps to reduce the black, cloudy moments and to foster the sunny ones.

Rivalry Has Justifiable Causes

There are many reasons why rivalry and resentment play a part in the way all children feel about their brothers and sisters. Every child would like to have exclusive possession of his mother and father. Small children cannot understand that the supply of parental affection is elastic enough to take care of two, three, six, ten, or more sons and daughters. In the thinking of the two-year-old or the six-year-old, love is like a chocolate bar. He believes that if a portion is given to another member of the family, that much less remains for the original owner.

You are familiar with what happens when you step in to stop one of your children from mistreating another. Even as you plead with the wrongdoer, a new wail arises from the victim, "Don't make Bud go upstairs. I won't let you talk cross to him."

Anger and loyalty are both present at the same instant. Such contradictory feelings, existing side by side, are one of the strongest forces in shaping human behavior. These inconsistent feelings play a part in the relationships which exist among children in the family. They are a second cause of resentment between children who are basically fond of one another.

Another reason for jealousy is that a small person prefers the receiving end to the giving end of any relationship. A certain amount of giving is, one way or another, a part of getting along with brothers and sisters.

Consider, too, how children who grow up under the same roof are continuously together, and how frequently they get in one another's way. It should be remembered that the very competitiveness of present-day living communicates itself to even the youngest member of the family.

Jealousy and rivalry are no cause for disgrace. They are the natural consequence of being human, of being childlike, and of living in the Western World in the twentieth century. Once you have accepted the inevitability of these feelings among children in the family, you have taken a first step toward keeping rivalry within bounds. Then you will be better able to cultivate the friendliness and affection which are also a force among children who are growing up together.

Should Competition Be Ruled Out?

It might seem as if forbidding competition would do away with jealousy and rivalry. But feelings are not subject to regulation. If children are led to believe that their normal, high-spirited drive to be first or best is wrong, and if they find it brings down parental disapproval, they may hesitate to try out their powers in any way. They may grow up to be the kind of timid souls who are always afraid to assert themselves. If a child cannot assert himself in suitable ways at appropriate times, he is not adequately equipped to cope with the world.

Should You Protect Your Child from Competition?

Some parents, and some teachers, too, have gone to the opposite extreme and made use of children's spirit of competition to enforce discipline or to stimulate achievement. For example, have you ever been tempted to say, "If you want ice cream for dessert, then you'd better be a good girl like your sister"? Too much competition can be discouraging, and can increase the rivalry among members of the family.

Children who are allowed to meet slightly competitive situations as they arise from time to time are likely to develop the capacity to live with their feelings of rivalry. It is as if these small amounts of competition serve as inoculations. They make it possible to take the inevitably increasing doses of competition.

New Babies Are Puzzling

The degree of rivalry and the amount of friendliness the children in a family feel toward one another are not always the same. They shift and change as the relationships of the children to their

Doubts mingle with pleasure as the older child meets the new baby. "What's so wonderful about her?" is likely to be a question that arises often in his mind.

parents also change from year to year.

The resentment a two- or three- or four-year-old child feels toward a new baby is especially intense, because small children are so possessive about their mothers and fathers. Whether or not a young child puts the feeling into words, deep inside himself he wonders, "If I were all right, why would they want a baby?" Or "If I were good enough, this wouldn't have happened."

When Should a Small Child Be Told a Baby Is Coming?

It is not easy for a young child to accept the new baby. No matter how careful your preparation may be, you cannot always hope—nor need you try—to make a three- or a four-year-old completely jubilant when the new baby arrives. Still, there are some ways of approaching the whole question that may keep the event from being too overwhelming.

The announcement about the new baby does not need to be made long months in advance. But *when* a small child is told is not as important as *what* is told or *how* it is told. When the announcement of a new baby should be made depends on how old the child is and on what changes are being made in the household.

Honesty Is the Only Policy

No matter what the age of the child, you can be honest when you talk about the new baby. It will not be a "nice little playmate." Nor will it be "your baby."

And at no time should a small person be led to believe that he made the decision to have the baby. Don't get yourself out on a limb by predicting whether it will be a boy or a girl. In fact, the one thing to avoid is any statement that will make a youngster feel he has been intentionally misled.

Rearrangements of beds, play space, or routines are best made long enough in advance so that the child is accustomed to them before the baby is actually on the scene. By all means let him talk about the baby. Answer his questions, even though the same one is repeated fifty times. If possible, let him see other babies being bathed, dressed, and nursed. But all life need not revolve around the coming event.

"Why Does My Four-Year-Old Act Like a Baby Now?"

The Ferrises had done all the right things to prepare four-year-old Tony to be a big brother. Yet, six weeks after the baby arrived, Tony was insisting on

"If I can get Mother to feed me, at least I'm sure of her for a few minutes." So runs the reasoning of the youngster who feels pushed aside because the new baby gets so much attention and love.

having his milk from a bottle. He was refusing to feed himself and he was even wetting his bed at night. Mr. and Mrs. Ferris were disappointed—in themselves and in Tony.

Fortunately, the children's doctor to whom Mrs. Ferris took the baby for the monthly check-up was accustomed to this sort of backsliding. Consequently, he always inquired about the welfare of the other children in the family when he examined the babies. When told of Tony's reactions, he reassured Mrs. Ferris by saying, "Tony's responding the way lots of them do. You see, it looks to him as if you love that baby just because she *is* helpless. Tony figures that the one who is the most helpless gets the most loving. Probably, without saying it even to himself, Tony feels that there is no use knocking himself out trying to be big and strong and independent when the baby gets attention just by yelling."

Backsliding Is to Be Expected

In answer to Mrs. Ferris' question about how to deal with Tony, the doctor explained: "Don't make him ashamed of himself. Let him know you are on his side. Let him feel you have confidence in him, and that he's pretty important to you even though you and his father *do* pay attention to the baby. Let Tony drink out of a bottle for a while, if he wants to. You'll spend less time feeding him than battling to make him feed himself. But be sure to keep emphasizing the fact that this is just a temporary state of affairs. Tell him, 'It's more fun to be grown up and to feed yourself. I know you'll want to do that soon. It's more comfortable to be dry.' That sort of line will help him keep his self-respect as well as his confidence in his own ability to grow up. Growing up will be easier if he knows you and his father love him."

Peculiar Behavior Is Not Unusual

Everything may go smoothly when the baby is tiny. Resentment often reaches a peak when the baby begins to crawl or walk, and seems to become a real menace. It helps to remember that the underlying cause is pretty much the same in all these instances. These children are afraid of losing the love of the parents who are all-important to them. A child can be reassured through what Mother and Father say and do and

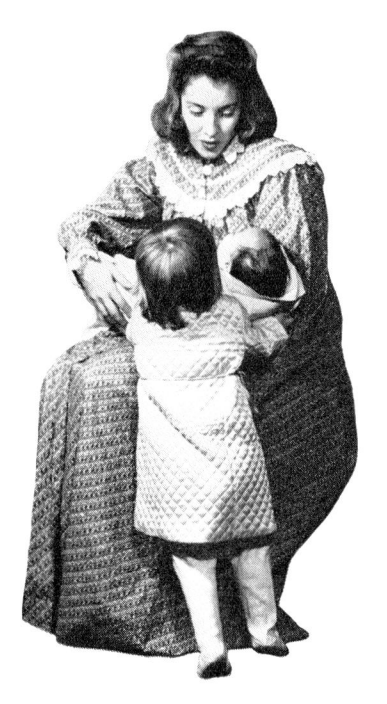

To a two-year-old or to a four-year-old, it seems as if babies get everything with no effort at all. But many hurts are healed if Mother takes time to cuddle the older child.

through affectionate attention. By having Mother or Father all to himself, occasionally, he learns in practice that he is still valued. Then he feels far less forlorn.

Events Are Often Misinterpreted

Routine care of one child may look to a brother or sister like a mark of special favor. When fifteen-month-old Kathy cut her head open in a bad fall and had to be rushed to the hospital, her sister Gwen, two and a half years older, was far more upset for days afterward than even this crisis warranted.

One night, she came tearfully into her parents' room. "If I got hurt in my head, would you take me right away to the hospital and leave Kathy home, and would Daddy come home from work to drive us?" she asked between sobs. Only after several patient explanations was she able to act like herself again.

Older Girls Care for Small Fry

Girls of seven, eight, or ten have a somewhat different attitude toward younger brothers and sisters. These girls are at the stage in their emotional development when imitating their mothers gives them real satisfaction. Mothers take care of babies; therefore, taking care of babies and smaller children appears to be an interesting occupation, at least some of the time. The motherly feeling that comes with a moderate amount of such care helps a little girl to make a further step on the road to becoming a truly feminine woman. She imitates not only what her mother does, but what her mother feels, as well.

Sometimes the older ones are gentle and protective. But their patience is short-lived and cannot be taxed.

How Much Responsibility Should Be Given to Older Children?

Some of these deputy mothers may grow much too bossy. Indeed, sometimes their bossiness only cloaks resentment pushed aside, for feelings of tenderness and annoyance are present at the same time.

Baby-sitting or caring for runabout children should not be the chief tasks of school-age boys or girls. Learning to get along with their own playmates is more important, as well as more fun. The amount and the kind of responsibility that older sisters or older brothers assume need to be worked out carefully and modified from time to time.

A suitable amount of such responsibility can draw the children closer together. Too much authority vested in an older sister can make her a petty tyrant. That state of affairs does not make a good basis for friendliness between sisters and sisters, or sisters and brothers, in childhood or in later years.

Jealousy of Older Brothers

Little boys are especially devoted to their mothers during the preschool years. They even regard Father as a rival for the exclusive possession of this desirable lady. Now, if a small boy has one or more older brothers, he may look upon them as serious rivals. Little does he know that they have grown beyond the stage where Mother is the center of the universe! The small boy is a bit afraid of these strong older brothers. Not only can they clearly get the better of him because of their superior size and skill, but also they are an unspoken threat to his position with Mother.

At the same moment that he is awed by them, he is fascinated by them. He learns a great deal as he takes them for models. Again there is the conflicting pull of opposing feelings! No matter what the older ones are doing, the younger one raises the persistent refrain, "Me, too."

Why Do Younger Ones Want to Copy Older Ones?

Being older does bring certain rights and privileges. These tend to make up for the annoyances of having tag-along brothers or sisters. Tommy, who is four, cannot stay up as late as his sister, who is seven. Nor can he wander as far alone or use sharp implements as freely as his brother, who is ten. This may be a bitter pill to Tommy, but it is a real fact; and some real facts must be accepted even at the tender age of four.

Tom will tend to resent his brother and sister less if his parents see to it that he has appropriate four-year-old satisfactions. The all-day picnic, the trip to the museum, or the motion picture that delights the older ones may be too much

This, too, is part of brotherhood. Scuffling and teasing may be limited, but the cost of forbidding them altogether would be high.

for Tommy's feet, digestion, temper, or understanding. Tommy will find more real enjoyment, and be far better off, if he takes a walk with his father to the railroad station to watch the turntable operate, if he eats supper in the back yard with the family, or if he looks at homemade movies of his birthday party or the lights and gifts of Christmas Day.

Like all younger brothers and sisters, Tom may clamor to do what the older ones do. His complaints are not so much because he enjoys their more highly spiced entertainment fare, but because such activities stand for the desirable state of being grown up. Still more acute is the occasional feeling that Mother and Father award greater privileges to the older children because the older ones are the favorites.

Balm for the Youngest

You can take some of the sting out of necessary restrictions if you let a younger child know that you find him just as interesting and just as good company as his older brothers and sisters. If the pictures he paints, or his performance in the Infant Choir, are as outstanding in parental eyes as were those of his older brother or sister, then the limitation he must endure will seem more bearable.

You can also help along the cause if you assure him from time to time that everyone was once small. Tell him the welcome news that he, too, one day will reach the dizzy height of being seven, and ten, and eventually twenty-one. But be sure to point out the good things possible right now.

It is a good idea to find some games, some projects, some excursions in which the younger ones can take part. If you can sometimes say "Yes" to the "Me, too" wail, things will not look so black when you must say "No."

How Can You Handle the Teasing of Older Brothers?

Among the crosscurrents in family relationships that may create some storms are the tensions between school-age brothers and two-, three-, or four-year-old sisters. Older brothers are sometimes heroes and protectors, but they can be equally notorious as experts in teasing.

Four-year-old fairy princesses and eight- or nine-year-old baseball players naturally see the world from different points of view. What one regards as

Small sisters give older brothers stiff competition for Father's attention.

A fishing expedition alone with Dad may make Big Brother resent his sister less. When resentment decreases, there may be fewer squabbles and arguments too.

treasure, the other considers junk. What one finds sidesplittingly funny has a flat and stale sound in the ears of the other. Differing tastes and interests are sufficient reasons for a frequent lack of cordiality between small sisters and older brothers.

There is still another cause for friction. The little girl between two and six is something of an enchantress, and the object of her enchanting ways is her father. She wants Daddy's time, attention, and wholehearted approval. That is exactly what her older brother wants, too. He is likely to be at the stage in his development where Pop combines all the remarkable qualities known to humankind. To have Dad lavishing praise and affection on that unspeakable smarty, little sister, almost makes any right-minded boy doubt Dad's good judgment!

As if this were not enough, fathers are likely to expect a good deal from a boy who is over seven. "When's he going to learn some sense? I never saw such manners. It's time I took him in hand. He's been babied too long" is often Father's attitude. The boy, who really is eager to cut a good figure in his father's eyes, may get a great deal of criticism. Smarting under this criticism, he is likely to turn on the younger members of the family, especially the feminine ones.

Rules and Threats Are Useless

What can you do when things have reached a pass where little sister cannot walk across the floor without brother sticking out a foot to trip her? An indirect approach to the problem may be the most effective. It is just possible that what Junior needs is more companionship and less correction from his father. The boy who is having a happy and satisfying life himself may have less need to tease a small sister.

There is always the possibility, too, that the most cherubic-looking little girl is herself no amateur at pestering. Perhaps she needs to know that older brothers have some rights and that their possessions and their confidences are to be respected. Perhaps she, too, needs more opportunities to play with children her own age. More activities that will give her a chance to let off steam and that challenge her powers may make her less of a pest and a busybody where her brother is concerned.

Again, it is worth real effort to find some common meeting ground for the children. Something they enjoy doing together, even for the briefest periods, can lead the way to more friendliness a little later on. All these devices may be helpful in any combination of ages or sexes.

Expect Ups and Downs

When there are two or three children of school age in a family, their relationship usually has an "on again off again" quality. At times they may be allies conspiring against the giants of the adult world, for they are all interested in achieving greater independence. At times, too, they may be good companions, willing and able to assist one another, laughing at the same jokes. The younger ones profit from the experiences of the older children and learn from them in all kinds of ways.

They are competitors, too. Old rivalries, although pushed out of sight, are still present. And yet, every fight may not be due to resentment left over from the earliest years. A boy or girl who is bullied or pushed around by playmates or adults may in turn use brothers and sisters as convenient scapegoats and push *them* around.

How Can You Deal with Outright Fights?

You *might* be successful in forbidding conflicts, but at far too high a cost. Squabbles and name-calling are usually less important than they sound to ears accustomed to the more restrained interchange of adult pleasantries. Words are a relatively harmless way of letting out feelings. It is, in fact, something of a relief to a child to find that, even though he comes out with the most violent threats, nobody is destroyed or even crushed by what he says.

Mr. and Mrs. Potter believed that there were worse things than name-calling, and even worse things than downright fights between children not too unevenly matched. They did try to limit the more spirited disputes to such times and places as they considered suitable. Therefore, calling anybody anything worse than a "dope" was not tolerated at the family dinner table, and physical combat was distinctly discouraged in the living room.

The Potters also made it clear that when you are angry, instead of pummeling your sister, it might be better to go out and run around the block. They frequently pointed out, too, that you can spank your dolls or smack a punching toy instead of hitting your baby brother when he annoys you. Pounding pegs with a wooden hammer rather than pulling sister's hair in moments of frustration was strongly recommended, even to the youngest member of the family.

Good manners did not automatically become customary among the small Potters as a result, but the children did find out that there are times when a slight degree of control is desirable. They also gradually discovered that getting angry at one another was not considered wrong. What you did about your angry *feelings* was what incurred parental approval or correction.

Forestalling Trouble

While one child cannot be allowed to get the worst of things on all occasions, the children can work out most of their disputes without adult interference. Parents probably can promote good relations more effectively if they avoid situations where difficulties are likely to arise than if they try to stop a pitched battle.

Before the children get so tired, so hungry, or so overstimulated that tempers are touchy, you can often provide glasses of fruit juice or some carrot sticks, or suggest some quieter but pleasing occupation. It may be worth while, both in terms of present peace and future friendliness, to stop whatever you are doing and take time out for a story or a little quiet conversation. Listening to music for a few minutes with the children may head off trouble when the air begins to crackle with the lightning of an oncoming storm among them.

Sometimes you can point to a tactful, face-saving way out of a difficult situation when two or three are ganging up on a brother or sister, or are excluding him or her from the absorbing secret of the moment.

You cannot hope to keep the climate of your home continually fair and warm. It is worth trying to understand some of the reasons for its changeableness throughout the day, and throughout the changing seasons of a child's emotional development. Then you may be able to make the moments when children are friends at least equal, or even outnumber, the times when they are rivals.

Music and a quiet time the children can enjoy together may avoid trouble at the end of an afternoon of strenuous play when children are tense and tired.

Hibbs

BUILDING FRIENDLIER FEELINGS

JOAN KALHORN LASKO, Ph.D.
Formerly, Clinical Psychologist, Children's Mental
Health Center, Columbus, Ohio

There are many sound bases for friendly feelings between children in the same family, but such feelings need cultivating. Brothers and sisters, or sisters and sisters and brothers and brothers, are not always fond of one another just because they have the same parents and share the same home. Just because they must share their parents, their toys, even their clothes and their candy bars, children growing up together in the same family are frequently argumentative, jealous, and resentful of one another.

Create a Friendly Atmosphere

If the frequent and conspicuous lack of affection among your children disturbs you, take comfort in the fact that it is usually children who are sure of their parents' love who can afford to be at odds with their brothers and sisters.

It is worth giving considerable thought and effort to the cultivation of friendly feelings. The importance of friendliness between your children extends beyond having peace in the nursery or at the dinner table. Early experiences with brothers and sisters influence feelings these children will have about one another all through life. Early relationships reach still farther. How a youngster treats and is treated by the other children in the family helps to form the pattern of his behavior toward schoolmates and neighborhood chums. Later, he may even transfer to the other fellows on the job, or to a marriage partner, the attitudes he had toward the baby who "always had it easy" or the older sister who always managed to get her own way.

Feelings about brothers and sisters are built out of the incidents that happen day in and day out. At dinner, Dad wants to tell his wife how his employer reacted to his request for a changed vacation schedule. Mother thinks the latest washing-machine breakdown may mean a big repair bill, or even investing in a new machine, and she would like to discuss that problem. Junior was asked to pitch for the fourth-grade team, and dreams of pitching for the Little League. Five-year-old Jane is worried as to whether she left her new doll at the

Not just to be loved "as much as the others," but to be loved in a special way is every child's heart's desire.

neighbor's or in some other place. The baby has decided that this is not the night to settle down in his crib upstairs without a doleful serenade. Who gets the floor and for how long?

There is no "right" way of handling this situation, or other situations where the needs of family members clash. Each family works out a few characteristic ways of dealing with the pulls and tensions of family life. This characteristic behavior is often described as the "family atmosphere."

It is this same family atmosphere that largely determines whether Bill and Tom, brothers aged six and four, are pals more often than antagonists. Family atmosphere, too, tends to shape the attitudes of Bill and Tom toward their sisters, now three months and a year and a half old. The small sisters, in their turn, respond in accordance with the general tone of the surroundings they soon learn to know well. WHAT CHILDREN NEED FROM LIFE and DISCIPLINE FOR SELF-RELIANCE in this volume give a general picture of a good home atmosphere, but there are special points to keep in mind in thinking about the relationships of the children.

Can You Avoid Favoritism?

If children are to grow up liking one another reasonably well much of the time, they need to know that their parents accept each of them as he is. If you give your children the feeling that you like each one just as he or she is, each one will in turn feel kindlier toward brothers and sisters.

The child who witnesses repeated evidences of a parent's preference for his brother or sister has serious reason to doubt his own worth. He has good cause for resentment and he is likely to behave in ways we label "jealous." The father who cannot resist the coy charm of his little girl need not be surprised if that same charm makes her brother "hopping mad." The little girl who hears again and again the phrase "we wanted a boy so much, and we finally got one" may well wonder if her mother really puts much value on girls.

It is to be expected that children seem cuter and more rewarding at one phase than at another. The traits of one child inevitably hold more appeal than another's. One child reminds you of something you prize in yourself, or in a loved member of the family. Another child may remind you of the very qualities you like least in yourself or in others. There is no reason to feel guilty about such altogether human and unavoidable attitudes. But you can still make an effort to meet each child's needs. You can still give each a sense of personal worth.

It is possible to avoid the kind of full-time favoritism that leads the other children to remark, "He can get away with anything—he's Mother's pet." You can test your own attitudes. Ask yourself, "If

"Fairness" does not mean "the same for each one," but rather that each will get love, care, and attention as he or she needs it.

there's an argument, a broken dish, a job left undone, do I automatically assume one child is to blame and the other innocent? Do I find it easier to say 'yes' to one and 'no' to another?" In big affairs requiring conscious decision or planning, most parents try to be scrupulously fair to all the children. Most parents insist that new clothes, special lessons, or vacation trips be apportioned with justice. In the "trivial" day-to-day matters it is more difficult to be unbiased, but a child can cope even with a situation of open favoritism, if he feels that he, too, is appreciated.

Can "Fairness" Be Overdone?

So much has been said about not playing favorites, parents have been told so frequently that they should be impartial, that almost every mother and father occasionally finds herself or himself carrying the idea of being fair to extremes. One husband whose wife set great store by treating all the children alike often teased her by telling their friends, "Frances is a stickler for treating all the children equally, but she treats some of them more equally than others."

If you keep in mind that because each of your children has a different temperament, each will also have different needs, you will probably not go far wrong. The children themselves will tend to be less insistent on mathematically equal divisions of candy, toys, or kisses if the atmosphere of home lets them know that everybody will be taken care of according to his needs. The seven-year-old who gets enough affection himself is less likely to be troubled if Little Sister cuddles up to Daddy.

There are times when one child or another needs special comfort or special attention. If you give that attention freely and cheerfully to each as he needs it, rivalry between the children tends to be eased rather than heightened.

Is it fair to spend the afternoon reading to Chuck, whose leg is in a cast, while his brothers are playing outdoors? Clearly, it would not be fair or sensible to let reading to Chuck interfere with having supper ready for the rest of the family. But this afternoon, Chuck's mother had some time free to spend with him, and it would have been carrying fairness too far to feel that "it isn't fair to the others for me to read to Chuck for two hours." By spending the time with Chuck, she was not taking anything away from the others. Parental affection and attention, fortunately, can expand to meet such emergencies.

Comparisons Are Odious

Probably the biggest single contribution that could be made to friendliness within any family is for parents to drop from their vocabulary those deadly statements comparing one child with another. "Johnny doesn't whine when *he* has to take a nap." "Why can't you take care of your things the way *Mary* does?" "Bill could tie his own shoes and dress

A friendly teacher can make the world far brighter when the going is rough at home, and spirits need a tonic.

Suzanne Szasz

himself completely when *he* was your age." Such comparisons seldom inspire the brothers or sisters to be like Johnny or Bill or Mary. More likely these comparisons will set up resentment. This resentment may from time to time find an outlet in a swift right to the jaw (or its moral equivalent) of the highly-praised brother or sister.

The child who is the model does not profit by being held up as an example,

either. Obviously, what he gains in being admired by adults, he loses by being teased or scorned by his brothers and sisters. Marion, a "model child," voiced her protest to an adored aunt. "All Mom and Dad like me for is 'cause I put my things away and hang up my clothes. I get sick and tired of hearing how nice it is that Marion's so neat. They never notice anything else about me. I wish they liked *me*, Marion, not Marion-the-human-carpet-sweeper."

Teachers Can Provide a Balance

Teachers are in a good position to help the child who has suffered an overdose of being second-best at home. They can interpret his behavior and personality to his parents. They can let Mother and Father know how a child looks to an outsider, how he shows up in positions where he is considered an individual rather than somebody's little brother.

If the first child took to school work like a duck to water, the parents may tend to have high expectations that the second will show exactly the same interests and aptitudes. If he doesn't, they may worry and begin to apply pressure. They even may forget their good resolution not to hold up the elder as an example.

A teacher who senses this situation can do much to forestall trouble. She can help the family recognize the special traits that *do* mark the less able student. A teacher can stress Nancy's ability to hold a group together when the others begin to fade out on a job, or Dan's flair for telling a story in pictures. Such talents are just as valuable as speed in doing multiplication problems or facility in reading.

Sometimes it is the Sunday-school

teacher, the Cub or Brownie leader, the group leader in the neighborhood center, or even one of the neighbors who can bring in a new note when the refrain at home has become wearisome because of comparisons.

Bringing Feelings into the Open

Teachers and group leaders can promote friendlier feelings among children in the same family by helping children understand better their own feelings about brothers and sisters. Stories and poems involving family situations can be the starting point for discussions. There are stories in FOLK AND FAIRY TALES and GREAT MEN AND FAMOUS DEEDS, Volumes 3 and 6 in CHILDCRAFT, that stimulate conversations of this kind. A host of other books for children are helpful.

It is good, sometimes, to get feelings off your chest, even when you are only six or eight or ten years old. Sometimes, too, it is easier to talk about feelings in a group whose other members give you sympathetic support when you declare that "My big sister is just like Cinderella's sister. She thinks she's so smart," or "My oldest brother is the one I like the best. He never lets the rest of them tease me and I like to have him taking care of me when Mom and Dad go away." With such feelings out in the open, a teacher has good clues for giving these children and their parents help in promoting friendliness among brothers and sisters.

What Makes Them Good Friends?

Friendly feelings are an outgrowth of the discovery that there is enjoyment to be had through doing things together. Children learn how to get along with others as they voice their opinions and desires on day-to-day questions of family living. They discover some of the things they must do to reconcile their own needs with the needs of other persons.

"Shall we go to the beach or shall we drive out to Uncle Dick's farm this Saturday?" That is the question before the house one fine summer day. The six- and eight-year-old vote for the beach. Teddy, the five-year-old, would like to go to the farm to see the calves. As the matter is talked over by the whole family, the eight-year-old ventures the opinion that "those old calves will keep until next time." Mother mentions that perhaps she and Dad could take Ted to the farm and the older ones could go to the beach with the neighbors this time. "Then I'll go to the beach," Ted announces. "Going to the farm's no good unless you guys come, too. I want to see those calves, but I guess they'll have to keep. I'll have more fun going with you."

Ted has the beginnings of the idea that certain activities are more fun if they are shared, and that compromising brings satisfactions in the long run.

It may take some thought and planning on parents' part to discover common ground where children of different ages can meet. In every family that common ground will be different, but it is usually possible to find some game, some excursion, some story that will hold everyone's interest for a time. In this connection, the stories and poems in the first three volumes of CHILDCRAFT and the games suggested in Volume 8 can be lifesavers.

If They Prefer Parents to One Another

Sometimes the children fail to form friendly relations with each other, not only because of friction but also because more satisfactions are to be had, with less effort, through activities with one or both parents. A girl may prefer to be alone with Mother on a shopping trip, a boy to fish with Dad. Every child needs time alone, for fun with Mother or Dad. The child who has Mother or Dad all for himself occasionally will be able to be more tolerant and generous with brothers and sisters, too. Any activity that the children could carry on jointly may seem pale by comparison.

The fact that children in the same family do not enjoy each other as much as they enjoy their parents need not be considered a bad sign, so long as they do enjoy play with other children outside the home. The child who gets along *only* with adults has not yet found enough satisfactions through other children, whether family members or neighborhood playmates. The pleasure scarcely seems worth the effort and sacrifice involved in playing with other children. It *is* effort and sacrifice! Other children, whether they are friends or relatives, insist on more give-and-take in the relationship than do parents or other adults, as a rule.

How Much Companionship Can We Expect?

If you were an only child, or if you have pleasant memories of family good times, you may have high expectations for your own children's enjoyment of each other. You may expect that enjoyment to start almost at birth. "What's the matter—don't you *love* your little brother?" you may ask. This question could frequently be answered with a frank, loud NO! Love is not a commodity automatically sent home from the hospital with the new baby. It probably took time for the mother and father to fall in love with each other. Once they were married, it still took time for them to adjust, and to learn all the small day-to-day compromises that make for harmony in living together.

Brothers and sisters, too, need time, years and years sometimes, to become friendly. Dorothy Aldis' poem, "Little," tells the story:

> I am the sister of him
> And he is my brother.
> But he is too little for us
> To talk to each other.
>
> So every morning I show him
> My doll and my book.
> But every morning he still is
> Too little to look.

And it is an unending disappointment to the two-, the three-, or even the five-year-old that he continues to be "too little to look," and is a liability rather than an asset for such a long time. Some of the things you can do to help the older child accept the new baby are explained in the preceding chapter, SOMETIMES RIVALS, SOMETIMES FRIENDS.

Is There Room for Quarrels?

Cheerful acknowledgment of one child's annoyance with another, or with the parent, can do much to ease tensions, and actually to improve relationships. "You don't *have* to play with your brother—or even *like* him—so why not try to find something else to do?" is an attitude that leaves the child some leeway to decide how he really feels about the brother or sister, and what he is going to do about it. This does not imply that the parents have to put up with constant battles among the children. Parents have some rights, too.

One mother used to tell whichever of her children were "at it"—"Why don't you go out in the back yard and argue? —then I won't have to listen to you."

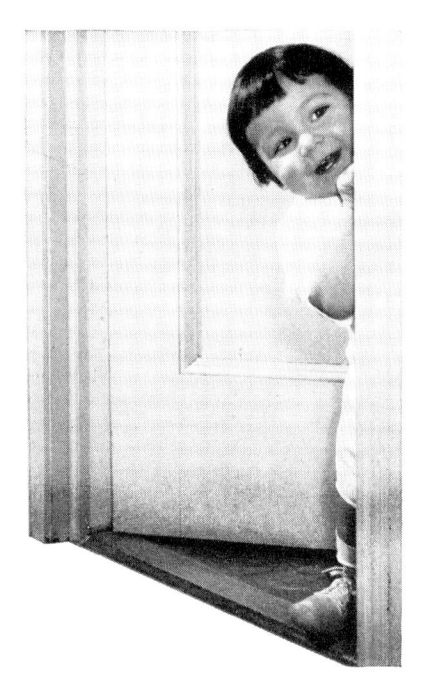

Small brothers or sisters can be real pests. The privacy the older ones treasure deserves protection at all costs.

The children realized that their mother was not upset by their anger and that they could settle their differences in their own way. They also recognized the justice of her demand for a measure of peace and quiet in her own vicinity. Usually, it seemed too hard to move somewhere else just to continue the squabble, and the children would come to terms with less noise and fewer blows. Of course there were times when this mother knew that she must step in to see that no one was mistreated, for might does not make right. But the children can often work out differences themselves.

Why Do Alignments Shift?

Once children have learned something about getting along together, you might hope that the learning would "stay put." But spurts in development create new needs. Sisters who last year were the best of playmates now seem capable of only a fleeting interest in one another. The eighteen months' difference between Dina and her four-and-a-half-year-old sister is suddenly of crucial importance now that Dina is in first grade. Little sister is labeled "that baby" and treated with scorn and condescension.

Dina has a right to some privacy. Her possessions need protection from little sister's explorations. She has a right, too, to play with her own friends without having sister tag along. If these rights are granted Dina, she will tend to be far friendlier with her sister, now and later, than if Mother and Father insist the two little girls play together as constantly as they did last year.

The four-year-old who has given his seven-year-old sister so much pleasure as she played at being a mother may suddenly rebel at taking orders from her. Either she must find new kinds of fun with him or lose him as a playmate, temporarily. His rebellion is a good sign that he is leaving babyhood behind. Some help from Mother and Father is called for here. Rather than trying to put a stop to Brother's defiance and protest, or to Sister's bossiness, it is wiser to plan more separate activities for these two. Maybe they will not be chummy in the next few years, but they will eventually feel kindlier if you do not force them to be together now.

Father may need to plan some excursions with Brother, to watch the trains at the turntable or the boats at the pier, so that young man will not devote his energies entirely to telling off his sister. And, of course, friends of his own age, who can satisfy his growing interest in the kind of building, exploring, climbing, and chasing so dear to the hearts of little boys, will help along the cause, too.

Only when you are sure of getting enough yourself, can you share cheerfully. Selfishness usually is based on the fear that there will not be enough to go around.

Can We Expect Generosity?

Probably one of the most frequent complaints parents make about their children, and children make about one another, is "He is selfish." It may be our demands rather than the children's behavior that need to be changed.

A toddler is not capable of great generosity. He cannot look ahead far enough to see that if he lets Tommy use his paints, Tommy will be more willing to let him play with his wagon. Enlightened self-interest comes about gradually as a child finds out through satisfactory experiences that a degree of unselfishness can make life more pleasant.

Children will tend to share more willingly if too much is not demanded of them in their early years. They share more willingly, too, if they themselves feel secure. A loved, happy youngster, who has confidence in himself and the world, will find it easier to be a bit generous. Parents can remember that some things do not have to be shared at any age. Certain precious dolls or stuffed animals, certain beloved treasures, should belong to their rightful owners, and to them alone. If you require too much sharing you can defeat your own purpose. But children *do* need to practice small, safe, and relatively painless experiences in generosity if they are to find the satisfactions it can bring.

Keep Your Eye on the Goal

As we try to balance friendliness between our children with the disputes and the resentments that are a part of their growing-up together, we need to keep the long-term goals in mind. Insisting on brotherly or sisterly devotion at the moment may not be the best way to build future loyalty and devotion. We can afford to overlook a great deal of coolness and indifference between the children here and now, if we are taking some of these steps that tend to lead eventually to better feelings.

SOME COMBINATIONS ARE A SPECIAL CHALLENGE

EDWARD LISS, M.D.
Lecturer in Psychiatry, State University
College of Medicine, New York, N.Y.

WHATEVER combinations of ages and sexes are found in families, each combination will have its strong and its weak points. But there are steps we can take to encourage the favorable features and also to soften the unfavorable ones.

Twins

Developing individuality in twins makes the usual family situations more interesting, but also more perplexing. No matter how identical the two may seem to be, there will be inner differences. There are two kinds of twins. Identical twins have developed from one fertilized ovum, while fraternal twins have developed from two distinct ova fertilized at the same time.

In the case of fraternal twins of the same sex, it is quite usual to find one larger than the other. The bigger one can easily outshine the smaller or weaker twin. In their earliest years the larger one may walk sooner or use his muscles more skillfully. While the twins are still small, he becomes the one who dominates. When they can talk, he is the spokesman who announces, "We don't like cereal," or, "We need a playhouse." It may be difficult to overcome this strong influence later on, unless the slower one avoids competition by choosing entirely different activities. Sometimes one twin is more subject to illness than the other, and is put at a disadvantage. More usually, we are struck with the way twins resist illness or get sick at the same time.

A boy and a girl who are twins will not tend to be as noticeably competitive as will twins of the same sex. If they are both lively children, it will be relatively easy to lead them into different activities and different interests.

Providing for the Differences

When twins develop at different rates, it requires extra effort to avoid having the weaker one overshadowed. Parents, with the best intentions, often dress twins alike. The children may be happier in the long run if they wear contrasting styles and colors at least part of the time. Parents can be prepared for quite different tastes and different responses from twins. There are tensions

She is happy if her brothers let her come along, but she must be a tomboy if she wants to follow the leader.

even in this close relationship. If members of the family keep in mind the special preferences of each twin, each will feel he—or she—has the right to be an individual. You encourage them to be individuals, too, when you talk to them and about them by their names, and not as a unit.

You can avoid playing up the twinship to such an extent that the children feel they are valued only because there are two of them. Each needs to feel worth while in himself or herself.

When Twins Have Different Interests

Twins can belong to different groups from time to time as they grow up. The extra-close flesh-and-blood ties may be preserved, yet the individual differences in each child will be allowed to flower. These occasional separations are good, even if the two are quite evenly matched and their closeness brings them mutual aid and comfort. If the twins become entirely dependent on one another, they may feel completely lost if separation should be necessary.

Twins' security may come largely from their togetherness. You can take care not to separate them at the expense of that security. But you can encourage them to make different friends whenever they show a desire to do so. Common sense must guide you in deciding when to impose the "second weaning" of separation on the twins.

The first school days are usually best when twins go together. Activities away from home can be similar at first, too. The right moment for separating twins will depend entirely upon their ability to stand upon their own two (not four) feet, and the pleasure they find in the company of other persons.

We can take care never to compare twins with each other. Teachers, particularly, must guard against this tendency. As always between children in the same family, love is deep but resentment can be even more intense.

One Girl with Several Brothers

A young woman of vigor and ability complained that in her community life she always contributed the most constructive ideas, yet she was never chosen as a leader. She was upset over this frequent disappointment.

Her early experiences threw light on her behavior. Edith had two older and two younger brothers whose interests, centered in sports. She was treated as a favorite, and at the same time included in her brothers' rough-and-tumble play. As a grown woman, she combined in her dress an attractive tweedy boyishness with a feminine emphasis upon charming hats and dainty shoes.

The Eternal Tomboy

Edith had the reputation of being an excellent manager and ran her home efficiently. She was intensely interested in community activities but she always wanted to be the leader. This trait annoyed not only members of her own sex but also all the men with whom she worked.

Edith chose as her friends among the girls those who were willing to let her be the queen. The whole picture recalled the tomboyishness we see in a preadolescent girl. Edith's unfortunate ways of behaving were brought about by an intense desire to be like her brothers. She turned her back on the more womanly qualities that would have made her a happy and appreciated member of her community. The average man, to her, was someone to compete with and dominate. The average girl was someone to look down upon.

Help the Girls Be Girls

Such a situation could have been avoided. The tendency for her brothers to treat Edith as if she were a boy could have been discouraged. Activities with other girls could have been encouraged. Her mother should have made special efforts to interest her in cooking or sewing. Feminine clothes and pride in her appearance could have been stressed as she grew up. She might have been urged to join a Girl Scout troop, a Camp Fire circle, or a dance group. Such a program has brought excellent results with other girls in a large family of boys.

There are, of course, advantages in living in a household with brothers. Here girls develop the know-how of getting along with the opposite sex. They will need this understanding and skill if they are to lead satisfactory, normal adult lives.

One Boy with Several Sisters

The only boy among several sisters, if he is the eldest, will have ample practice in acting the part of the strong man. Our world will expect such masculine behavior when he grows up. With the encouragement of a good father-son relationship, his numerous sisters may serve a useful purpose, although he would be the last to admit it when he is growing up! He learns to know the interests and the favorite activities of girls. Wholesome fatherly guidance can curb the impulse to bully the younger sisters. When such a boy is old enough to seek the companionship of girls, he will probably find it easy to get along with them.

If the Boy Is the Youngest

Should the only boy be the youngest or the middle child, he can easily become the victim of too much adoration. It can even happen that, during the years when his sisters are working out their own adjustments to everything masculine, they may take out on him resentments they feel toward boys in general. Their "what are boys good for anyway?" attitude may make him doubt the rightness of being a man. In the same way, too much mothering from older sisters, too much emphasis on the feminine way of feeling, talking, and thinking can sometimes result in the little boy's taking over the feminine manners he sees around him.

Parents can take care that older sisters are neither overprotective nor extremely bossy toward a small brother. In many families, giving the girl, or girls, a puppy or a kitten to mother and to boss has taken the pressure off the one boy.

How to Balance Petticoat Rule

These boys need many contacts with men and other boys in their out-of-school activities. Phil's three lively sisters babied him. Too much kindness smothered initiative and effort on Phil's part. To offset the disadvantages he suffered, his father and a bachelor uncle took him along on fishing and camping trips just as soon as he could travel without falling out of a boat. A boys' camp, when he was older, served as a balance against the abundant feminine influences at home.

The One in the Middle

The middle child has his own troubles. Unless he gangs up with the older or the younger, he finds himself squeezed between the two. To avoid having the middle child ground between the domineering oldest and the protected youngest requires watchfulness.

Parents can play up the special abilities of the middle child and highlight his contribution to the family whenever possible. The middle child can have a chance to go places with Mother or Father without the other children. Then he will be more likely to get that feeling of being "special." Everyone needs this feeling occasionally. As the children get older, it may be possible to arrange for the middle child to have a week or two, once in awhile—or even once in a lifetime—when he is the only one at home. His needs and tastes can be especially considered. Don't forget what your middle child likes best to eat, what *her* favorite color is, or what team *he* watches with greatest interest.

As the children grow older, the middle one often allies himself with the youngest. With a united front, the two can hold their own.

When the children are all girls, the mother has a more than full life. Father may long for male company and make a tomboy out of one of or all his daughters. Girls need to know their father likes them *because of*, rather than *in spite of*, the fact that they are girls. They need companionship from their father even more than if they had brothers.

How About the All-Boy Family?

In a family of boys, antagonisms are likely to be shown more frankly than in a family of girls. Rivalry among girls

F.P.G.

If a "great little mother" grows too bossy with brothers and sisters, give her a pet. Kittens can absorb unlimited quantities of mothering.

Nothing like a pillow fight when lively boys need to let off some steam!

may be equally intense but less open. Brothers can be great allies, but they can at times be enemies. A group of boys is certainly more of a handful than girls. There is more noise, more mischief, and more high spirits.

A mother who has been disappointed in not having a daughter may sometimes overprotect one of her sons. Frequently she seeks in her youngest son the understanding and companionship she had hoped for in a daughter.

Some female color is needed in an all-boy household. Grandmas and aunts should be welcome visitors. Visits from girl cousins, or opportunities for the boys to visit in homes where there are girls, add the balance and variety in such families. It is a matter of record that girls are seldom reluctant to visit in these jolly households.

In the all-one-kind families there are always enough individual variations between the children to keep life interesting.

Wide Differences in Age

Great differences in age among the children can bring about many interesting relationships. To a certain extent, these relationships are determined by the causes of the spacing in births. The wide spacing may be due to some misfortune, such as unsuccessful pregnancies between the births of the children, or to the death of a child. Then the tendency to overprotect the youngest is likely to be strong. The older children can be condescending, or they can be resentful toward the youngest. There may be a great deal of motherliness or fatherliness on the part of the older children, and it is by no means pure good will. It is sometimes an indirect way of bullying. It may be interference with the younger one's freedom. The younger one, in turn, may become too easily led, and develop into a flabby adult. If the older children become overwhelmingly annoying, the youngest may remain in a constant state of anger and rebellion.

Older Ones Can Be Interpreters

None of these misfortunes need happen. If parents are aware of the risks, they can guide the children carefully. It is possible that the older child, although he may be condescending, will not feel so strong a sense of rivalry if his parents have not let him feel that the younger child is the favorite. Often he can serve as a bridge between the parents and his brother or sister. It is he who explains the ideas of one generation to another. Through his firsthand knowledge of the manners and customs of the younger generation, he can keep his parents posted. At the same time, he can lend a sympathetic ear to the younger child, for he will not be as distant as the parents in years and experience.

Respect the Privacy of the Older Ones

The older children, who have reached a point where privacy is precious, are entitled to it. A heedless youngster barging in at all hours may be more than they can stand. Parents may need to take firm measures to protect the older ones, especially where space is limited and rooms must be shared.

It is hard to insist to a four-year-old, "You must stay out of sister's room when her club meets," or "Brother's snapshots are not to be touched unless he says it's all right." It is even harder to enforce these rules, but that may be the price of peace. The rights of the older children will be easier to protect if you make sure that the youngest child has the kind of activities and the sort of fun he can enjoy at his age.

Sometimes parents have grown tired of the noise and confusion several lively youngsters can create in a house. The youngest one is not encouraged to have his own friends come to play. Trips to the zoo and similar outings may have ceased to appeal to parents, but the six-year-old finds them as thrilling as his older brothers did. It may take some extra thought to see that these children who bring up the rear in the family procession have satisfying lives of their own.

How Can We Bridge the Years?

Let us not burden the oldest with too much responsibility for his younger brothers' welfare, or remind him that he must set an example lest Junior copy his misdemeanors. Somehow we overlook

Great difference in age may be a bar to companionship in the early years, but understanding will ripen in time.

the good qualities Junior also copies!

Sometimes parents have become a little stiff with the years, and physical activities do not come as easily as they used to. Here is where the older brother or sister can take over.

A long interval between children can be beneficial, for parents can learn by experience. Through their own growth and accumulated knowledge they can become more competent and more assured.

The Only Child

The only child is a child with special problems. Too much concentrated contact with adults, with whom he is the center of attention, can initiate him so thoroughly into the ways of the older generation that he finds it hard to get along with his playmates. He becomes thoroughly accustomed to being the only child among adults. This may make him less flexible. He may also shy away from larger groups because he finds them overwhelming.

Parents who find satisfaction in their relationship with one another are especially important in the case of the only child. If one parent should attempt to find in the child the satisfaction properly found in the companionship of husband or wife, it would be harder for the child to grow up emotionally strong and free. It would not make for the emotional health of the parents, either.

The mother who is too absorbed in her child may become the proverbial overprotective "hen with one chick."

The Only Child Needs Playmates

There are no rivals to teach the only child about sharing and co-operating. The extra measure of affection concentrated on him at home can give the only

When only children are lonely children, you may need to make extra efforts to find congenial playmates.

child false ideas of what to expect in the outside world. He has no opportunity to learn that it takes all kinds of people to make a world. Other children absorb this fact as they learn to get along with the different traits and characteristics that are bound to show up in a larger family.

From his earliest years, an only child needs plenty of experiences with other youngsters. Play groups and kindergarten can be helpful. The only child needs the chance to learn about sharing, and about being a leader. Most of all he needs to learn about playing a minor role. Neighboring children are lifesavers and should be encouraged to come and go freely. Overnight visits are a great treat and give the only child the chance to see what other parents are like. He is apt to have a rather limited idea of how mothers and fathers act, because he is unable to see how his parents react to different members of the same family.

Only children are not necessarily selfish, but they are apt to be self-centered. They have had no experience in the gentle art of teasing and banter. The mischief which comes about naturally in a larger family is unknown to them. They miss the adventures that go with family conspiracies. They are likely to be greedy for attention and unwilling to be just part of a group.

If parents can cultivate a casual attitude, they will avoid the danger of turning an only child into a hothouse plant. A certain amount of easygoingness is good preparation for being part of a group.

The Only Child Goes to School

Many only children find going to school something of a shock. They are not accustomed to sharing the attention of an adult with other children. The casualness of even the friendliest teachers is a great change from the undivided attention of mother and father. The first days of school are of great importance to the only child. Teachers need to be especially co-operative and patient with only children, for the break from home puts real strain on them.

The Child of Older Parents

Tommy came somewhat unexpectedly when his parents were in their late forties, and set in their ways. Their social rounds were clocklike in their regularity, and their ties to each other all the closer because of being alone. In the early stages of their marriage there had been a certain amount of yearning for a child. With the passing years their desire for children had been somewhat gratified by being uncle and aunt to many of their friends' boys and girls. It was with mixed emotions that they received the information that Tom was on the way.

Older Parents Can Keep Flexible

After Tom's arrival, his parents were extremely conscientious in their efforts to do the right thing. Schedules were ironclad. Wisely, they sought professional help early. The counselor suggested that Tommy be turned out to grass with other, more lively, youngsters. Nursery school and kindergarten were of great assistance. The mother's conferences with the teachers, and discussions at parent-teacher meetings, helped the parents become more flexible.

It would be difficult now to realize from his behavior that Tommy is not a member of a large family group. His parents have taken on a youthfulness along with Tom's growth. Father is not as agile as he used to be, and muscles get a bit stiff when exercised in baseball. Tom and his dad have found fishing and canoe trips or long hikes in the country good ways to be together. These excursions have more than made up for the lack of more strenuous activities. There is a solidarity in their relationship which comes from moments spent intimately in the out-of-doors. Youth has returned to the father through the common interest in outdoor activities, and the boy has profited by the mellow quality of his mature parent.

. . .

In every one of these combinations of sexes and ages there are possible hazards, but in every one there are, too, possible advantages. The good points can be realized if parents understand the situation and are willing to take the trouble to meet the challenge.

SHARING PLEASURES AND RESPONSIBILITIES

USDA-Knell, Monkmeyer

20. SHARING THE WORK

21. FAMILY CELEBRATIONS

22. FAMILY VACATIONS

23. THE FAMILY KEEPS RECORDS

24. READING TOGETHER

25. BUILDING A HOME LIBRARY

Sharing is the keynote in good family life. The more your family is able to find satisfaction in working and in having fun together, the stronger and the more elastic will the family ties tend to be.

Celebrations, vacations, the quieter times of reading and remembering together are pleasures that increase when they are frequently shared with those we love.

In order that the memory of the events, great and small, that are woven together in the fabric of family life shall stay fresh, families may want to record events. Out of the shared past and present can come increased family flexibility and family strength.

SHARING THE WORK

DOROTHY LEE, Ph.D.
Chairman, Division of Social Development, Merrill-Palmer School, Detroit, Mich.

Triangle

Teaching Children to Work

IN YOUR day-to-day living in your family, you are bringing up children who have to learn skills they will need as men and women. You are making a home, not just doing housework. Through working, children learn skills and learn to get the job done. Through sharing in the family work they learn to co-operate, to work as members of a team. Through helping you and doing things for you, they learn to do things for others.

In a happy home full of the warmth and security so necessary to healthy development, the children are given a full share in whatever may be going on. That is why you ask the children to help, even though you could perhaps do the work more quickly and easily yourself. Even though your son makes a litter around the trash can when he empties the garbage, or your daughter leaves puddles on the floor when she helps you with the scrubbing, you want them to take part in the life and work of the family.

There is no virtue in just working or in just knowing skills. Skills are important because they are necessary to living. He who learns to do necessary things well is free to do creative work. Helping with the work of the house is good because it gives your sons and daughters a chance to participate in the running of the family affairs. It gives them a chance to share in the life of their parents, to be creative, to learn responsibility, to be co-operative. In itself, work is neither good nor bad. It may be interesting or boring. Whichever it is, when it is an essential part of something important and enjoyable, such as getting the family meal, it has meaning.

Preschool children see work as part of their parents' lives. They do not separate work from other activities. When they build tunnels, make mud pies, or set the table for their dolls, they are doing something creative and enjoyable. They do not call it either work or play. They want to "work" like Mother, and with her. Since this is what her life seems to

When a job contributes to family comfort, it makes sense and appeals to a youngster as worthy of her best.

consist of, they are eager to be a part of it. At this early age, they do not have to be urged to help Mother, or to work with the family. All you have to do is to give them the opportunity to share in the work.

It is different with the older child. His world does not end with the home. He goes to school and he has outside contacts. He has learned to make a distinction between work and play. Any work he is asked to do will have to be challenging, so that it can catch his imagination.

Can You Correct Without Scolding?

Give your child work that is real and needs to be done. Let him hammer in that nail that has been snagging your stockings. Then he can feel he is doing something that counts. Give your daughter the beans to string. Don't just let her wash pea shells that you are going to throw away later. When she has washed the beans, doing her five-, or seven-, or nine-year-old best to follow your instructions, accept her work as a real contribution. Washing the beans over again yourself may benefit the beans, but it will not teach your daughter to participate in group undertakings. She has had a lesson in stringing beans, yes, but her work has gone for nothing. If you put them in the boiling water as they are, your daughter's work has meaning. She is having a share in getting the family dinner. She is learning a skill by participating in this important work. In this way she learns to be creative, not just to keep busy.

Since you are teaching your daughter, you have to show her what she has done wrong, and how she can improve her work, but you can correct without scolding. When you do it this way, you are guiding, not blaming. It is also important to show the child where she has done right. This, too, is guidance. Be appreciative, but don't overpraise.

To exclaim, "Look what Mary has done all by her little self," in that special tone of voice, shows that you did not really think her capable of doing it. This hurts her dignity. You can point out mistakes without making her feel small and foolish, and you can show your appreciation without being condescending, if you have respect for her work. Above all, make sure that nothing in your comments leads her to feel that she

Willing hands make light work, and, if the children have fun at the same time, the job is usually done well.

has to succeed to win your approval. After all, value lies in the *doing*, not in the *success*.

What Kind of Jobs?

In addition to making the job one that needs to be done, give your child full scope, but limit the job to what she can do. There is no use in turning over the job of making an angel-food cake to your five-year-old, because it is beyond her ability. But perhaps you can trust her with preparing hamburgers for you to cook. You can turn over this job to her completely. She can mix the ground meat and shape the patties. You do not have to keep interrupting her with directions. At worst, the patties will be every size and shape.

School-age children can understand that sharing in the family means also working in the family. You will find that they will work more willingly when their jobs make sense to them. Give them a voice in choosing their jobs. You may find that they will prefer to rotate them each week or each month. And a call for volunteers is always better than "forced labor."

Do They Have Manageable Tools?

The working surfaces in your kitchen have been designed with you in mind. Their height is just right for you, not for your youngsters. Have a low, wide stool, and keep it where your little girl can pull it out whenever she wants to scrub your pans for you. The tools you use may be too heavy for a six-year-old, or even a ten-year-old. When you buy household equipment, from egg beater to vacuum cleaner, plan with your growing children in mind. Other things being equal, don't get the heaviest kind of equipment. The children can do better with tools that will not tire them.

Should Johnny Wash the Dishes?

In some few families, jobs still seem to be divided into "girls' work" and

The hands that pitch a curve can also wash the dishes. Nowadays nobody considers doing necessary household tasks unmanly.

"boys' work." Bedmaking, dishwashing, and dusting are not required of the boys, or at least the boys feel such jobs should not be required of them. Cooking is usually not so controversial a subject, for boys can see the advantage and the fun of having that accomplishment!

From a practical point of view, there is no sense in separating what men should do and what women should do to keep a home comfortable today. The various skills are valuable to both of them. There is nothing unmanly about any job connected with keeping house. Most young husbands today take it for granted that they should share in the work of making a home, and your boys will be husbands in another fifteen years or so.

There are some jobs that seem to be the special province of the boys, although girls can learn to carry them out too. When a fuse blows out, nine-year-old Tim will come to the rescue and put in a new one, proudly showing you he knows he must first disconnect the main switch.

In a home where the father never lends a hand with the household jobs, or openly disdains them, the boys will hardly be willing workers. Boys need to know Father thinks that doing the work necessary to keep the family comfortable is important, and worthy of a man's best efforts.

A Child Copies Your Feelings

The children take their cue from you in their attitudes toward work. If you gripe about having to work, your children will come to see work as a nuisance. If you let your children see that you enjoy working with them, and if you give them a significant share in this work, they can learn to enjoy co-operative work.

If you hate one special job, such as bedmaking or scrubbing the floor, you won't be able to fool them. In such a case, find some work you do enjoy, and use it as a basis for family work. If you like the out-of-doors, you may find that making a family enterprise out of cutting the lawn is the answer. Father or big brother pushes the lawn mower, while the three-year-old picks up the sticks and stones. Mother rakes the grass, and sister carries it off to the mulch pile. If you have a fourth child, there is always the grass along the edges to be clipped. Find some work that everyone enjoys doing together, and where everyone's contribution counts. Then, when your children like one kind of work, it will not do them any harm to learn that they do not have to like all kinds. They can accept the fact that you do some jobs not out of pleasure, but because they have to be done. They can understand that you are ready to scrub the floors and make the beds because those jobs are part of the work of making a good home.

What About Jobs and School?

The pattern of daily life changes when children start going to school. By this time, they are not so interested in sharing everything you do. They need to play and work with their age-mates. School provides them with some such experiences. It is good for them to have the opportunity to form their own groupings out of school, also. Plan their work with this in mind.

Remember that school takes up most of the weekday for the older child. Allow time for homework, Cub Scouts, or the committee meeting after school. There will still be some time left to help with the dishes, or to make their own beds. See that your children continue doing some of the daily work, however little. Apart from this, you can concentrate their work during the week end.

You can respect your children's time. Even the preschool child embarks on activities that are important to him. Older children may be doing something with friends, or may be engaged in some project of their own. Do not interfere or interrupt with small errands, unless this is absolutely necessary. Let children know what their jobs are, and keep the jobs regular. Then they can plan their day accordingly. They will like family work much better when it does not keep breaking into their play, or even into their work. If you respect their time, you will be giving them a chance to learn to organize their time and their activities. You can set an example for them by organizing your requests. Perhaps you can make a list of errands as you think of them. Your son then can take these on as his daily or weekly job.

What Jobs for the Older Ones?

Give your school child a challenging job. Catch her, or his, interest. Try having your eleven-year-old get Saturday lunch or Sunday supper. Or turn over to the children the whole undertaking of getting a meal. They may want to make a group project of it. Perhaps the sisters will plan the menu, and the brothers will do the marketing and set the table while the sisters get lunch. Give your children something worthy of their skills and intelligence.

Teaching Responsibility

Much of what we have said about work applies to responsibility also. When responsibility is taught gradually, as a part of the work, it furnishes interest and a reason for doing the job, instead of being a burden.

How much responsibility do we allow a child? There are no hard and fast rules. You can be careful not to overload your child. You must see his capacities clearly, so that what you offer him is opportunity and not license. In general, it is important to watch your child, to know his limits and abilities.

Jobs Need Boundaries

Give your child clear limits. Choose a job that he can do, but make sure that he knows where his responsibility stops. If your seven-year-old is fascinated by lamps and cords, have him be responsible for replacing the light bulbs, and for making a note of this on your shopping list. Let him know that after he has learned to carry through this responsibility, showing proper care and taking adequate precautions, he can graduate, at a later age, to the job of replacing plugs and frayed cords. In this way, you offer responsibility as a privilege as well as an incentive.

Try to give a child full responsibility within the limited job. Once he knows how to do a job effectively and safely, and has a job suited to his abilities, let him work things out by himself. Unsolicited offers of help, or explanations about the next step, are often insulting to an interested worker.

You can expect a child to do well, according to his own abilities. Do not set up general standards for him to meet. Each child is different. Each has his own temperament, his own way of doing things. One may have a quick eye, one a quick and sure hand. Another may be slow or unobserving. Younger children and older children cannot take on the same kinds of responsibility. To hold them to a set standard in performance may stunt their initiative and creativeness, and make for anxiety.

Try to see your child as a separate, unique individual. You can be appreciative when he has done his best, crude though it may be. Be ready to understand, to give him support and help if he has fallen short of his own abilities. If he falls down on the job repeatedly, question the job you have given him. Perhaps it is beyond him, or its limits are not clear. Perhaps he is confused and is worried because he cannot meet your standards. If this is the case, adjust the job to his abilities. You can be satisfied if your child does his own particular best.

How Much Reminding Shall We Do?

A gentle reminder, when necessary, is different from nagging. A reminder assumes your child will live up to his responsibility. The spirit behind nagging is different, for it assumes your child is not going to fulfill his obligations. You can teach and help without finding fault. If a job has piled up through neglect, do not allow your child to stagger under the consequences. Every child occasionally lets his room get too messy. Then the job of ordering and cleaning it looks overwhelming. You can help him, in a friendly way, to bring it back to the point where he himself can undertake its care again. If you let him be crushed, he may learn to hate or fear responsibility, or even become irresponsible. Give your help in such a way that it is not a form of punishment.

How Shall We Foster Initiative?

There are regular responsibilities, and others arise which you cannot predict. Encourage your child to be guided by the demands of the situation, and to act without being asked. Perhaps your small daughter notices that you are hot, and brings you a glass of water. Drink the water, even if it is warm, even if there is an ant floating in it. If you find it sickening, you can still accept it and swab your forehead with it, but don't belittle her efforts. If she feels appreciated she will be encouraged to be sensitive to a situation, and she will not hesitate to use her initiative another time. There will be time enough to teach her about the refreshing qualities of cold water, and about germs, as she grows older.

How Shall We Handle Failures?

Every child occasionally falls down on a job. If your eight-year-old daughter let the cat eat the hamburgers she prepared, you can all help her with the tunafish salad you have to eat instead. You don't

No use crying over spilt milk! When accidents happen, you can show the children how to do better next time, without humiliating them.

have to pretend that you like this last-minute confusion. But you do not have to remind her of the incident with every mouthful you eat, either. Help her meet reality, and give her your support, so that she will neither be overwhelmed by it nor refuse to recognize it. With your understanding and help, she will have the support and security necessary to learn from this situation. She will recognize that you were not unreasonable when you warned her about the cat, and that care brings desirable results.

You can afford to have faith in your children. Give them real responsibility and then depend on them. Do not insure yourself against their failure. See that the job is worthy of their skills. See that their responsibility is clear and limited, not beyond them, but not too easy, either, or it will not hold their interest. Then trust them. If the ten-year-old is making the cake for supper, or even for your party, don't make a batch of brownies secretly "just in case." There is a nice balance to be maintained here, for you also need to guard against making her feel that it will be disastrous if the cake is not perfect. When responsibility is backed by your understanding and support, it can be a reason for doing one's best, and for being truly creative.

Should You Pay for Work?

Both allowances and paid work should contribute to a child's experiences in using money, and to the security he feels in sharing the life of the family. Your decision in such matters should take into consideration the whole picture of the child's development and the family's needs.

Allowances are discussed in detail in CHILDREN LEARN TO HANDLE MONEY, in Volume 15. Here we are concerned with allowances only in connection with family sharing.

If your children have a share in the work of the family, and share in the family income for their food and shelter and clothes, then they also rate a share in the family pin money. Allowances are not a reward for good conduct or for work done, and should not be confused with pay. An allowance helps your son to learn responsibility about money, how to spend and how to save. When you allow him full responsibility within the limits of the allowance, remember that he can choose to spend his whole nickel on you, or on a family project, if he wants to. As you feel free to go without that spring bonnet and add the money to the fund for the new car, so does your son have a right to add his nickel to the fund.

The preschool child probably cannot understand pay. For the older child, the specific situation should be your guide. It is good for a child to know that there are some things one does as a matter of course. For example, it might be best not to pay for things like making one's bed, helping with the dishes, or dusting the stairs. This work is part of the daily routine.

How About the Special Job?

There is also the special job, or the occasional job. This is not done as a matter of course. Your son can make his individual decision about it, and undertake it on a voluntary basis. He may want to do it for you as a special favor, or in exchange for something special he wants you to do for him. If he decides he wants money, he may want to do it for pay. If you are dismissing the boy who has been cutting the lawn, because now your own son is old enough to mow it, you could offer the mowing to your son as a paid job.

There is no hard and fast rule. One working mother decided that her children were sufficiently grown up for her to dismiss her part-time help. This meant, of course, that the children would have to help with the housecleaning and the laundry. The children voted that, instead of being paid, they would like the help's wages to be set aside toward a new family car. A different family of children might have preferred to be paid for the work so they could use the money for individual purposes. Then, being paid for doing the work might be better for the children than sharing in the buying of a car. If the family income is suddenly diminished, and any outside help has to be dismissed, the whole family can discuss the situation. The solution here may be that the children undertake the work without pay.

If you handle the work in this way, you may find that your home is more full of warmth, and your housework has a new significance. And suddenly, on top of all this, you discover that the children are actually a help with the work after all!

Sometimes the spirit is willing, but small fingers are clumsy. Good will is more important than perfect performance. That comes with practice.

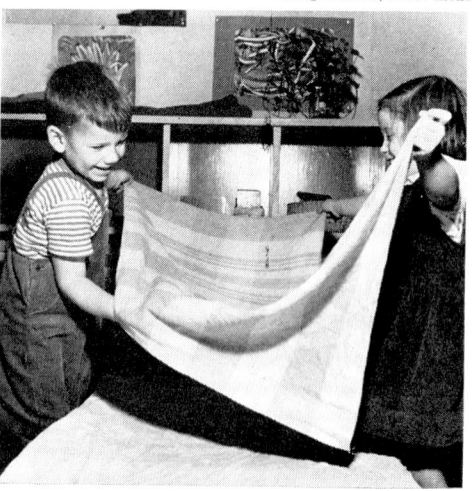

George Pickow, Three Lions

FAMILY CELEBRATIONS

ANNA ROSE WRIGHT, B.A.
Author, "Room for One More,"
Upper Montclair, N. J.

THE WHOLE family had spent the snowy Sunday afternoon coasting. As they ate supper in front of the fireplace, Patsy, the eight-year-old, sighed contentedly. "This was super. Let's make coasting and having supper in front of the fire a family tradition once every winter." "And what," asked Father, with a twinkle in his eye, "do you think a tradition is, young lady?"

Patsy thought hard. "A tradition is when you do something just your family, and nobody else, does, and it's lots of fun."

Making Traditions

Whether or not Patsy's definition agrees with the dictionary is not important. She had caught the spirit of traditional family celebrations, great and small. When a child says proudly, "At Christmas we always . . . ," you can be fairly sure these family traditions are one of the bonds that tie the family together. Family holiday customs, repeated from year to year, strengthen the feeling of belonging. Customs can be tailored to fit each family's needs. It may take a bit of experimenting to find what best suits your family. When you distribute the presents on Christmas, whether Thanksgiving dinner is at noon or six o'clock, will be traditions of your own making.

The Andersons are musical and no event would be complete at their house without songs. Their neighbors, the Santers, cannot boast even one member capable of carrying a tune. But they like to decorate the house for special occasions. The Santers would consider it no holiday at all if they did not make wreaths and a crèche for Christmas, gay and fanciful rabbits for Easter, and daisy chains or chains of colored paper for the chair of the birthday boy or girl. Still another family might center its traditions around reading holiday legends. Special dishes or special costumes mark the holiday in some families. Others like to share the holiday season with friends who are far away, by means of a family chronicle written and illustrated by the whole family.

Children love repetition. They will

Singing makes it a real celebration. The fine old songs strengthen the family traditions and forge a lasting bond.

want to do the same thing over and over again, and protest if you leave one ornament off the Christmas tree or one place card off the Thanksgiving dinner table. It takes a certain amount of foresight and flexibility to see when a tradition needs some slight modification to keep it from becoming flat and stale. But it is always the parents' job, in celebrations as well as in weightier matters, to keep one jump ahead of the children and set the stage or alter the program in line with family needs.

The Lesser Holidays Have a Charm

As we build family solidarity through the closeness of our celebrations, let's not overlook the minor holidays such as Valentine's Day, Halloween, or the delightful regional holidays of some parts of the country.

"Valentine's Day," one mother was fond of saying, "was not meant for lovers. It is the special joy of children housed with colds." Certainly, the origin of the holiday has less than nothing to do with sniffly youngsters, but colds in February are as traditional in most families as red candy hearts. Sniffly or not, children enjoy making their own Valentines.

Halloween is another occasion when families can do the traditional celebrating together. A family party, with masks and the good old games, is a good way to keep the children out of mischief. The smaller children will love dressing up and ringing a few near-by doorbells under Father's watchful eye.

Keeping the Religious Values

The religious holidays, like Christmas and Easter, can be joyful, but we can take care not to substitute overstuffed stockings and mythical reindeer, or rabbits and candy eggs, for real religious thought and feeling. To do so would be to cheapen the occasion and cheat our children. Whatever our religion is, we can hand it down unspoiled to our children. Through the services in church, through talking about the meaning of the holiday, and through using the family devotions of our own faith, we can make the spiritual values more vivid and more full of meaning.

We are likely to be a little confused ourselves as to how some of the secondary features of our holidays crept in. It might be helpful, in our reading together as a family, to turn to a reference book or a story that tells how holidays grew, and where some of their well-loved symbols came from. Fun can still be included in the celebration, for fun seems to fix the occasion pleasantly in mind. But we can keep a balance and interpret the true values to our children.

Sentiment Varies

The degree of sentiment varies from one home to another. You can find the amount that seems to agree best with your own family. Most children have a taste for ceremony, and it is a taste worth cultivating. It is worth going to some trouble, and taking time, to give members of the family a chance to express those deeper feelings of regard and affection that are too often lost in the hustle of daily living. Children need "emotional nourishment," and holiday celebrations can provide it. The ability to express appreciation and warmth enriches life. The presents they make for members of the family, the thought they put into planning celebrations, give children a happy sense of doing for others and working together.

There may come a time when the preadolescent nine- and ten-year-olds will turn against some of the family customs, even the celebrations. If they are not forced to do so, they will come back to them again. And of course, for children of all ages, there is a world of difference between stuffy family affairs, where everyone is stiffly dressed and stiffly mannered, and those that bring out spontaneous warmth and good spirits.

Keep the Past Alive

There are many delightful celebrations that tend to get lost in the uniformity of our present-day living. It is often rewarding to find an older member of the family who remembers some customs brought along from an earlier home. These have a specially precious flavor. They may be adapted to suit your own tastes in holiday celebrating. There is nothing to prevent your going to see, and perhaps taking over (even if you have no connection with them), some of the features of the festivals that are celebrated by people from other lands in your own community.

Your young guests thrill over the familiar, simple things. Even the humble hot dog gets a big hand at the party.

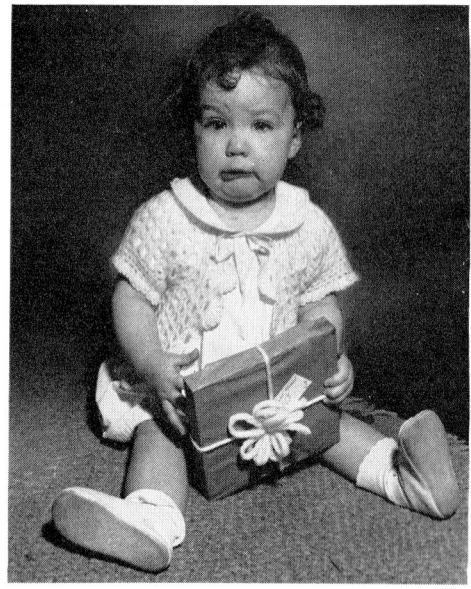

Spotlight on Birthdays

The big national or religious festivals belong to everyone, but there is something specially precious about a birthday. The person whose birthday it is can hold the spotlight for that day. Do not be so afraid of making your children conceited or self-important that you forget that the best way to develop consideration for others is to give a small person a big dose of consideration and importance for himself, once in a while. Then he can afford to let other people have their share, too. Birthdays are the logical time to let a girl or boy be queen or king for a day.

Birthday parties have their place, but it is more fun if there are special family birthday traditions, as well. In some families everybody marches to the birthday breakfast table singing. The presents set out on the table are opened with great ceremony. In one family, the making of decorations for the birthday child's chair is a project for the other children.

The children usually decide that the

A two-year-old may feel slighted when another member of the family gets all the birthday presents. He knows he is not forgotten if he gets a trifle, too.

birthday boy or girl is entitled to choose the day's menus, and perhaps even to be exempt for that one day from the usual household jobs. If that is the tradition, it can apply to Mother and Father, too, when their turns come.

What Kind of Birthday Party?

Small children may find more real pleasure in the simplest party than in something elaborate that adults may choose. Many children under five are likely to be somewhat overwhelmed by large, noisy groups. A dozen three- or four-year-olds can be extremely noisy! The rule of "as many children as you are years old at your birthday party" worked well in one family, until each one reached the age of six. The years from six to nine are the years when birthday parties seem to reach their peak.

Suggestions for the actual carrying-out of the affair can be found in PLANNING A PARTY, in Volume 8. The children should certainly be allowed to choose their own guests and to plan their own parties. The simplest kind of home affair is preferable, under most circumstances, to just taking the children on the block to the movies. A simple gathering of friends at home can give a youngster an idea of what hospitality really means. Children can learn, without anything being said about it, that there are pleasures and values in life over and beyond going to the movies.

What of the Non-Birthday Child?

When Sister holds the spotlight, how shall we keep Brother or another sister from feeling left out? The relative ages of the children will determine how the situation is handled. A preschool child whose younger brother or sister is celebrating may need some small present. Preschool children's memories are short. A three-year-old or four-year-old will not be able to look forward with joyful anticipation to his next birthday, when he will know the sweet taste of being important. Neither will he derive sufficient comfort from remembering the time last year when he was king pin. Some slight gift may prevent hurt feelings and an undesirable outburst. As the children

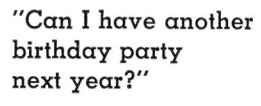

"Can I have another birthday party next year?"

get beyond the age of five, the custom of presents for the brothers or sisters may gradually taper off. In some families it persists, with the birthday boy or girl giving a small gift to brothers and sisters. And what a happy custom that can be!

The part brothers and sisters play in the birthday party again needs to be determined by the relative ages of the children. If they are near in age, there may be no problem at all. They are all part of the party. If they are far enough apart in age, the oldest one, with the consent of the birthday child, may proudly take on the role of master of ceremonies, or may run off the games and generally keep things moving along happily.

The older ones can find satisfaction, too, in preparing the birthday refreshments and decorations for the table, and other surprises.

But there may come a few years when the age difference seems to be all wrong for any useful purpose! The older one may be going through an unpleasantly bossy streak, or may not have the right touch for the master-of-ceremonies role. When the younger is the non-birthday child, he may seem to be in the way. Here is a dilemma, for birthdays rightfully should not banish anyone from the house. One good solution has been to let the non-birthday child invite one friend of his own. These two may elect to have their ice cream or some other favorite dish at a separate table. Eight- or nine-year-old boys with younger sisters may scorn eating in the same room with mere girls, and may retreat to the back steps, with a boon companion and an ice-cream cone. This gives the non-birthday boy a sense of being included, and yet forestalls his being in any way a disrupting or dominating influence.

Surprises for Mother and Father

Some of the best family celebrations are those the children plan for Mother and Father on their birthdays, wedding anniversaries, Mother's Day, or Father's Day. In some families the children always make the gifts themselves. Certainly, a gift made with loving care should be used as well as treasured by the fortunate parent who receives it. In some families the present for Mother or Father, or both, is a new piece played on the piano, or whatever instrument the youngster plays. It might be a playlet put on by all the children, or perhaps a dance by the family's dancers. In some families the children, when they get to be of school age, take over the party for Mother or Father completely. They plan both food and entertainment, invite guests, and act as hosts.

How About the Overambitious Planner?

Of course, such events are not always an unqualified success. Six-, eight-, or ten-year-olds may attempt more than they can handle. They may even plan unwisely. If they make plans that are too ambitious, it is not always necessary to clip their wings. It is good to dream good dreams and have the courage to plan. How else can one grow up? We can be gentle with the planner whose good intentions have not been entirely realized, and generous with praise for the aspects of the affair that were successful.

We can be ready with counsel when it is asked, and yet not take the enterprise out of the children's hands.

Some Occasions Have No Labels

There are some traditional events

Ewing Galloway

Each season brings its own delights. Easter eggs or Jack O'Lanterns, family feasts or religious festivals, can all serve to draw the hearts of parents and children closer together.

J. C. Allen & Son

which are not grand and glorious enough to be called "celebrations." They have no names, but they may be precious nonetheless. These "small" occasions require less effort on the part of adults, but just the presence of parents and relatives increases the children's fun.

Such an event in one family was "Sunday hopscotch." On Sunday afternoons in spring, when uncles, aunts, and cousins gathered at Grandmother's house, the children played hopscotch while the grown-ups watched from the front porch.

This was an occasion to indulge the familiar "look, Mother, watch me," and to encourage friendly applause. Sometimes a grown-up jumped up to take a clumsy, laughable turn or two. As the children's legs grew longer through the years, "one old cat" replaced hopscotch, but the day was still referred to as "Sunday Hopscotch Day."

As years passed, reference to these Sundays was made so often by the children in the three families involved, that it became clear how much the fun and the sense of happy security had been enhanced because the whole clan shared in them. Repetition made them dearer to the children, too. Each spring some child was sure to remark, "Forsythia's out! Time for Sunday hopscotch."

It had become the children's own ritual for welcoming spring and it was precious to them. These small occasions can sometimes mean more than the great big, overwhelming holidays that seem to have grown almost unwieldy.

The Values in Celebrations

Every family will not find its satisfactions in the same kind of celebrations. Surely, it would be pointless to enforce a celebration because some other family enjoys it, or out of a sense of duty. It takes a grown-up who is having a really good time himself to give a good time to a child.

But when occasions are celebrated with warmth and genuine kindness, they bring home the joys of giving and of receiving. They can help children learn that there is an art to receiving graciously, as well as to giving generously.

One small girl said with enthusiasm, "I'm so glad I have another Mary Poppins book just like the one I have. Now if I wear one out, I can read the other." She had already learned a lot about being gracious. She had absorbed it largely, we may safely guess, from the graceful way her mother accepted *another* pot holder from her daughter each Christmas!

The memories of these happy occasions draw the children closer together now, and keep the bonds between them closer in later life. One young married woman wrote to her sister, who was also recently married, "Bert's family doesn't know the first thing about keeping Christmas. But I guess nobody except our own family could do it the right way for us."

Through the years this young family gradually made for itself its own ways of celebrating holidays. They were ways different from either the wife's or the husband's family's ways. But the children in the family came to feel it was the only way to celebrate. As they go out into the world, they will feel that only their brothers and sisters understand what a holiday celebration should be. Of such memories are family traditions made, and through such happy events is family strength increased.

FAMILY VACATIONS

HELEN W. PUNER, A.B.
Author, "Daddies: What They Do All Day," Ossining, N. Y.

Have you ever taken a good look at the word "recreation"? It breaks down into re-creation. Ideally, that is what we all want out of a family vacation. A vacation should be more than a change from routines and obligations. A vacation can and should be the kind of fun and spontaneous enjoyment that is an enrichment and a re-creation of family life.

Vacations like this do not just happen. Good vacations, like good family life in general, need thought and planning. No vacation will be perfect, but there are things you can do to avoid serious disappointments. Your family's attitude toward the holiday plays a greater part in its success than the time or money available.

Vacation Give-and-Take

Often, individual members of a family need and want different kinds of vacations.

A vacation, in the end, is as good as the happiness and satisfaction you feel when you remember it. Your vacation may be a week end or a series of day

Devaney

"Where do we go from here?" Vacation fun starts with planning. When everyone is in on the making of the plans, there is little question but that good traveling will follow.

The great day finally dawns! "Operation Loading" is under way and adventure lies ahead. All aboard!

Ewing Galloway

trips. It may be a two-week stay at a resort, a whole summer in a waterfront bungalow, or a family trip by car across the country. Whatever form it may take, everybody's needs and tastes should be weighed and considered before the final choice is made. Of course, you cannot please everyone, not even everyone in a family, all the time.

In many families, Mother's idea of a perfect vacation is a rest from housework. Dad may pine for a fishing trip, and that involves Mother's cooking the fish! Six-year-old Eddie needs the companionship, not of fish, but of children his own age, for his sister Phoebe is twelve and his brother Bill, ten. Bill wants to do anything that spells *adventure*. Phoebe says she'll die, just *die*, if she can't go off to the work-camp to which her friends Marilyn and Patty are going.

Compromise is called for. But compromise need not necessarily mean the wholesale sacrifice of the parents' desires and rights to the children's. If either parents or children are making great sacrifices, nobody is going to have much fun.

Take what happened to the Moores. Travel-happy Father Moore reluctantly decided that his six-year-old son, Jimmy, really ought to have other children to play with on his vacation. He made up his mind to sacrifice his own inclinations. But martyrdom did not make him agreeable. He was irritable with Jimmy during the two weeks they spent at "Klamber Inn—Bring the Kiddies and Be Carefree." Grumpiness descended like a pall over all three Moores, and none of them look back with any pleasure on that venture!

The Wald family reached a happier solution for all its members. Parents and

176

children decided together that one week would be spent doing what the children wanted. In this case, it was camping out. The second week would be devoted to the kind of traveling the parents relished.

It is not always easy or possible to provide exactly the kind of vacation each member of the family wants or needs. But it *is* always possible to recognize that differences exist. It is possible to try to reach a decision that serves the greatest good of the greatest number. Nobody needs to be a martyr. There is always another summer. In a family that respects the individuality of its members there is a feeling of give-and-take elastic enough to withstand temporary disappointments.

When Are Separate Vacations Wise?

Some years, the best kind of compromise seems to be not to make the vacation a family affair. A family may decide that the most comfortable plan for all concerned is to split up for the holiday.

The Brodericks have two children, Ned, eight, and Maggie, six. There is considerable friction between Ned and Maggie. Last summer the Brodericks sent Ned off to visit a friend for a month. Maggie bloomed, and Mrs. Broderick's temper improved. Ned returned in such a state of well-being that getting Maggie's goat seemed to be a less attractive occupation.

In other families, the center of friction may be between a mother and one of the children, or a father and one of the children.

Children over nine years old may want to get away for a few weeks with friends their own age, and may benefit by the experience. A Scout, YMCA, YWCA, or American Friends' camp might be the answer. If that is not possible, a visit to a friend's house might be arranged, as it was in Ned's case. A summer's stay at a camp, if the family can afford it, often provides a happy time for a child old enough to enjoy separation from his parents.

Parents need to be by themselves at times. A shorter vacation for Mother and Father, with part of the budget spent on a reliable, friendly person to stay with the children, might make everyone happier.

There is strength in union, but the seeds of a fortified solidarity may lie in reunion.

Planning Is Half the Fun

A vacation is one of the best opportunities a family has for really being with one another, instead of living side by side.

Being with your children can begin before the vacation. Even young children can be involved in the family's planning. They can be told about the places you are going and how you will get there. What you expect to see on the way and what you expect to do once you have arrived will make fascinating dinner-table conversation in the weeks before the trip begins.

If your children are older, they can help plan. With a few tips from you, older children can collect travel folders and information. In large cities, department stores often have travel bureaus. Motor clubs, or even gasoline stations, will help you plan the way to go on an automobile trip. Railroad and bus offices and the travel agencies may all be called upon.

Planning together is often nearly as much fun as the vacation itself. The children have a feeling of closeness as the family plans. They gain status as their opinions are asked and their contribution of maps, brochures, and schedules proves useful.

It's a Vacation, Not a Marathon

Too many places, spaces, and faces should not be crowded into your two or three weeks. Children are not capable of absorbing more than a limited number of impressions. Fatigue has spoiled more trips than flat tires or poison ivy.

Allow time for spontaneous side trips, or you may miss the finest adventures.

One family, the Strangs, stopped at every roadside point of interest they encountered. The children saw Gila monsters, abandoned gold mines, roadside geysers, two-headed calves, caverns, and museums, and enough soft-drink dispensing machines to stock a warehouse. During hours of driving, they chatted happily about what wonderful thing was going to turn up next. Of course, the trip across the country took two weeks. Maybe it could have been done in six days if the senior Strangs had been intent on following the crow instead of following the lure of delightful byways. The family had a wonderful time. That, they agreed, was better than the empty satisfaction of achieving a schedule.

Some Rules Hold—Even on Vacations

Some of us unconsciously paint the joys of vacation in such glowing colors that the trip itself is an anticlimax. There will be rainy days on any vacation. There may be bruised knees or the lake may be too cold for the youngest children to enjoy. Mosquitoes, irritating people, and sunburn are always with us!

A good way to prepare a child for what to expect, is to play out situations beforehand. Pretend that the family is already in the dining room of the hotel, or about to breast a wave at the ocean's edge. Perhaps going to sleep in a Pullman berth, or exploring a mountain trail, may be the situation that will be excit-

"You explain it to her."

ing to your child. As you act out the event, you can make it clear that some rules hold—even on vacations.

It is a good idea to discuss privileges, responsibilities, and traveling manners before you set off. If your children know what is expected of them, they are much more likely to conform.

Remember there is a happy medium even in the matter of preparation. Too much planning with the children may prove unduly exciting.

Enjoying the Journey

Places of interest along the way can be pointed out and discussed. You can arm your children, if they are old enough, with simple maps, so they can identify for themselves the new cities or whistle stops they pass. If you go by train, show them how to use timetables. Most children love to check up on how efficiently the locomotive is locomoting. You can get out with them and walk around stations whenever stops are long enough. GAMES FOR TRAVEL, in Volume 8, has a wealth of suggestions for avoiding boredom and the fidgets.

Less Haste Makes More Fun

The Strang family, who traveled across the country and learned the anatomy of every soft-drink machine and Gila monster along the way—or so the senior Strangs thought—illustrated how a long automobile trip can be accomplished happily.

The Strangs started out with the recognition that frequent stops forestall the natural restlessness built into every child. They recognized, too, that frequent snacks serve the same purpose. They armed themselves with sour-balls, potato chips, fruit, and vacuum bottles full of lemonade. They accepted the fact that their children might eat less at regular meals.

They did not forget their daughter's teddy bear, for they knew it would provide familiar comfort for her in the series of unfamiliar beds. They took along a soft ball, a bat, and a jump rope. When they stopped for the night, all four would often have a game of catch before dinner. The physical exercise was a welcome change after hours of sitting, varied only by ambling around the Gila monsters and soft-drink dispensers.

The Strangs tried to get variety into the trip. Where there were caverns and mountain trails to explore, they explored them. Whenever possible, they made a point, too, of selecting a stopping place for the night in a good natural setting. A few nights they just sat and loafed and looked at the scenery and refreshed their spirits.

It would not be true to say that the Strangs never had a cross moment in their two-week trip. The children quarreled now and then. Occasionally they all were hot and tired. Good food or good beds were not always to be found, but the over-all experience was one of pleasure and fun.

Precautions for Health and Safety

There are some basic rules for health, safety, and traveling courtesy that everyone can observe. You know your own children and the special signals they send out when they are beginning to get overtired. Stop driving, or exploring, or sight-seeing before they become overfatigued. If you are suspicious about the drinking water in a strange place, don't drink it. Carry a thermos for emergencies, or order bottled water in a suspect eating-place. Don't allow your babies and young children to drink unpasteurized milk. Avoid eating foods you know spoil easily in hot weather. Observe the rules for regional safety hazards. If you are planning to go to an unfamiliar region, make it your business to find out its danger spots in advance. Write the local Chamber of Commerce. Consult a travel bureau or someone who knows the region well. Don't let your children litter beach fronts, or violate the rules for mountain trails. Never throw trash or lighted cigarettes out of the windows of your car.

It is also wise, if you are visiting an area new to you, to find out about its plants and animals. If you learn to recognize its poisonous plants, its insects, and its ticks, you can take steps to protect yourself and your children. No one swollen to twice his normal size because of poison ivy or insect bites ever had a happy vacation.

While You Are Away

The Lewises took a house on a lake one summer, near other families who had children. Mr. and Mrs. Lewis felt that it was important for Tim who was eight, Linda who was seven, and five-and-a-half-year-old Mike to be near other children. They had chosen the place with foresight. There was a life guard in attendance at the beach all day.

How Can Mother Have a Vacation, Too?

The only fly in the ointment was the fact that Mrs. Lewis was sick and tired of housekeeping. But she was a sensible woman. She used her wits and reduced housekeeping to its simplest.

Laundry was kept at a minimum. There was a silent conspiracy among the mothers around the lake to make seersucker shorts or swimming suits the usual clothing for the children.

Cook-outs were held as often as possible, and two nights a week Tim and Linda took over the supper preparations. The cottage had been chosen with ease of housekeeping in mind. Once you had swept the sand out of the door it looked fairly presentable. Tim and Linda pitched in and helped with the dishes and the beds. They enjoyed bicycling down to the community store to pick up extra groceries or to get the mail.

Mr. Lewis helped, too. Some week ends he took the children off on side trips. One week end he packed his wife off to stay with a friend of hers who happened to be near by. The house was a little dirtier when Mrs. Lewis returned. It cannot be claimed that the children and Mr. Lewis were exactly neat and tidy, either, but everyone had enjoyed the change. Mr. Lewis told his wife later, "I really got to *know* the kids the week end you were away."

Help the Children Feel at Home

If you are spending your vacation in a hotel, select one that welcomes children. Youngsters have a natural tendency to stick to adults and to parrot their behavior in new places. In the long run, the children will be more willing to look out for themselves if you spend the first few days with them. Telling them not to "hang around" is not helpful to anyone. Stay with the children and show them the points of interest. Look around for good spots where they can play safely by themselves. Younger children may need some assistance in making friends with others.

If Your Children Talk to Everyone

"Stop it, Frank! Now don't annoy the man." How often have we heard parents snap at their children this way on train or bus trips!

Most travelers enjoy friendly children. You do not have to be self-conscious if your children make friends with strangers en route. Of course, this does not mean that you should allow them to make pests of themselves. But a friendly move on your children's part is not always an annoyance to the stranger. After all, we talk to those others who are traveling. There is nothing wrong in showing a friendly spirit.

Making Vacations Endure

If you have had a good vacation with your children, the chances are they will never let you forget it. The Strang children acted this way.

To be sure, they did not mention the

trip at all for some months after they returned home. Then reminiscences began to pour out. Now, a year after the trip is over, they sound as if the experience were woven into the fabric of their lives. "When we were on the trip—" one of them will begin. Or, "Remember the lady who said 'Put your nickel in the machine and out comes a cooooool bottle of pop'?"—and they will dissolve into the same giggles they giggled when first they heard this remark.

The Records Speak for Themselves

The Strangs took pictures as they wound their way across the country. Often now, on rainy days, the children take out the album and spend a happy afternoon re-creating the trip. Jim Strang kept a record of all the new and unfamiliar kinds of gasoline he encountered on the way. This gasoline log is still one of his treasured possessions. He entered it, with its crayoned illustrations of gas stations, in his school hobby show last year. Both children are delighted when they come across books set in regions they have seen. Somehow, the information in these books is more wonderful and more easily remembered than the information in others. Many of the pictures they draw and the stories they tell draw inspiration from the trip. So, too, with much of the play acting they do.

The trip was fun, and the experience has been kept fresh for them all. Undoubtedly it will continue to live in their minds and hearts. The vacation has become a never-to-be-forgotten part of their life together as a family. It was a happy time which brought them all closer together. Their adventures proved to be the kind of true *re-creation* of family life a good vacation can and does provide.

A. Devaney; Bell and Howell

These are sights they will never forget and events it will be pleasant to remember in the years to come.

THE FAMILY KEEPS RECORDS

MARJORIE K. REYNOLDS
Author of Magazine Articles, Indianapolis, Ind.

WHEN our parents were children, and for hundreds of years before that, the Family Bible was the place where information about various members of the family usually was kept. Dates of births, deaths, and marriages were carefully set down, and made available for future reference.

This is still a good custom, but there are other kinds of information as well that are so important or delightful to preserve that a fuller record is desirable. Such a record might be called a *Family Log*. On every voyage the captain keeps a record of the most important events. This is called the *Ship's Log*. The Family Log would do the same thing—keep a record of main events. In most homes, space is at a premium, so a family needs to travel light as far as its records are concerned.

Each family may have its own ideas about keeping records, and, indeed, there are infinite possibilities. Undoubtedly, some variations will occur to you as you think about the suggestions made in this chapter.

You can buy all kinds of record books, but it is more fun and less expensive to make your own. A Family Log can be kept in any kind of expandable loose-leaf notebook. For obvious reasons, you will want to use only one side of each page. The covers and the decoration can be as simple or as elaborate as suits your family's taste. The Log does not necessarily take the place of the usual baby book that records the progress of each individual child, although it may do so. Usually families find a Log Book a good way to keep the records that concern the whole family, as well as the information that has permanent value.

Some Vital Facts and Dates

We live in a complicated world where it is all too easy to become snarled in red tape. Did you ever try to replace a missing birth certificate? You can save yourself endless trouble if you make sure that problem, and others like it, will never arise. Let us suppose you start your family record, or Log Book, with the essentials, and then take it from there in the directions that appeal to you.

Begin with the vital statistics. Put in your marriage license and each child's

The Family Keeps Records

Our Family Group

Father:
  Birthplace and date: _____
  Parents: _____
  Brothers and sisters: _____

Mother:
  Birthplace and date: _____
  Parents: _____
  Brothers and sisters: _____

Add as many records as may be necessary or desirable.

We were married at: _____
Date and hour: _____
We were married by: _____
Members of the bridal party: _____

Our Children:
  Name: _____
  Where born: _____
  Date and day: _____
  Time: _____
  Weight: _____
  Hospital: _____
  Doctor: _____

birth certificate. Attach them in such a way that they can be taken out easily. Better still, use photostats of the birth certificates in the Log Book and put the originals in the safest place you have for valuable papers.

It is not always easy to remember the names of various churches or synagogues to which the family has belonged. This is especially true if the father's work has made it necessary for the family to live in different towns. You may even want to remember the name of the minister, priest, or rabbi.

You will want to record all kinds of other information for future reference. You may want to remember when and where each of your children was baptized, christened, or blessed. Who are the child's godparents? When was he confirmed and when did he take his first communion?

Churches We Have Attended

CHURCH	PLACE	STATE	DATES	PASTOR
St. Luke's	River Park	Ill.	1948–1954	Rev. J. Goodfellow
Trinity	Madison	N. J.	1954–	Rev. John Hall

Church Records

(You can adapt this to the ceremonies of your own faith)

CHILDREN	BAPTIZED CHRISTENED BLESSED	PASTOR OR RABBI	GODFATHER	GODMOTHER	CONFIRMATION	FIRST COMMUNION
John	St. Patrick's March 5, 1940	Rev. A. L. Brogman	E. Murphy	J. Cassidy	St. Patrick's April 2, 1954	St. Patrick's April 7, 1954
Ann						

Before your babies are a year old, they will probably have had immunization for whooping cough and vaccination for smallpox. Immunization for diphtheria will come along in the early years and then, possibly, protection from tetanus.

There are many times in their lives when it will be important for your children to know exactly when they were given inoculations and vaccines. It is all too easy to forget or to become confused. If you devote one section of your Log to "Health Data" you can keep there this essential information, with the dates, or paste in the certificates your doctor, clinic, or health department gives you. You will have the facts all together and easily available if the children enter a new school or go to camp, or if there should be an epidemic, and evidence of immunization is needed. Then, too, if you have the dates clear you know when "booster shots" or additional immunizations should be attended to.

You Can't Trust Your Memory

You will find it equally necessary to keep a permanent record of when each child had such diseases as measles, mumps, and chickenpox. "It will be a long time before I forget this siege,"

Records of Immunization

DISEASE	JOHN Date	LOIS Date	ANN Date	BILL Date
Whooping Cough				
Smallpox Vac. (1)				
Vac. (2)				
Diphtheria				
Booster				
Tetanus				
Booster (1)				
Booster (2)				
Typhoid				
Temporary Immun. (1)				
Immun. (2)				
Other Immun. (1)				
Immun. (2)				
Immun. (3)				

one mother declared, after nursing her children through severe cases of measles. Ten years later she was amazed to find herself unable to recall whether the baby had caught the disease at the same time or whether it was just a cold he had that same week.

You need to have these facts straight every time you fill out one of those admission blanks or questionnaires about the children—and how many each one of us fills out in the course of a lifetime! After the children are grown, the information may be even more valuable to them.

If your family enjoys figures, you may want to keep a record of each child's physical development, emphasizing the many "firsts" in each baby's life. His

Record of Illnesses

DISEASE	JOHN Date	LOIS Date	ANN Date	BILL Date
Chickenpox				
Whooping Cough				
Mumps				
Measles				
Scarlet Fever				

The occasions you want to remember, the facts you need to preserve, are always at hand if you keep a Log.

Ewing Galloway

first smile, his first tooth, the first step, the first words are all interesting to look back upon. The dates on which they occurred are forgotten all too soon. Yearly growths in height and weight are interesting, too, but how much of this you keep in the Log Book will depend on how record-minded a family you are.

"State the Schools You Attended"

"Give names and dates of all schools you attended." Here is another direction that appears on all those information blanks and questionnaires. "Can't any of you remember the name of the school Paul went to the year we lived in Riverside?" "Was Rosemary in school when the rest of you went to that wonderful school in Oak Grove?" The answers to these questions might make a real difference some day. Be sure there is a space in your Log Book marked "Schools," and that the dates that each child entered and left are duly put down. It might be helpful to have the principal's name, too.

You may want to keep a page for camps the children go to. Such a record has real meaning to the boys and girls, even though no one may ask them to produce it in later years.

The Log Is a Link with the Past

In this country, we are not, as a people, particularly concerned with our ancestors. Interest in family trees is the exception rather than the rule. We may carry this so far that in this day of widely-separated relatives the children know almost nothing about their grandparents, and less about great-grandparents. This data has more than purely sentimental value. It should probably be considered in the "necessary information" department. At any rate, a simple diagram, showing the names and dates of birth and death of at least the parents, the brothers or sisters, and probably the grandparents and great grand-

Schools Attended

NAME	SCHOOL	TOWN	DATE ENTERED	DATE LEFT	PRINCIPAL
John	Highland	River Park	Sep., 1950	June, 1954	James McNeill

parents of the mother and father in the family, is interesting and almost indispensable. Again, those questionnaires and information blanks are always asking for these facts.

Aside from the strictly practical value, such a diagram gives the children a sense of having some roots. It can increase the sense of belonging. It can strengthen the ties with relatives.

It might be well to record, too, the jobs or positions Father has held. Mother's jobs may be included, if she has worked. Names and addresses of employers may be confused or forgotten, and certainly belong with the important information.

It's Fun to Remember

In addition to the information that is necessary, there is a great deal that is worth keeping for the sheer pleasure it can give you. As the family grows, the records grow along with it. Some families make a hobby of keeping a written record of precious moments. The story of a vacation, jotted down along the way, can be delightful reading around the fire on winter nights. Along with the account of things seen and done—and if the children have a part in it you can be sure things eaten will be included—Father may enjoy keeping a record of how many miles to the gallon "we got out of the old bus."

Family celebrations and family projects may make equally good subjects for records. Where did we eat Thanksgiving dinner two years ago? Was Grandpa here for Christmas four years ago? These and a host of other questions are difficult to answer correctly as time passes. Records, when carefully kept, will leave no room for guesswork.

Not every family likes to keep its records in written words. Clippings, programs, announcements, invitations, place cards, even receipted bills may tell the story well for some people.

Of course, pictures are indispensable. Snapshots serve the purpose admirably, but pictures the children draw themselves—or that Mother and Father draw—are even more personal and revealing.

In addition to a place for pictures of the family and their friends, you would want in the record book a place for pictures of the houses the family has lived in. At the rate most of us move about, that could be quite a revealing story.

Family Vacations

WHEN	WHERE WE WENT	HOW WE TRAVELED	MILES TRAVELED	WHO WENT	WEATHER
May 15–30, 1954	Great Smoky Mts.	By car	690	Mother, Father, John	

Special Occasions

OCCASION	DATE	WHERE CELEBRATED	GUESTS
Thanksgiving	1953	Grandpa Dunn's	Us and Uncle Jim's family
Christmas	1953	at home	Grandpa and Grandma Dunn; Aunt Emily

Memories will stay bright for years if you tell the story in pictures.

Houses We Lived in

```
Leave
Space
for
Snapshot
```

Address: _____

We lived here from August, 1947, to May, 1948.

The house was built of brick and had five rooms, all on one floor.

What we liked best about the house was: It was new when we moved in and it had a built-in breakfast nook.

The Children Are the Authors

Let the children compose the captions under the pictures of the houses in which you have lived or the pictures of people and events. You may be surprised at their telling comments!

Stories of family experiences told in the children's own words are always a delight. Sometimes it is fun to tell the story in rhyming doggerel or in a song parody. The smaller youngsters can dictate their contributions. When they are able to write their own impressions of family celebrations or undertakings, they can be encouraged to set down their ideas in the Log Book.

Keeping records should never be a drill in penmanship, spelling, or composition. The best kind of record is the natural, spontaneous one, complete with misspelled words, ink blobs, and some dubious grammar. Enthusiasm is better than accuracy, and interest is more to be prized than great neatness, in young authors and artists.

The collecting and the pasting-up of items for the Log Book can be the special responsibility and joy of the children. Perhaps a few bits will be pasted askew, but that is no great fault.

"If I'd Only Written It Down!"

How often do you or some other member of the family exclaim, "I wish I'd written that down. I just can't remember." Different kinds of information are of value to different families, but many kinds can have a place in the Log Book. One family liked to remember friends they made on their travels —a list that came in handy in sending out Christmas cards. Another family found it useful to write down in the Log Book the names and addresses of such family helpers as sitters, seamstresses, and "yard men."

Still another household found that, by pasting each year's Christmas-gift list in a place provided in their particular book, they could avoid making a tea cozy for Aunt Sophie three years in a row, or duplicating the game sent to the small cousins.

Another family kept the three or four choicest Christmas cards received each year in the Log Book as a remembrance of that particular Christmas.

Some families like to make a guest book a part of their permanent record.

How Can You Keep Interest in a Log?

You cannot nor need you try to maintain the whole family's interest in keeping the record at an even pitch. Some years will see more recorded than others. One member of the family may be immensely interested for a time and then turn it over to a brother or sister. Mother and Father take responsibility for the essential facts, but, beyond that, interest can be the guide.

With a little planning, the keeping-up of the Family Log can be woven into family activities. If Mother or Father has a good sense of timing, he or she will bring out the Log Book at one of those "What Shall I Do Now?" moments. Being allowed to page through the Log Book may stimulate a boy's or girl's interest in working at it, too, and the youngest may catch up on what happened before he was born.

Then, too, the record may change with the family's tastes and interests. There is more than one good way to keep a record, or to keep records.

A Log Reinforces Solidarity

The family that works on such records as a hobby is likely to be an intimate group with that precious feeling of security, closeness, and unity that families, and only families, can provide. The opportunity of working side by side, doing something that includes all members of family, is not offered by many activities. Emphasizing the common background and common heritage forges links that will tend to be strong, no matter how great the distance between the members of the family may be. The record keeps alive happy moments that might be lost in the hustle of everyday existence. It can provide something, too, for each taste. The practical person interested in facts and figures, the dreamer interested in embroidering on those facts, and the artistic one who likes to make the facts, the figures, and the dreams come alive through pictures or well-arranged mementos—all contribute when the family keeps a record.

READING TOGETHER

JEAN BETZNER, Ph.D.
Visiting Professor of Education,
Queens College, New York, N. Y.

READING together can be enjoyed by every member of the family. All who like to read know well the great pleasure found in exploring the infinite variety in the world of books.

In literature one can find the familiar in pictures and words, the past presented briefly or in detail, the future suggested. Books can open new worlds, stimulate imagination, give understanding of other people and their ways of living. Books even make possible a keener understanding of one's self. Book friends can be depended upon through life, and without doubt their value is increased because they can be shared.

Enriching Family Life

In a family where book friends have come alive, communication takes on a new richness. One eight-year-old came into his mother's kitchen on a glorious spring afternoon announcing, "It's a regular 'mole and rat' day."

"So it is," said his mother.

At this point a neighbor who happened to be present, broke in, mystified, "Whatever are you two talking about?"

"You know, the kind of a day the Water Rat and Mole had their picnic in *The Wind in the Willows*," explained the eight-year-old.

All families do not find reading equally rewarding. Some people find other means useful for high-lighting the advantages of doing and being together. Travel, construction, working with creative materials, and other shared pursuits build similar bonds and may frequently accompany or stimulate reading together. Surely, among the various activities through which families are finding enrichment, reading together is worth trying.

How Shall We Begin?

The ideal setting does not happen often. The phone rings, the potatoes boil over, and the baby cries. But in spite of interruptions and distractions, reading together is well worth the effort.

An essential ingredient is time, even a small amount of time. A comfortable spot—probably a welcoming lap and the security of two strong arms—and someone who wants to share the moment of being together in that spot are really all it takes to begin. The sound of a familiar loving voice and the frequent reference to the small person make the moment of great importance. The accompanying pictures, with their additional meanings, help him conclude that this is good.

Later, the sight of the book, the empty lap, the sound of the voice, the picture, or the spot may remind this little one that he likes being read to. Clutching the book he makes his uncertain way to that familiar voice and demands a repeat performance.

Reading Is Where You Find It

The question, "Can I take the time for this now?" must be faced. If a child came asking to have zippers zipped or shoes tied, the answer might come more quickly, because the necessity is clearer.

"You're droning again."

But it is doubtful that it is greater. Certainly, if one wishes children to grow up loving books and reading, one must be willing to arrange time for this learning.

The setting for reading together varies with the nature of family life. In some families, the precious quarter- or half-hour before the children's bedtime is made memorable through the shared enjoyment of reading together. In other families, happy memories accumulate about the reading aloud as an accompaniment to household tasks such as shelling peas, washing dishes, ironing, or sewing. In still other families one finds Father and Mother, after the day's absence from the family, picking up the loose ends broken by separation, and renewing their touch with each member under the spell of a common experience.

A day under trees and sky, at the shore or in the woods, a pause in the day's motor journey, a high note in a family celebration, or a brief respite from pain or anxiety can be lifted from the commonplace by those who have in mind the endless delights in reading together. When parents believe that this is worth doing, they provide the time or just seize it, so that members of the family may become accustomed to sharing the riches found in books with one another.

Happy By-Products for Adults

Fortunately for adults and children alike, the appeal of many children's books is not limited by age. In fact, the boys and girls have claimed as their own many stories and poems planned originally to appeal to grown-ups. Intriguing situations such as Robinson Crusoe's, Heidi's, and the Pied Piper's capture the interest of old and young alike. A good horse or dog story, another interpretation of the adventures of Daniel Boone, an account of the limitless powers of Paul Bunyan, the sound advice of James James Morrison Morrison Weatherby George Dupree, or the nonsense of the "Courtship of the Jongy-

Story time is the finest hour for all ages. Family unity grows when delight in books is shared from day to day.

Bongy Bo" or the "Yarn of the Nancy Bell" find willing listeners of different ages.

The portrayal of children's life with its pleasures, misunderstandings, difficulties, and struggles is accurately and vividly set forth in their books. Acquaintance with these serves as another means of understanding the difficulties and triumphs of those children who are nearest and dearest. In fact, such true-to-life characters as Carolyn Haywood's Little Eddie or Eleanor Estes' Moffats are worth several stout volumes of child psychology.

One cannot know children, or be in their company even for a short time, and fail to be caught up in their enthusiasm for the world about them. They readily communicate their wonder and their direct approach for finding answers. Their naïve and partial explanations and interpretations open the door for the fuller and more appropriate answers of the adult.

When children are being helped to explore, to understand, and to know, adults are always challenged.

The rewards are intangible but nevertheless real. Who would forego the companionships, the friendships, the fresh outlooks, and the deepened convictions that accompany exploration in books with children?

When Should They Read Alone?

Children enjoy demonstrating their ability to manage a newly-acquired skill or to exhibit a much-sought independence. Children want to and should do much of their own reading. As soon as they show an inclination to interpret printed symbols, this attempt should be respected and encouraged. The freedom and power which comes with the ability to wander at will through the world of print is too rewarding to be thwarted by any lesser values.

Reading for yourself does not need to mean reading alone. The family's reading together provides the perfect setting for the small one to take his part in this shared pleasure.

One six-year-old who was encouraged to take her turn in reading to the family, made her contribution at first with obvious effort and only with considerable assistance, for she usually chose something that was not easy for her. As the group accepted her reading she became proud of her attainments. She could be heard many an afternoon trying out

Each to her own taste! They may not always like the same books, but looking at books is always companionable.

on the doll family something she would read in the more critical circle of brothers, sisters, Mother, and Father later in the day.

The shared reading aloud of all members of the family, both young and old, sets up for children definite standards in reading, and furnishes goals. One busy mother unconsciously set such a standard for her small daughter. The mother read to the child on many occasions as she ironed. Later, when her teacher complimented the little girl on her progress in learning to read, she quickly responded, "Oh! I don't read well yet. Just you wait until you see me read and iron."

Understanding Their Tastes

Children do not conform to expectations or to any precise patterns in anything they do. They must grow, each in his own way, and out of the selections each makes from the world that lies about him. No child can be his mother or father all over again, in taste and preference or in conclusions and values.

With each succeeding year there are books from which children can make their choices. In this fast-moving world, it is no wonder that children do not follow their parents' tastes exactly.

"How *could* you have liked *Little Women*, Mom? It's positively *sappy*," says a ten-year-old who has no more connection with the world of Louisa Alcott than with the world of the ancient Greeks. And even the *mother* of today's ten-year-old may confess that she read Alcott, and perhaps some of the other so-called "children's classics," under pressure from *her* mother.

Some books are, of course, timeless, and the books from long, long ago may have more to say to a child of today than the books of a generation recently past.

Suit Reading to the Listener

You need to live with children to learn to know their individual reading tastes. Broadly speaking, the youngest children want to hear about themselves, about the things and people around them. They respond to definite rhythm and pleasing sound, and both prose and poetry delight them. As children grow, they move out with curiosity into farther-away times and places. Before one is quite aware of their expanding interests, they are seeking tales of fancy, adventure, and danger, all highly improbable. But at the same time, in other moods, they give eager attention to specific and exact information that keeps them in touch with their own everyday affairs. The struggles of mankind as set forth in folk tales with their simple structure and clear-cut characterizations can generally be relied upon to hold an audience of mixed ages. Ballads and humorous narrative poems make their appeal much as do music and songs.

Why Do Young Children Want Repetition?

There is a great deal for young children to grasp in even the simplest stories. They are attempting to get hold of and manage the ideas that are there, and the business of doing this is agreeable. We accept the young child's satisfaction in having familiar objects about him and in enjoying familiar routines at the same time he is making mild advances into the less familiar. Grown-ups may grow weary of the Gingerbread Boy or even of "Little Toot" or "Ask Mr. Bear" on the fifty-ninth reading; but for the three-, four-, or five-year-old it is a chance to be sure he really understands all the wonders of the tale.

How Shall We Choose?

With so little time for the many activities that can enrich family life, one wishes to be certain that the time given to reading together is used profitably. There are many guides to help in selecting stories and poems for reading aloud. CHILDCRAFT has furnished just such a service in BUILDING A HOME LIBRARY, the next chapter in this volume. STORIES FOR YOUNG CHILDREN are discussed in Volume 13.

Local, school, public, and state libraries; organizations such as American Library Association, Association for Childhood Education International, National Council of Teachers of English, as well as others, make available not only excellent current annotated lists of children's books but excellent personal help and advice. In Volume 14 you will find a chapter on MAKING THE MOST OF YOUR PUBLIC LIBRARY which will suggest ways of using the library's services. Current book reviews in book sections of newspapers and magazines can be studied by all reading members of the family. Anyone who has access to that all too rare but precious source, the friendly bookshop, knows well the services rendered through the opportunities for browsing and seeking advice.

But there is another source through which quality in books is disclosed. That is in the tastes of the members of the family. In reading together, each has a chance to share the best he has with the others, in terms of its suitability to them. Each person's taste is revealed in what he shares. Probably at this point the greatest value of reading together lies. This means of knowing what those closest to one find good, and believe to be of service to others, is a good way of insuring common understand-

Devaney

When they enjoy a fascinating tale together, everything else is forgotten.

ings and strengthening family ties. One six-year-old became something of a hero in the family because he discovered that remarkable lady, Mary Poppins. The ten-year-old who introduced her parents to *Charlotte's Web* gained practically the stature of a literary critic.

No fairy tale worth reading aloud is set in the realm of pure fancy. In fact, a well-constructed tale which reaches farthest into the field of fancy has most realistic boundaries. Only by destroying the hedge of caution, fear, and the unknown was it possible for Sleeping Beauty's prince to waken her from the sleep of fear, revenge, and disobedience. Hans Andersen in his story of *The Nightingale* is giving the lucky reader another chance to see again that the true glory of nature cannot be reproduced. Many ideas lifted out of the blurred vision of realism are made clearer and hence more significant when treated imaginatively.

It is the children of six years and older who find the greatest delight in fairy tales. For the smaller ones, it is harder to keep the fanciful and the real separated.

Are Fairy Tales Confusing?

One need not fear that children will be made unable to distinguish truth from untruth by an extensive exposure to and use of books. When a group is reading together, some member is bound to question the probability or authenticity of the matter in hand. It is then that the importance of an imaginative as well as a realistic approach to life can be made clear.

Can Reading Hold Its Own?

Radio and television, the modern instruments for bringing literature to children, are real competitors for the family story hour. If one would use some of the same inducements for reading together that are present in these modern instruments, much of the competition would disappear. The regularity and dependability found in the radio program, the television show, the motion-picture theater, and the comics are appealing to boys and girls.

No one compels the child to look, listen, or read, and no disapproval attends his failure to do any one of the three. Alone, practically unaided, he can find what he wants, use it as he will, and dismiss it without embarrassment. The chapter Radio and Television, in Volume 15, discusses in detail radio and television in our children's lives.

The variety of material, its contemporary quality, and the fact that much of what is heard, gazed upon, and read is the coin of exchange among one's friends, all combine to make a tremendous appeal to children, especially of school age.

There may be times when reading as a family will seem to be losing out. There may be even less of it than there was a few generations ago, but reading together can offer the same attractions as do radio and TV, and even more. The chance to share in reading, to plan for such times, to include one's special friends on occasion, to talk things over where one feels comfortable and is not afraid of being misunderstood—all these are too much prized by children to be easily cast aside. No mechanical device can really replace the personal, intimate quality of the small face-to-face group, aware of the flexibility for adjustment to the needs of those present, and trying in all earnestness to give of their best.

BUILDING A HOME LIBRARY

ANNIS DUFF
Author, "Bequest of Wings," Scarsdale, N. Y.

THE books that are gradually assembled on the shelves in a home are evidence not only of the tastes and interests of the people who live there, but of their growth in companionship.

The building of a family collection of books is fun. It is subject to no hard and fast rules. Its only purpose is to give pleasure and satisfaction to a special group of people living together in their own special way.

Choosing the Books

A limited budget can be a great advantage. The need for careful spending often focuses attention on the really choice books that give long-lasting enjoyment, and these are by no means necessarily the most expensive. It is better to have ten books that are really loved and used, than a hundred that serve only as a display in the living-room bookcase.

A family library can afford to grow slowly, especially at its start. One of the best ways of helping it grow is to make sure books you will want to keep are included in the birthday and Christmas lists for each of the children. Another way to make a timely addition might be to let a boy or girl go to the bookshop with you. Browsing and choosing for oneself can make the book selected especially dear.

Little children do not need, nor can they enjoy, a great many books. They love to look at the same books, and listen to the same stories, over and over again. It is wise to start off with a few books that have pictures and text that wear well for both the listener and the grown-up who reads aloud.

No great knowledge or experience is needed to find such books. To a new child every book is new, so it is safe and sensible to choose the first ones from among the time-tested favorites. A good edition of *Mother Goose*, for example, is a fine cornerstone for any family library.

Reading and looking at books with a child is the happiest way there is of learning to recognize the book qualities that have lasting appeal. Familiarity with books of proved quality is a great help to parents in judging the quality of unfamiliar books for any child.

How Can You Decide What to Buy?

A good deal of "sampling" is necessary, for the sake of widening children's reading interests, and to discover their preferences. Generous use of the public library is highly recommended wherever it is possible. It provides opportunities for extensive and varied reading, and is a sure and inexpensive way for children to find out what books they really want to have "for keeps."

Some families have no library near enough for regular borrowing. There are often services available from state and county libraries to help in book selection. Sometimes there are bookmobiles. Always there are good booklists. In most cases, advice by letter to individuals asking for information about books to fit specific situations is available from the state or county libraries. It is a good plan to find out from the nearest state library what is available in your locality.

Reference Books Are Basic

No matter how children differ in their tastes in pleasure reading, they are all the same in one respect. They ask questions! Every family should own certain basic reference books so that reliable answers can be forthcoming at the moment of need.

A good standard dictionary is essential, preferably one that gives word derivations. An encyclopedia is a sound investment.

A sound, well-written book on physiology is invaluable in answering children's inevitable questions about the structure and functions of their own bodies. *How Your Body Works* by Herman and Nina Schneider (Scott, 1949) would be a good choice.

Other reference books may be added as children develop special interests. Any keen and active interest, from stamp collecting to baseball, is stimulated by reading a good book about it. Public libraries constantly supply information about good books on children's hobbies. If your local library is unable to make suggestions, a request by letter to any large city library may bring a satisfactory reply.

The business of finding the right books for pleasure and to satisfy growing appetites for learning is bound to require a certain amount of effort. The time to make the effort is when the child has the urge to know. There are few endeavors that yield such rewards in companionship and lasting joy.

Books About Children's Reading

These books tell what kinds of books to look for, how to find them, and how to introduce them successfully to children.

Bequest of Wings, a Family's Pleasures with Books. ANNIS DUFF. Viking, 1944. One family's companionship in enjoyment of books, art, and music. Booklists.

Children and Books. MAY HILL ARBUTHNOT.

Scott Foresman, 1947. Sympathetic discussions of a wide range of reading interests, with penetrating comments on related subjects such as the comics, radio, movies. Booklists.

Reading with Children. ANNE THAXTER EATON. Viking, 1940. Long, rich experience as a librarian working with children gives warmth and practical usefulness to a book that deals with almost every phase of young people's reading. Booklists.

Unreluctant Years, The; a Critical Approach to Children's Literature. LILLIAN H. SMITH. A. L. A., 1953. A guide to basic qualities of good literature.

Booklists and Reviews

The New York Public Library compiles each year a list of "Children's Books Suggested as Gifts." The Chicago Public Library *Book Bulletin* for each November is devoted to children's books. Both are available on request, with a stamped, self-addressed envelope. Your own library may have such lists, too.

The leading newspapers in most large cities carry reviews of the new books for children, especially during the pre-Christmas season. The New York *Times* and the New York *Herald Tribune* have especially good, comprehensive children's book review sections in the spring and during Book Week in November.

The Horn Book Magazine has excellent annotated current booklists in each of its six issues a year, and a variety of authoritative articles on children's reading.

Books for the Family Library

The following lists are intended to suggest the variety of good books for children in age groups up to ten years. The purpose is to satisfy and supplement tastes and curiosities aroused by those who enjoy the stories, poems, and information in CHILDCRAFT. A list of books is necessarily limited. Not all children like the same books at the same ages. Titles are grouped under the age span at which children usually begin to enjoy the books, but enjoyment, as a rule, continues beyond the age indicated. It is wise to allow your own knowledge of a child's interests and ability to guide the selection of books for purchase. Lists of books will also be found at the ends of chapters in Volumes 7 and 8 of CHILDCRAFT.

For Children Two to Four

Mother Goose Rhymes. Many satisfactory editions are available, varying in the number of rhymes included, in size, shape, illustration, general make-up, and price. The two following are especially recommended:

Real Mother Goose, The. BLANCHE FISCHER WRIGHT, illustrator. new ed. Rand McNally, 1941. Over three hundred rhymes and many colored illustrations in this large flat volume.

Ring o' Roses; A Nursery Rhyme Picture Book. LEONARD LESLIE BROOKE, illustrator. Warne, 1922. The choicest of all collections, with pictures that are a never-ending delight. A wonderful first item for the family library.

Alphabet Books. *A B C Bunny.* WANDA GÁG. Coward-McCann, 1933. Every letter is an adventure for Bunny, who goes frisking down from A to Z in pictures alive with fun and action. *A-Apple Pie.* KATE GREENAWAY. Warne, 1928. new ed. An old classic.

Angus and the Ducks. MARJORIE FLACK. Doubleday, 1930. About a mischievous and lovable Scottie whose curiosity got him into trouble. *Angus and the Cat.* 1931. *Ask Mr. Bear.* 1932.

Friendly Animals, The. LOUIS SLOBODKIN. Vanguard, 1944. Easy jingles and three-color pictures of dogs, cats, and other friends.

Jeanne-Marie Counts Her Sheep. FRANÇOISE (FRANÇOISE SEIGNOBOSC). Scribner, 1951. A delightful first counting book, with charming lifelike pictures of a little girl and her pet sheep. *Thank You Book, The.* 1947.

Johnny Crow's Garden. LEONARD LESLIE BROOKE. Warne, 1904. Most wonderful nonsense about animals in gay little jingles with beautiful playful pictures. *Johnny Crow's Party.* 1907. *Johnny Crow's New Garden.* 1935.

Look! ZHENYA GAY. Viking, 1952. Charming baby animals scamper across the pages, inviting little children to listen to the rhymes. The best invitation of all comes at the end.

Where's the Bunny? RUTH ROBINSON CARROLL. Oxford, 1950. The puppy plays hide-and-seek with the bunny in this picture storybook.

For Children Four to Six

All Together; a Child's Treasury of Verse. DOROTHY KEELEY ALDIS. Putnam, 1952. Selections from her previously published volumes.

Bears on Hemlock Mountain, The. ALICE DALGLIESH. Scribner, 1952. There are no bears on hemlock mountain, tramped Jonathan's feet, but—. Helen Sewell's illustrations are the perfect accompaniment for this tale based on an American legend.

Biggest Bear, The. LYND KENDALL WARD. Houghton, 1952. The author-artist has brought humor and imagination into both pictures and story in this worthy recipient of the Caldecott medal.

Billy and Blaze. C. W. ANDERSON. Macmillan, 1936. A favorite story of a little boy and his pony.

Caldecott Picture Books. RANDOLPH CALDECOTT. 2d ed. Warne, 1928. Favorite old stories illustrated by a great artist, with humor, beauty, and all the detailed simplicity that children love.

Cock, the Mouse, and the Little Red Hen, The. FELICITE LEFEVRE (MARGARET SMITH-MASTERS). Macrae Smith, 1945. The old story of the clever little hen who saved her companions from the wicked fox. It is full of the repetitions that little children love.

Complete Nonsense Book. EDWARD LEAR. Dodd, 1943. Century-old nonsense in rollicking verse that never wears out its surprise.

Curious George Takes a Job. HANS AUGUSTO REY. Houghton, 1947. When the pet monkey escapes from the zoo, he has a riotous time.

Fishing Cat, The. GRAYCE SILVERTON MYERS. Abingdon-Cokesbury, 1953. How Old John's cat Skipper caught the fish when Old John was hurt, with storytelling pictures by Paul Galdone.

Golden Goose Book, The. LEONARD LESLIE BROOKE. Warne, 1906. "The Golden Goose," "The Three Bears," and "The Three Little Pigs" in a beautiful book with pictures that simply couldn't be better.

Happy Easter. KURT WIESE. Viking, 1952. A humorous story of colored chickens emerging from colored eggs.

Little Boy Brown. ISOBEL HARRIS. Lippincott, 1949. Pictures and text describe the delight of a city child who spends a day in the country.

Little Tim and the Brave Sea Captain. EDWARD ARDIZZONE. Oxford, 1936. A small boy goes to sea, weathers a wreck, and comes home in triumph. Story and pictures are a delight.

Little Toot. HARDIE GRAMATKY. Putnam, 1939. A lazy little tugboat makes a heroic rescue and learns that it's fun to help with the world's work.

Little Train, The. LOIS LENSKI. Oxford, 1940. Sheer delight for little boys! *Little Auto, The.* 1934. *Cowboy Small.* 1949.

Magic Michael. LOUIS SLOBODKIN. Macmillan, 1944. Hilarious account of a small boy who imagines himself to be many things and many people. *Clear the Track for Michael's Magic Train.* Macmillan, 1945.

Make Way for Ducklings. ROBERT McCLOSKEY. Viking, 1941. A friendly Irish policeman sees Mr. and Mrs. Mallard and their eight ducklings safely through traffic in the city of Boston. Funny and beautiful. Caldecott medal winner.

Mike Mulligan and His Steam Shovel. VIRGINIA LEE BURTON. Houghton, 1939. A perfect story for little boys, with a steam shovel as heroine. *Katy and the Big Snow.* 1943

Millions of Cats. WANDA GÁG. Coward, 1928. The little old man couldn't decide which was the prettiest cat, so he came home with "hundreds of cats, thousands of cats, millions and billions and trillions of cats."

Mr. T. W. Anthony Woo. MARIE HALL ETS. Viking, 1951. A small mouse joins forces with a dog and a cat to keep peace in the house where they live with a gentle old cobbler.

Mittens. CLARE NEWBERRY. Harper, 1936. You can almost feel the softness of the fur in the pictures of a little boy's lost kitten.

One Morning in Maine. ROBERT McCLOSKEY. Viking, 1952. Sally loses her first tooth on a sparkling, blowy day in Maine, and gets her wish. Distinguished pictures full of humor and beauty. *Blueberries for Sal.* 1948.

Poppy Seed Cakes, The. MARGERY CLARK. Doubleday, 1924. The lively adventures of Andrewshek, full of excitement and laughter.

Prayer for a Child. RACHEL FIELD. Macmillan, 1944. Lovely, gentle pictures of a child at home make this beautiful prayer very real to children. Caldecott medal winner. Illus. by E. J. Jones.

Real Santa Claus, The. MARGUERITE WALTERS. Lothrop, 1950. Too many Santas at street corners can puzzle a small youngster, but this explanation is just right for meeting the problem.

Red Light, Green Light. GOLDEN MACDONALD. Doubleday, 1944. The rules of safety deftly taught in a delightful story with beautiful pictures by Leonard Weisgard. *Little Lost Lamb.* 1945.

Story of Babar, The. JEAN DE BRUNHOFF. reissue. Random House, 1937. Gay and amusing adventures of a little elephant, with enchanting childlike pictures.

Tale of Peter Rabbit, The. BEATRIX POTTER. Warne, 1903. The classic story of Flopsy, Mopsy, Cottontail, and Peter, not to be missed by any child. *Tale of Benjamin Bunny, The.* 1904. *Tale of Tom Kitten, The.* 1907.

When We Were Very Young. A. A. MILNE. Dutton, 1924. No child can resist the fun of these endearing verses written for and about the poet's own beloved little boy. *Now We are Six.* 1927.

White Snow, Bright Snow. ALVIN R. TRESSELT. Lothrop, 1947. All the beauty and fun of winter. *Hi, Mr. Robin!* 1950. *Follow the Wind.* 1950. *Sun Up.* 1949. *Rain Drop Splash.* 1946.

For Children Six to Eight

The children will not be able to read all these books for themselves, but they will enjoy hearing them read aloud.

Abraham Lincoln. INGRI and EDGAR PARIN D'AULAIRE. Doubleday, 1939. Profuse illustrations, fascinating in color and detail, combine with vigorous text to bring a great man to life for boys and girls. *George Washington.* 1936. *Benjamin Franklin.* 1950.

And to Think That I Saw It on Mulberry Street. DR. SEUSS (THEODOR S. GEISEL). Vanguard, 1937. A small boy's active imagination turns a horse and wagon into a circus parade. Ridiculously funny pictures add to the enjoyment of the rhymed story.

Andy and the Lion. JAMES DAUGHERTY. Viking, 1938. Boys especially love this hilarious yarn of Andy's adventures with a lion.

Big Book of Real Boats and Ships. GEORGE J. ZAFFO. Grosset, 1951. (Big Treasure Books series) Oversized picture book, one of a series that is popular with many ages.

Boats on the River, The. MARJORIE FLACK. Viking, 1946. All the fascinating details of life on a river near the sea, with magnificent pictures.

Bojabi Tree, The. EDITH RICKERT. Doubleday, 1923. Adapted from an African folk tale, this amusing story of animals and what they like to eat has the repetition and quiet drama that little children love.

Child's Garden of Verses, A. ROBERT LOUIS STEVENSON. Oxford, 1947. All the delights of a child's own world, in verses singing with music and rhythm. Many good editions available.

Christ Child, The. MAUD and MISKA PETERSHAM. Doubleday, 1931. Pictures of great beauty and reverence illustrate the story of the Nativity. There is a Catholic edition and also a Protestant edition.

Dash and Dart. MARY and CONRAD BUFF. Viking, 1942. The growing-up of two beautiful fawns in a simple, poetic story. Magnificent pictures in color and black and white.

Dick Whittington and His Cat. MARCIA BROWN. Scribner, 1950. Bold illustrations printed in two colors give this old tale fresh appeal for young children.

Down, Down the Mountain. ELLIS CREDLE. Nelson, 1934. An endearing story of two children and a new pair of shoes, with pictures that give a real feeling of life in the Blue Ridge Mountains.

Egg Tree, The. KATHERINE MILHOUS. Scribner, 1950. A warm-hearted story of children and a charming old Pennsylvania Dutch custom. Families can make their own egg trees from the directions given. Caldecott medal winner.

F. P. G.

Finders Keepers. WILL and NICOLAS (WILLIAM LIPKIND and NICOLAS MORDVINOFF). Harcourt, 1951. A dog story with a moral, brilliantly illustrated. Caldecott medal winner.

Fish in the Air. KURT WIESE. Viking, 1948. A little Chinese boy, a huge kite, and a gale of wind make an entertaining story.

Five Chinese Brothers. CLAIRE HUCHET BISHOP. Coward, 1938. Story and pictures bubbling with fun.

500 Hats of Bartholomew Cubbins, The. DR. SEUSS (THEODOR S. GEISEL). Vanguard, 1938. One of the funniest stories imaginable. Improves with every reading.

Follow the Sunset. HERMAN and NINA SCHNEIDER. Doubleday, 1952. The whole world says good night as the earth and the pages turn; customs and lullabies shown in picture, text, and melody.

Four Little Foxes. MIRIAM SCHLEIN. William R. Scott, 1953. Distinctive full-page drawings by Luis Quintanilla supplement this well-written nature tale.

Gone Is Gone. WANDA GÁG. Coward, 1935. A comical retelling of the old tale of a man who "thought he could do more work in a day than his wife could do in three." Wonderful pictures.

Great-Grandfather in the Honey Tree. SAMUEL F. and ZOA SWAYNE. Viking, 1949. Storytellers will love telling this tall tale again and again.

Hundreds and Hundreds of Pancakes. AUDREY CHALMERS. Viking, 1942. All the animals escape from the zoo during a cyclone, and Mrs. Frizzlewit calms them down with pancakes.

In My Mother's House. ANN NOLAN CLARK. Viking, 1941. The life of Indian children in New Mexico, described in lovely graphic language with superb pictures.

It's Mine. ELSE MCKEAN. Vanguard, 1951. A foreword tells parents how to teach the concept of sharing, and the photographs and main dialogue show children how to enjoy things together.

Jerome Anthony. EVA K. EVANS. Putnam, 1936. This affectionate story of a little Negro boy on a visit to the city is much loved by children.

Judy's Baby. SALLY SCOTT. Harcourt, 1949. A delightful, warm-hearted story for "expectant" brothers and sisters, about a little girl's happy welcome for "her" baby. Charming pictures.

Little Dermot and the Thirsty Stones, and Other Irish Folk Tales. RICHARD BENNETT. Coward-McCann, 1953. This author-artist returned to Ireland to hear again and record the tales he remembered from his boyhood.

Little House, The. VIRGINIA LEE BURTON. Houghton, 1942. How the city grew up around a little country house, and how it was moved to the country again. The loveliness of the four seasons shines in the pictures. Caldecott medal winner.

Little Pear. ELEANOR FRANCES LATTIMORE. Harcourt, 1931. A little Chinese boy's everyday life described in vivid detail, in a delightful story.

Madeline. LUDWIG BEMELMANS. Simon & Schuster, 1939. Twelve little Parisian schoolgirls in a spontaneously amusing story with gorgeous pictures of Parisian scenes.

Mei Li. THOMAS HANDFORTH. Doubleday, 1938. A little girl of North China goes to the Peiping Fair, in an endearing story with beautiful pictures. Caldecott medal winner.

My Father's Dragon. RUTH STILES GANNET. Random, 1948. The fabulous adventures of a boy who learned to fly and went off to rescue a baby dragon. Fine excitement and some narrow escapes.

Night Before Christmas, The. CLEMENT CLARKE MOORE. Illus. by Arthur Rackham. Lippincott, 1936. There are many attractive editions of this perennial favorite, and one of them should be in every family's library.

Olá. INGRI and EDGAR PARIN D'AULAIRE. Doubleday, 1932. The adventures of a little Norwegian boy. Handsome, authentic illustrations in color and black and white.

Painted Pig, The. ELIZABETH MORROW. Knopf, 1930. Humorous and imaginative story of a Mexican boy and girl and a lovable toymaker.

Penny and Peter. CAROLYN HAYWOOD. Harcourt, 1946. Happy family relationships result when adopted Penny urges his parents to adopt a big brother. Another series concerns *Little Eddie*. Morrow, 1947.

Picture Tales from the Russian. VALERY CARRICK. Lippincott, 1913. Simple, vigorous folk tales with humorous pictures to match.

Puss in Boots. CHARLES PERRAULT. Freely translated from the French and illustrated by Marcia Brown. Scribner, 1952. A gay, a distinguished, a memorable picture book.

Riding the Rails. ELIZABETH OLDS. Houghton, 1948. History of railroads and kinds of cars today with many colorful pictures.

Ring-a-Round. MILDRED P. HARRINGTON, compiler. Macmillan, 1930. A distinguished collection of real poetry, appealing to little children.

Rocket in my Pocket; the Rhymes and Chants of Young Americans. CARL WITHERS, compiler. Holt, 1948. Just about all the rhymes, jingles, riddles, songs, and sayings that children dance, skip, and jump to throughout the United States.

Roundabout Turn, A. ROBERT H. CHARLES. Warne, 1930. Jacob Toad's adventurous expedition to see the world, in verse. Wonderful for reading aloud. Leslie Brooke illustrations.

Silver Pennies. BLANCHE JENNINGS THOMPSON. Macmillan, 1925. A companionable and inexpensive little volume of poems, with a nicely varied selection. *More Silver Pennies.* 1938.

Small Rain. JESSIE ORTON JONES and ELIZABETH ORTON JONES. Viking, 1943. Brief and beautiful passages from the King James Bible, with good drawings of everyday boys and girls.

Stone Soup. MARCIA BROWN. Scribner, 1947. A new and charming version of the old tale about co-operative soup-making.

Storm Book, The. CHARLOTTE SHAPIRO ZOLOTOW. Harper, 1952. A mother tells her little boy about the storm in such a way that the reader feels the calm that follows. Pictures by Margaret Bloy Graham are appropriate.

Story about Ping, The. MARJORIE FLACK and KURT WIESE. Viking, 1933. A naughty little duckling runs away from home on a Chinese houseboat.

Story of Ferdinand, The. MUNRO LEAF. Viking, 1936. Everybody enjoys the story of the bull who loved flowers and wouldn't fight until he sat down on a bee.

Taxis and Toadstools. RACHEL FIELD. Doubleday, 1926. Sparkling poems of the child's world.

They Were Strong and Good. ROBERT LAWSON. Viking, 1940. The story of the author's parents and his four grandparents, important as Americans not because they were prominent or famous but because they were typical of the strong, good people who built this nation. Caldecott medal winner.

This Is the Way. JESSIE ORTON JONES and ELIZABETH ORTON JONES. Viking, 1951. Brief prayers and meditations from the scriptures of the great religions, with pictures that convey the joyous serenity of children in following the Way.

Tim and His Hearing Aid. ELEANOR C. RONNEI and JOAN PORTER. Dodd, 1951. Both illustrations

Building a Home Library

and story help young children understand the why and how of mechanical aids for children who need to hear better.

Tommy and Dee-Dee. Yen Liang. Oxford, 1953. The differences and likenesses that characterize the daily activities of a Chinese boy and an American boy, with a full-page picture to each line.

Torten's Christmas Secret. Maurice Dolbier. Little, 1951. The little gnome who thought Santa forgot the bad children learned what really happens.

Very Young Verses. Barbara Peck Geismer and Antoinette Brown Suter, eds. Houghton, 1945. Poems for enjoyment, selected by two experienced teachers.

We Are Thy Children. Hymns by Lois Lenski. Music by Clyde Robert Bulla. Crowell, 1952. Original music and words, simple but dignified, on themes of brotherhood.

Wee Gillis. Munro Leaf. Viking, 1938. The comical account of how a boy learned to play the biggest bagpipes in Scotland.

When the Mississippi Was Wild. Le Grand Henderson. Abingdon-Cokesbury, 1952. A rollicking tall tale about Mike Fink, the river worker, who tied up the alligator's tail so he could make only "half-tail" storms on the Mississippi.

Who Goes There? Dorothy Lathrop. Macmillan, 1935. A wintertime picnic in the woods provided by two children for the little animals. Beautiful pictures.

Winnie-the-Pooh. A. A. Milne. Dutton, 1926. Reprint, 1950. No family should miss the fun of reading about Christopher Robin and his friends. *House at Pooh Corner, The.* 1928.

Wise and Otherwise; the Do's and Don'ts of Sundry Proverbs. Anne Marie Jauss, comp. and illus. McKay, 1953. These large, literal pictures will be fun, and useful in stimulating discussions with individual children or groups.

Wonderful Farm, The. Marcel Ayme, translated by Norman Denny. Harper, 1951. Two friendly little girls and their "just right" father and mother on a farm where the animals talk exactly as animals should.

Wonderful Story of How You Were Born, The. Sidonie Matsner Gruenberg. Doubleday, 1952. Direct explanations of sex and reproduction, in correct terminology, with guide to parents.

Yonie Wondernose. Marguerite de Angeli. Doubleday, 1944. True-to-life story of a little boy who wondered about everything.

For Children Eight to Ten

Some children will not be able to read all these books themselves. Some books have been included just for reading aloud to the children.

Abraham Lincoln. Genevieve Foster. Scribner, 1950. Simply and pleasantly written, with just the right emphasis to give young readers a feeling of greatness.

Adventures of Odysseus and the Tale of Troy, The, or *The Children's Homer.* Padraic Colum. Macmillan, 1918. The stories of the *Iliad* and the *Odyssey* told simply and beautifully in vigorous, rhythmical prose.

Adventures of Pinocchio, The; The Tale of a Puppet. Carlo Collodi (Carlo Lorenzini). Macmillan, 1951. The story of a frisky wooden doll who, after a series of adventures both gay and awesome, becomes a real boy.

Alice's Adventures in Wonderland and Through the Looking Glass. Lewis Carroll. Macmillan, 1950. Incomparable nonsense, with a great deal of beauty and wonder. John Tenniel illustrations.

All-of-a-Kind Family. Sydney Taylor. Wilcox & Follett, 1951. These five little Jewish girls enjoyed growing up in New York a generation ago.

American Folk Songs for Children; in Home, School and Nursery School. Ruthy Torter (Crawford) Seeger. Doubleday, 1948. A book to look at as well as a book from which to sing.

America's Paul Revere. Esther Forbes. Houghton, 1946. An authentic brief biography, written in a sparkling style, and illustrated with magnificent pictures.

And There Was America. Roger Duvoisin. Knopf, 1938. Brief, dramatic stories of explorers from Leif Erikson to the Pilgrims, with splendid pictures in color. *They Put Out to Sea.* 1943.

Appleseed Farm. Emily Taft Douglas. Abingdon-Cokesbury, 1948. Aunt Millie tells a bored ten-year-old girl how the farm got its name from Johnny Appleseed.

Arabian Nights. Andrew Lang, editor. Longmans, 1946. Twenty-one well-chosen stories that make a good introduction to the brilliantly colorful tales of Eastern romance, adventure, and magic.

Art for Children. Ana M. Berry. Studio, 1934. An introduction to painting, with an inviting selection of beautiful pictures, excellently reproduced, from the works of great artists of all periods.

At the Back of the North Wind. George Macdonald. Macmillan, 1950. There is a lovely spiritual quality in this most enchanting imaginative story.

Away Goes Sally. Elizabeth Coatsworth. Macmillan, 1934. A little girl travels with her three aunts all the way from Massachusetts to the Penobscot Valley in a little house on a sledge drawn by oxen. A story that fairly purrs with contentment!

Ben and Me. Robert Lawson. Little, 1939. The life of Benjamin Franklin, as told in the diary of his mouse friend, Amos. Delightful nonsense.

Big Music, or Twenty Merry Tales to Tell. MARY NOEL BLEECKER, compiler. Viking, 1946. A collection of folk tales of unusual appeal and quality.

Blue Fairy Book. ANDREW LANG. new ed. Longmans, 1948. The old romantic fairy tales, beautifully told. There are also the *Red, Green, Yellow,* and other "color" *Fairy Books,* a whole rainbow of them!

Caddie Woodlawn. CAROL RYRIE BRINK. Macmillan, 1935. The madcap adventures of Caddie and her two brothers in the frontier days in Wisconsin. Newbery medal winner. *Magical Melons.* 1944.

Call It Courage. ARMSTRONG SPERRY. reissue. Macmillan, 1951. The stirring account of a Polynesian boy's victory over his fear of the sea. Spirited drawings. Newbery medal winner.

Charlotte's Web. ELWYN BROOKS WHITE. Harper, 1952. Friendship between a spider and a pig in this blending of fantasy with the realistic background of a farm and a county fair.

Cottage at Bantry Bay, The. HILDA VAN STOCKUM. Viking, 1938. The work and fun of a happy Irish family.

Dolls' House, The. RUMER GODDEN. Viking, 1947. A little gem of a book for all doll-lovers.

Eskimo Boy. PIPALUK FREUCHEN. Translated from the Danish. Lothrop, 1951. A stark and stirring tale of real-life adventure and courage.

Fables of Aesop. Selected. Told anew and their history traced by JOSEPH JACOBS. Macmillan, 1950. (New Children's Classics.) Old favorites are well told and well selected in this collection.

Fairy Tales. HANS CHRISTIAN ANDERSEN. Oxford, 1945. Thirty-one favorites with enchanting pictures by Tasha Tudor. Other collections available.

First Thanksgiving, The. LENA BARKSDALE. Knopf, 1942. A little girl, spending Thanksgiving at a family gathering, hears her grandmother's vivid reminiscences of the first Thanksgiving at Plymouth.

Floating Island. ANNE PARRISH. Harper, 1930. High adventure on the sea, and shipwreck and island rescue—all in a world peopled by dolls.

For a Child; Great Poems Old and New. WILMA K. MCFARLAND, comp. Westminster Press, Philadelphia, Pa., 1947. Large flat book of favorite poems with colorful thumbnail sketches.

Gaily We Parade. JOHN BREWTON. Macmillan, 1940. A fine variety of poems about people. *Christmas Bells Are Ringing.* 1951.

George Washington; Leader of the People. CLARA INGRAM JUDSON. Wilcox & Follett, 1951. The format and illustrations are attractive and the style is warm and friendly.

Good Master, The. KATE SEREDY. Viking, 1935. A marvelous picture of country life in Hungary, permeated with the flavor of ancient traditions and customs.

Great Geppy, The. WILLIAM PÈNE DU BOIS. Viking, 1940. The witty story of a horse who turned detective. Beautifully comical drawings by the author.

Hansi. LUDWIG BEMELMANS. Viking, 1934. A little boy spends Christmas with an aunt and uncle in the Tyrolean Alps, in the lovely excitement of all the traditional celebrations.

Heidi. JOHANNA SPYRI. Lippincott, 1948. Still fresh and appealing after more than seventy years, this story of a little Swiss girl wins immediate affection.

Hitty, Her First Hundred Years. RACHEL FIELD. Macmillan, 1929. A little ashwood doll, made in the early 1800's, tells her own story of journeyings and adventures, strange encounters, and the changes she observed in the American scene. Newbery medal winner.

Homer Price. ROBERT MCCLOSKEY. Viking, 1943. Absurdly funny accounts of the doings of a super-American boy of today.

Honk, the Moose. PHIL STONG. Dodd, 1935. Gloriously funny things happen when two Finnish boys in Minnesota find a moose in the stable.

Hundred Dresses, The. ELEANOR ESTES. Harcourt, 1944. The growth of understanding between a little Polish girl and her more fortunate playmates.

Inheritance of Poetry, An. GLADYS ADSHEAD and ANNIS DUFF, compilers. Houghton, 1948. A wide selection of poems, ranging in period from Bible times to the present, and in mood from the nonsensical to the spiritual. Intended as an invitation to all ages to the enjoyment of poetry.

Jack Tales. RICHARD CHASE. Houghton, 1943. The themes of most of these English-American stories are old favorites, but they have a delightful, fresh flavor from being retold by the people of the southern mountains. Their gusto and humor recommend them especially to boys of all ages.

Johnny Texas. CAROL HOFF. Wilcox & Follett, 1950. A German family homesteading in 1834. *Johnny Texas on the San Antonio Road.* 1953.

Jungle Book, The. RUDYARD KIPLING. Doubleday, 1932. Truth and imagination in the telling of these stories of the East Indian jungle give them timeless interest and importance.

Just So Stories, The. RUDYARD KIPLING. Garden City Books, 1952. Marvelously told nonsense stories of how the elephant got his trunk, how the camel got his hump, and how the leopard got his spots. This refreshing edition is illustrated by Nicolas Mordvinoff.

Light at Tern Rock, The. JULIA LINA SAUER. Viking, 1951. At the moment when Ronnie puts a light in the window on Christmas Eve, he comes to forgive completely the old man who had almost spoiled his Christmas.

Lightfoot, the Story of an Indian Boy. KATHERINE B. SHIPPEN. Viking, 1950. Simply and graphically written, an excellent introduction to the customs and traditions of the Iroquois Indians.

Little History of the United States. MABEL PYNE. Houghton, 1940. A fine introduction. Pictures full of color and action, with clear, interesting text.

Little House in the Big Woods. LAURA INGALLS WILDER. Harper, 1953. This is the first in a series of stories of the author's pioneer family that no child should miss. *Little House on the Prairie.* 1953. *On the Banks of Plum Creek.* 1953. *By the Shores of Silver Lake.* 1953. *Long Winter, The.* 1953. *Little Town on the Prairie.* 1953. *These Happy Golden Years.* 1953.

Little Vic. DORIS GATES. Viking, 1951. A distinguished story of a boy's faith in his beloved horse.

Little Women. LOUISA MAY ALCOTT. World Pub. Co., 1950. The adventures of the March family are as dear to girls of today as they were to their first readers almost a hundred years ago.

Magic Money. ANN NOLAN CLARK. Viking, 1950. A lovely picture of family life in Costa Rica, and a little boy's loving efforts to earn enough to give his grandfather two white oxen. Beautiful pictures.

Many Moons. JAMES THURBER. Harcourt, 1943. A lovely, amusing story of a princess who wanted the moon. Good for reading aloud.

Mary Poppins. PAMELA TRAVERS. Harcourt, 1934. There's fun for the whole family in the adventures of the Banks children with their magic-making nursemaid. *Mary Poppins Comes Back.* 1935.

Matchlock Gun, The. WALTER EDMONDS. Dodd, 1941. A fine, exciting story of a boy's courage at the time of the French and Indian Wars. Newbery medal winner.

Melindy's Medal. GEORGENE FAULKNER and JOHN LEONARD BECKER. Messner, 1945. A Negro girl saves her school from burning, and wins Grandma's praise.

Mr. Popper's Penguins. RICHARD and FLORENCE ATWATER. Little, 1938. Hilarious nonsense, told matter-of-factly, about a family of penguins brought up in a city house. The whole family will enjoy hearing it read aloud.

Misty of Chincoteague. MARGUERITE HENRY. Rand McNally, 1947. Two present-day children help tame a wild pony.

Moffats, The. ELEANOR ESTES. Harcourt, 1941. A story of family life in Connecticut. Strikingly true to life and both droll and hilarious. *Middle Moffat, The.* 1942. *Rufus M.* 1943.

Mousewife, The. RUMER GODDEN. Viking, 1951. A caged dove longed for freedom, and a tender-hearted mouse opened the cage door. Beautiful pictures by William Pène du Bois.

Mozart, The Wonder Boy. OPAL WHEELER and SYBIL DEUCHER. Dutton, 1934. Simple, interestingly written life of Mozart, with emphasis on his boyhood. Selections from his music included. *Joseph Haydn, the Merry Little Peasant.* 1936.

Nino. VALENTI ANGELO. Viking, 1938. This story of a boy in a Tuscany village about 1900 is autobiographical.

One God: the Ways We Worship Him. FLORENCE MARY FITCH. Lothrop, 1944. The forms of worship in Christian churches and in Jewish synagogues are given meaning and beauty in fine photographs and simple text.

Paddle-to-the-Sea. HOLLING CLANCY HOLLING. Houghton, 1941. The geography of the Great Lakes comes alive in this marvelous story of the journey of an Indian doll in a tiny canoe. *Seabird.* 1948. *Minn of the Mississippi.* 1951.

Pancakes—Paris. CLAIRE HUCHET BISHOP. Viking, 1947. Two American soldiers, distressed by the poverty in Paris after the war, make a gay party for a French family.

Paul Bunyan Swings His Axe. DELL J. MCCORMICK. Caxton Printers, 1936. Lusty tall tales of the fabulous woodsman, hero of American lumbermen.

Peacock Pie. WALTER DE LA MARE. Holt, 1913. Enchanting poems. Out of print, but worth looking for.

Pecos Bill. JAMES CLOYD BOWMAN. Whitman, 1937. Rollicking tall tales of the greatest cowboy of them all.

People Are Important. EVA KNOX EVANS. Capitol Pub. Co., Irmington-on-Hudson, N. Y. 1951. Humorous style in text and pictures helps even young children understand the reasons for differences in food, shelter, clothing, and manners of people around the world.

Pepper and Salt. HOWARD PYLE. Harper, 1887. Modern tales of imagination based on old themes and told with humor and distinction. *Wonder Clock, The.* 1887. A classic story for every hour of the day.

Peterkin Papers, The. LUCRETIA P. HALE. Houghton, 1924. Inspired nonsense, all about the doings of a family with a positive genius for "dimwittedness." Indispensable for reading aloud.

Peter Pan. J. M. BARRIE. Scribner, 1950. A new edition of the old favorite, with drawings by Nora Unwin that are right and appealing.

Picture Tales from Spain. RUTH SAWYER. Lippincott, 1936. Eleven tales and some riddles. Delightful for storytelling.

Plain Princess, The. PHYLLIS MCGINLEY. Lippincott, 1945. A practical fairy tale for every little girl, about how the plain one became beautiful.

Prairie School. LOIS LENSKI. Lippincott, 1951. A true picture of a little rural school in South Dakota, with thrilling adventures in a blizzard.

Quaint and Curious Quest of Johnny Longfoot,

the Shoe King's Son, The. CATHERINE BESTERMAN. Bobbs, 1947. A tale that is both adventure and fairy tale, full of marvels, yet the hero is a boy such as anyone might know.

Rabbit Hill. ROBERT LAWSON. Viking, 1944. Love of the countryside and its furry creatures shines in every page and picture of this lovely, friendly story. Newbery medal winner.

Rainbow in the Sky. LOUIS UNTERMEYER. Harcourt, 1935. A wide selection of good poetry, excellent for introducing young readers to the works of many different poets.

Rip Van Winkle and The Legend of Sleepy Hollow. WASHINGTON IRVING. Macmillan, 1951. The first tale is the ever-popular story of the "Weary Willie" who slept for twenty years in the Catskill Mountains.

Rootabaga Stories. CARL SANDBURG. Harcourt, 1922. A great storyteller at his best in delightful imaginative tales full of wisdom, poetry, and nonsense.

Saturdays, The. ELIZABETH ENRIGHT. Rinehart, 1941. Four enterprising children devise wonderful ways of spending their allowances. *Thimble Summer.* 1938. Newbery medal winner.

Spunky. BERTA and ELMER HADER. Macmillan, 1933. A wild pony is taken first to work in the mines, next across the Atlantic, then into a circus, and finally to the happiness of a good home.

Stories of the Gods and Heroes. SALLY BENSON. Illus. by Steele Savage. Dial Press, 1940. Classic myths skillfully selected and retold with imagination and simplicity.

Story of Doctor Doolittle, The. HUGH LOFTING. Lippincott, 1920. A kind-hearted doctor gives up his work with people to care for the animals he loves and understands. Convincing fantasy. *Voyages of Doctor Doolittle, The.* 1922. Newbery medal winner.

Tales from Grimm. WANDA GÁG, translator and illustrator. Coward, 1936. This free translation and inimitable drawings will delight the individual child as well as the storyteller.

Talking Cat and Other Stories of French Canada, The. NATALIE SAVAGE CARLSON. Harper, 1952. An old-time storyteller visits a French-Canadian household on a winter evening, and entertains the family with stories full of laughter.

Thomas Alva Edison, Inventor. RUTH CROMER WEIR. Abingdon-Cokesbury, 1953. (Makers of America series.) A story which makes Edison's boyhood come to life, and shows its bearing on his later years.

Thunder of the Gods. DOROTHY GRANT HOSFORD. Holt, 1952. Retelling of the Norse myths for both the child and the storyteller.

Told Under Spacious Skies. ASSOCIATION FOR CHILDHOOD EDUCATION. LITERATURE COMMITTEE. Macmillan, 1952. (Umbrella Book series.) Thirty regional stories about people throughout America, to follow up interests aroused by CHILDCRAFT, Volume 5.

Tom Sawyer, Adventures of. MARK TWAIN. Harper, 1917. No American childhood is complete without long, friendly association with this and its companion book, *Adventures of Huckleberry Finn.* 1912. Several attractive editions.

Treasure Trove of the Sun. MIKHAIL M. PRISHVIN. Viking, 1952. Distinguished story of two Russian peasant children lost in a cranberry swamp. Full of the sights and sounds of nature. Beautiful pictures by Feodor Rojankovsky.

Twig. ELIZABETH ORTON JONES. Macmillan, 1942. A cheerful little girl makes a house out of a tomato can and lives there with an elf.

Up the Hill. MARGUERITE DE ANGELI. Doubleday, 1942. The customs, legends, and music of Poland are richly interwoven into a delightful story of a ten-year-old Polish girl, her family, and friends, in a Pennsylvania mining town. *Henner's Lydia.* 1936. *Thee, Hannah!* 1940.

We Live in the South. LOIS LENSKI. Lippincott, 1952. (Roundabout America series.) Four short regional stories.

Willow Whistle, The. CORNELIA MEIGS. Macmillan, 1931. Pioneer days in the Western prairies, with friendly Indians and buffaloes.

Wind in the Willows. KENNETH GRAHAME. Scribner, 1933. Unforgettable stories of small animals, full of beauty, humor, and imagination.

Wind Island. HEDVIG COLLIN. Viking, 1945. A Danish story with real people and a sense of place.

You Among the Stars. HERMAN and NINA SCHNEIDER. William R. Scott, 1951. A sense of wonder pervades this simple book which explains the system of the universe.

Zuska of the Burning Hills. ALVENA VAJDA SECKAR. Oxford, 1952. This story of an immigrant Czech girl growing up in the mining country presents a warm family picture.

Some of the favorite children's stories may also be had on records. You will find a list of these in MUSIC FOR THE FAMILY, Volume 11 of CHILDCRAFT.

FAMILY CRISES

Rae Russell

26. LOSSES THROUGH DEATH

27. DIVORCE AND SEPARATION

28. FAMILY UPS AND DOWNS

Every family at one time or another experiences some degree of misfortune, some illness, or even loss through death. Unfortunately, some families have to go through the tragedy of separation or of divorce.

What any of these events means to the child, how he feels about it, how you interpret it to him, and most of all how you respond to it yourself, will largely determine how it affects him.

Indeed, many times feelings about events count for more than do the events themselves. Facing misfortune honestly has helped many families grow in strength, understanding, and mutual affection and respect.

Suzanne Szasz

LOSSES THROUGH DEATH

ADELE FRANKLIN, M.A.
Assistant Administrative Director, All-Day Neighborhood Schools of the Board of Education, New York, N. Y.

WHEN death strikes close to the home, be it a pet, a member of the family, or a friend, it always comes as a shock. It is profoundly disturbing. We are face to face with a reality that is painful and frightening. It is not at all the same as something read about in the newspaper, or something that happens to other persons.

What Does Death Mean to a Child?

Our own attitude toward death and grief is none too clear, and the children are even more confused. Perhaps it would be more accurate to say that we are confused by their reactions. Our behavior often lets them know that death is a topic to avoid. We do not—frequently we cannot—answer their questions satisfactorily. As a result, some children avoid *feeling* about death as well as *talking* about it. These children are afraid to show their feelings. In order to escape the fact when it occurs, they pretend nothing has happened. They may ask no questions at all, in a pitiful attempt to do what they think adults expect them to do. They engage in a kind of play acting to protect them from facing an emotion too deep for words.

Other children are able to show sorrow or worry openly, when anyone close to them dies. These children are perhaps more fortunate, for they can be helped more readily by comforting adults. We need to remember that even in the same family, each child will react differently. We must therefore approach each child differently, to help him best.

Are the Children "Bloodthirsty"?

Children's play is often deceiving to adults. Even very young children love to play with guns and gleefully "kill" each other. But they become frightened quickly if the play becomes too realistic and a companion insists that they stay "dead." Nine- and ten-year-olds assume vivid poses and imitate, with surprising realism, the death agonies they have seen portrayed in the movies or on television. But even at this age they have trouble deciding who has "killed" whom in the battle. Often the "dead"

"You're a dead duck," may not be as bloodthirsty as it sounds. "Stick 'em up—or else!" does not mean to seven-year-olds what it does to us.

Three Lions

arise as new recruits, not so much to prolong the game as to reassure themselves that this is play after all.

We adults are often shocked by children's ability to show the aggression we have learned to mask and hide. "How can children understand and be sympathetic when they are so bloodthirsty?" we cry. A large audience of children from three to fifteen years of age sat watching the Walt Disney picture, *Snow White and the Seven Dwarfs.* The jealous stepmother caused general alarm, especially among the younger members of the audience. When she went hurtling over the cliff to her death there were cheers and great rejoicing. This eager acceptance of the death of an enemy or wicked character may make us believe children are unfeeling. Our attitude further convinces the child that death is a topic he cannot talk about freely.

Children Exaggerate Their Power

In bursts of anger, children often express violently a wish that a parent or relative would die. They do not really want a permanent separation. They want immediate relief from being made to conform. A three- or four-year-old will give voice to such a wish. When the older child says, "Oh—drop dead!," of course he only means, "Let me alone."

The parent may be wise enough to understand and accept the outburst. A mother may tell the child, "I know you are angry because you do not want to do what you have to do, but Mommy loves you anyway." But sooner or later the youngster gets a violent reaction from Grandma or a friend. A neighboring child whose parents have been shocked by a similar response may tell him, "It's bad to talk like that." The simple, meaningless outburst is blown up into something of importance. The child begins to feel that his words and even his thoughts carry great power. Adults frequently increase this feeling in children by telling them that their behavior has made, or will make, Mommy sick. Children have a tendency to attribute magical powers to their thoughts. They often believe that they are responsible for what has happened.

The apparent indifference a child sometimes shows, and his failure to talk about a lost relative, may not be lack of feeling, but a deep sense of fear that if he talks he will reveal his guilt. The relatives of little Mary, aged six, were astonished at her insistence that she did not remember her grandmother at all. The grandmother had been a devoted member of the household until her death the year before. Here indeed was proof that children were really heartless!

Mary had been playing in the back yard at the time her grandmother died. In order to keep the child quiet and out of the way, a neighbor had told Mary that if she would be a good girl her grandmother would get well. When her grandmother failed to recover, Mary did not dare tell that she had disobeyed rules and run out of the yard. For years, Mary carried a feeling that she was responsible for her grandmother's death.

Losing a Pet

Children sometimes seem to show more emotion for a lost pet than they do when they hear of the death of a relative. Actually the pet may be closer to the child than the relative. Even fathers can seem remote to young children, and the child is not aware of the immediate implications of such a loss. It is sometimes safer and less frightening to show emotion over the loss of a pet, just as some adults can shower devotion on a pet when they seem cold and aloof to other human beings. Parents should never belittle a child's feeling for a lost pet. Telling him that it was "only a cat" or "just another goldfish" adds to the child's sorrow. It is better not to increase the child's suffering by suggesting that the pet died because of neglect. It is hard enough to bear the loss without adding a feeling of guilt which can so easily transfer itself to guilt feelings in other relationships. Incidentally, a pet can often offer great comfort and solace to a child at the time of the loss of a relative.

The Children Feel Shut Out

The mystery and solemnity with which adults surround death is in itself a frightening experience. Children sense our feelings from the tone of voice and the general atmosphere in the home, more accurately than they grasp the meaning of the words we speak. The common belief that "children don't understand" or "have no feelings" makes it far easier to exclude the child than to attempt to discuss the event. It is especially difficult to talk about what has happened at a time when we are overwhelmed by our own emotions. But this adds to the child's feeling of being shut out and neglected. The child knows something is wrong, and the silence about the cause of the disturbance increases the feeling of fright and isolation. Furthermore, with death, the child's ever-present fear of being abandoned becomes a fact. The silence and withdrawal of the family increase a sense of guilt. The child hides this guilt deep within him. He becomes further convinced that the subject of death is something too frightening to talk about. Since he often assumes that adults are all-powerful, he imagines that their silence indicates a knowledge of his guilty secret which may be used against him.

Explaining Death

It is not morbid for children to be curious about death and about dead things. Small Johnny had been taught to be careful of his belongings. One day he marched in with a dead cat in his

The customs surrounding death may be as confusing as death itself. Simple answers can often clear up a child's mistaken ideas and reduce his fears.

arms, shouting, "Look, Mommy, here's a perfectly good cat someone threw away." We do not know whether Johnny was scolded for handling a "dirty old cat," or whether his mother used this opportunity to explain to Johnny that the cat had stopped living and was dead. Too often such opportunities to discuss death with children are overlooked because of our aversion to discussion of a topic with painful associations. The child cannot know our personal reactions. He merely gets his first strong sense that there is a forbidden subject, and that he cannot get help from adults.

You can help your child by being casual and answering his questions simply. If the three- or four-year-old asks, "What is 'dead'?," simply stating that the person or animal "stopped breathing" or "stopped moving" will generally be sufficient. Saying that death is like going to sleep may make a child afraid to go to sleep. If you answer questions without emotion and without fear or anxiety, your child will accept the answer in the same way. As your child gets older, he may ask why people have to die, or even when he or his parents will die. Just how you answer some of these questions will depend on your religious beliefs. Your minister, priest, or rabbi can give you guidance in answering some of the children's questions.

It is well not to get too involved or to answer more than the child asks. In most cases, the child is seeking reassurance for himself. Children often want to know who will take care of them if their parents die. A direct statement that you do not expect to die for a long time, but that Aunt Susie will take care of him if anything should happen, is often the most comforting answer.

It has already been mentioned that it is important not to tell children that being naughty will cause the illness of a parent, or that a parent will leave them if they are not good. If death occurs, the child remembers his naughtiness and may hold himself responsible.

Why Do Children Worry About Death?

It is well to point out that most people live a long time and that most sick people do get well. Making a child too conscious of his health makes him overanxious about illness and creates a fear of death. Tommy's mother had died at the time of his birth. His father had so impressed the child with the importance of staying healthy that Tommy was in a constant state of fear. At the age of eight, he sought reassurance at all times before he would participate in normal activities.

When a child seems unduly worried about illness or morbidly concerned about death, try to find what is disturb-

LOSSES THROUGH DEATH

ing him. Long explanations in words are apt to confuse him further, and will not get at the root of the difficulty. Sometimes he has been frightened by talk he has overheard but not understood. Certain movies and comics may be the cause of his fear. An older brother or sister may be deliberately terrifying the child by telling him "tall" tales or threatening him.

Worry About Death Reflects Other Worries

A child may develop anxieties about death for less obvious reasons. There may be a great deal of violent quarreling between the parents in his presence. Financial worries discussed in his hearing may make him feel insecure, even though he seems apparently unconcerned. The older child who feels pushed out by a younger brother or sister, or a child who feels unloved or unwanted, may give much attention to death and constantly dwell on related topics.

Eight-year-old Martin was an attractive, intelligent, seemingly happy little boy. His play always consisted of killing and death, and he was always the victim. He was the animal killed by a cruel hunter. At the time of the war with Japan, he had to be a Japanese who was killed by an American pilot. In any dramatic play started by other children, Martin invariably got himself into some role where he could die dramatically. Most conversation was punctuated by remarks such as, "Did someone get hurt?"—"He could have been killed if he did that."—"I would have shot him if I had been there." Actually, Martin never was the killer. He was always the victim.

Martin's mother realized that something was troubling him and sought expert help. Martin was an adopted child and was deeply concerned about his place in his adopted home, even though he had been there since infancy. He felt sure that his younger sister was the favorite of his parents. When the source of the difficulty was discovered, it was possible to help Martin accept his place and the genuine love of his parents.

Today, fortunately, many communities have child-guidance facilities to provide help for parents. We are beginning to realize that it is far wiser to seek the help of experts at the earliest signs of disturbance. FAMILY GUIDANCE SERVICES, in Volume 15, will tell you more about finding such help.

Sorrow Can Be Borne

It is relatively easy to explain things

When sorrow comes, children need to be with an adult they love. A child who is shut out may suffer more than one who shares his family's grief.

F.P.G.

to children when we ourselves are not involved. It is therefore important that children should have been able to discuss death before it strikes a crushing blow to those on whom the child most depends. It is seldom necessary to create an artificial situation and make a point of bringing death into the conversation. In the natural course of events, questions will arise that can help the child to understand that death is sad, but can be met.

Children *can* be saved from morbid details, but a change in the conversation, or complete silence when the child enters the room, is not wise. He gets a feeling of fear and mystery that makes a real loss more difficult to bear. Seeing a person who is suffering from a loss is not apt to be too disturbing to a normal, healthy child, unless the adult is hysterical and uncontrolled. Seeing the adult on whom the child depends for support in a state of *collapse* may be frightening, but most adults can manage to check their more violent feelings, at least in the presence of the children.

A child should not be expected to show grief or emotion he does not feel or understand. He cannot be asked to keep quiet all the time, or to refrain from playing. Nor must he be made to feel that his natural desire to play means that he is showing a lack of love and respect for the dead. Long-drawn-out periods of association with sadness can be depressing for children. When adults are so overcome by grief that they cannot give their children a normal outlet, they should try to have the children visit friends or neighbors for part of the time.

Share Your Feelings Honestly

Children are not fooled by an unnatural attempt to have life go on just as though nothing had happened. A girl of ten whose dog was killed was immediately offered another dog by her family. A fresh outburst of tears met this offer. "How can you think any dog could take Chum's place?" she cried.

When children see no outward sign of grief on the part of adults, they wonder if the adults are completely heartless. They may come to think that it is wrong to show any emotion, and so they bury their feelings. Seeing an adult express the emotions of grief may help the child to realize that it is natural to express his feelings.

Two frightened little girls sat with stony faces when they were told their father had been taken sick during the night and was dead. The grief-stricken mother was at the hospital and the children's aunt was making a determined effort to keep from crying as she talked with them. The silent, rigid little girls stared back at her and seemed to recede from her as she spoke. Finally, the aunt began to cry and the two children flung themselves into her arms. They needed to be able to share the emotional release with their aunt. They could not let themselves go in the face of her unnatural control.

If Death Comes to the Family

It is important that the person who tells the child about a death be someone the child knows and trusts. Often the surviving parent cannot take on the task, because the state of emotional shock may make it too difficult for both parent and child. Although the immediate effect of the grief of the survivor would be overwhelming for the child, the parent must realize that the child has a great need, too. The child must not feel that he has been abandoned by the dead

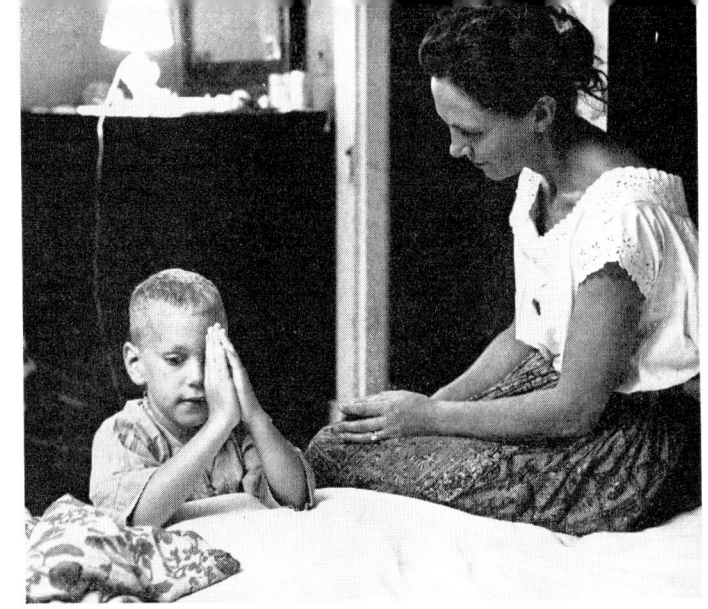

The attitudes toward death of the family's religious faith may help to comfort the child who has lost a beloved relative.

parent and by the living one as well. He should be allowed to share his grief with the parent for at least part of the time.

In the first shock of tragedy, it is normal for some parents to push the children aside completely. Only when the effort is made to accept the situation, can parent and children recover from the bereavement. Gradually the parent finds that by helping the child who needs him so badly, he in turn is helped.

The children can be spared some of the too-realistic details of life's ending. For that reason, children are often sent away from home when death occurs or is expected. It is doubtful if much is gained by this separation, for parent and child need each other at this time. Particularly, the separation should not be made into an effort to shut the children away from all knowledge of death and all experience of grief.

In any case, a child should be with someone he knows and likes. He should not be left with a stranger at such times. If a child is in school at the time of a death in a family, the teacher should be told. She will then be able to prepare the other children and help the bereaved child make the adjustment in school.

Feelings About the Survivor

A child who has lost a favorite parent may express resentment toward the survivor. "Why couldn't you have died instead of Mommy?" cried a small boy to his father. It takes patience and understanding for the father to realize that it is far better for the child to express such feelings. By getting sympathy from his father at such a time, he can overcome his resentment toward him. He can also find solace in the new friendship that can develop between them.

What if a Brother or Sister Dies?

Parents sometimes fail to realize that the death of a brother or sister is extremely difficult for the remaining child or children to face. Frequently adults think only in terms of their own grief, and forget that many mixed emotions are probably troubling the children. Death of a young person may be harder for children to take, as it strikes nearer home. Feelings of guilt for real or fancied wrongs to the departed are mixed with a sense of loneliness. The tendency on the part of the parents to place the lost child on a pedestal confuses the living children. In one family, a particularly troublesome youngster died. His younger brother, Philip, had always been considered the "good boy." Philip suddenly found himself competing with an older brother who, until his death, had been the "horrible example" of what not to do or be. It is not surprising that Philip became "difficult."

Should Children Go to Funerals?

Whether or not a child should attend a funeral depends on the individual circumstances. It would be generally agreed that a child under seven should be spared this experience if possible. The solemnity of the occasion and the grief displayed by the close relatives are apt to be disturbing to the young child. One wise parent took her seven-year-old child to the funeral of a friend of the family because she believed that sharing the experience with her parents would help the little girl face more intimate losses which might occur. Here again the attitude of the parent is all-important. The religious beliefs of the family strongly influence such decisions.

It is unwise to keep a boy or girl of twelve or thirteen, or even younger, from a funeral if the child feels he wants to attend. A child who is fond of a relative may want to pay this last tribute to him, even though he finds it painful and difficult. Sometimes the attempt to keep the child away from the funeral or the wake may invest death with more horror than if he shared the experience with the family and accepted it as part of the routine. It is important, if he does attend, that he be with an understanding and well-loved adult. The grief of a surviving parent should not be met by the child without such an adult to help.

If the child does not attend the funeral, someone should stay with him who can talk helpfully about the member of the family who has died. It is hardly necessary to say that the conversation will not remain on this topic, but in the course of the day the child should be able to refer to the relative, to ask questions about the funeral, and to recall some of the things he liked about the person who has died.

When Children Ask About Burial

It is seldom necessary to go into details with children on such subjects as embalming, cremating, or burial. But if children overhear conversation of adults, they sometimes become curious. In that case, it does not help to evade these questions. But, just as in the case of any difficult problem, we can be careful to answer only what is asked, and not to elaborate and confuse the issue. We can discuss things we like to remember about the relative who has died.

Children often ask about cemeteries. Here again the way the adult replies will make a difference in the way the child feels about burial. If the adult acts frightened or tries to evade the question, the child may develop fears and anxieties about cemeteries. The whole question of burial will then be imbued with a feeling of aversion and dread.

It is comforting to realize that children can face almost any trouble if they have confidence in and the support of the adults who love and care for them. In order to give children this support and keep them emotionally healthy, we must share our joys and our sorrows with them from the earliest years. A strong family bond is the greatest bulwark against disaster, not only for the individual, but for the nation as well.

DIVORCE AND SEPARATION

DOROTHY W. BARUCH, Ph.D.
Consulting Psychologist; Author, "New Ways in Discipline" and "One Little Boy," Los Angeles.

Divorce, regardless of the circumstances leading up to it, is almost always an unhappy experience for one or more members of the family who are directly involved. It is particularly difficult for children. But if you have decided there is no other solution, then you can tackle the problems it brings. You can get through the difficult moments. So can your child. As you gain in courage, so will your children.

What Divorce Means to a Child

Sometimes a child gets more upset by divorce than need be, because he does not understand enough of what is happening.

Children have vivid imaginations. They "cook up" in their own minds reasons for their parents' separation. Left to their own devices, they may, for instance, pick out and misinterpret something they have heard. This is what four-year-old Ruth did.

After her father left, she became exceedingly rebellious toward her maternal grandmother, who had always lived with the family.

"I don't like her. She'll pull my hair," Ruthie would whimper.

"That's nonsense, Ruthie," Mother would insist, but to no avail. Then, following the suggestion of a counselor, she tried to find out what Ruthie had on her mind. "Why do you think Nanna will pull your hair?" she inquired.

" 'Cause she pulled my daddy's hair and made him go 'way."

Then the reason became clear. Over and over, the husband had threatened, "I'll leave if your mother doesn't stay out of my hair!"

When children try to explain to themselves what has happened, they are apt to grow far more insecure and fearful than when they are taken into their parents' confidence.

If we tell our children about the divorce or separation, in so far as we can, we may prevent fears from accumulating.

What Shall We Tell About Divorce?

Nothing short of the truth will be good enough. A child feels it when we try to make things seem different from what they are. For his own sense of security, he needs to be able to count on us to share the truth with him.

First come the facts. We must have them clear to ourselves before we can make them clear to a child.

Say them out loud to yourself before you try telling your child. Put them into spoken words that your ears can actually listen to. If you can be brave enough to do this, you will be braver in telling your child.

The child three years old or under ordinarily will not want reasons. "Daddy moved away to another house. We're getting a divorce," usually suffices, and serves as a ground for further details later on. If he is more than four years old, even though he does not ask, he will wonder about the "whys."

You can tell him simply, "Daddy loved somebody else better than he loved me," if there is another-woman reason. Or, "I made him so unhappy and he made me so unhappy we had no time left for being friendly." Or, "When you're married you like to feel real good when you are close to each other. But it didn't feel good to Daddy and me any more because we no longer loved each other, and so we decided to get unmarried." Or, "We weren't happy together and so we're trying out a plan. We're going to live in different houses to see if we're happier that way. If we are, we'll get unmarried—divorced, they call it. We'll tell you about it as soon as we know for sure ourselves." The assurance that you will keep him posted is important.

If possible, try to help the child feel that the other parent is a good person, even though not good for you. Don't do this if it is not true. It is better for a child to hear a harsh truth from the parent who loves and cares for him than to have it slip out of the mouth of a stranger.

If you believe your former spouse has deserted his family, never to return, hold out no false hopes. Waiting for something that will never happen is worse than any blunt answer could be.

Your Attitude Can Give Courage

You don't want to weigh down your child by using his shoulder to weep on. But if you do weep, and he hears it, it is best for him to know that you have been feeling sad. The reassurance of your hope that life can bring many new experiences, and that the pain of today can heal as time moves on, helps him. If you cannot feel this, try to get some professional help for yourself from a psychologist, a qualified marriage counselor, or a family-counseling service. FAMILY GUIDANCE SERVICES, in Volume 15, may have good suggestions for you.

Rae Russell

An honest sharing of feelings with hope and courage for the future may make a child feel more secure.

It is not wise to keep up a pretense of love when love has flown out the window. Sweet, martyrlike forgiveness in such an instance almost always is false. If you cannot help being bitter, do not hide it. Your child will feel more secure if he has the sound, solid truth of your feelings right out in the open than if he senses something shaky and insincere in what you say.

Feelings Can Be Shared

Steve's mother said to her five-year-old son, "Your Daddy's a wonderful man, Steve. Lots of people think so and you think so, too. I know that. But he wasn't wonderful to me and I don't like him."

"You're mad at him, Mom?" Steve asked.

"I'll say I am."

" 'Cause he got mad at you?"

"That's one reason."

"But you won't ever get that mad at me?"

"No, darling. Never!" she assured him. "I get mad at you, but it's a different kind of mad."

"Not the divorcing kind?"

"No, Steve. You never divorce children. They're yours for good."

But still, in spite of her reassurance, Steve went on worrying. What bothered him was the fear that his mother might send him away because he, too, sometimes was angry at her. When he was able to talk about his angry feelings and when he found out that his mother understood them, he was able again to be a happy, more independent boy.

Worries in Disguise

Children need to bring out their questions and worries. Most of all, they need to bring out their feelings of being

A small child often misunderstands events. "What if Mother leaves me, like she left Daddy?" is sometimes a worry.

"bad," and to know it is safe to be angry.

There is no child alive who does not occasionally have feelings of resentment toward both parents, especially when the parents are first separated or divorced. It is only natural that he should resent one or the other from time to time. Even children whose parents are getting along well have such feelings. Most often the child says nothing about his resentment, but his actions talk for him.

Nancy, who was eight, went on a hunger strike after her father left.

"It hurts me to see her sit and stare at her food," her mother confided to the psychologist from whom she sought help.

The psychologist told Nancy's mother that refusal to eat, lying, nail biting, and a dozen and one other kinds of disturbing behavior, even a cough for which the doctor finds no physical basis, can be expressions of anger. She told Nancy's mother to help Nancy put her feelings into words, instead of into naughtiness.

Permit the Words, Curb the Actions

Pete's father opened the subject to nine-year-old Pete. "I think you must be mad at me, Pete, for separating from Mother. Children always are angry at both parents when they start to get a divorce."

"Yes," said Pete thoughtfully. "You shouldn't have left Mom. I've had it in my mind to bust all your tools and bust up your car and everything."

"You can't do those things to let out your anger. I won't let you. But you can tell me how you feel any time you want."

Younger children, even two-year-olds, feel the insecurity that the decision to divorce invariably brings to the parents. Bobby takes his rubber doll and hits it, and calls it alternately, "Bad Mommie. Bad Daddy."

Bobby's mother knows that little children play out their feelings. She does not scold him, because she knows it is important for Bobby to keep sharing his feelings with her.

Steve worried that his mother would send him away because of his "badness." Nancy translated her mad feelings into roundabout "bad" acts. Some children fear that their "bad" thoughts have caused their parents' separation. If a child thinks it is wrong to have "bad" thoughts, all sorts of troubles grow. Parents can help their children know that "bad" feelings are a natural, normal part of life.

A child needs one home if he is to know where he belongs. Visiting the other parent is fine, but let it be a visit, not equal division of time.

Should a Child Have Two Homes?

Unless there are unusual circumstances, a child needs to see and visit with the parent who has left. These visits tend to assure him that he has not been deserted. Ordinarily, a child needs two parents, but he should have only one home.

Equal division of time is apt to be confusing. A child feels more secure when he can say, "Here is my home; this is where I live," and "There is where I visit."

For a child under four or five, the visits are ordinarily best confined to daytime. As he grows older he may ask, "May I spend the night?" It may be well, if the parent whom he wants to visit has room for him, to try it out. If the experience proves a comfortable and happy one for him and does not increase strain between his parents, he can try it again.

When he is around seven or eight years old, the child may want to spend several days or weeks during vacations with the other parent. At the age of nine or ten he may even elect to spend more time with him (or with her). There are no hard and fast rules as to how much time should be spent with which parent at what ages. What is most important is that the child feel easy and comfortable. It is important, too, that things be so planned that both parents feel as easy and comfortable as they can.

Clear-Cut Plans Ease the Strain

In most cases it is best to have arrangements about visits definite, and to have them put in legal terms. When they are fluctuating and lax, the child feels less secure.

"Hasn't my Daddy come yet?" weeps Susan. "It's almost noon. Last Sunday he came at nine o'clock. Something must have happened or he'd be here!"

"Oh, no, he wouldn't!" Mother flares. "That's typical of him. I know!"

Such scenes, obviously, only increase tension.

The parents should agree on definite details, and the information should be shared with the child.

"I'll pick you up every other Saturday," Ned's father tells his seven-year-old. "I'll be by for you between nine and ten in the morning and I've promised to have you back Sunday evening between six and seven."

Ned nods. He knows what he can count on, and that seems good.

"But I won't come into the house," Father continues. "Mother gets too upset. So I'll just ring the bell."

"Yes," says Ned, understandingly, "I think that's a good idea."

As a child grows, the legal arrangements concerning visits, and possibly also custody, may well be reviewed and revised to fit changed circumstances, interests, and needs.

When a Parent Remarries

One of the circumstances that brings changes is a parent's remarriage. Some children take the event casually. Says Barbara, five, with the pride of possession, "I got one new mother and one new father. I call them by their first names so I remember the real ones best. And I got two new grandmas and two new grandpas! Did you ever hear of so many new ones in your life?"

Other children feel left out when a parent remarries. "My Daddy kisses June and listens to her now, instead of me."

When a parent plans to get married, the fact should be shared with the child. "Tom and I are thinking of getting married. We're together a lot to see if we love each other enough. We'll let you know how things go."

In visiting the parent who has been remarried, the child still needs time for himself alone with his parent. A half-hour walk, a fifteen-minute talk, time alone for reading together, are desirable, as well as times when the child, his parent, and his stepparent have fun.

The parent should not suddenly give up the caretaking to the stepparent.

"I won't go driving with my Daddy! I don't like Nell," shrieks Bill, who is not quite four. "Daddy used to take me to 'Men's' and now I have to go to 'Ladies' with Nell."

How About Stepbrothers and Stepsisters?

When new children arrive on the scene, jealousies are bound to enter after the first flush of excitement. Half-sisters and half-brothers are no more immune to rivalry than are full sisters and brothers. Letting the "bad" feelings toward the new brother come out into the open in words, rather than deeds, is still our cue.

"I liked it more when you took me to the park instead of staying home with the smelly baby," says one five-year-old to his mother.

"Yes, dear, I know you did. You don't like either me or the baby, now. But pretty soon I'll be able to go to the park again with you."

"Hm!" with a sniff, "and take that brat? "I'm going to my daddy's to stay."

With the complaints out in the open, accepted, and understood, more peaceful days could come.

There is one actual advantage that the new baby enjoys which the older child often begrudges. "Mother's new baby has Mother's new name."

"When we both go to school, she'll be the one they think belongs in the family. And when you introduce us to people, you'll say, 'I'm Mrs. Smith and this is Mr. Smith and this is Judy Smith.' But I'm no Smith. I'm Eleanor Brown. So they'll look at me and wonder, 'Whose are you?'"

It may be to the child's best interest to bear the new name also, either through legal adoption by the new father, or by friendly consent. The matter should at least be freely discussed.

The new stepbrother or stepsister may seem like the final blow. The older child will need generous reassurance that she is still wanted.

What of the Part-Time Parent?

"Why do I have to go?" moans Stephanie.

"It's necessary, dear. Neither of us has a choice. It's . . . well, it's a law."

"Like 'Stop' when there's a red light?"

"Yes, only now it's 'Go'!"

Sometimes what Father does or thinks or feels influences the picture. Sometimes what Mother does or thinks is just as important.

"Mother didn't use to like me to go to Daddy's, and I didn't like to go, either. But when she got married, she changed her mind. It's okay for me to like to go now," a six-year-old confides.

Each individual parent of a child can work on his own adjustment. But neither one can successfully dictate to the estranged parent what to do. Sometimes, if both are willing, parents can talk things over. But, in the last analysis, nothing but the wish on the part of the parent himself will accomplish what is needed.

Where good will is lacking, the one parent cannot, need not, and should not try to make up for the other, for this may tie a child too close. It is better to permit the child his griping as a safety valve, and to help him, as he grows, to have his own interests, his own friends, and a life of his own.

If the Part-Time Parent Is Preferred

"His father is just as much of a child as Joe is. No more discipline than another nine-year-old! Joe comes home loaded with presents, lollipops and ice cream, dimes and baseball bats. How

Divorce and Separation

am I supposed to compete?" wails Joe's mother.

Competing is not the answer but, unfortunately, parents do compete. They may use the child as a weapon with which to carry on their battling. The child may use his parents similarly as weapons against each other in order to let his "bad" feelings out, especially if he has not been given opportunities to talk about his worries.

"What am I going to do with Lucy?" Lucy's mother asks. "She goes over to her father's and talks about me as though I were a witch. Then she comes home and talks about him as though he were Santa Claus. He glowers at me for treating her too badly, and I could kill him for treating her too well."

Ordinarily, children do protest more to the parent who has them most of the time.

"It's easy to have fun with a holiday parent," Beth's father told Beth. "But if I were to become the parent you stay with, you'd think I was just as bad as Mother."

"No, Daddy," said nine-year-old Beth, "I think I'd think you were worse."

Possibly more fun with you as the "stay-with" parent is indicated. Perhaps you have been a bit grim and have worn the weight of responsibility too heavily. Possibly you do not spend enough time enjoying your child rather than improving him.

Lollipop gifts do not cement the relationship. In the long run, there are things that are far more important. The honest sharing, the true understanding, the straightforward, non-mollycoddling but warm, down-to-earth caring for him count for more than ice cream and circuses. Give a child the feeling that he is accepted. Give him that secure sense that you love him and that with you he can be himself, and you build the deeper, more enduring relationship for the long pull.

These are the things that really count, for both parent and child!

The estranged parent may overload the child with presents, but these are no substitute for continuous, kindly care.

Ewing Galloway

Fun and laughter with the "stay-with" parent are an important part of life.

Korling

FAMILY UPS AND DOWNS

JAMES LEE ELLENWOOD, D.D.
Author, "It Runs in the Family" and "Just and Durable Parents," Westbury, N. Y.

Ups and downs in family life are a normal part of everyday living. Like measles or television, few families escape them. No one is to be blamed and it is a waste of time to search for culprits.

Two acute causes of family ups and downs are fluctuation in finance matters and the distressing difficulties that go hand in hand with the critical illness of a parent. Here are two eventualities that may strike any home at any time, even without warning. If parents have given some thought to meeting these trying situations, family crises may be weathered with far less strain.

Let Children Know

There is a significant reason for telling the children what is happening, and telling them promptly. Although they seem to possess the capacity to sense change and unrest, they may ascribe it to false and exaggerated causes, and imagine things to be worse than they are. Children lack the ability to express their deepest emotions in words. They build up dire fears and forebodings that can result in worry that has no foundation in the facts. Reasoning in a typically childish way, a small boy or girl may conclude that his own misdemeanors are the cause of all the trouble.

What Shall We Tell?

In confronting the children, we had better tell the truth, and nothing but the truth. Young people want to know the facts, and need to know them, for their picture of the situation will influence the way they act.

All doleful circumstances need not be related in detail. You can avoid creating worry and confusion and still not omit any essential facts.

How the children are told will count for exactly as much as *what* they are told, so be as direct, as simple, and as reassuring as possible. Self-pity has no place in the recital.

Responses Differ

Some youngsters make so few comments that you think they are not interested. Often the response of a six-year-old or an eight-year-old is so far off the main line that you feel he has not understood the full meaning of what he has been told.

"Will there be a place to roller-skate?" was the only concern one small person expressed when she was told the family would be moving half way around the world, because of her mother's illness.

We should not expect the same reactions from all the assorted ages, nor is the same approach to be used for all the children as we acquaint them with family difficulties. Each child needs to have the situation presented in ways appropriate to his years, and in terms that he may quickly understand.

It is not a waste of time to make careful explanations, even if a child grasps the facts only imperfectly. Children lose confidence in their parents and experience a sense of acute uncertainty if they are told nothing, or if you try to fool them. They may feel that they do not belong to the family group at all. Some children figure out that the reason they are not being told the facts is that it would be unbearable, or actually dangerous, for them to know the truth. Eventually, when they grow up, these children may shrink from accepting any unpleasant facts, just because they have the impression, "It would be bad for me to know. I should be protected."

Either of these states of mind can cause real unhappiness. What is more, the feeling of being pushed aside may be at the root of a great deal of children's misbehavior.

Children often have their own methods of expressing their resentment when they are shut out. A child may sulk in his room, or refuse to pick up his things or eat his dinner. In extreme cases, he may even run away from home.

Belonging Is Essential

Knowing that you are a part of the family is more important than eating bushels of carrots and spinach, picking up playthings, or being nice and polite to dear Aunt Susie.

A boy or girl of any age, from one to one hundred, desperately needs to feel wanted, and ardently desires to be considered an indispensable part of his group.

One family, out for a ride, was stopped by a state trooper. In the front seat, next to Father, sat five-year-old Ruth. The trooper must have been in a kindly mood, for instead of turning on the humiliated father he said, "Young lady, why do you permit your father to drive so fast?"

Ruth felt tremendously important over this unexpected turn of events and promptly answered him, "We were driving fast because we are going to my grandma's house and I am in a hurry to get to the bathroom."

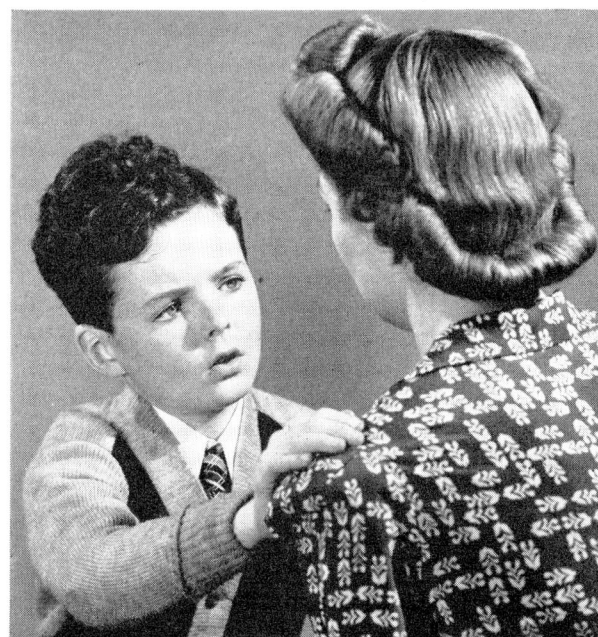

You can usually give a child an idea of the actual state of affairs without frightening him. He worries less if he knows he is in your confidence.

The trooper had no ready reply for that one, and gallantly waved them on. Ruth's elation was complete. "Well, I sure helped you out of that mess," she said proudly.

Beyond doubt, her intense delight was caused by the fact that she had been recognized as an important member of the group. Furthermore, she was immensely gratified that she had been able to extricate her family from a bad predicament.

Since Ruth was in this case telling the truth, perhaps we do not need to worry about the ethics of the situation. Being part of the family does not always mean rising to heights of nobility.

In far more serious matters, children may help when they are acquainted with the situation and are given a chance to do their share. They derive a fine sense of family solidarity and a great amount of self-confidence, when they can make a contribution.

It is worth taking some trouble to figure out how each child can be useful, and how he can find satisfaction in making his contribution. If a child volunteers to assume a responsibility which might prove too hard to carry out, you can suggest a sensible compromise and avert a painful failure.

How Discreet Are Children?

Too often, parents have kept things from the younger generation because of a dreadful fear that family secrets might be circulated in the neighborhood.

The young are usually quite dependable as guardians of family secrets. The tender generation is extremely reluctant to discuss family evils with outsiders. You can trust them more, for instance, then you can trust Uncle Billy or Aunt Emma, or any gossipy adult. No fear of undue revelation should prevent family teamwork.

Facing Financial Reverses

An acquaintance of ours was faced with a long period of illness, and a resultant drop in family income. Suddenly, spending had to be cut to a bare minimum. Economizing meant moving to a smaller house in the country, giving up the car, and forgetting all notions of new clothes.

The parents were disturbed about the effect on the children. One would be forced to give up his cherished dream of going to camp for the summer. Another would have to leave her friends and the school which gave her special opportunities in music. All would undergo drastic changes in their way of life.

Wisely, the parents decided to call together the entire group. Junior, who was five, might be too young for complete comprehension, but no chance could be taken that he might feel that he was being left out of things.

"Children," Mother said, "we need your help. Dad's income has been cut away down, and will be low for the next few years. You know he can't work much, now. We will have to move to the country where living will be cheaper. We will all need to give up things we have become accustomed to."

They Rise to the Occasion

To her great surprise, the children seemed disturbed only by their parent's illness, and not at all worried about the economies. As a matter of fact, if parents are not upset by necessary economies, the children usually follow their lead, and are reasonably cheerful.

"Suffering cats, Mom," Joe said, "why didn't you tell us sooner? We knew that

A change in the family's fortunes may bring out unsuspected strengths, new satisfactions, and deeper respect, as everyone puts a shoulder to the wheel.

Dad wasn't well, and we could see that something was bothering you, but we didn't know anything we could do about it. Let's go!"

And they are still going strong and having a great time of it. This could not have happened had not the crisis been faced together by the entire family unit.

Recently we visited the group, and only then did we learn how painful and difficult the adjustments had been. Each member had lost much and, being only human, had felt the pinch. But the losses were offset by newly discovered assets and capabilities. Working together, each confident of the other, informed about the situation, and aware of the need for co-operation, a family can tackle almost any crisis that comes along. But leadership and inspiration must come from the parents.

It Has Happened Before

As adults, we have had enough experience with the world to know that people have had illnesses, reverses, and troubles of all kinds before. We know, too, that others have surmounted, or at least muddled through, their troubles. Children have no idea that troubles come to everyone.

It is good mental hygiene to point out to the children that others have lived through this sort of thing and still managed to enjoy life. If some families the children know have weathered similar storms, it does no harm to point out that fact.

Offer a Program

Concrete suggestions that give the children a notion of what they can do to help are in themselves encouraging. You are less likely to go into a panic if, under any circumstances, you know what you can do and what is expected of you.

"Now be good." "Be careful." "Behave yourself." "Be thoughtful." Such admonitions are too indefinite for the youngster of seven or eight or ten.

It is better to be specific, making clear, for instance, just what being "careful" should involve. If it means fewer sodas or fewer parties, no trips on the train, treating our clothes so they will wear longer, or giving up our pet projects, say so frankly. If parents can give guidance and suggest a method, children will tend to accept whatever comes more readily. They know their parents are doing something to protect and care for them. They feel that their parents are equal to the situation.

We can take care not to be so detailed that we deprive our young people of any initiative. We can try to make each member of the family feel that his advice is needed, and that his suggestions will be considered. Then each will sense that he has a vital part in the new program. Adults can pay youth no finer compliment than to ask, "Well, what else do you think we should do now?"

"What do you think we should do?" can follow some positive suggestions from parents. The problem is, after all, primarily the adults'. If children felt all the decisions must be theirs, the responsibility would be overwhelming.

Daily Life Goes On

If possible, children should not have every event of their daily lives colored by the need to count the pennies. Parents can avoid emphasizing at every turn, "We can't do the things we did last year." Then children are more likely to take in their stride stew instead of steak; a picnic instead of a movie party on birthdays; and patched overalls instead of new ones.

Parents do their children no favor if they make tremendous sacrifices so that the children will not be affected in any way by the need to economize. If ten-year-old Alice does not go to Miss Uppish's dancing school this winter, she will be none the worse for it. If dancing school and all that it involves is out of keeping with the scheme of things in the family, Alice will probably not be the gainer in any way if she attends.

It has even happened that giving up certain "advantages" has appeared to the children as a blessing in disguise.

A bit of sensible philosophizing with the children will be found useful, but it must be real and it must be sensibly expressed. It must, above all, be something we really believe and are willing to put into practice ourselves.

When Fortune Improves

Now and then there develops a situation of quite different nature. A family suddenly faces unexpected wealth and good fortune.

Difficulties that come with greatly increased resources may not be as obvious as those faced in financial depressions, but they may be far more insidious.

How Shall We Take Prosperity?

Sudden wealth always brings real tests of character. Some of the more dangerous traits, to be avoided rigidly, are negligence and wastefulness, selfishness and extravagance, self-indulgence and social snobbery. If we are not careful, the security that comes with money is permitted to become a substitute for the practice of our better qualities.

Children in a family suddenly enriched will need to be taught that virtues of modest living may not be discarded. In large measure they are essential in the more affluent state of affairs. Toys should be used carefully and habits of thrift should continue. Friendship is to be maintained, and social relationships must rest on a sound, democratic foundation.

If a Parent Is Ill

The inevitable visitation of illness in the home, particularly when one of the parents is afflicted, brings about crises, too. At these times children undergo intense worry and strain. You take the first important step when you give an explanation. Naturally, what you say depends on how old the children are. No matter what words you use, the tone of your explanation is the important matter. You can stress the things that are being done to aid recovery. Older children may worry about what a father's illness means as far as loss of the family income is concerned, and they can be told what provisions the family has made for such a rainy day.

For the smaller children, the bottom drops out of the universe the day Mother takes to her bed, or goes to the hospital.

Giving Reassurance

If Mother herself can tell the children about her illness or her coming hospitalization, things will not look so black. Unless it is absolutely unavoidable, and it rarely is, no child should ever experience the shock of having his mother whisked away to the hospital in his absence. Coming in from play or from school to be confronted by a stranger or an empty house, and the news that Mother is in the hospital, is enough to send a boy or girl under ten into a tailspin. And it usually does!

If Mother is sick in bed at home, the children can probably come to the door and talk to her, and that is a comfort to them. They know she is there. She can be called on to give the last word on such vital matters as whether Bobby must have a bath before supper, as that valiant pinch-hitter, Cousin Mathilda, is insisting he should, or whether he may wait until bedtime as is his custom.

Show How They Can Help

Children, even young ones, have a great capacity for rising to the occasion when definite and suitable ways of helping are suggested to them.

One mother put it this way to her three sons, seven, nine, and ten years old: "I know you boys are the kind we can count on. I'll be in the hospital about a week. Nothing very much is going to happen to me, and when I come home I'll probably feel much better. You boys know where everything is, so you'll have to help Daddy get breakfast and do some of the straightening up. You'll have to fix your own lunch boxes, and Minnie, whom you all like, will be here when you come home from school. She'll get supper for you and Dad. We'll talk to each other on the telephone, and probably Dad can bring you to see me on Sunday. You'll have to help Minnie take care of things, and while I'm gone you'll have to remember about feeding the goldfish and Jip without anybody reminding you. How about an ice-cream cone all around right now?"

There are no signs of fear or panic in such an explanation. Alarming details are omitted, and there is no frightening uncertainty. A simple appeal is made for co-operation, and there is sensible effort to maintain family morale. No undue responsibility is placed on the shoulders

The youngster who is away from home knows he is not forgotten if Mother and Father telephone him frequently.

of those who may not yet be up to it.

There may be a temptation to say to the three- or four-year-olds, "You must be good, so Daddy (or Mommy) will get better fast." Small children cannot understand cause and effect. Obviously, no three- or four-year-old will be "good" consistently. If he feels there is any connection between his "badness" and his parent's illness he may feel overwhelmingly guilty.

It cannot be said that no chins will quiver, or that there will be no doubts and protests at an announcement that Mother is ill or going to the hospital. But at least the doubts can come out in the open and can be dealt with. "Minnie, whom you all like," or a reasonable facsimile of her who will make life agreeable for the children, is important. She may be a relative, a neighbor, or that rare and precious jewel, a family helper. Even a child who is a worrier will worry less if somebody who is comforting is around part of the time. As much of Father's time as he can give to the children, and his cheery reassurance that Mother is on the mend, will be invaluable.

Should a Child Be Sent Away?

Sometimes, in case of sickness in the family, it may seem advisable to send one or more of the children to a neighbor's house for a visit until the trouble blows over. When this becomes necessary, care should be taken to do a number of seemingly small things that may ease the worry and fears of the young deportee. Calls on the phone, short visits, a little present of some sort, information about things at home—these and many other deeds of thoughtfulness will help the visitor understand that he is a vital part of the family. They will keep him conscious of his most cherished relationship. In any case, he should know that he is wanted back at home, and soon.

Ready for Anything

Emergencies of any kind may be tided over when parents take the entire family into sensible confidence, maintain a serene attitude, and offer a program of mutual faith and help.

Too often we find ourselves beaten by emergencies, and unable to cope with difficulties, because we have not made preparations in advance. It will help if we try to figure out ahead of time the best method and mood for us to assume. Then we can make even emergencies occasions for drawing family members closer together. Then we can probably surmount obstacles in a way that furthers rather than threatens the growth of each individual.

SPECIAL FAMILY SITUATIONS

29. THE ADOPTED CHILD

30. STEPPARENTS AND STEPCHILDREN

31. GIFTED CHILDREN

32. THE HANDICAPPED CHILD AND YOUR CHILD

33. THE HANDICAPPED CHILD IN THE FAMILY

34. SPECIAL NEEDS OF VARIOUS HANDICAPS

    Children Who Cannot See
    Children Who Are Hard of Hearing
    Children Who Are Crippled
    Children Who Have Cerebral Palsy
    Children Who Are Epileptic
    Children Who Are Mentally Retarded
    Children with Rheumatic Fever

Some families have adopted children, stepchildren, or children who are exceptional in some way.

Because of their experiences or because of their native endowments, some of these children are particularly vulnerable. They may require special understanding, special attention, or special interpretation in varying degrees in certain situations.

If the child feels that the adults around him accept him, he is free to be himself, to grow, to make his contribution in the family and the community. Then the family can grow in solidarity, too.

THE ADOPTED CHILD

MAY REYNOLDS SHERWIN, Ph.D.
Author, "Children From Seed to Sapling," Wappingers Falls, N. Y.

THE adopted child in the home is no different from any other child, for children are children wherever you find them. My husband and I adopted our two boys and two girls. The six of us have had fifteen years of unusually happy family life together. Adopted children are just as naughty, just as lovable, just as annoying, and just as satisfying as children the world over.

No two children are alike, of course. Each child is different from all the others because he is himself. Adoption has nothing to do with that difference.

This Is Adoption

Adoption brings together parents who want children and children who want parents. Once they are together and the legal hurdles are over, the situation is the same as it is for all parents and children. The problems of the adopted child in the home cannot really be separated from those of any other child.

Good Adoption Practice

Most people picture the adopting parents coming away from a hospital with a baby in their arms, as if the mother herself had given birth to the child. Adoption does not work this way. Tiny babies are seldom available for adoption. Good adoption practice encourages a mother to take time to decide whether she can care for her baby herself. Only after careful deliberation and helpful counsel is a parent permitted to give the baby out for adoption. By that time the baby has started to grow. He grows more while the agency takes time to study the youngster and make sure that he will develop normally. No wonder there are not enough babies for all the adopting parents who want them!

The best way to find a child to adopt is to work with a recognized adoption agency. Finding a child or children for adoption may be rather confusing. Adoption is a relatively new development. It has grown in popularity faster than the social-work machinery that is supposed to control it. The time factor is important. You must exercise real patience, for adopting parents may have to wait a few months, or even years.

Now he is really yours! Be proud of the fact that you adopted your child, and he will grow up proud of it, too.

There is more involved in an adoption program than meets the eye of adopting parents. It is not just a matter of finding a child for you. A good adoption agency also helps those who are giving up the youngsters. The agency's staff bends over backward to provide the best for the child, too. The agency often works on a small budget and with a limited staff. In one way, the work of an adoption agency is like an iceberg. Seven eighths of it you never see, but it is there just the same. It is well to have a wholesome respect for it. A good agency is your protection. It makes sure that the youngster is ready for adoption, and forestalls any possibility of his being taken from you once he is settled in your home.

Where Shall I Find My Child?

Go first to the agency nearest your home. Your State Department of Welfare or Welfare Council will direct you to the right place. Get their help and advice. Work with this agency as long as you receive any encouragement from them. If time drags on and you do not seem to be getting anywhere, find another agency in some other part of the country. It is easier to work with the agency nearest your home, but no law says you have to limit your activities to any one agency. Put out as many lines as you can, and some day you will find just the youngster or youngsters you are looking for.

In adopting our children, my husband and I took the attitude that somewhere in these United States there were children for us. We felt it was up to us to find them. We did find them, in three different states, five hundred or more miles away from our home. Although it took us almost ten years to bring our

You may discover that a six-year-old is even more fun than a baby if you are willing to take a lively, interested youngster into your home.

family together, it was worth it, many times over.

Two to Get Ready

There are steps parents can take to get themselves and their home ready for the youngsters they hope to adopt. What you do depends on whether your adopted child will be the first child to come into your home, or whether you already have a child and are adopting one to enlarge the family.

In either case you will want to make sure that your own attitude toward adoption is good. If you want your child to feel proud about his adoption, to accept it naturally and easily, you must be able to accept it yourself. You will be your child's teachers. He will learn from each of you. He will learn from the way you feel even more than he learns from what you may tell him. The starting point is for you yourself to feel proud about adoption. Then you can help him meet the bewildering situations adopted children sometimes face. If your own attitude is good, you are ready for any emergency.

Books and articles on adoption will be valuable. Talk with parents of adopted children to get their advice and suggestions. The ideas you get from such reading and conversation will help you decide whether you can accept an adopted child comfortably and happily.

Learn About Children

Should this child you plan to adopt be your first child, the best preparation will be for you to spend some time with children.

If you do not like this idea, if being with children is a burden and a bore to you, you had better take your name off the agency waiting list. Adoption is not for you. You cannot fool yourself that "It will be different with our own child." Children are children wherever you find them. They are fun at all ages, if you understand them and know what to do for and with them. If you do not understand them, they are likely to scare you. Then you might take refuge, as so many scared grown-ups do, in a stern "do it because I say so" attitude toward children. That is no basis for a successful family relationship. Love and understanding make the family wheels go round smoothly. You undoubtedly have the love or you would not be wanting to adopt a child. You might as well use the waiting time to develop an understanding of how youngsters grow, what they need, and how they feel.

If you do not know children very well, look around for opportunities to be with them. Lend a helping hand to the parents you know. Volunteer at a children's hospital, playground, or day nursery. You might change your ideas about the age and kind of youngster you would like to adopt.

Most people start out looking for a curly-headed baby girl. After you have learned what fun toothless, six-year-old boys can be, you may want to tell the agency that you will take a youngster of any age or sex whose personality appeals to you. That would shorten your waiting period a great deal. Agencies have more older children available, and fewer demands for them. The satisfactions are just as great. Here in our home we speak from experience. All four of our youngsters had passed their sixth birthdays when they came to us.

Becoming Acquainted

One day, word will come from an agency that there is a child for you. Off go the adopting parents to the agency office to talk over the youngster's background. Possibly you will see the child himself right then. The social worker will tell you all that she knows about the child. The final decision is up to you, and no one can really help you with that. It is how you both feel that counts. Are you drawn to the youngster? Do your personalities click? If it is not a case of love at first sight, take time before you decide.

If there are other children in your family old enough to have opinions about a new brother or sister, by all means let them get acquainted with the youngster you are considering. Everybody loves babies, so there is seldom any question about them. Older children are more reserved. They are apt to be on their best behavior in the first interview, and it is hard to tell what they really are like. Other children will help them thaw out and feel more comfortable. Then the real personality of the youngster comes through. That is the time to tell whether or not the child appeals to you.

You Need a Trial Run

If you do decide that this is the youngster for you, then you can begin to do all those things that you have put off for so long. Fixing up a room for the child, buying toys and clothes are delightful experiences. At last, you can do something definite to make ready for your child.

Most people think that adoption begins the day the youngster is first placed in your home. Technically, it is not quite as simple as that. Usually there is a trial period of about a year before the formal adoption can take place. Adoption agencies feel that this gives both parents and child a chance to become accustomed to each other. They need a trial period in order to make sure that

Suzanne Szasz

Angry words may be frequent until a child is sure he belongs in the new family. The youngster needs reassurance and parents need patience until he feels this is "for keeps."

the arrangement will work out satisfactorily. But to all intents and purposes, at least in your minds, adoption begins when you bring the child to your home. What a happy day that is and how you want to shout it from the housetops!

Once the youngster is with you, the problems are no longer those of adoption. They are just the usual run-of-the-mill family problems—the kind that all families have. The child-training books that help other mothers will help you, too. In this volume, the chapter WHAT CHILDREN NEED FROM LIFE will be most helpful.

How Can I Help Him Feel at Home?

There is a period of adjustment in the beginning. This is the time when all members of the family are learning to get along with the newcomer. It is like the period in any family after the new baby comes home from the hospital. Don't rush things at this stage. Take it slowly and easily. Don't expect too much of the youngster, the family, or yourselves.

One of our girls was almost eleven when she came to us. She was fiercely independent at first. It was some time before she accepted us as her family. She insisted on paying her own way when we went to the movies, and paid other small expenses. She even bought from us any stamps she used, though we encouraged her to help herself from the family supply. It was her way of showing that she did not yet feel safe and secure with us. We respected her feelings and let her take her time. Finally, one day, we rejoiced to see her use one of our stamps without paying for it. That was the sign that our family had passed the test. Our new daughter and sister was ready to become one of us. She felt at home at last.

Let Him Be Himself

The core of feelings and behavior that is the real child may not be visible at first. Years may pass before you can be sure what the youngster wants or needs from life. But you can be ready to let the child grow and develop in the way that nature intended him to. No child, either adopted or born to you, should be allowed to grow into a selfish, unpleasant person. You cannot make a musician out of him if he would rather be a carpenter. You need not try to make him a conservative if he is cut out to be a reformer. Let him be himself, but take into account the effect of his behavior on the other persons with whom he has to live and work.

Ups and Downs in Feelings

Parents usually feel loving and sentimental when their youngsters first come to them. They are sure that they will always feel that way. They are surprised one day to find themselves upset and angry with their children.

One mother with a saving sense of humor used to say, "I'm so cross with the kids this morning, I'd like to put them in the ashcan with their feet sticking out!" When she felt like that, she called them her "ashcan babies." All parents feel that way at times. It has nothing to do with adoption. It is just a normal part of the ups and downs of family life.

The youngsters' feelings about parents are changeable too. We would like to think that they are overwhelmed with love for us all the time, but they are not. Our four used to burst out against us, either singly or in a body, from time to time.

One time the four children ganged up. They were angry at us, although no one remembers now what was the cause. The children stamped off to bed, telling us in no uncertain terms to let them alone. Mysterious noises went on upstairs. With difficulty their dad and I restrained our curiosity until we were sure they were sound asleep. Then we went to investigate. We found all four

You need a sense of humor when the children shut you out. Don't take it personally, for it happens sometimes to every mother and father.

youngsters asleep in the same room on mattresses strewn about the floor. A large penciled sign was pinned on the door.

Keep Out!
This Means Parents

The children apparently knew that we would not obey these orders. As we crossed the room to open the window and make sure that each child was properly covered, we stumbled over another sign. It said "Can't You Read?"

It is well if parents can handle incidents like this with a light touch and a sense of humor. Even then, there are times in every family when things get a little "thick." At these moments, it helps to remember that it is good for parents and children alike to blow off steam now and then. Family life cannot and should not always be smooth and pleasant. We really would not like it that way. It is the ups and downs that add zest to life.

Explaining Adoption

Many adopting parents are afraid of the questions that their youngsters *might* ask. The parents' attitudes determine what the adoption questions will be, as well as the kind of answers they give. That is why it is important for adopting parents to get things straight in their own minds and hearts before the questions arise.

Every child should know from the beginning that he is adopted. It should be so much an accepted fact that the question of "When shall I tell my child?" never comes up. Parents and friends should talk about this child's adoption in his hearing, even when he is a tiny baby. Long before he can understand what it is all about, he will *feel* that he is something special.

Many adopting parents have sent out announcements in order that there can be no doubt in anyone's mind. One of the most gracious of these announcements read:

Mr. and Mrs. James Brand
are happy to announce that their
chosen daughter
Mary Jane
is now in her nursery at
19 Oak Lane

A Favorite Story

As soon as the child is old enough to be interested in stories, you can tell him the story of how he came to live with you. All children like stories, especially about themselves. Adopted children like to hear from their parents how "We looked and looked until we found just the baby (or youngster) we wanted. And who do you suppose that was? It was you, of course." Soon the child will ask for this story himself. "Tell me about the time you first saw me," he will say, or "What was I like when I came here?" Over and over again, you will have to repeat the story of his adoption. As you tell it, the child will fill in the details. He will like to answer the questions himself.

If the story is told and retold, a youngster grows up knowing that his parents really wanted him. He feels their joy and pride in his adoption. Retelling the story also helps parents feel right about adoption. You cannot think of adoption

> Doubts children may have from time to time can be set at rest when the story of "how we chose you for our very own" is retold frequently.

as an unfortunate secret when you share a youngster's joy in the story of how he came to you. You will never have to worry about when to tell your child, in any formal sense, if he knows from the beginning that he is adopted. You will both be proud of his adoption.

Older Children Welcome Adoption

You could not keep the facts from the older children even if you wanted to do so. If adopting parents could know what it means to a youngster to be adopted into a home of his own, any doubts or hesitation they might feel about telling him would be swept away.

To have no home of one's own, to live in foster homes, in children's institutions, or with relatives who do not really care is a sad fate. The older a child is the more he realizes that these are not substitutes for a real home. He wants desperately to be adopted. He wants to be placed in a home of his own—for keeps. He wants to know, as one child put it, that he "won't have to be moved again." He longs for a "real mommy and daddy."

This yearning for a family of one's own was brought home to us forcibly when we first saw the six-year-old who was to be our daughter. She put her hand in mine and said, "You have two children now and when you take me, you'll have three." She was as ready to

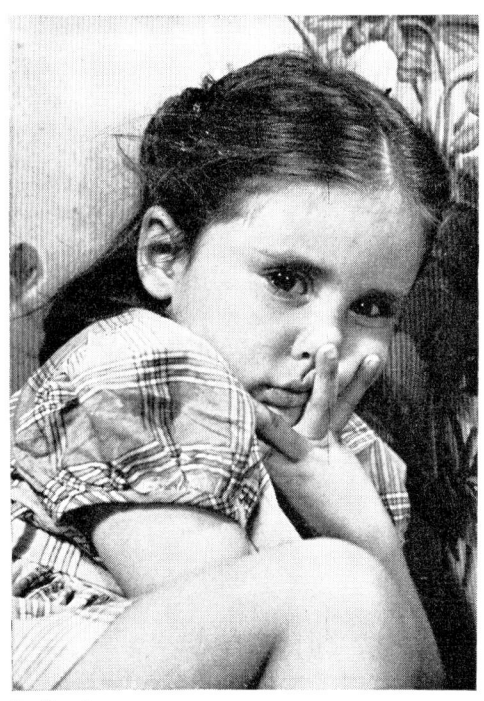

Rae Russell

be adopted as we were eager to have her.

"Who Was My Mother?"

A child whose questions about adoption have been answered honestly as he was growing up probably would never ask questions like "Who was my real mother?" "Why did she give me away?" He would already know, from the stories about his adoption that have been his steady fare for years, that you are his *real* mother for good and always. You are his mother and father legally and because you *feel* that you are. His "other mother" was "the lady who borned him," to use an expression our youngsters coined. He would not feel that she "gave him away." He would understand from what he had been told that she only let him go because she could not take care of him properly herself. She wanted him to have a better home and family life than she could give him. It was a hard thing to do but she did it for his sake. She went to the Child Welfare Association and asked the lady there to find a mother and father for him who would love him as much as she did and who could give him everything she wanted him to have. That was how he came to be adopted. All this the child would know from the beginning, as a part of knowing about his adoption. A child with a background of understanding like this would probably never ask why his real mother gave him away, any more than he would ask "Am I adopted?"

Preserve the Information

It is well to be prepared for the other questions adopted children will ask about their backgrounds. You cannot count on your memory to retain the details the children have a right to know some day. The years blot out the things that were so fresh in your minds when the youngsters first came to you.

There is one way to have this information available to the children when they are ready for it. The agency will prepare a written summary of the child's background and give it to the adopting parents at the time of the child's adoption. The parents can keep this in a sealed envelope marked with his name. Keep it in a safe place, with the rest of the family papers. The family safe deposit box, if you have one, is the best place. It is reassuring to the child to know that, even though you cannot give him the details now, some day he will know. You can say to him as he is growing up, "Honestly, dear, I don't remember. But I do know that it is all written down. You will want to know those things about your other family. Some day when you are old enough, you can read it for yourself. It's all in a sealed envelope, marked with your name. Even if something happens to us, you will have it. It is being kept for you, and nobody can open it but you."

"We're Proud of Adoption"

Here, as in all matters pertaining to adoption, your attitude is the crux of the matter. If you talk of adoption naturally in your home, the children will easily learn and accept the facts. If you cultivate that comfortable feeling in yourself, you will not need any guide to tell you what to say or when to say it. You will act as you feel, and it is your feelings that are important.

We feel proud and comfortable about adoption in our home. The *feeling* comes first with us. The mechanics of adoption and child training take second place. Adoption merely brings together parents who want children in their homes and children who want homes. Each then may give to the other what is peculiarly his to give. We speak from experience when we say the satisfactions work both ways. Our four youngsters, Bob, Ray, Janet, and Ruth, have done more for us than we will ever be able to do for them.

STEPPARENTS AND STEP-CHILDREN

MARY H. FRANK, B.S.
Co-author, with Lawrence K. Frank, "How to Help Your Child in School," New York, N. Y.

IN "REAL" parenthood, as most parents realize, love grows and deepens with the years, as the child and the parent build on memories. This is true in stepparenthood, too. And in real parenthood, there are moments of discouragement and doubt, just as there are in stepparenthood.

Your Feelings About Yourself

When parenthood is a brand new relationship, it may bring with it feelings of unsureness and doubt, even, at times, despair. It may bring occasional feelings of dislike for children, or anger at one's spouse, and perhaps jealousy of the other parent's relationship to a child. And yet, despite all the old fairy stories, stepparenthood can be richly rewarding.

"Slow But Sure" Builds Confidence

Stepparents often expect far too much of themselves. Just as you have, in many jobs, a few weeks of training time, so, in parenthood, you need to allow for "getting-acquainted" time. In this time there will be mistakes, irritability, tears. But occasional insecurity is an "occupational hazard" of parenthood. Stepfathers and stepmothers can expect some of it.

Preconceived Theories May Not Work

A stepparent must also be willing to change some of his ideas about children. If you come to stepparenthood with no children of your own, you may have made up your mind about what children are like and how they should be reared. Some of these theories may have come from your own childhood days, some from observing other children. Some notions stem from your own wishes and dreams about married life and parenthood.

If you have children of your own, and acquire a new family with remarriage, you are likely to consider what your own children do as "normal." You may lose sight of the infinite variations in behavior and in personality that can be good and useful.

Feelings About Your Marriage

Stepparenthood is a relationship that involves a great deal more than just being a parent. In stepparenthood, the happiness of the husband-and-wife relationship often depends on the parent-and-child relationship.

For example, if you are a stepmother married to the father of one or two or more children, you may be worried about doing the right thing with the children. You are also worried for fear what you do to the children will make your husband less fond of you. You feel that, to keep your husband's love, you must be not a stepmother, but a "supermother."

Much of the tension in all parent-child relationships comes not from *one* parent, or from the way *one* parent talks to one child. *It arises from the whole family system, from Father's and Mother's relationship to each other and to the children.* Parents need to give each other understanding in their difficulties so that they can rear children confidently. The chapter PARENTS ARE ALSO HUSBANDS AND WIVES in this volume discusses the effect of the relationship of the parents on their children.

What Are Stumbling Blocks?

Parents, "real" or "step," are more relaxed and happier when they know ahead of time how children may be expected to act.

The stepparent family may be one of a number of combinations. Whatever combination your family may be, there are certain kinds of problems you may meet as a stepparent. These problems seem to be the ways in which the worries of a child who has a stepparent will frequently show up, no matter how good the stepparent may be.

You will, in many cases, find some demonstration of antagonism. It may be open rebellion or sulky silence. You may run into learning problems. A child may have difficulty in learning to read, or may show a sudden and marked resistance to school work.

A child may steal small things such as desirable objects from other children, or a trinket belonging to a parent. "Tall tales" are not unusual.

Stepchildren tend to worry about their own possessions more than "own" children. This worry may come out in terms of wanting many things, or wanting to hold on to things and refusing to discard anything. Sometimes the child becomes unduly concerned about money as a possession.

What Causes the Antagonism?

The loss of a parent by death, divorce, or abandonment usually involves some kind of deep hurt for a child. The baby or child feels helpless and frightened. "Fight" is a common way of dealing with fright. Withdrawal and retreat are other ways of reacting to helplessness. Children may do either one.

Antagonism—a Response to Loss

For instance, Derek, a four-year-old in a preschool group, had been deserted by his father when he was two. At four, he made the other children in his group miserable by appropriating, each morning, whatever toys or possessions they had. He was also a "biter." He did his biting unexpectedly and for no apparent

The infinite variety in children's personalities may hold a few surprises for you. It takes all kinds to make a happy family.

Suzanne Szasz

Korth

Pinney, Monkmeyer

One finds delight in any toy. Another is absorbed in tinkering, while baseball, and only baseball, makes life worth living for many lively boys.

reason. To adults he was a sweet, almost overaffectionate child, eager for hugs, for attention.

Even though his mother had remarried, he spread exciting stories in his group about his "real" father. "My daddy has a big car." "My daddy is going to take me to the circus." These stories were wishful thinking. They were his response to the spontaneous remarks of other children whose daddies took them places and gave them presents. He was jealous of the other children, and of the fact that they had something valuable which he did not have. Therefore, almost *all* the possessions they had seemed to him infinitely desirable. Such behavior is a child's defense. It is not "badness," nor is it the stepparent's fault.

It Is Hard to Share a Parent

If a parent remarries when a child is between six and ten or eleven years, another kind of resentment may appear.

A child normally and naturally, especially in the years from two to six, becomes attached to a parent of the opposite sex. If a little boy has lost his father, and lives with his mother for a number of years without another male in the household, his normal attachment to his mother may be prolonged. Normally, he would become interested in masculine pursuits about the time he entered grade school. If his mother marries again, a boy, after five or six years of having Mother to himself, may show marked antagonism to his new father. Such a child may be disturbed. He may, for example, show sudden learning problems or be extremely withdrawn and unhappy. He may need special guidance in order to get along with friends and to accept the changed family situation.

A similar problem may occur when a mother dies and a daughter remains with her father for many years. She may start to keep house for him and feel possessive about him. She may show acute jealousy when he speaks of remarrying.

The real parent is wise to stand firm in his or her resolution to marry. Even though the child objects, the marriage will eventually produce a happier and more wholesome family life for the growing boy or girl.

Why Do Children Feel Guilty?

Another reason for a child's antagonism to a stepparent is his guilt. Children often say to their real parents, "I hate you . . . I wish you were dead." Or they say, "I hate you," and then privately wish you were dead. If the child is told often and emphatically that it is wrong to hate someone, especially Mother or Father, he may feel guilty. Most children hate, or have hated, someone at some time in their lives. We cannot feel love for everybody all the time. Children, who are constantly told what to do and what not to do, are especially likely to have these strong, but brief, feelings of resentment.

Now, a child may have had such strong feelings toward his parent, and may have been told that these feelings are wicked. If, then, that parent dies, his guilt may become intense. He feels that, by wishing it, he has caused the death of his parent. It is hard, then, for the child to accept a new parent. A stepparent is a constant reminder of his guilt. The happiness the stepparent shows in his new relationship is a blow to the child and adds to his emotional burden. The upset child may need to talk to a person skilled in understanding and helping children, in order to talk out, and thereby release, his guilt feelings.

Past Experiences May Create Suspicion

The behavior of an upset child does not indicate willfulness or bad temper. It is, rather, a sign of profound feelings of unhappiness that often disturb his behavior and appear in his attitude toward a newcomer.

Other earlier experiences may have made the child more vulnerable, less secure about people in general, and, therefore, less able to accept a change in his family situation.

Most little children have had some experiences that have left them a bit worried and uncertain about the world and people beyond their immediate family. Sickness will do it, or a constant turnover of people responsible for the child's care in the household. The death or divorce that preceded a second marriage is in itself enough to have made a child wary. All these experiences and anxieties will play a part in the child's attitudes toward a stepparent. A stepmother or stepfather may be kind and generous and loving, but, to the child, he or she is at first a stranger.

Strengthening the Relationship

Stepparents must not expect statements or demonstrations of love from children, especially in the beginning. For a long time the youngster does not know whether or not he loves a stepparent. As the child grows, the stepparent will be not only a parent, but also a close and good friend.

From the beginning, *fairness* is the keynote of friendship. This fairness has to be shown again and again, and perhaps stated openly. As a stepparent, you have to show that you do not demand obedience simply because you are a "boss," but because you have to help all the persons in the house live happily together.

Perhaps you have tried to impose a few rules just at the points where your stepchild is most easily hurt, or at an age level when he is most "touchy," and would be touchy with a real parent. You may get the normal response of a normal child. There may be stiff resistance, a sulky look, or the statement, in so many words, "I don't belong to you," or "You're not my mother." As a stepparent you need to learn to take antagonism or resistance without fear or anger, or without being completely "squashed" by the child's attitude.

This sounds like a tall order, but ideally it is what most real parents need to learn. Children *are* going to resist and resent demands. It is foolish to pretend that they must like everything their parents do. You, as the stepparent, will probably get more *open* resentment than a real parent would. If resentment does come out in the open, so much the better. There will be less buried resentment to clear up in the future, and there will be more face-to-face honesty in your relationship.

How Can You Let Them Know You Care?

With any child, but especially with a stepchild, the one most important idea to give him is the feeling that *he helps to govern and discipline himself.*

Give him the feeling that he can choose things. Help him see that the world is not slowly closing in on him in a "squeeze play." For example, at bedtime a child may not want to put out his light. If you say, "Put it out immediately, because *I* say so," you may succeed in getting the light out, but actu-

Tears and black looks are not a sign you are failing. Days like this are unavoidable as a child grows up. Good humor helps you weather such storms.

ally you only increase the tension in the child.

It might be better to say, "All right. When you have finished looking at the book (or doing the puzzle), call me and I'll put out the light." A child who has been hurt has a sense of the world's harshness. Remember, *the world is people*. The world is you, at the moment, and you can help the child see that it is not necessarily all harsh.

You give the child a sense of his ability to manage for himself, also, when you respect his possessions. At the expense of tidiness, give the child the right to have and to keep his own things, even his "junk" collections. They are silent protection and defense for him. They reflect him. Just as your grown-up trinkets —a necklace, an old pipe, a knife, a picture—are invested with meaning far beyond their temporary value, so are his treasures valuable to him.

Take the Stepchild into Partnership

Go easy on "changing things around," especially in the child's room. If you must change, give him a "say" in the proceedings. Try to let him know about events or changes in the household beforehand. This is wise for all children, but especially for a stepchild. Then he has time to think it over, to offer comments, and to feel that he has had an actual part in deciding about changes.

Do not be afraid to be flexible. Think a bit about rules; do not be trigger-quick at saying "No" or "Do it."

Make room for a child's friends. This is the best way of proving your own friendship. The quickest way to a child's heart is through your respect for his possessions, his ideas, *and his friends*.

How About Being Firm?

Firmness does not mean harshness. If your are fair and flexible, then, usually, you are clear-minded and firm about what you want in the family. The simpler the rules the better, for then the child can understand them. It helps if a boy or girl knows that you are not just "picking on" him. You can take the attitude that every family has rules. For

Take time to make friends with your stepchildren and trusting love will more than repay your efforts.

every child there are some demands. This understanding makes life gradually easier.

Too often, "firmness" means sticking to a rule until you and the child are exhausted, or it may mean punishment. Your stepchild wants the protection of adult regulation and help. But punishment is frightening, and may provoke rages and tantrums terrifying for him and miserable for a stepparent.

The chapters DISCIPLINE FOR SELF-RELIANCE, in this volume, and WHEN THINGS GO WRONG, in Volume 14, will be helpful to read in this connection.

Stepbrothers and Stepsisters

Many times, two people remarry who have children of their own, so that there may be two "sets" of stepchildren, and, later, other children of that union.

In such cases, of course, favoritism has to be avoided. But it is not necessary to bend over backward and neglect one's own children in such a family. That may be confusing and damaging for them.

In families where there are unusually happy stepbrothers and stepsisters, par-

Respect his treasures and you have a good start in stepparenthood.

ents are likely to be happy with one another. Each parent makes a determined effort to consider the children and their special needs. Plans are made with an eye to the tastes of each person. This helps avoid favoritism, and at the same time gives each child a special importance. The parents do not demand that the children show great love for one another. They do ask that one child show consideration for the other, as well as respect for his possessions and his privacy. The parents, too, respect the children's rights.

This only proves once again that a parent who gets the support and affection of his spouse makes a good parent and builds a happy family. Happy stepparents make happy stepchildren.

Stepparenthood No Secret

It frequently happens that a parent remarries while his or her child is still a baby, or at least too young to have any memory of a time when the stepparent was not in the family picture. Then parents wonder what and how much to tell.

The truth is, on the whole, wisest. But first, convince *yourself* that the truth is nothing shameful or hurtful to the child. Do tell the child the truth with the conviction that you are a good person.

Why Should They Know the Whole Story?

A young child is not disturbed by information about stepparents, nor does he think it unusual. But an older child who has not been told may not only feel cheated, but also may suddenly feel "different." He wonders why he was not told, and he resents the silence. Normally, as he grows into later childhood, the child may idealize his real parent. He may reject the stepparent at one time or another, and think how beautiful life would be in another existence. But that is normal. As they grow, children rebel. They show resentment to a parent, real or step. It is not special animosity against you or against your household.

Sometimes parents fear that the true story will involve all sorts of embarrassing "facts." Sometimes parents think that the child will blame them. They feel almost guilty about remarriage. Often a stepparent thinks, "If the child knows I'm not his 'real' parent, he'll lose his love and allegiance for me." It is natural to want to hold on to the child's love, but telling him the truth will not destroy love.

As regards the "facts of life," remember that children absorb only as much as they are ready for at any point. Young children are not concerned (and should not be concerned) with the intimate facts of the adults' life. Also, what we consider unusual is only everyday life to the child. A small child is ready to accept almost anything at face value. If he is happy and loved, the fact that you are a stepparent, or that he has stepsisters and stepbrothers, is interesting but not astonishing or hurtful.

The parental love and affection you have given a child cannot be lost by the addition of the word "step." Most of the child's attitude will come from you —if you feel apologetic and guilty, the child will wonder why. If you are happy about your position, if you love the child, then "step" is a pleasant name.

It is the child's right to know the facts. If you want to keep his confidence, never put yourself in a position where he can say, "You fooled me; you didn't tell me the truth."

GIFTED CHILDREN

HARVEY ZORBAUGH, B.A.
Director, Counseling Center for Gifted Children, School of Education, New York University, New York, N. Y.

In order to judge how original and creative a child may be, one must have had experience with many children. Some parents, with understandable pride, overrate the originality of their children. Others take unusual creativeness as a matter of course. Your child may be gifted, even though he is not strikingly original.

Fortunately, today there are advisers in some of our counseling centers and schools who can advise parents on how to handle their children if they are particularly gifted.

Gifted Is as Gifted Does

A six-year-old composed a musical suite to accompany the Arabian Nights stories. An eight-year-old was intent on proving that New York City could not grow larger. To uphold his belief, he drew a cross section of the intersection of Broadway and Forty-second Street, from the pavement down. His diagram showed the arrangement of subway tubes, water and gas mains, electric conduits, and sewers. A nine-year-old gave his entry in an essay contest the title "The Meaning of the Life of Theodore Roosevelt in the Development of the American Idea."

Compared with other children of their ages, these children are highly original and creative. We would have every right to decide they were gifted.

Gifted Children Talk and Read Early

The gifted child is likely to learn to talk at an early age, and to have a large and varied vocabulary. An interest in ideas and in the interrelationship of things is also a sign of giftedness.

A father took his two-year-old boy for a walk. They passed a place where the pavement was being repaired. At the curb stood a tool cart. Hitched to it was a cart in which tar was being melted. The two-year-old made a circuit of the carts, squatting to look at them from every angle. "Look, Daddy! Attached! Attached!" he cried, fascinated by his great discovery.

Some gifted children start to read long before they go to school. They seem almost to teach themselves, with little help from anyone.

What Can Intelligence Tests Tell?

There is little doubt that superior intelligence is essential to giftedness, but a high score on intelligence tests is not in itself a proof that a child is gifted.

Black Star

The Gifted Child and His Family

If your child is gifted, he will still be essentially like other children. Forget the dismal, alarming old wives' tales about children who have special talents. You can be reassured by the findings of science. Lewis Terman's thorough studies of gifted children have shown them to be fully as sturdy, healthy, well rounded, and friendly as children who

Gifted children will enjoy the same things other children like, if they are given the chance to experiment.

You can appreciate a child's special gifts without giving him the feeling he is "different" from the others or making him self-conscious.

Black Star

You can read about mental tests in the chapter MEASURING ACHIEVEMENT AND ABILITY in Volume 14.

The originality and creativeness we call being gifted depends on a child's whole personality, not just on his intelligence. Mental tests are, therefore, not a reliable guide in determining who is gifted.

Some children are "late bloomers." Their unusual originality and creativeness do not show until later adolescence or adult life. Paderewski, the great pianist, and the humorists Mark Twain and Will Rogers, are examples of such individuals. "Late blooming" may be due to the fact that children grow at different rates in mind as well as in body. Some children use up most of their energy in working out their relationships to those around them. When these emotional problems have been straightened out, their outstanding abilities begin to show up.

are average. Gifted children have a head start toward a happy, successful adult life.

The gifted child does not need to be overprotected, nor does the family need to make itself a slave to his future. Of course, he should not be pushed, but he should not be squelched, either. Let him grow in his own direction and at his own rate! Relax and enjoy growing with him!

There will be times when he will need support and help, as all growing children do. Since gifted children differ greatly from one another, some will need more and some less help in learning to live with others.

If he is to get along reasonably well with his brothers and sisters, there is one rule you will need to observe. Never hold up the child with marked abilities as an example to the others. It is well to remember, too, that in spite of his grown-upness in some directions, he is still a child in other ways. You can avoid giving him more responsibilities than you would give any child of his age.

Taking Giftedness in Your Stride

All children need to feel they belong. Occasionally, parents are amazed to find themselves with an extraordinarily bright youngster on their hands. "How do you suppose this family got such a 'brain'?" may seem to be a properly modest attitude. If it is carried to an extreme, the youngster gets the feeling that he is an outsider. He may really begin to worry that he does not belong in the family at all.

You do not want to make a child feel he is "different" because of his talents. But you want to give him opportunity to use his ability and find satisfaction in it.

One gifted child was asked by a guest if there were fairies in the woods. He replied politely, "I don't know, but there are plenty of edible fungi."

The father accepted the reply as a normal part of the conversation. It would be a temptation to some parents, under such circumstances, to prod the youngster to go on with the subject and show off his gifts. Other parents might be inclined to let the silence lengthen after such a remark. Their attitude might be that this was the answer of a "show-off" who had better be squelched at once.

Common Sense with Gifted Children

Gifted children are ahead of their years and ahead of their age-mates. Their conversation often is different from the chatter of the other boys and girls of their age. They need to feel that their gifts are valued, and they need the chance to express and try out their ideas, just as all children do. The more matter-of-factly you accept your child's gifts, the more comfortable the youngster will tend to be about himself. This does not mean that you are ignoring him. You do not need to worry about the child's getting an exaggerated idea of his own importance. If you can take his giftedness easily and happily, he will probably be able to do the same. He will feel that you like him just as he is.

Occasionally thirst for knowledge may unexpectedly cause disciplinary crises. One father who lived in New York took his young son to the Hayden Planetarium, for the little boy had become immensely interested in the stars. The boy was fascinated and wanted his own telescope. The father was able to get hold of a small telescope for him. Then the boy wanted to stay up all

The youngster who is far advanced in "book learning" will get along better with the other children if he is good at doing things they admire.

Fredric Lewis

night stargazing! Humor, common sense, and a reasonable program will solve these problems.

The Gifted Child's Friends

You need not worry about the talented child's ability to get along with other children. If they are given the chance, most gifted children will get along with their playmates.

If your child's special abilities have led him into interests far beyond those of the other children of his age, he may find it somewhat harder to make congenial friends. He may want to spend his time with older children because his ideas and his conversation are more like theirs. But since his ability to play games, to control his feelings, and to get along with others may not be as advanced as his mental development, the older ones may shut him out. As a result, he may feel lonely and complain that he belongs nowhere.

How Can the Gifted Child Fit into a Group?

You may need to put some thought and effort into planning things that will interest other children and attract them to your home. With patience, you can help your child develop the skills that other children in the community value.

The father of a nine-year-old with marked literary ability heard a group of children jeering "cry baby" at his son. Looking out his window, he saw the little boy standing at home plate. Tears streamed down his face. He had just struck out, and the twelve- and thirteen-year-olds, with whom he desperately wanted to play, declared that they were through with him. There he stood, weeping and reciting poetry! In this black moment when he could not hold his own in the ball game or control his feelings, he fell back on the one thing he knew he could do better than the other boys!

That evening the father suggested to his son that they play ball together. We cannot claim that the friendly coaching from his father made the little boy into a Babe Ruth, but it did improve his batting average sufficiently to make him an acceptable member of the team.

Sometimes a child who is advanced mentally or artistically does not find close friends until he reaches the teens. If that seems to be happening to your child, you can still let him feel that he is the kind of person whom people like. You can explain that some people come into their own a little later.

GIFTED CHILDREN

You can take care to avoid discussing his difficulties in front of him. If well-meaning relatives or neighbors say, in your gifted daughter's hearing, "Isn't it too bad Dorothy hasn't any nice little friends?" you can be quick to answer in a way that will let Dorothy know you have confidence in her ability to be liked and to like others. Dorothy should not get the idea that she is a problem. She should not feel, either, that you are disappointed in her, or that she is "different." Keeping up the confidence of the gifted child without letting her feel she is too good or too smart for the other children requires tact on your part. For further suggestions, read Friends Are Important in Volume 14.

If you live in a large community, you may be able to find other children who are mature beyond their years. Two or three such children can be happy together and have a great deal to offer one another in play, or in pursuing hobbies.

The Gifted Child and His School

A worried mother brought her six-year-old first-grade daughter to a reading clinic. The little girl repeatedly held her book upside down as she read. The child engagingly explained to a psychologist that she always finished her reading before the other children. She had nothing else to do, so she thought it would be fun to read upside down.

Gifted children often find the reading material "easy" and "silly," and become bored in the early grades. School does not become more challenging as they reach higher grades, either.

If Children Lose Interest

Gifted children have learned from other experiences much of the material that the school sets out to teach their age-mates. Finding it "old stuff," they

Let the gifted child share his abilities. His classmates are more likely to think him "a good guy" if they get some pleasure from sharing his many talents.

Merrim, Monkmeyer

may lose interest in school. Some children resign themselves to doing nothing, but others rebel. A boy was brought to a counseling center by his mother, who was in despair because his school had called him unmanageable. He constantly disturbed his class by throwing chalk. He confided to a counselor that he threw the chalk to make the teacher send him to the principal's office. That was at least an escape from the boredom of long division. He had mastered long division two years ago!

If your child shows signs of being uninterested in school, it is well to have a talk with his teacher. She probably will be as aware of his boredom as you are. She will know that boredom discourages learning. If you work with the teachers, you will find them more willing to help you.

To Skip or Not to Skip?

"Skipping" a grade may help. Whether to skip or not to skip depends, of course, on the whole child. His intelligence and his achievement need to be considered. His health, physical development, ability to control and express his feelings, and how he gets along with others are also important in determining the age group in which he can happily live and learn. There is always a limit to how much skipping is desirable or even possible. Most gifted children can stand a year of skipping, and some can take more. The question of skipping grades is discussed in REPORTS AND PROMOTION, in Volume 14.

The school may feel it is wiser to enrich your child's program while keeping him with those of his own age. Enrichment means taking advantage of the gifted child's zest to know, and of the wide variety of his interests. He can be encouraged to follow out the interests the course of study stimulates, and to report back to the rest of the class. The opportunity for such reports not only satisfies his need to know, but also at the same time enriches the classroom experience of other children.

A resourceful teacher will also provide experiences in the arts or other creative work as a stimulus to, and outlet for, his interests. Given opportunity and encouragement, gifted children will often do their own enriching. They may take the lead in following the school program into all its fascinating relationships with the world around them. You can provide much enrichment at home, too. The section on THE WORLD OF KNOWLEDGE, in Volume 14, points out some specific ways that reading, spelling, arithmetic, language, and social studies may be enriched for the child who learns easily.

How About Special Classes?

If you live in a larger community, the school may propose a special class. You will hear debates over the desirability of special classes for gifted children. Many people feel it is not desirable to separate gifted children, because it sets them apart. Other children lose out on what the gifted children contribute. If skipping and enrichment are not successful or possible, a good special class often admirably meets the gifted child's educational needs.

Children, particularly gifted children, have a way of taking care of many of their problems for themselves. The majority of gifted children find school reasonably satisfying, just as they find their whole lives interesting and satisfying if parents are encouraging, accepting, and matter-of-fact about their giftedness.

THE HANDICAPPED CHILD AND YOUR CHILD

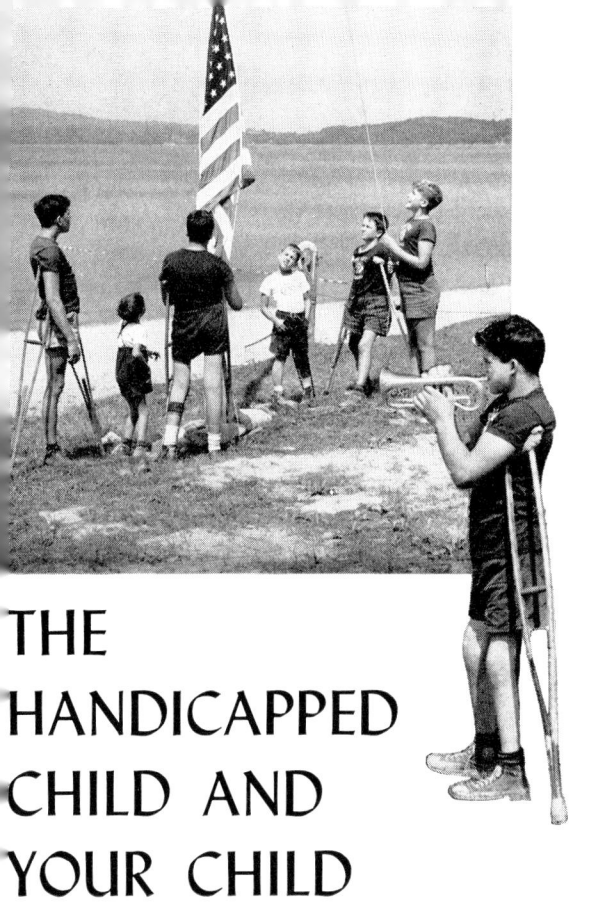

ELEANOR P. EELLS, M.A.
Co-director, Herrick House—for Children Convalescing from Rheumatic Fever, Bartlett, Ill.

Every parent, teacher, or group leader has an opportunity and a responsibility to help children learn to accept and to get along with handicapped children. The handicapped child's disability usually affects only a part of his activity. In most respects he is like other children. Your focus must be on the child as a person. You need to see his abilities, not his bad leg, his poor sight, his damaged heart, or his crippled arms. As you, in your own thinking, see the handicap in proper perspective, you increase the possibilities of a more normal life for the child.

The Handicapped Need Friends

All children must learn to accept and to be accepted.

For the normal child, there are values in experiences with many kinds of people. He can learn to be easy and friendly, rather than curious and afraid, with children who have handicaps.

Children who are overprotected, insecure, or obviously disadvantaged need acceptance even more than other children. They must gain acceptance in many different situations, if their confidence is to be built up and their development is to be normal. Acceptance in the family is a basic need. Beyond this, all children need recognition and acceptance by friends of their own age.

Any child deprived of friends and playmates will feel solitary and become unhappy. He may even become antagonistic. This is especially true of the handicapped child who already feels "different" because of his physical disability. "Feeling different" is a cross for any child to bear. He may have been hospitalized for long periods and he has probably had painful treatments. His school attendance has been irregular, if he has been able to go to school at all. He has watched from his window while other children played. Finally—after what seems to him ages—he is able to get out with other children. Everything depends on the way they accept him.

Many handicapped children find their friends easily and naturally. They learn new games and new skills readily, and find congenial playmates in their home neighborhoods and on the playgrounds. Other handicapped children need much more help from adults. They may be shy and fearful, or awkward at games. One child may lack skill in athletics in a neighborhood where ball and active games are all the rage. Another child, with good physical skills, may be out of place in a school or recreational group where the emphasis is on creative and artistic achievement.

How Can You Play up Abilities?

For such children the stage must be carefully set by the adult. The handicapped child must be helped to discover that he has some talent, some contribution to make. He must be encouraged to develop his abilities further and at the same time be guided toward new interests. He must be helped to grow in appreciation of the things other children hold dear. Any special gift must be used (with help from the adult) so that he gets satisfaction and recognition naturally, along with the other children. Parents and teachers, without being obvious about it, can make casual suggestions to other children about playing with him. Children can be cruel to a child who is "different," or they can just as easily accept him. The feeling of the adult can turn the trick.

If adults are interested and relaxed when handicapped and non-handicapped children play together, the children will usually be at ease. Mary and John become "our playmates," not "that girl with the brace" and "that boy who can't play ball." The children will form friendships around shared interests. Mutual pleasure in one another's company is a far sounder basis for friendship than tolerating the "different" child out of duty. Whenever a handicapped child is ridiculed and excluded from play, all the children concerned are harmed.

Does Seeing Handicaps Upset a Child?

Your child comes home from school one day with the exciting news that there is a new child in his room—"and, Mother! he acts funny, but the teacher says he's real smart." You suddenly realize that here is a seriously handicapped child. Can you accept it as an opportunity and a challenge? All the old wives' tales come to your mind, and for a while you are nagged by fears. Will my child be frightened or harmed by association with the spastic child? Will he be afraid this can happen to him, too? Then you think of the crippled child himself. How will he be treated? Will the other children tease him? Or will they pity him too much? Will they ignore him and leave him on the sidelines?

The Children Follow Your Lead

Adults are likely to be fearful about the effects of a handicap, but if adults can be casual about and accept marked differences, children will quite naturally handle themselves well. It is true that anxious or disturbed children tend to pin their disturbance upon another child's problem. This is as evident in interfaith and interracial situations as in the association of the handicapped and non-handicapped. If a child seems unusually disturbed by another child's difference, his anxiety may be the clue to a problem or a worry of his own.

As you are friendly, thoughtful, and accepting of the handicapped child, your own child will follow your lead. If you show repulsion or avoid mentioning the disability, your child may feel that this child is to be shunned.

Explaining a Handicap

It is important that you as a parent, teacher, or recreation leader understand this new playmate. His parents will be happy to tell you about their child's

Handicapped children usually feel more at ease when they are treated just like everybody else.

disability and discuss with you their way of handling it. They will let you know what they and the family doctor hope for in this child's associations. His mother will be delighted to work out plans for including her child in neighborhood games, trips, and parties. When you understand the handicapped child's condition, his needs, and his parents' approach, you can make a simple and natural explanation to your child.

It is usually sufficient to tell your child that nobody knows why some people are born with handicaps. Certainly it is nobody's fault. It is sad and it is hard for the child and for his parents. Everybody can help. You may feel sorry, but you must not pity openly. Try to accept and understand the handicapped child as he is. Tell your child that everyone has limitations. Those of the handicapped child may be greater or more obvious in some directions. In the same way, his ability may be greater in others.

How Can You Avoid Pity?

Where the handicap is the result of an injury, or an illness such as polio, the explanation is easier. Your child knows that the crippling is the result of an illness and that the child's doctor has given him instructions to be followed. It may be that the important thing is not to help him too much, and not to worry too much if he falls or fails. A news item appeared recently telling of the graduation of a handicapped girl from eighth grade, after a heroic struggle. As a parting gift she gave her principal a box of band-aids to replace the many bandages used upon her, and thanked the principal "for letting me fall so I would learn not to."

Considering Limitations

You can point out that the child with heart trouble should not play in competitive games or go on an overnight hike; that the deaf child needs special attention on the streets and wherever his lack of hearing may constitute a danger. The child with a brace is obviously at a disadvantage in athletics and in most physical activity. When a handicapped child uses such equipment as crutches, braces, or a hearing aid, it often helps to let other children see and handle it. As they understand how it works and how it helps the child, they can more readily include the child in their play.

When a diabetic child is along, other children can learn to pass up soft drinks, candy, or ice cream for the time. If they can understand why he must have special refreshments at a party, they can save him the embarrassment of explaining.

Give any necessary information around the situation as it arises, rather than make too many explanations. If the adult is understanding and natural, his attitude is easily communicated to children. Attitudes are always better caught than taught.

Everyone Has Limits

You do not expect to have your child at all times entirely accepting of and helpful to all children with handicaps. You do expect to develop the attitude that everyone has limits beyond which he should not go. You do want your child to understand that the handicapped child has a smaller sphere of activity and a slower pace. Within these limits, the handicapped child's talents and abilities may have a greater chance to develop.

Values in Handicapped Friends

You want your child to have a variety of associations and experiences. You know you will need to help him find and use such experiences. You want your child to grow up without shrinking from defects and deformities. You want him to learn to accept people for what they are, in spite of external appearances. He cannot do this if he is too long protected from sights and sounds which might be unpleasant.

Wise Handling Promotes Understanding

An epileptic seizure can be a frightening thing to witness. The different ways two similar episodes were handled may suggest how children can be helped to accept illness and deformity in others.

A ten-year-old boy was reciting in class at the front of the room. Suddenly he stuttered, fell on the floor in a convulsive seizure, frothed at the mouth, and uttered guttural sounds. The teacher was as frightened as the children. She sent for the principal of the school, but nothing was done until he arrived. He promptly dismissed the class without any explanation. For many of the children, the return to that room and association with that child were frightening experiences for the remainder of the school term.

A different story was Ann's experience at camp. Ann had suffered severe epileptic seizures for many years. She had recently been given a new medicine to control the convulsions. Her doctor arranged for her to attend a girl's camp, and gave careful instructions to the staff. During the first month she had a bad attack in the dining room. The counselor immediately gave her necessary care until a nurse arrived. The rest of the children were calmly dismissed to

There is sure to be something the handicapped child can do with other children without being at a serious disadvantage, so play it up!

their cabins for rest hour with the explanation that Ann was ill and needed rest. Each counselor was then given suggestions about explaining this spell to her own cabin group. The children were given freedom to ask all the questions that troubled them. They were told they could help Ann when she returned to the group by being natural and asking her no questions.

Ann required considerable help from the counselor before she felt ready to rejoin the group. She feared the other girls would "ask questions" or "make fun of me." The following morning she voluntarily said she felt well and ready "to get back into things," although the day before she had wanted to go home. Several years later, at a camp reunion, Ann and some of the girls who had been in camp at the time discussed the experience freely. Ann felt that through it she gained much security and confidence. The girls felt they had gained understanding and had been helped to handle well what might have been a deeply shocking experience.

They Learn Difficulties Can Be Met

You do not want your child to take the attitude of "how much more fortunate I am." You want your child to know people who have faced difficulties and who have accepted a handicap as a natural part of their existence. It gives anyone courage to see evidences of the strength and capacity of the human spirit.

No one would ever want any child's association to be exclusively with handicapped children. The child who is physically normal needs to play active games and indulge in strenuous physical activity. No one expects him to *limit* his playmates to children who cannot join in active play of ordinary children.

All photographs in this chapter from Nat'l Soc. for Crippled Children and Adults

Other children benefit as they discover that the girl on the strange "trike" is still a good companion.

Any relationship has its good and bad sides. A handicapped child may have the personality difficulties any child might have. His problems and the effect of his illness may have been unwisely handled so that he has become an unhappy, belligerent, and difficult child, or a shy, withdrawn, unstable one.

At first you tend to explain his behavior as related to the handicap, and then you realize that this is not so. His behavior is the result of that child's life experiences and the ways in which they have been handled. The handicap and its effect upon the child are only parts of the picture—not necessarily the significant parts.

There are no dangers inherent in the handicap. Your child may imitate the stutterer for a bit, or he may copy briefly another child's mannerisms or random movements. This is a phase that will pass naturally, if you do not become too disturbed about it.

The long-term gains for your child will far outweigh these passing mannerisms, for he will have a deeper understanding of all kinds of people.

THE HANDICAPPED CHILD IN THE FAMILY

EDITH M. STERN, B.A. Silver Springs, Md.
and
ELSA CASTENDYCK, B.A. Washington, D. C.
Authors of "The Handicapped Child: A Guide for Parents"

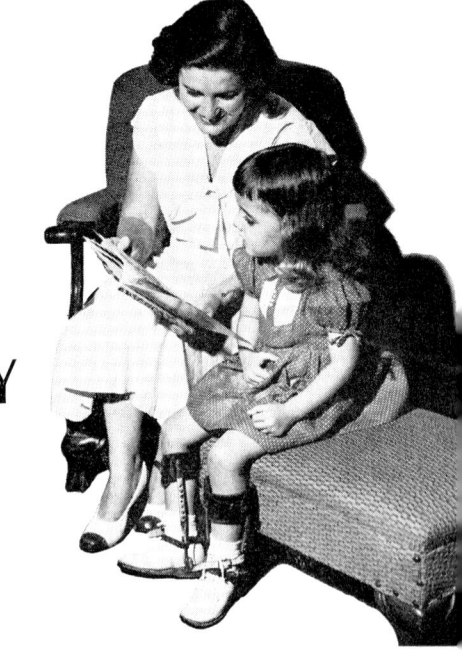

WHEN a child is crippled, has epilepsy, impaired sight or hearing, or is mentally retarded, it would be nonsense to say that there is no shadow over his life and that of his parents. But that shadow need not become a blackout. Fortunately, when children are handicapped, their physical or mental differences from other boys and girls are only part of what shapes the course of their lives. An even greater influence is the way parents look upon and deal with such children.

Facing a Handicap

The parents of a handicapped child can help him to make the most of himself within whatever limits are set by the handicap. They may even determine whether he is going to belong comfortably at home and in the community, or whether he will continually feel like a misfit. If they look upon his handicap as an unbearable calamity, so will he. But if they take it in their stride, he will, too, for children take their viewpoints from adults.

Some parents cannot even accept their child's handicap with their heads. "The doctor saw him only a little while; I'm with him all the time; it's not as bad as the doctor says," they may protest. Many, though they accept it with their heads, cry out against it in their hearts. "Why did this happen to my child?" is an age-old, almost universal reaction. Though the full answer brings peace, it may take years to find, for only faith can give it.

A handicap is by no means all there is in life. This is a vital fact for mothers and fathers to grasp with their heads and with their hearts, and in their very bones. Many famous individuals, including Charles Steinmetz, Thomas A. Edison, and President Franklin D. Roosevelt, led full, rich lives in spite of handicaps. A child may not be doing what his parents wish he were, or he may never be able to fulfill all the hopes and ambitions they had for him. But that does not mean he misses out on everything.

Stress What He Can Do

Always, with a handicapped child, it is important to concentrate on what he can do rather than on what he cannot do. Some handicaps, like epilepsy, are in effect only part of the time. In between seizures, an epileptic child can do pretty much what all children do. Other handicaps, like defective vision, affect only part of a person. Aside from what must be seen, a blind child can use and fully enjoy his other senses.

Sometimes disabilities loom so large that they seem to swallow up everything in the child's make-up. But it must never be forgotten that behind and beyond and above any handicap is an individual, a temperament, a personality. The child as a person, and some of his senses and abilities, are undamaged by a particular handicap. Overemphasize the handicap and its limitations, and a youngster is doubly handicapped from the start. Consider the human being, encourage use and development of his abilities, and he can have a satisfactory life in spite of his handicaps.

Of course, this does not mean that the handicap can or should be overlooked. Pretty little May, who at eight had a mental age of four, was punished by her mother for not doing better at school. Such an ostrichlike attitude can be as harmful as one of despair. The handicap needs to be honestly faced for exactly what it is and how it limits the child.

The ability of parents to talk about a handicap in a matter-of-fact way, with the child as well as with others, is fairly good evidence of their frank, wholehearted acceptance of it. The probabilities are that the child, taking over from his parents, will also accept his handicap, and will be able to go on from there successfully.

See the Child, Not the Handicap

A handicapped child is first and foremost a child. His handicap is only secondary to the wants and needs he shares with all children.

Like all other children, a handicapped one needs the reassurance that he is loved. This includes being accepted as he is and for what he is, rather than as his parents would like him to be. The ways of showing him love are as many and diverse as the ways of showing love to all children, but a handicapped child especially needs warm and affectionate support for the things he tries to do. Above all, he needs reassurance during his moments of discouragement. If he is crippled, for instance, his stumbling attempts to walk should be encouraged. If he is deaf, his efforts to pronounce words properly need recognition. If he

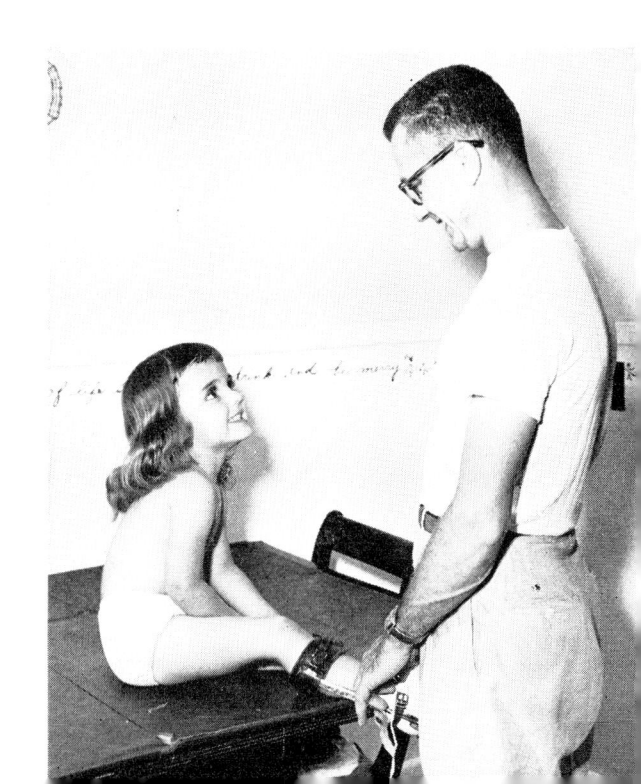

This little girl knows the doctor is her friend, and her confidence in him will help her along the way.

is mentally handicapped, praise for even the smallest improvement in accomplishing little chores or mastering simple book learning gives the needed assurance that Mommy or Daddy is pleased with him.

He Needs a Sense of Achievement

Boys and girls who are handicapped, like all others, need to have a sense of achievement. Some things they cannot do because of their handicaps, but they can still enjoy success if they are provided with suitable experiences and activities. Lame Harold, for instance, cannot be on the baseball team at school, but he is one of the leading members of the glee club. Betsy's cerebral-palsied hands cannot be entrusted with dishes or glasses, but she takes great pride in drying the kitchen silver. While the rest of the family watches television, blind Elinor listens to her radio and weaves place mats which, later, the others admire and use.

Handicapped children ought not to be exposed to what overtaxes and discourages them, but their tasks and amusements should not be too easy. As they grow older and more competent, the nature of their jobs can be varied accordingly. Only through meeting challenges and attaining progressive goals, can any of us experience the joy of feeling successful.

Like all other children, handicapped ones ought to have every possible chance to become self-reliant. They should dress themselves as much as they are able. Unless they would be in real danger, there is no reason they should not go out alone. Whenever it is reasonably possible, they should make their own choices. What to wear today or what cereal to have for breakfast are the kind of simple choices many children can make happily even at an early age.

He Needs Wider Experiences

Handicapped children need every chance to broaden their experiences. Excursions, reading, story hours at the library, or games are among the kinds of experience you can often give a handicapped child. As many different kinds of experience as are not ruled out by the nature of the particular handicap can be provided. If the experience can be had with other children, in groups, so much the better. Fun in itself is an experience. Though a child with a handicap may not be able to have fun in some ways, he is able to have it in others.

How Can He Make Friends?

In common with every other boy and girl, a handicapped one needs to have friends. Some parents have the idea that it is not good for their children to associate with others who are likewise handicapped. They think that it might be depressing. They are afraid that, through imitation, their children may take over inabilities, bad habits, or mannerisms, or that their progress may be hampered by lack of necessity to live up to ordinary standards. Actually, it is good for a child to have some friends handicapped as he is, for among them he does not suffer undue competition.

He ought also to have friends who are not handicapped, even though such associations may require some paving of the way. The mother of the handicapped child, for instance, might invite other children to visit. If the child has to wear a hearing aid, or braces, or thick eyeglasses which obviously set him apart as "different," they might be shown to other children with a simple explanation as to why they must be used. To pretend they are not there will cause more embarrassment than frankness will.

If the parents of the handicapped child have been able to accept the handicap, they will be able to talk about it casually. Then the child and his playmates will be better able to do so, too. Though a disability may require naming, and explanations, it does not require apologies. When children who are not handicapped play with those who are, the favors are not all on one side.

A delightful relationship, for example, exists between mentally handicapped Sue and normally intelligent Jane. Sue looks up to Jane, who warms under the admiration. Jane has many ideas for play and Sue likes to follow them. Sue can always be relied on to be a good, steady companion, to keep the doll house in order and follow housekeeping routines, while Jane does most of the talking and creating.

Finding Common Interests

Some skills or interests may make a child able to meet other children on common ground. Such interests are a great help in stimulating friendships. Many mentally handicapped children, for example, like music, and can share in group singing or enjoyment of radio programs with other boys and girls. A lame child may become an expert checker player. One who is hard-of-hearing can often join successfully in arts or crafts. One who is subject to seizures might be a marbles champion. Other children can see a handicapped child as a congenial playmate with tastes and interests similar to their own, rather than as someone peculiar and set apart. Then the chances are better for friendships.

When handicapped children associate with others, there is always the possibility that their feelings may be hurt if they are pushed aside. At times, they will be left behind by their friends who are not handicapped. Perhaps the "gang" decides to go on a long walk. This would be too much for Rose, who is convalescing from rheumatic fever, or for George, who wears a brace.

Through such slights to their children, parents are even more intensely hurt. Their own pain should not make them discourage their children from taking part in everyday social life. There is some comfort in the thought that even the healthiest, most attractive children, without handicaps, have similar experiences at one time or another.

Parents of handicapped children can be careful not to *force* their sons and daughters into friendships with children who do not have like limitations. As in setting goals or tasks of any kind, there is a nice point between expecting too much or expecting too little.

What Attitudes Are Helpful?

Grief is inevitably felt by all parents of handicapped children. But they need to be careful not to let it be expressed in pity, for pity is not good for anyone. Pity implies that the person you pity is inferior to you. If parents can manage to substitute for pity the sympathy and respect they give to an equal, a handicapped child will have a more wholesome attitude toward himself.

It does not help a handicapped child, either, for parents to indulge in pampering him. More often than necessary, parents say, "Let me do it for you"; "That's too hard for you"; or "Never mind, I'll look after it." Some mothers and fathers give handicapped children everything they want, or let them always have their own way. As a result, a boy or girl is made more helpless than his handicap itself would make him. What is more, to the unavoidable physical or mental handicap is added the needless handicap of that unlikable personality—a "spoiled" child.

At the other extreme, some parents are overcritical of their handicapped children. Mothers and fathers may set their own standards of accomplishment and behavior, rather than the ones possible in the light of the handicap. They may make demands that it is impossible for the child to meet. In so doing, they add to the child's other burdens.

Finding Medical Care

Parents of handicapped children of course want the assurance of good medical care. Sometimes this leads them to chase from doctor to doctor in the hope of finding one who can correct or markedly diminish the handicap. Sometimes they even seek out quacks who promise sure-cure miracles. A seesaw of false hopes and real disappointments is good neither for the parents nor for children. The best course is to rely on a reputable doctor or clinic, and to follow through on the recommended program consistently and conscientiously.

Help in a child's emotional guidance can come from many sources, such as a child-guidance or mental-hygiene clinic, a public-health nurse, a family-service agency, or a school counselor. In some states, training classes for parents of handicapped children are offered.

The chapter SPECIAL NEEDS OF VARIOUS HANDICAPS, in this volume, as well as the chapter FAMILY GUIDANCE SERVICES, in Volume 15, will be helpful in this connection.

The Parents Have Needs

The parents of handicapped children have the wishes and worries of other parents. They want their sons and daughters to be happy and successful. Their hopes and ambitions are limited, like those of all parents, by what the children are able to do—for all children have some limits beyond which they cannot go. Their problems differ from the problems of other parents more in degree than in kind.

But sometimes the degree may be so great that their problem seems overwhelming, and in order to meet it they need special kinds of help.

Why Is My Child Handicapped?

Nearly always, parents feel that they

When a child can do some things other people do, she will feel less handicapped and more contented.

All photographs in this chapter from Nat'l Soc. for Crippled Children and Adults

Braces can be forgotten, and little girls can meet on an equal footing when the doll family is being lovingly tended, for they all want "to be like Mother."

are somehow to blame for their child's handicap. But very few handicaps are anyone's fault. For many, like certain forms of mental deficiency or of seizures, the cause is unknown. With others, even where a cause is recognized, it may still have been unavoidable.

A sense of shame over having a handicapped child is another common feeling among parents. Sometimes this is related to the guilty feeling, "Maybe this was my fault." Sometimes it comes from the normal, human desire to have a child of whom you can be wholly proud. Sometimes it is the result of undue emphasis on what other people may think. But whatever the cause, a sense of shame can be overcome by remembering always that there is nothing disreputable in the nature of any kind of handicap. It is something like the color of a child's eyes, simply a fact for which no one is responsible, and in which there is no disgrace.

Others Have Similar Problems

Membership in a group of parents whose children are similarly handicapped holds particular solace and inspiration for parents of handicapped children. It is profoundly comforting to meet with others who share your difficulties.

Groups for parents of handicapped children hold informative lecture and discussion sessions. Valuable for individual parents, as well as for the community, are the projects through which these groups improve services for handicapped children. They organize and finance their own special schools. They crusade for improved legislation for handicapped children, or for better conditions in state institutions. They stimulate the establishment of clinics or research projects.

It is too bad that sometimes, instead of working together for common ends, the parents' groups for children with different handicaps compete for dollars, publicity, and services. Each group is concerned with children who need medical care, schooling, and community services. The emotional needs of all the children, and of all the parents, are identical. "We are all in the same boat" is a much sounder stand for every group of parents of handicapped children than "Nobody matters but us."

Parents Need Recreation

It is even more fruitful emotionally for most parents of handicapped children to take part in activities outside their homes than it is for other parents. In groups of parents of handicapped children, aimless grief is channeled into doing for others. Some parents find it more refreshing to get a complete change of scene and interests than to take part in anything connected with their troubles. Nearly all, at times, need and want this kind of change. Sheer fun, occasionally, is as important for the parents of handicapped children as it is for the children.

Consider the Whole Family

The needs of others in the home of the handicapped child have to be considered if family life is to be harmonious.

Sometimes parents expect brothers and sisters who are not handicapped to make too great sacrifices for the handicapped. In the long run, even he is not benefited when he gets a disproportionate share of the family's attention or money. He is better off being loved and accepted by his brothers and sisters as one of themselves. If he is always standing in their way, their feelings toward him will not be kindly.

Every family has to decide for itself how much of its money ought to go for the medical care or special schooling a handicapped child may need. But no decision ought to be made before everyone's needs and rights are taken into account. For instance, will a brilliant older brother or sister have to forego a college education if a mentally handicapped little sister or brother goes to an expensive private school?

Shall the Handicapped Child Share the Work?

Each child's home duties ought to be budgeted with equal thought and care. Like the other children, the handicapped child should contribute what he can to family living. Doing his part is good for him, and makes for better relations with his brothers and sisters. If they feel "he gets out of everything" they are likely to resent him.

Perfect, unbroken harmony among brothers and sisters is, of course, a pipedream in any home. All children in the same family quarrel and have their moments of indignation against one another. Where one is handicapped, there are bound to be times when the other children feel that he is a burden, just as his parents occasionally do, too. When this happens, they should be allowed to blow off steam by expressing their feelings freely to their parents. Otherwise these feelings might explode to the hurt of the handicapped child.

The fewer occasions for jealousy or annoyance that parents can give the other children, the more kindly they will tend to feel toward the handicapped brother or sister. Indeed, when they give him service out of love, rather than because their mother or father demands it of them, they can be invaluable allies. Brothers and sisters have proved amazingly resourceful in helping the handicapped one to share in what they do. They are often heartwarmingly proud of his accomplishments.

Shall the Handicapped Child Live at Home?

For some handicapped children, a residential school may be preferable to living at home. If it alone can provide certain kinds of medical care or schooling the child requires, he should not be deprived of them. Or perhaps only at a residential school can he get necessary companionship. Whether or not a child is better off away from home depends on the home, the school, the handicap, and the resources available in the community. The right answer might change at different times and at different ages for the same child. Plans ought to be periodically talked over with medical advisers, teachers, and social workers. It is always hard to have a child away from home, but whether or not he should go must be answered by "What is best for the child?" regardless of any ache in the parents' hearts. If your child lives at home and goes to school, you will want to read THE HANDICAPPED CHILD IN SCHOOL in Volume 14.

Brief periods away from home are likely to benefit everyone. They are good for the handicapped child for the same reasons that they are good for any child. They afford a breathing spell for him as well as for his brothers and sisters and parents. Special camps for the handicapped work well for some children. Others may do better in a regular camp.

Whether a child is away from his parents for a long time or temporarily, he needs letters, visits, and gifts to assure him of their love and to keep him in touch with his family.

The ideal for handicapped children is a balanced life between two worlds. One is the world geared to his special needs, where he is provided with the combination of stimulation and relaxation right and fitting for his handicap. The other is the world where people are not handicapped. If he can feel he belongs, and has his own little niche that no one else could fill in his home and community, he will be aided in developing. Passing over easily from the more-protected to the less-protected kind of life, he can, despite his physical or mental limitations, become what every parent wants—a well-adjusted, contented child, making the most of himself and of life.

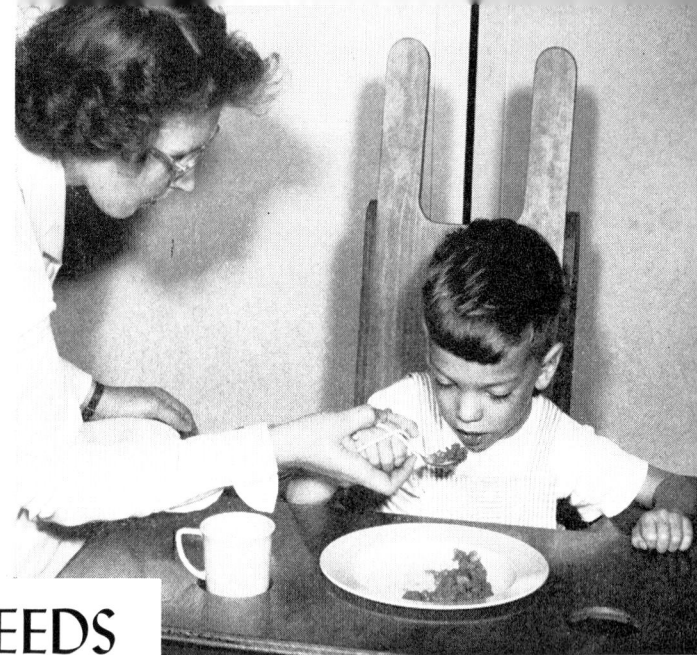

SPECIAL NEEDS OF VARIOUS HANDICAPS

Mildred Shriner

THE handicapped child is basically just like every other child. He has the same need to feel that he is loved and that he belongs. He has the same craving for friends, and for a sense of accomplishment. If you accept him, you can give your child these feelings, as you live with him day by day. "Accepting him" means really thinking of him and treating him as much as possible as a normal child.

If you have a handicapped child, you may sometimes say, "I want to do what's best, but I don't know where to find help. I don't know how much I can expect of a child who has this handicap."

Understanding and intelligent handling, based on sound information, can go a long way toward solving many of the problems of handicapped children. They can grow up to become happy, useful, and reasonably contented individuals. They can be a credit to themselves, to their families, and to their communities as they mature.

This chapter is designed to give you increased understanding of the specific needs, limitations, and possibilities of children with different kinds of handicaps. This chapter points out what help is available for a particular handicap, and how it can be obtained. Recent discoveries in medicine, in mechanical aids, and in ways of teaching have brought new hope and reduced the disadvantages for many children with handicaps. As a result, these children can be more independent and can live more like other children than would have been possible a generation ago.

Here you will find recommendations from specialists who are familiar with the needs of crippled or mentally retarded children. Here you will find suggestions, too, for helping children who have poor eyesight or poor hearing, cerebral palsy, epilepsy, or rheumatic fever.

N. Y. City Bd. of Educ.

CHILDREN WHO CANNOT SEE

BERTHOLD LOWENFELD, Ph.D.
Superintendent, California School for the Blind, Berkeley, Calif.

IT IS only natural that those who find themselves parents of a blind child should have strong feelings about it. They consider their task of raising the child a difficult one, for two beliefs about the effects of blindness are uppermost in their minds. Although widely accepted, neither is true. Most people believe that the blind child's lot is a sad one because he feels sorry that he cannot see. They also believe that blindness makes a person completely helpless and dependent.

We know, from practical experience and research, that blind children do not yearn for sight, and that they take things in stride. They act and react with all their other senses. These they learn to use efficiently and to their complete satisfaction. During preschool and school age, blind children learn to master their environment, with more or less success, just as seeing youngsters do. As adolescents or young adults, they acquire the usual professional or vocational training. This, in time, gives them economic security and helps them to participate fully in community life.

It is true that the visual handicap must be taken into account during certain phases of the child's development. But the blind child is first of all a child. Most of his problems are the same ones parents meet and solve with all children. The blind child also develops just as seeing children do, although his speed of progress may vary.

Where Special Help Is Needed

In three areas, the child will need special attention and consideration because of his blindness. These are acquiring a workable knowledge of the world around him; learning to get about; conforming to the generally accepted social and behavior patterns.

Finding Out About the World

The blind child gains most of his knowledge of the world around him through touch. He hears about many things, but, to acquire concrete experiences, he must apply his touch senses. For this reason, the blind child should be encouraged to make use of his hands from early childhood. Give him playthings that appeal to the touch. Allow him to get messy by playing with wet sand and by finger feeding. Encourage him to explore with an ever-widening "touch horizon."

Give him opportunities to handle models and replicas of things he cannot experience in reality. His touch experiences do not happen in isolation. He also hears, smells, and tastes. Stimulate him to apply these other senses. Give these opportunities to a blind child and he shares common experiences. He is then better prepared for life with others.

Learning to Get Around

The blind child learns to walk when he is ready for it just as all children do. He may need to be shown how to move his legs. He will also want things to hold on to, and free space to move. But total blindness does restrict him in his ease in getting about.

See to it that the blind child has opportunities for moving around and for exploring. Encourage him to make use of them. His area of activity gradually expands from his crib to his play-pen, to his room, to his home, and to his back yard. Much will depend upon your attitude in following the blind child's growth. Overcome your fears and anxieties, as much as you can, in order to give him the needed opportunities, and you will be well rewarded as you watch your child develop from day to day.

Opportunity for Activity and Self-Expression

Many things which seeing children learn because they observe others doing them, have to be taught to the blind child. In trying to grasp and hold, in learning to walk and talk, and in playing alone and with others, give the blind child the opportunity to observe with all his senses. This will often make demands on your patience and ingenuity. One case in point here is when a blind child changes from liquid to solid foods. The change from standing to walking, from playing alone to playing with others, and, in general, from having things done for him to learning to do them by himself, will tax your best efforts. Give him opportunities for self-expression in play and through such materials as plasteline and clay, through songs and dances, rhythm and noise-makers.

Out of every three children who are called blind, only one is *totally* blind. One of the three has enough sight to get around and to recognize larger objects. The third one of every three has enough sight to learn to do most tasks, except those requiring recognition of details such as are needed for reading and writing. Children are generally considered blind if they cannot see at twenty feet with the better eye, and, with correcting glasses, what persons with normal vision can see at 200 feet (20/200 Snellen measurement).

All parents should be concerned in preserving the best possible amount of sight for their child. The family doctor will refer parents to an eye specialist or to an eye clinic. Parents who are unable to provide the needed medical care should write to their State Department of Public Health. The Department will advise you how to secure assistance for medical care for your visually handicapped child.

Educating the Blind Child

Information on educational facilities for blind children is available from local, state, and national organizations. For the blind preschool child, services of special teachers who visit him in his home are available in a number of states. A request to the State Department of Education or to the State School for the Blind will bring such services to parents and child. The child of school age may go either to a residential school or to a public-school class for blind children.

Nearly all states have residential schools for blind children. Most of these are under the State Department of Education, which will be glad to refer parents to the proper agency. Classes for blind children are maintained in the local public schools in larger communities. Schools and classes for the blind provide an education equal, grade by grade, to that provided in public schools. This means not only Braille reading and writing, but also the teaching of other skills by methods especially developed for blind children. (Braille is a system of touch-reading and writing. Varying combinations of six embossed dots, arranged in two rows of three, represent letters, letter-combinations, and words.) Whether a child should go to a residential school or to a public-school class for blind children depends upon such factors as location, home environment, quality of available facilities, and on the child himself. Both residential schools and public school classes for blind children have been successful in producing graduates of whom they can be rightfully proud.

Booklets to Read

Helpful information on educating the blind child will be found in the following booklets which also contain more extensive reading lists.

SPEER, EDITH L. *A Manual for Parents of Pre-School Blind Children.* The New York Association for the Blind, 111 East 59th St., New York 22, N. Y.

UNITED STATES OFFICE OF EDUCATION. *Education of Visually Handicapped Children: The Blind —The Partially Seeing.* Bulletin 1951, No. 20. Superintendent of Documents, U. S. Government Printing Office, Washington 25, D. C.

The following agencies will be glad to assist with information if you write to them and request it.

American Foundation for the Blind, 15 W. 16th Street, New York 11, N. Y. Help on all matters pertaining to the blind; also has a free lending library.

National Society for the Prevention of Blindness, 1790 Broadway, New York 19, N. Y. Particularly on the education of partially seeing children.

American Printing House for the Blind, 1839 Frankfort Avenue, Louisville 6, Ky. For books and appliances used in the education of the blind.

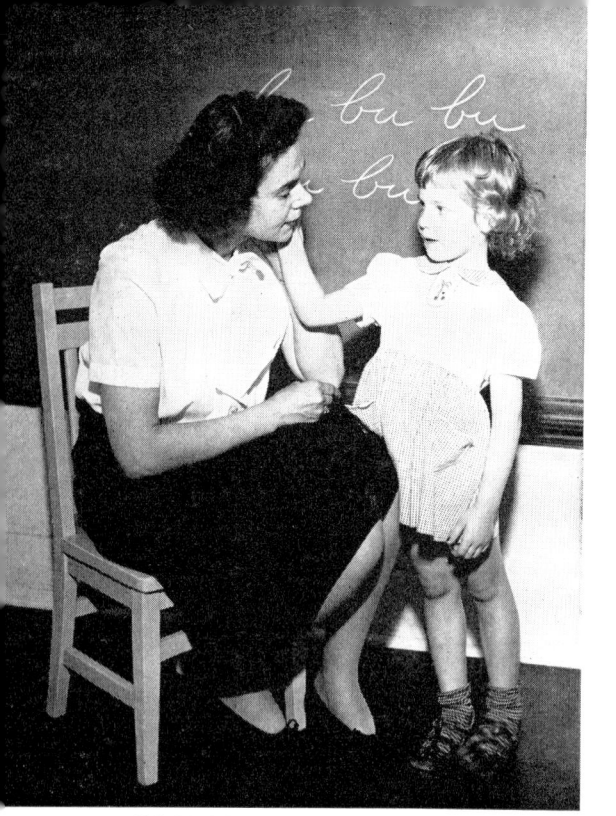

N. J. School for the Deaf, West Trenton, N. J.

HELPING CHILDREN WHO HAVE DEFECTIVE HEARING

RICHARD G. BRILL, Ed.D.

Superintendent, California School for the Deaf, Riverside, Calif.

Unlike most other handicapping conditions, defective hearing is not readily apparent. For that reason, a child's defective hearing is frequently not discovered promptly.

Deafness and Hearing Loss

There are two groups of children with defective hearing, the deaf child and the hard of hearing child.

The deaf child is one who cannot hear enough sounds in the speech of those around him to be able to understand connected speech, even if he wears a hearing aid. The child who is deaf from birth does not learn to talk. He does not know the meaning of words, because he has never heard people talk. Nearly all deaf children have some slight ability to hear, called *residual hearing*. If a sound is loud enough, and of a certain quality or tone, they are able to hear it. Sometimes parents think a child is not deaf because he hears an airplane fly overhead, or he hears a truck roll by. The child hears these sounds because he has residual hearing for the quality of sound that is being made by the airplane or truck. But he cannot hear the quality of sound or tone used in speech.

The hard of hearing child has a hearing loss, but he can hear and understand speech. We talk the way we hear speech spoken. A person who is hard of hearing will have a speech defect until he has had special speech lessons. He will say words the same way he hears them, but usually he will not hear all the sounds in every word.

See the Child, Not the Hearing Loss

The child who has defective hearing is first of all a *child*. He is going to live with, play with, and work with other people all his life, just as everyone else does. He should be treated by the members of his family in the same way that others of his age are treated. He should be expected to become toilet-trained, to dress himself, and to assume responsibilities that are assumed by other children of his age.

Why Can't the Deaf Talk?

The deaf child will not learn to *talk* when other children do, because he does not *hear* the speech of others around him. Many parents think that this lack of ability to get words out is the major problem of the deaf child. Actually, this is not so. Lack of *language* is the basic handicap of the deaf child. The word *run*, for instance, is a word a deaf child can easily learn to speak. But the word *run* has at least twenty-three meanings. The child can learn to pronounce the word *run* more quickly than he can learn all its various meanings. Examples: The boy runs down the street. The girl has a run in her stocking. There is a run of fish up the river. Several men run for election. The word *run* conveys a different idea in each use.

Learning the Meanings of Words

Because the child who is deaf does not hear others speak, he does not at first realize that the things around him have names and that words are used to communicate ideas. Deaf children need to be spoken to in the same way that other children are spoken to. The deaf child does not hear the parent's voice, but in time he comes to associate the movement of the lips with a definite action that follows. Sentences should be brief, and words should be repeated constantly.

When the child is getting dressed and undressed, you can use the words *shoes*, *stockings*, *dress*, and so on, each time the child is putting on or taking off that piece of apparel. In the same way, the child should learn the names of the pieces of furniture and other things around the house. The names of the various objects can be printed in manuscript lettering or printing, with letters at least two inches high on pieces of cardboard, and attached to the appropriate objects. In this way the child will learn such needed words as *door*, *bed*, *table*. As long as the letters are made large enough so that the eyes of the small child are not strained, these labels can be used with children as young as three years of age.

How About Speech Training?

Teachers skilled in helping deaf children learn to speak are the only ones who can successfully give speech instruction. The person who is not trained in this work is likely to instill bad speech mannerisms that are difficult for the child to overcome when he is older. The parents and others can work a great deal with the young deaf child and with his lip reading. Parents can help him develop his senses of sight and touch through such sense training as matching colors, forms, and materials, and doing puzzles. Sand pies, mud, water, dough, and other materials around the house offer good learning experiences. They can assist him in beginning the matching of words to objects.

Hearing Aids for Children

It is difficult to test accurately the hearing of a child under six years of age. If a child has such a great hearing loss that he does not learn to speak naturally, it is doubtful that he should have an individual hearing aid and be expected to wear it all day. There are table model hearing aids that are more powerful than the individual aids a person wears. Such aids can be used for about fifteen minutes at a time with the child, at specific times during the day. Learning to distinguish between sounds that are clearly different, such as those of a bell, a horn, and a drum beat, might be the first exercises. Later, the child learns to identify the number of drum beats and then their pattern.

Still later, the child may listen to recordings of the various animal sounds and nursery rhymes set to music. During this time his hearing is not improving, but his discrimination for what he hears is being educated. A carefully worked-out program such as this is usually more beneficial than just wearing a hearing aid all day and trying to make sense out of all the sounds that are heard.

Who Can Use Hearing Aids?

The child who hears well enough to pick up language and speech, but whose speech is faulty because his hearing is defective, probably should begin to wear an individual hearing aid as soon as possible. Hearing aids are expensive and delicate instruments. You will need to use your judgment in determining whether an active child should be required to wear his aid when out playing with the other children.

School for the Deaf Child

Almost every deaf child should receive his education in a school for the deaf. The school may be a special day school of the kind provided in large city school systems. It may need to be a residential school. The school should be large enough so that the children are well graded according to both educational achievement and age. Most deaf children will always require special education because of their language handicap, their lack of general knowledge, and their lack of speech.

Throughout their school careers, hard of hearing children need some special help in lip reading, speech correction, and language development. They may need such help in subject matter, too. The hearing they have may need to be developed through special training. Specially trained teachers in the public-school system can give them this extra attention.

N. J. School for the Deaf, West Trenton, N. J.

Careful testing will help you decide whether a hearing aid is the answer.

The following agencies will provide information on educating the deaf and the hard of hearing child:

Each State Department of Education.

The Volta Bureau, 1537—35th Street, N. W., Washington 7, D. C. Pamphlets and information can be obtained here.

The John Tracy Clinic, 806 West Adams Boulevard, Los Angeles, Calif. A correspondence course, free to the parents of pre-school deaf children, is furnished.

Books to Read

The following books may be helpful:

DAVIS, HALLOWELL. *Hearing and Deafness, A Guide for Laymen.* Murray Hill Books, Inc., New York, 1947.

LASSMAN, GRACE HARRIS. *Language for the Preschool Deaf Child.* Grune & Stratton, New York, 1950.

MYKLEBUST, H. R. *Your Deaf Child.* Charles C. Thomas Company, Springfield, Ill., 1950.

CHILDREN WHO ARE CRIPPLED

JAYNE SHOVER, M.A.
Associate Director, National Society for Crippled Children and Adults, Chicago, Ill.

CRIPPLED children, like all children, need to know they are loved and accepted. When we accept a child's handicap, we see him for what he has and not for what he lacks. Crippling is hard to define. It may be so mild that it passes unnoticed, or so severe as to result in permanent and total helplessness. It may be a defect a child has at birth, or be the result of accident or illness in childhood. In between these two extremes are "moderate" cases. To these we devote most of our effort in care, education, and treatment.

Use All the Resources

There are wide variations in emotional reactions. A mild handicap may be more disabling to one child than a severe handicap is to another. Also, the very intelligence of the child has a profound influence on his ability to profit from treatment.

Thus, each child is different, and an individual plan must be made for each. Our first need, then, is a plan of action—a blueprint to guide us in what we are going to do to help the crippled child toward a happy, useful life.

The central figure in this blueprint, when the child lives at home, is the parent. It is through the affection and security given him by his parents that the child will learn his most difficult, but most important, lesson—how to accept and live with this handicap.

Of the trained workers whose task it is to set up and carry out the plan of action, you can look first of all to the doctor. He will tell you what you need to know about your child's handicap. From him you can learn what you can expect in the way of progress and improvement, what you should do now, and what you will leave for the future. And, always, you need the doctor for regular checkups to keep you on the right path, to give you new goals as old ones are attained.

But the doctor is not alone. For the crippled child, the doctor is a member of a team. He works with the nurse, the physical therapist who assists in training muscles, the occupational therapist who teaches handicrafts, the speech specialist, the social worker, the teacher, the psychologist, and the parent. Each has his special part to play.

Where Can Help Be Found?

There are many public and private agencies to which parents may look for assistance. In each state there is a statewide crippled children's service to help those who need it in securing diagnosis, hospitalization, and convalescent care, as well as other services. The types of cases eligible for this help vary from one state to another. But help is available in all states for children handicapped in the development of bones and muscles.

Supplementing and extending these services in every state, the Society for Crippled Children offers many services in the rehabilitation of crippled children. In some states, the Society sends mobile clinics and traveling therapists into the rural and sparsely populated areas. Convalescent homes, treatment centers, nursery schools, camps and recreation programs, curative workshops, and many other services have been developed by the Society.

Agencies that will offer helpful advice and guidance are:

The National Society for Crippled Children and Adults, Inc.
11 South LaSalle Street
Chicago 3, Illinois

National Foundation for Infantile Paralysis
120 Broadway
New York 5, New York

United States Children's Bureau
Crippled Children's Services
Washington 25, D. C.

United States Office of Education
Dept. of Health, Education and Welfare
Washington 25, D. C.

School for the Crippled Child

Almost every state has made special provisions for the crippled child who is ready for school. When he can attend regular classes and schools, he should do so. Some children need no extra attention. Others need an adjustment in their school tasks, an extra rest period, help in going up and down stairs, or transportation. When several children in a given area need special help and attention, special classes may be formed, taught by a trained teacher. In large cities, special schools have been set up, with buses to take the children to and from school. For those who cannot attend, but are confined to their homes, to hospitals, or to convalescent institutions, special teachers may be provided. Other special arrangements may be made, also, such as the school-to-home or school-to-hospital telephone which enables a child to share in classwork and recitations, even though he may be in bed.

For those children whose disability is severe, or who, for other reasons, cannot be cared for at home, care may be provided at residential centers where the doctor, those who give treatments, and other members of the team can keep a close watch on their progress.

New Help for the Crippled

We can all be heartened by the remarkable advances research on crippling conditions has made. With early diagnosis and new treatment methods, infantile paralysis does not so often leave children paralyzed. Drugs now control some diseases which formerly caused years of hospitalization, and permanent crippling. Great strides have been made in fitting, and teaching the use of, artificial limbs. Much is known about bringing useless muscles back to work; and teaching crippled children to walk, use their hands, and talk. New techniques in special education are opening a whole new world to these children.

Perhaps the greatest change is in people themselves. We are coming to the realization that a whole body is not always needed. The horizons of a child's world need not be limited by his bodily imperfections. The crippled child should be a part of, not apart from, our society.

Helpful Reading Material

The Handicapped Child; a Guide for Parents by EDITH M. STERN with ELSA CASTENDYCK. A. A. Wyn, Inc., 23 W. 47th Street, New York 19, New York. 1950.

"Letter to the Parents of the Cerebral Palsied Child," by MARY HUBER. (Reprinted from *The Crippled Child*, June, 1952.) The National Society for Crippled Children and Adults, 11 S. LaSalle Street, Chicago 3, Ill. *The Crippled Child* Magazine. Bimonthly. The National Society for Crippled Children and Adults.

CHILDREN WHO HAVE CEREBRAL PALSY

MILDRED SHRINER, B.S.

Formerly, Consultant in Special Education and Parent Education,
National Society for Crippled Children and Adults, Chicago, Ill.

CEREBRAL-PALSIED children have the same needs as normal children. They have the same problems, too. Like all children, they want and need to learn to do for themselves and to become increasingly independent of their families. But the occurrence of cerebral palsy presents additional problems.

What Is Cerebral Palsy?

Cerebral palsy is a general term used to define a condition resulting from damage to nerve centers in the brain that govern muscular control. This damage to the motor control areas of the brain may occur before, during, or after birth. The degree and nature of the handicap depend upon the amount of damage that has been done and the areas of the brain which have been affected.

We find children who have mild, moderate, or severe problems in learning to talk or to use their hands, or in being able to sit, creep, stand, or walk. In some cases, problems in hearing or in seeing may be present. If the injury should extend to portions of the brain other than the motor control centers, a child's ability to learn may be affected. In the majority of cerebral-palsied children, this type of injury does not occur. When adequate educational and medical treatment is available, many such children can complete elementary school, high school, and even college.

Parents should realize that cerebral palsy is not inherited and that it is not contagious. It is the result of an accident which probably could not have been prevented. The damage has been done. With understanding, patient care, and training, the child can be helped to improve his condition.

Meeting the Special Needs

Parents of a child having, or suspected of having, cerebral palsy should immediately seek advice from a private doctor, a good hospital, or a clinic where the problems of cerebral palsy are understood and treated. Parents will want to know what they can do to help. When a skillful doctor who understands the child's problems is found, parents should consult him regularly. Stay with him, for it wastes precious time and money to go from one doctor to another. Progress and improvement in a cerebral-palsied child are best made by carrying out the day-by-day home exercises. Such suggestions are usually recommended to parents by the doctor and the other professional workers who are called upon for assistance.

How Can Co-ordination Be Improved?

If a child cannot walk, exercises or physical therapy may be recommended. A person trained in giving exercises, a *physical therapist*, working under the doctor's direction, will show parents what exercises the child needs. These exercises will aid a child in learning how to develop and maintain the balance and reciprocal leg motion needed in walking. From the doctor and physical therapist, parents will learn what special equipment they can make for their child to use at home and at school. These equipment aids may be specially built chairs which give proper support. Perhaps modified tricycles which help build a walking pattern will be recommended. Standing-tables may hold a child in correct position for practice in standing. Parallel bars, crutches, or canes are easily made and may help the child learn to walk.

If a child cannot use his hands, he may have difficulty in reaching, grasping, placing, and releasing his toys. He may be unable to feed or dress himself, or help with his personal habits. He may have difficulty in learning to hold a pencil for writing, or in being taught to type. A person trained in helping people use their hands constructively, an *occupational therapist*, working under the doctor's supervision, may be called upon.

Help with Speech

If a child has speech problems, parents will need to see a *speech therapist*. Speech is produced by muscular coordination. Speech problems are related to the kind of cerebral palsy present in the child. Like all other children, a cerebral-palsied child goes through stages in developing speech. First he babbles and repeats sounds like "ba-ba." He next plays with sounds, and echoes what he hears. Finally, he puts sounds together in words and sentences. A speech therapist will be able to offer suggestions.

There are many ways parents can provide a child with experiences which stimulate speech and language development. They can give a child a need and a desire to talk. Speech progresses more rapidly when it is stimulated but not forced. Parents can talk to a child in simple words and sentences about everything he does as he goes through his daily activities of dressing, eating, playing, and working. The child can be told about everything that he sees in his home and his neighborhood.

The child can be included in family conversation and can help to plan family activities, even though he has limited or imperfect speech. New experiences, such as visits to stores, to a farm, to a fire station, to the zoo, or to an airport, will help to increase his knowledge of the world about him. Inviting other children to share these excursions may help his speech and give him the companionship he needs. Hobbies and play interests he can share with other children also will help.

Parents can provide a child with a wealth of pictures to discuss and storybooks to read, selected according to his interests and understanding. The saying of rhymes or poems and the singing of simple songs will add to his vocabulary. All these experiences will build speech readiness and real speech, and will give the child a readiness for learning in school.

School for the Cerebral-Palsied Child

The age at which a child may be enrolled in school, and the amount and kind of instruction he may have through the years, will depend on the community in which he lives. Many large cities, and an increasing number of smaller communities throughout the United States and Canada, now provide some educational facilities for the cerebral-palsied child.

For the child who is severely handicapped, some states provide residential schools where he may live for a period of time. Intensive therapy and special education are given.

When a child is severely handicapped, and no provisions are made in the local community or in the state, a *homebound* program may be the solution. The teacher comes several times a week to teach the child in his home.

A good educational program for cerebral-palsied children costs three to four times that for a regular class. Many states have passed legislation providing financial aid to local school districts for such a program. Crippled children's societies, fraternal organizations, and cerebral-palsy parent groups often provide for needs that cannot be met by public funds. State legislation and local school boards willing to assume a fair share of their financial responsibility are necessary if children with cerebral palsy are to be given the opportunity they need.

Parents Work Together

Parents of cerebral-palsied children will benefit if they seek out other parents who have the same problems. By organizing as a parents' group, they may learn more about cerebral palsy. They may plan co-operatively with both public and private agencies. When problems are shared with others, and when parents work co-operatively, difficulties become less of a task and more of a challenge. Parents may then work more easily and confidently to bring out the best in their children.

Resources for Help

Parents need all the help they can find in giving their child his chance. Fortunately, in many communities help is obtainable outside home and school.

State and Community

To discover medical and educational facilities available for a cerebral-palsied child, parents may call upon the family doctor; the local health department; the Crippled Children's Services of the State Department of Health; and the local or state Crippled Children's Society (affiliated with the National Society for Crippled Children and Adults). The local, county, or state Department of Education will have information that may be of assistance.

National

Parents may obtain information and guidance from the following agencies: The National Society for Crippled Children and Adults, Inc. (Cerebral Palsy Division), 11 South La Salle St., Chicago 3, Ill.; United Cerebral Palsy Associations, Inc., 50 West 57th St., New York 19, N. Y.; Division of Physically Handicapped, U. S. Office of Education, Department of Health, Education and Welfare, Washington 25, D. C.

What to Read

EARL R. CARLSON. *Born That Way.* New York, John Day Co., 1941.

JULIETTE MCINTOSH GRATKE. *Help Them Help Themselves.* Texas Society for Crippled Children, 3703 Worth Street, Dallas, Tex.

ROMAINE P. MACKIE. *Crippled Children in School.* U. S. Govt. Printing Office, Superintendent of Documents, Washington 25, D. C.

Parents' Study Guide, A Manual for Parents of Cerebral Palsied Children. National Society for Crippled Children and Adults, Inc., 11 South La Salle Street, Chicago 3, Ill.

MILDRED SHRINER. *Foundations for Walking—A Practical Guide for Therapists, Teachers, and Parents of Cerebral Palsied Children.* National Society for Crippled Children and Adults.

EUGENE J. TAYLOR. *Help at Last for Cerebral Palsy.* Public Affairs Pamphlet No. 158. Public Affairs Committee, Inc., 22 East 38th Street, New York 16, N. Y.

CHILDREN WHO ARE EPILEPTIC

JOHN W. TENNY, M.A.
General Adviser, Special Education, College of Education, Wayne University, Detroit, Mich.

MEDICAL science in recent years has discovered real help for epileptics. It has now been firmly established that children who have epilepsy may still have normal mentality. Epilepsy is not inherited as such, although there may be a family tendency toward epilepsy, just as there is toward diabetes and disabilities of the heart. There is no such thing as an epileptic type of personality.

All Convulsions Not Epilepsy

An infant whose temperature rises rapidly to around 105 degrees may go into a fit of unconsciousness with violent spasms or movements of the body. This is known as a *convulsion*. The first convulsion is such a frightening experience that the family doctor is quickly consulted. Few medical men will treat a convulsion lightly, but fortunately they can bring much in the way of assurance to the parents.

If the child is younger than three or four years of age, and if the convulsions occur only with a fever, and not too often, it can be expected that they will stop. If the convulsions or seizures occur without fever and continue after the child is older than three or four, or start after this age, the doctor will think of epilepsy.

Medical Care for Epilepsy

The doctor will need the full co-operation of the parents in making a careful study of the epileptic child. The treatment of epilepsy is more hopeful where the cause may be an inherited tendency rather than the result of previous injury or illness. Parents should, therefore, be completely frank in answering questions about family history.

The doctor may ask the parents to take their child to a hospital or clinic for special examinations. A machine has been perfected to measure the faint electrical impulses of the brain. This machine can help to determine injuries or disease in the brain which may be causing the convulsions. The machine has a long name, hard to pronounce, *electroencephalograph*. This examination is painless and harmless.

After careful study of the child, the doctor will begin treatment. Since 1935, medicines increasingly helpful in the treatment of epilepsy have been developed. About three fourths of all cases of epilepsy may be controlled, or the frequency or severity of seizures reduced.

What Is a Seizure?

The major convulsion is called *grand-mal* epilepsy. There is often a warning sensation of some sort just before consciousness is lost. This sensation may permit the patient to protect himself from falling. This is called an *aura*. In the convulsion, the patient's muscles may stiffen or become rigid, and will then begin to twitch and jerk, first rapidly, then more slowly but more violently. Saliva may flow more freely during convulsions and is not swallowed. Therefore, we say the victim is "foaming at the mouth." Often bowel and bladder control is lost, and the patient may soil himself. The convulsion usually lasts only a few minutes, but the patient frequently remains drowsy and perhaps sleeps for a time.

Frequently, seizures occur at night, or at a particular time of day. Sometimes parents can tell by a change in the child's behavior that a seizure will occur in a day or so. Then they can take precautions, and be especially watchful.

What Can Be Done for a Major Seizure?

There is not much one can do to help the child in a convulsion. If a coat or pad can be placed under the head, and objects moved away from jerking arms or legs, injury may be prevented. If possible, a folded handkerchief or other soft object may be placed between the teeth to prevent biting of the tongue or cheek. Generally, onlookers try to do too much rather than too little.

The Minor Seizure

There is also a minor type of seizure in children, often called *petit-mal* epilepsy. In this minor seizure, consciousness is lost for a few seconds, but balance is maintained and the patient does not fall. Afterward, he may appear dazed momentarily, then he resumes conversation or normal activity. Minor seizures may occur so frequently as to interfere seriously with school or other activities. Minor seizures may occur in children who have major seizures. Some medicines have been developed that are effective in the control of minor seizures.

Medical care in epilepsy requires full co-operation from parents. The particular kind and amount of medicine most beneficial to a child takes weeks, perhaps months, to determine. Then the medicine must be taken faithfully—sometimes for years. Indifference or carelessness on the part of parents in giving medicine and providing proper care may offset the doctor's efforts.

Contact with the Outside World

Epilepsy itself is usually not a serious handicap, but the attitude of the child's playmates and of adults may create difficulties. Parents can often improve the situation by giving some of the friendlier neighbors accurate information about epilepsy. If seizures occur in public it is best not to pretend they are fainting spells. Understanding parents can help their child to a reasonably wholesome adjustment by their own acceptance of and frankness about the disease, for children form a picture of themselves from the way their parents see them.

Epileptic children need the same kind of affectionate guidance, patient understanding, and satisfactions from life that every other child needs. Parents will find that the suggestions for living with children, and for furthering their growth and development, set forth in these volumes will apply to their epileptic children as well.

What About School?

If the principal, teacher, and school nurse are correctly informed, they will be more willing to give the child a place in school. Often a telephone call or a letter from the doctor carries considerable weight. A teacher will want to know what to do in case of a seizure. If she understands what to do when a seizure occurs, and how to handle the other children's reactions to it, she can prevent some unfortunate effects on the whole class as well as on the epileptic child. Parents will find it is worth going to considerable trouble to share with the teachers everything they have learned about the child and his reactions.

It has been estimated that one in every hundred children has convulsive disorders. Most of these children are in regular schools, either because their epilepsy is not evident, or because their seizures are infrequent and do not create a major problem.

For other children whose seizures are more serious, some school systems provide special schools or classes where the teachers and school nurses have been specially trained to care for handicapped children. Others provide teachers who go to the homes two or more times each week. With the help of the parents, they arrange a fairly satisfactory educational program.

What if There Are No Services?

Unfortunately, there are still communities where special medical and educational services are not available for children whose illness is severe. Under these circumstances, parents will need to be resourceful if their child is to be prevented from needless handicap. The local doctor or medical society can usually advise you as to where special medical help can be secured. In some cases, parents may need to arrange special educational services themselves. Often a former teacher in the community can be secured to help in the home with the child's education.

In extreme cases, either through lack of local services or the severity of the illness, parents will need to think of the state residential schools. Increasingly, these institutions are providing good medical care and programs of education. If, through these services, the child can be sufficiently improved, he is returned home. If this is not possible, lifetime protection and care are available.

In the light of present-day medical knowledge, epilepsy is not the discouraging picture it was a few short years ago. There is additional hope, too, from ever-increasing medical knowledge.

Agencies which may assist with additional information:

THE NATIONAL EPILEPSY LEAGUE, 130 North Wells Street, Chicago 6, Ill.

THE INTERNATIONAL COUNCIL FOR EXCEPTIONAL CHILDREN, 1201 Sixteenth Street, N. W., Washington 6, D. C.

U. S. OFFICE OF EDUCATION, Dept. of Health, Education and Welfare, Washington 25, D. C.

Books to Read

BRIDGE, EDWARD M., M.D. *Epilepsy and Convulsive Disorders in Children*. McGraw Hill Co. New York, 1949, p. 670.

INTERNATIONAL COUNCIL FOR EXCEPTIONAL CHILDREN AND NATIONAL EPILEPSY LEAGUE *Education for All American Children—Do We Really Mean It?* National Epilepsy League. Chicago.

LENNOX, WM. G. *Science and Seizures*. Harper and Brothers. New York, 1941, p. 258.

PUTNAM, TRACY, M.D. *Convulsive Seizures*. J. B. Lippincott Co. Philadelphia, 1945, p. 160.

YAHRAES, HERBERT. *Epilepsy—The Ghost Is Out of the Closet*. Public Affairs Committee. New York.

Nat'l Soc. for Crippled Children and Adults

CHILDREN WHO ARE MENTALLY RETARDED

ELISE H. MARTENS, Ph.D.
Consultant, Education of Exceptional Children, Berkeley, Calif.

THERE was a time when parents felt that any suggestion that Johnnie or Mary was "mentally retarded" would bring disgrace to the home. Fortunately we are wiser today. We know that many accidents and deficiencies can happen to the mind as well as to the body.

When a little child's mind seems unable to grow normally, fathers and mothers naturally hope for signs of improvement as the months and years go by. They seek advice and often spend all their savings in trying to find a "cure." When at last they are told by a competent authority that Johnnie's or Mary's mind will probably never grow as other children's minds do, there is sure to be heartache. If the parents are wise, they will determine to help Johnnie or Mary live a happy and useful life in as nearly normal a way as possible. In so helping the child, parents will also help themselves and other members of the family to keep in the home a spirit of happy sharing and companionship.

Needs of the Mentally Retarded

We should always remember that the mentally retarded are, first of all, children. As children, they have the right to all the love and security that can be given them. Most mentally retarded children have a place in the community and can make some contribution to the workaday world. Some, severely retarded, may at some time in their lives need the more sheltered environment of the boarding home or school. But they, too, can learn to take part in the activities of the institution. They can also enjoy work and play with others who, like themselves, need its protection and guidance. There are a few so seriously retarded that they must have continuing physical care, sometimes even as bed patients.

Get Expert Advice Early

If you notice that Johnnie or Mary seems markedly slow in learning to do the things that children of the same age ordinarily do, do not delay in finding what may be causing the trouble. It may be only a temporary slowness of growth, for not all children develop at the same rate of speed. In that case the condition need cause no concern. But it may be something much more serious, and the sooner you know about it the sooner you can plan intelligently for the child's future.

Some parents who suspect a child is not developing normally are afraid of the verdict a capable specialist might give them. They fail to get help and, as a result, they waste precious years when early training might prove to be helpful.

Patient Guidance at Home

When it is plain that your child is mentally retarded, the home and the family have a special responsibility. There must be day-by-day patience in teaching him things that other children acquire with little or no difficulty. He will need many repetitions of the same instructions, the same activities, the same simple lessons, before an idea or habit can become his. Do not allow yourself to push him beyond his ability. Be satisfied with progress that seems painfully slow and with accomplishments that to you seem small indeed. Judge his progress not by what other children in the family can do but by what he can do today as compared with what he did last month or last year.

But work for progress—progress consistent with his ability. Let no fond relative pamper the retarded child because "he is such a baby." Certainly let no one shun or despise him. He is a member of the family in his own right. As such he has his privileges and his responsibilities, sharing in the family duties and the family fun as he is able.

Parents Work with the School

Going to school is always a great adventure for the six-year-old. For our retarded Johnnie and Mary, it will be fraught with unhappiness and frustrations, unless special provisions are made to give them the type of instruction needed. Many school systems have special classes for retarded children. There they are taught the practical things they need to know for self-protection and safety.

The teaching of health habits and muscular co-ordination is an important part of the program. Handwork helps to develop manual skill and provides interesting things to make. Nor are the fundamental skills neglected. As each child is able to make progress, he reads, writes, spells, and does number work. All these are related to everyday problems and activities within his own experience. With them, the teacher helps the children to grow in ability, to make friends, and to work and play together, both in their own group and with other pupils in the school.

Wise Planning for the Future

As Johnnie and Mary approach adolescence, there always arises the question: What next? Shall they continue in the local public day school? Shall they be sent to a private school? Should they be enrolled in one of the public boarding schools that the state maintains for the severely retarded? For what type of self-supporting occupation, if any, can they be prepared? Even parents of young retarded children are disturbed by such questions as these, as they look into the future with misgivings. The answers can come only as the result of careful study of each girl and boy for whom plans are being made. Physical and emotional problems may make it wise for some to have the protective care of a public or private boarding home or school as they grow older. Others may find all the special help they require in the local schools. The matter is one that needs to be studied carefully. Get all the expert advice you can from physicians, educators, and child-guidance specialists.

Where Can I Get Help?

Advice on educational matters should come from your local school superintendent, in city or county, or from someone he suggests. He can direct you also to local health and welfare services, to psychological assistance, and to community clinics. He will know if there is in your community an organized group of parents of retarded children through which you may secure further information.

In most states there is, in the State Department of Education, a division giving advice on the education of retarded children. State departments of Health, Welfare, Mental Hygiene, and Vocational Rehabilitation give advice in their respective fields. Every state has the use of one or more boarding centers to which it can send the mentally deficient needing protective care.

Several national groups have a special interest in the mentally retarded. The following may be of help to you:

Association for the Help of Retarded Children, 31 Madison Avenue, New York City, N. Y.
American Association on Mental Deficiency, P.O. Box 96, Willimantic, Conn.
National Association for Mental Health, 1790 Broadway, New York City, N. Y.
Department of Health, Education and Welfare, Washington, D. C. The Office of Education and the Children's Bureau are especially helpful in problems of the mentally retarded.

Materials to Read

All the agencies that have been named will send you a list of materials available from them, either free or at nominal cost. In addition, you will find helpful suggestions in books and pamphlets that you may borrow from a public library. A few of these are:

BUCK, PEARL. *The Child Who Never Grew.* New York, John Day and Company, 1950. 62p.
STERN, EDITH M., with ELSA CASTENDYCK. *The Handicapped Child: A Guide for Parents.* New York, A. A. Wyn, Inc., 1950. 179p.
Teach Me. St. Paul, Minn., Mental Health Unit, Division of Public Institutions, Department of Social Security, 1945. 31p.

CHILDREN WITH RHEUMATIC FEVER

IRENE M. JOSSELYN, M.D.
Staff Member, Institute for Psychoanalysis,
Chicago, Ill.

IF YOUR child has rheumatic fever, you can help him feel that the most important parts of his life are the things he *can* do, rather than the things he *cannot* do. Give him opportunity to find, and encourage him to use, those pleasurable experiences in life that are not forbidden because of restrictions on his activity. Then it will be possible for him to develop a well-rounded personality and enjoy his life, even though certain activities are not permitted.

Facts About Rheumatic Fever

The cause of rheumatic fever is not definitely known. Your child may be ill a few weeks, or the illness may extend into months. There is no certain treatment except to keep him as quiet and as comfortable as possible. More definite medical treatment may be available soon, if the early reports indicating that Cortisone and ACTH are effective are borne out by further study.

Your child may recover from this attack without any damage to his heart. He may in the course of the illness develop indications that tell the doctor his heart has been damaged. Once a child has had rheumatic fever, there is always a possibility of a recurrence, and damage to his heart.

Don't be alarmed by publicity that says that rheumatic fever is the commonest cause of death in children. This is true, but other childhood diseases have come under medical control to such an extent that childhood illnesses seldom end fatally. When the statement is interpreted in this way, it becomes far less alarming. Most children who have rheumatic fever do not die during the illness. Their life span is not necessarily shortened, nor need they become permanent invalids.

The care of the child with rheumatic fever involves a longer program than do most children's illnesses, and has to be considered in three steps.

Acute Illness

During the time the child is acutely ill with fever and swollen joints, he needs complete rest in bed. Often the doctor recommends hospitalization at this time, chiefly because it is easier to keep a child in bed in a hospital than at home. In the hospital he may be protected from exposure to an additional cold or other illness.

If Your Child Is in a Hospital

This is a hard time for you and for your child. He feels lonely without his family and may be frightened by the hospital routine. Try not to let your child see that you are worried. His own anxiety is heightened if he senses that his parents are frightened. It is vital that he follow the doctor's orders, but it is better not to talk about the serious consequences that may follow if he does not do as the doctor tells him. It is not wise to deny completely to the child the real meaning of his illness. A child, by the time he is seven or eight years old, can understand a simple explanation as to why he needs to follow the program the doctor outlines for him. If the doctor can talk to him in a friendly way, he is the one to give this explanation.

You will want to visit your child as often as the hospital will permit. Hospitals vary greatly in their attitude toward parents' visiting. In those hospitals where visiting is kept to a minimum, the child will be unhappy when other parents visit and his do not. When children are in the hospital for long stretches of time, parents sometimes grow careless about coming when visiting is permitted. A child may feel deserted just when it is particularly upsetting to be deserted. When you are allowed to visit, bring books, or the kind of toys he can enjoy while lying quietly in bed. These presents may help to tide him over some bad moments when he feels lonely because you cannot be with him.

Convalescence

When the child leaves the hospital, or if he has remained at home and is able to be out of bed, you may notice a change in his personality. Before his illness he probably was normally independent and dependable for his age. Now he may behave in more babyish ways. This is due in part to the long period of not feeling well, when he wanted the comfort given to a small child. Also, during his illness he was taken care of, rather than having any responsibility of his own. He is uneasy about assuming the responsibilities he carried before his illness.

Do not expect him to resume his former independence immediately. Let him experience gradually the pleasures that come from more grown-up, independent behavior. You can continue for a while to meet some of his more babyish needs casually and warmly. In a few months he will be more like his old self.

How Can You Keep a Convalescent Content?

Convalescence is trying for the child, for he now feels quite well. He wants to resume his former activities, but he tires easily. He is apt to ignore his fatigue. The doctor will not wish him to take part in much active play for a time. Gradually he can be permitted more strenuous play as his general condition improves.

The child will often be rebellious unless interesting activities that are not a strain on his health are provided. You can help him choose activities in line with his own interests. A child who does not like to work with his hands is not going to enjoy handicrafts. Another may find a great deal of fun in such activity. Still another child may love baseball and be satisfied for a while if he can watch games. Volume 8, especially the chapter on QUIET PLAY, may have helpful suggestions.

During convalescence, your child needs a chance to be with other children. Let him return to school as soon as the doctor feels he is ready. Be sure you know just how much the doctor actually wishes him to do.

If a convalescent home especially equipped to care for children recovering from rheumatic fever is available, your doctor may recommend that your child go there. The benefits of contact with other children and the variety of quiet activities a good convalescent home can provide may outweigh the difficulties of a longer separation.

After Convalescence

After the child's period of convalescence is over, the doctor will tell you how much permanent restriction of activity is necessary. Many children who have had rheumatic fever, with the sometimes resulting damage to the heart, can, after the convalescent period, resume relatively normal activities. Only the doctor can determine with any measure of accuracy what any particular child's permanent heart condition is.

Within the limitations established by the doctor, the child should be given an opportunity to live a normal life. Any kind of cold, cough, sore throat, or bronchitis needs prompt medical attention, for there is always danger of another attack.

The child who has or who has had rheumatic fever is not "just a heart." Certainly, the program of care and activity laid out by the physician must be followed with the utmost care. But the total needs of the child should be considered, too. Do not restrict his activities more than the doctor tells you to. Just because your doctor says the child should not play baseball for a time does not mean that he will be better off if he takes part in no physical activity. The child who has had rheumatic fever will tend to get along better if you remember he wants and needs the same things that other children want.

If you want more information or reading material about rheumatic fever, your local medical society or heart association, or the American Heart Association, 1775 Broadway, New York 19, N. Y., can help you.

HAPPY
FAMILY LIVING

H. Armstrong Roberts

35. BUILDING THE STRONG FAMILY

The home is the most important influence in shaping the life of a child. Feelings about themselves and about other persons, attitudes toward work and play, beliefs about right and wrong which children learn at home in their earliest years stay with them throughout their lives. It is these feelings, attitudes, and beliefs that play an important part in making an individual what he is.

Homes as well as schools help to educate children. Homes as well as churches and synagogues contribute to children's spiritual values and to their faith. Homes have the opportunity to make tomorrow better by guiding children wisely and by fostering all-around growth.

A family can sustain its members better in joy and sorrow, in venturing into what is new, or in adding vitality to what is old and familiar, if all its members have confidence in one another, in themselves, and in the purpose and order of the universe.

BUILDING THE STRONG FAMILY

EDUARD C. LINDEMAN, LL.D.
Formerly, Professor of Social Philosophy, New York School of Social Work, New York, N.Y.
and
MELVIN A. GLASSER
Assistant to the President, National Foundation for Infantile Paralysis

H. Armstrong Roberts

THE family is the rock on which our society is founded. It is the oldest, and it is unquestionably the most important, of all human institutions. Only the family can give individuals the warmth, the closeness, and the feeling of belonging that are essential to the healthy growth of personality. No satisfactions are greater than those associated with happy family living. The home is a strong influence for stability throughout an individual's life. Children who learn to give and take in a happy family group have the best foundation for becoming well-adjusted adults. Later, they will in turn contribute to the building of strong families of their own.

We are what we are mostly because of the influence of family relationships. Communities and nations are nothing more than collections of families whose combined unity and strength are derived from family strength. Nothing can be of greater importance than finding and understanding the resources for building strong families.

The Strong Family Is Flexible

The way in which we get along with other persons is closely connected with the kind of relations which exist within the family. It is primarily through the family that the child is enabled to express himself freely and to develop satisfying emotional attachments to parents, brothers, and sisters. These relationships in turn make it possible for him to move out and form positive ties with others.

Family relations based on warmth and affection give all the members the kind of balance they need to enable them to live successfully in our competitive society. By and large, in jobs, schools, and other aspects of American life, major value is placed on achievement and success rather than on emotional satisfactions.

The resources of the average family group are greater than we realize. Not the least of these resources is flexibility. New conditions which are sometimes imposed by the rapidly changing world in which we live demand that families be flexible; and the flexible family accepts changes cheerfully.

When one father lost his business because improvements had outmoded the product he was selling, he got a job in a factory more than a hundred miles away. The family had to move. This meant giving up old friendships and associations. But the family lost no time crying about the situation. They simply said, "We belong together and we'll get along fine. The big thing is to get Pop started on his new work." Their ability to adjust themselves to new conditions gave this family the morale necessary to get over this rough spot.

Vacation habits changed completely with the coming of the automobile and hard-surfaced roads. Joe Brown liked to spend his vacation fishing but Mrs. Brown thought it would be no vacation for her to take a housekeeping cottage near a trout stream. She preferred to go on an automobile trip and see as much of the country as she could. Her husband said that "only gypsies would go from place to place like that."

But this family was flexible. They sat down and talked it over. They finally decided to travel around this year, and to go fishing next year. So their vacation trips became pleasant for everybody involved. "Give-and-take" had solved what appeared for a time to be a most difficult problem which had no immediate answer.

Individual Differences Are Recognized

Each individual member of the family group is a whole person in his own right. In the strong family, the many ways various members of the family differ are recognized, accepted, and respected, so long, of course, as such differences are not harmful to anyone. Recognition of these special differences gives unity to the family and strengthens it immeasurably. In times of crisis, this makes for a greater solidarity than uniformity can ever give.

In a democratic society, only strength founded upon respect for individuals is

Gendreau

The strong family rallies round in time of need. If Mother is ill, family solidarity gets a real test.

The school paper collection may be a way of fostering the sense of community responsibility in the family that reaches out to those beyond its circle.

Elizabeth Hibbs

sound. Strength may be based upon uniformity in an autocratic society. But such strength is on the surface only. In times of crisis, such regimented families usually "go to pieces," unless they are held together by fear and force. But, in the democratic family, strength is based upon affection and respect. Each individual learns how to use freedom.

The men in the Whiting family had always been engineers. So it came as a shock to Edward Whiting when he discovered that his oldest son wanted to be a tree surgeon. His first impulse was to object strenuously because of the break in the family tradition. But as he listened to his boy talk about trees and forestry, and as he watched him spend his time around the evergreen nursery during his vacations, he became reconciled. In fact, he began to encourage his boy to make this absorbing interest his lifework.

The recognition of individual differences made this family even stronger than it was before. And, later on, every member of the family could point with pride to the fine work of the oldest boy. They even admired him for having the courage to break with family tradition and go into work that he loved more than anything else.

Rules Are Necessary

Life in a democratic family is not "all sails and no rudder." Order and freedom are not opposites. Besides, no form of human association can exist without rules. No rules at all means confusion and license—not freedom. In the long

Vivienne Lapham

Family life provides the setting for appreciation of spiritual values when children learn to express thanks to our Heavenly Father through prayers.

run, when sensible rules are adopted with everyone's needs in mind, it means more freedom. A strong family operates on the basis of fair rules clearly understood.

Problems Are Shared

It is the fortunate family that does not occasionally have to meet and surmount difficulties of various kinds. It is true, too, that, when these obstacles are frankly discussed in the bosom of the family, the burden is almost automatically lightened through the sharing.

The character of the problem and the ages of the children have much to do with the way the problem can be discussed. Perhaps money is one of the main difficulties facing the average family. Junior, maybe, cannot understand why his parents are unwilling to send him to a summer camp. Mary is unable to understand why she cannot have a new dress for the Junior Prom.

Obviously, such difficulties will not be solved if the finances of the family are shrouded in secrecy. It is not suggested that total family income and the mortgage on the old home be discussed by the younger members of the family. They cannot be expected, at their ages, to have much understanding of such matters. But if Bill is home from college for the Christmas holidays, and has been studying family budgets in a course in economics, then that is another matter.

Discussions about the family's income and expenses can be the source of a lively exchange of differing ideas of values. Family budgets should be openly arrived at. All members should take part in decisions concerning the use of income, in proportion to their ability to appreciate and understand.

But money matters are not the only problems members of the family can share helpfully. There are other things such as daily chores and duties, or running the household when Mother is ill. A host of similar problems come up from time to time. The family that has unity and strength makes the load lighter by sharing the burden.

A Strong Family Reaches Out

Families are not self-sufficient. They do not exist in a social vacuum. Clusters of families make up neighborhoods, and combinations of neighborhoods form communities. Families cannot separate themselves from neighborhood and community influences and relations. Standards of dress, ways of playing, working, and getting along with others cannot be kept up indefinitely in a single family if they conflict markedly with those of most other families.

Parents who hold fast to standards of behavior that differ sharply from those about them frequently create confusion and conflict for themselves and their children. Wise parents recognize that the prevailing forms of our behavior tend to come from neighborhoods and communities. If a family is markedly different from its neighbors, it is important that its members be aware of this. They need to recognize that in our world today there is more than one right way of doing things. It is helpful therefore to review such things as the family's way of dress, its customs, and its regulations, in relation to the variety of existing standards. The strong family is then able to select those ways that are most satisfying to them, that fill their own needs, and that at the same time will be acceptable in the general community.

A strong family is aware of the way

neighborhood and community influences affect family life. They realize that if they want a good neighborhood to live in, they must get out and work in it. Each member takes part, according to his ability, in the affairs of the church, the school, the neighborhood center, the library, and the other institutions that make up community life.

Facing Misfortune Bravely

The principal tragic experiences of life are happenings affecting families. The place where tragedy is felt is in the family circle. In weak families there is no expectation of tragedy, and hence no emotional and spiritual preparation. When tragedy strikes these weak families, they frequently suffer a shock so devastating that they never again regain their internal strength. One normal and apparently strong family never regained its solidarity after the serious illness of the mother. Many similar breakdowns in family life have occurred during times of depression when the family breadwinner for the first time found himself unemployed.

It is not a sign of fear to be prepared for tragedy. Nobody says that tragedy should be the daily fare of family discussion, but we should not run away from it.

Two girls, eight and ten years old, knew that the father of one of their friends had died and that the mother had gone to work. They said to their own mother, "If Daddy died what would happen? How could you get a job when you don't know how to do anything?"

Their mother explained to them that she and their father had thought about this problem. She told the children what provision had been made to take care of them and of her in case the father died or fell ill. She explained, too, how the training she had had before they were born might make it possible for her to find work more readily than they realized.

The little girls seemed reassured. Surely family strength was reinforced because the mother did not say, "Hush, you mustn't think of such things."

Humor Goes with Confidence

Family humor, its presence and its absence, is also a significant index of family strength. Genuine humor, as distinguished from the "wisecrack," is founded upon a solid base. Genuine humor rests upon confidence. Where there is a feeling of security and trust, it is possible to use humor as a means of seeing events in their true proportions. Then life becomes a kind of drama. Members of the family group may think of themselves as actors in the play, and at the same time as a part of the audience. Humor then becomes one of the ways of seeing bits of truth otherwise concealed. It also acts as a "lubricator," easing difficult situations and making interrelationships simpler and kindlier. Families often do use humor in other and less-beneficial ways. There are secret and rather childish forms of humor shutting out nonmembers of the family group. Humor, when it takes on the form of wit and satire, can become a cruel instrument, but in its kindlier forms it can strengthen and sustain family life.

The Anchor of Society

When these qualities of family strength are combined, we see a modern family group involved in an experiment. Families begin with love and affection between two persons. A fam-

H. Armstrong Roberts

When grace before meals is a treasured part of each day's plan, ties grow stronger, and there is a deeper sense of gratitude, wonder, and reverence.

ily becomes a group concerned with giving attention to the individual differences of its members. Each person is permitted to develop his or her powers and capacities. Certain tensions and conflicts are likely to arise just because families are a close-knit group. A strong family has so much solidarity and basic unity that these conflicts can be dealt with by talking things over in a friendly fashion. The strong family then becomes a group moving toward unity. It is flexible enough so that no member completely dominates another. Being a member of a strong family is a preparation for life in the world of stress and struggle. At the same time it is a haven of release from the sterner demands of modern life. Where there is a sense of such strength and resiliency, family life adds courage to affection, and thus faith is reinforced.

Even though family life involves problems and difficulties, it is the core of modern living. Because of human frailty, the age-old institution sometimes breaks down. But without the comfort, the affection, the security, and the training that the home offers, the world would indeed be a sorry place to live in.

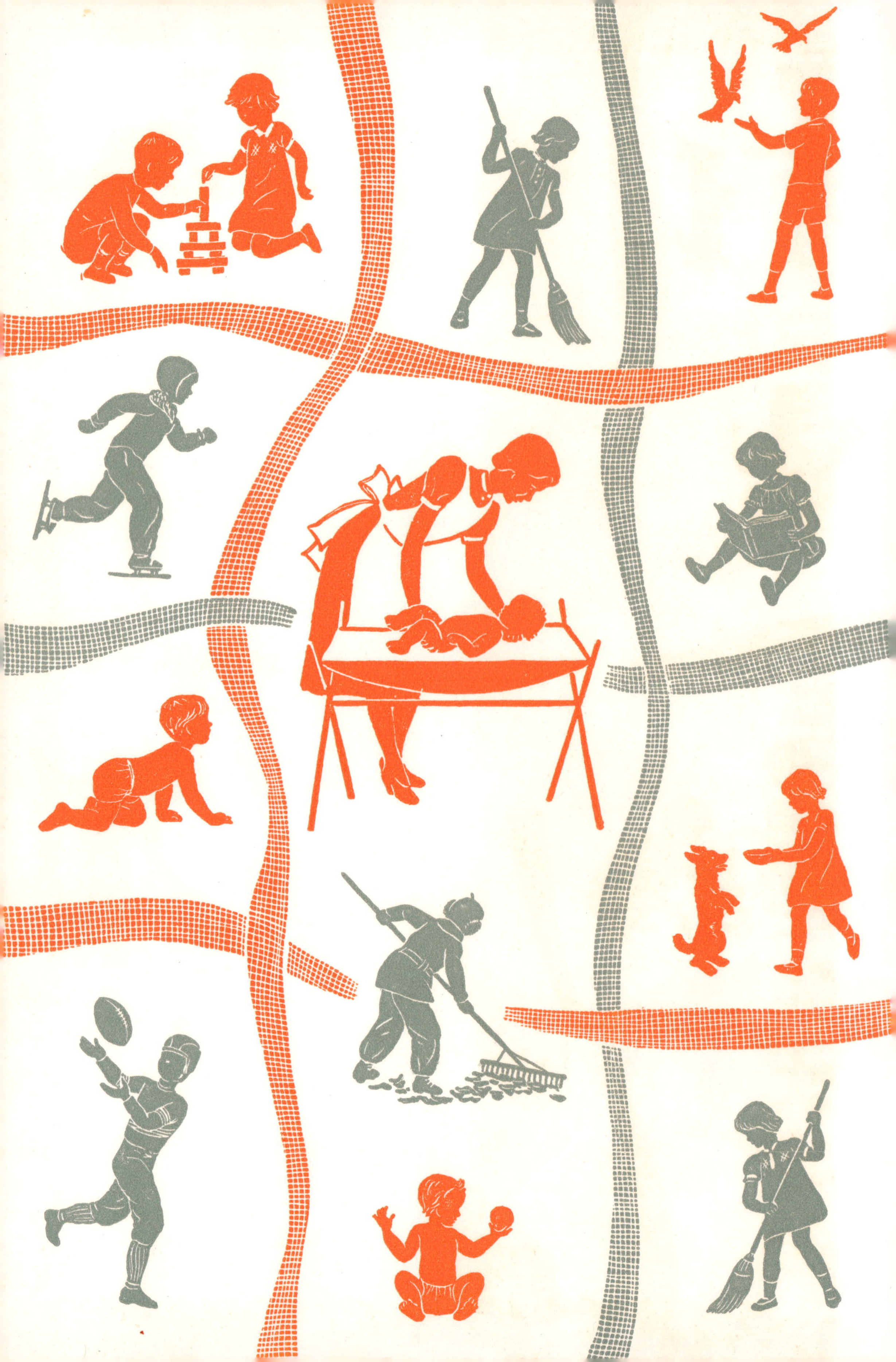